For:

Young Professionals | Mid-career Individ

Design a Life on Your Terms

A Roadmap to Financial Independence and Career Fulfilment for Every Life Stage

ISBN 978-981-94-3685-9 (Paperback)
ISBN 978-981-94-3742-9 (Hardcopy)
ISBN 978-981-94-3686-6 (Digital)

Disclaimer

The information contained in this book is intended for educational and informational purposes only. It is not intended to be a substitute for professional financial, legal, or career advice. While the author has made every effort to ensure the accuracy and completeness of the information, readers should consult with a qualified professional before making any financial or career decisions. The author and publisher disclaim any liability for any loss or damage incurred directly or indirectly as a result of the use of the information presented in this book.

This book is dedicated to:

My children, and to all who aspire to achieve financial independence, embrace a meaningful re-career—or early retirement—and live a life of purpose.

And to you, the reader:

- **Undergraduates:** May you find the courage and clarity to turn aspirations into actionable plans, shaping a future aligned with your dreams.
- **Young Professionals:** May this book inspire you to build a strong financial and career foundation, setting the stage for a lifetime of success.
- **Mid-Career Professionals:** May you discover the tools to reflect, pivot, and take charge of your journey toward greater satisfaction and success.
- **Aspiring Retirees:** May this book help you transform retirement into an opportunity for reinvention and renewed purpose.

To all who dare to dream bigger and believe in the power of reinvention—May this book be a trusted companion on your journey to financial independence and a life well lived.

https://BooksByYK.PharmacistCoaches.Com
https://www.Linkedin.com/in/ykpng/
www.CoachToring.Com
www.PharmacistCoaches.Com

Contents

Prologue: A Life by Design, Not by Default

In a world where busyness is often mistaken for success, many find themselves on a treadmill—working harder, climbing faster, yet feeling increasingly disconnected from what truly matters. The traditional narrative of career and retirement, shaped by decades of societal norms, rarely questions whether the path leads to fulfilment or freedom. It simply asks for compliance: study hard, work long, save later, retire eventually.

Financial Independence, Re-career Early: Work Less, Live More challenges that script. It offers not only a roadmap to financial independence but also a new lens through which to view work, money, time, and purpose. Rather than deferring joy to a distant future, it calls for a life built around autonomy, intention, and meaning.

Drawing from personal lived experiences, multidisciplinary insights, and real-life transitions, this book offers a roadmap for those who sense that something more is possible. Whether standing at the start of a career, reassessing the mid-career grind, or exploring new directions post-retirement, *F.I.R(Re-career)E* provides tools to navigate toward a life aligned with values—not obligations.

The chapters ahead explore practical strategies—financial planning, income diversification, tax optimisation, property, investing, re-careering, and legacy—through the lens of intentional living. Each part builds toward a central idea: success is not about having more, but about living well on one's own terms.

This book is an invitation to reclaim agency, challenge assumptions, and craft a life with clarity, courage, and purpose.

Let the journey begin.

~ YK Png

Introduction: The F.I.R(Re-career).E Journey

Have you ever felt your life was more about surviving than truly living?

That quiet question shaped my journey. I still remember sitting alone in a hospital canteen at 3 PM during a break from my early pharmacist shifts. Surrounded by routine, I felt grateful—but also restless. I asked myself: *Is this what the next 40 years will look like?* Stability was there, but fulfilment was missing.

That moment sparked a conscious mission—rooted in earlier life values—to achieve financial independence and re-career into a life aligned with my true purpose and desired lifestyle. Not escaping work but redefining it. Not early retirement, but intentional living—with autonomy, purpose, and time for what truly matters.

What This Book Offers

F.I.R(Re-career).E: Work Less, Live More is the roadmap I wish I had then—and the one I now offer to others. It goes beyond conventional views of early retirement. It is a flexible and strategic framework built on three pillars:

- **Achieving financial independence** through clear planning, disciplined habits, and smart investments.
- **Re-designing one's career** to reflect evolving passions, purpose, and lifestyle goals.
- **Creating a fulfilling life**—not someday but starting now.

This book integrates technical strategies with reflective prompts, frameworks, and practical tips—across different life stages and transitions. It is for those who seek more than just success. It is for those ready to shape a life of significance.

Book Structure

The chapters are structured into three parts to guide readers across the F.I.R(Re-career).E journey:

Part I: Building the Foundation for F.I.R(Re-career).E

This section explores the mindset, resilience, and planning required to begin. It includes my personal story and shares how early adversity, intentional design, and redefinition of success shaped my path.

- Chapter 1: My Journey Towards Financial Independence and Re-careering.
- Chapter 2: The F.I.R(Re-career).E Mindset.
- Chapter 3: Planning for the Future – Career, Finances, and Health.
- Chapter 4: From Mindset to Action – Navigating Transitions.

Part II: Mastering Financial Planning for F.I.R(Re-career).E

This section provides essential financial strategies. With expert contributions, it covers CPF, insurance, investing, property, tax, and legacy, tailored for different life stages.

- Chapter 5: Financial Foundations for Freedom.
- Chapter 6: Maximizing CPF for Financial Freedom.
- Chapter 7: Insurance – Protecting What Matters Most.
- Chapter 8: Investment Strategies for Financial Growth.
- Chapter 9: Property – A Wealth-Building Strategy.
- Chapter 10: Tax Planning and Wealth Preservation.

Part III: Transitioning into the Re-career Journey

The final section supports readers in designing a second career or lifestyle aligned with freedom and fulfilment. It covers practical preparation, career redesign, and sustaining a meaningful life beyond traditional success.

- Chapter 11: Preparing for the Leap.
- Chapter 12: Designing Your Unique Re-career Path.
- Chapter 13: Living a Life of Purpose, Growth and Fulfilment.

Why This Book Matters

F.I.R(Re-career).E isn't idle early retirement, but flexibility to live meaningfully. It's about reclaiming time and choice for a portfolio career, social contribution, family, or simply a different pace.

The journey starts now.

Part I: Building the Foundation for F.I.R(Re-career).E.

"You can't go back and change the beginning, but you can start where you are and change the ending."

~ C.S. Lewis

Chapter 1: My Journey Towards Financial Independence and Re-careering

"Financial independence is not about escaping work—it's about reclaiming the freedom to do the work that truly matters to you."
~ YK Png

Definitions: F.I.R(Re-career).E.

- **Financial Independence (FI):** Freedom from money stress, enabling work by choice, not necessity.
- **Re-career:** Shifting to a new, fulfilling career path, emphasizing growth and reinvention.
- **Early Retirement (E):** Retiring from traditional work to pursue chosen activities, driven by financial freedom.

Every journey has a beginning, and mine was rooted not in privilege, but in perseverance, planning, and purpose. Long before I understood what financial independence truly meant, I knew I wanted more than just a conventional career path. From growing up in humble circumstances to navigating corporate life and eventually re-careering into coaching and entrepreneurship, my story is one of transformation—fuelled by values, intentionality, and a deep desire for freedom.

This chapter outlines key turning points in my journey—marked by challenges, pivotal decisions, and transformative mindset shifts—that led to the intentional design of a life beyond the conventional career track. The experience shared here is intended to serve as both mirror and map: reflecting the possibilities available beyond traditional employment and offering a guiding perspective for those seeking to define their own version of F.I.R(Re-career)E.

From Adversity to Opportunity

From the very first day I started working, I was already thinking about financial independence and early retirement. My upbringing instilled in me the value of resilience, hard work, and financial prudence. The lessons I learned from my family's struggles and sacrifices shaped my approach to career and financial planning.

1. ***A Flood That Reshaped My World:*** *I was born and raised in Kelantan, a small state in the northeastern part of West Malaysia. My parents ran a small family business that provided us with a simple but secure life. They made biscuits and cookies for schools and shops and also manufactured bottled drinks, which they supplied to food outlets across the state. The business always thrived during festive seasons, and the period leading up to Chinese New Year was a time of high anticipation and preparation.*

   In 1967, a catastrophic monsoon flood struck without warning. The rising waters submerged our home and business, completely wiping out our inventory, equipment, and savings. As a five-year-old, I was too young to grasp the devastation. I later understood that my family, with no insurance or safety net, lost everything they had built.

   My parents, however, chose to rebuild. This defining moment showed me that resilience isn't just about survival; it's about choosing to rise from adversity. Their example taught me to see setbacks as opportunities to grow stronger—a lesson that became foundational to my life and resonates deeply with the principles of resilience and adaptability.

Key Takeaway: Resilience is built through adversity.
Even when everything is lost, the decision to rise and rebuild shapes the path forward.

---

2. ***Family, Sacrifice, and Aspiration:*** *Behind every success story is a network of unwavering support. For me, it was my family, particularly my parents, brothers and sisters, who played a pivotal role in shaping my journey.*
   Their selflessness inspired me to aim higher, not only for my own growth but also to honor their trust and sacrifices. This

phase of my life taught me that success is rarely an individual accomplishment. It's built on a foundation of love, encouragement, and collective effort. This sense of togetherness remains a cornerstone of my values and has shaped my approach to overcoming challenges.

Key Takeaway: Success is never a solo journey.
It is often the product of unseen sacrifices and unwavering support from those who believe in you.

---

3. ***New Horizons in Singapore:*** *My early education began in Kelantan, first in a Chinese-medium school and then a Malay-medium secondary school. The most significant shift came when I moved to Singapore, an English-speaking environment where I could barely string a sentence together. This challenge forced me out of my comfort zone, teaching me invaluable lessons about resilience, adaptability, and perseverance—qualities central to achieving success.*

   As a foreign student, I faced high tuition fees. To ease my family's financial burden, I took on part-time jobs and tutoring during school holidays. This instilled a strong sense of financial discipline and responsibility in me from a young age.

   This phase of my life became a masterclass in embracing challenges and turning them into steppingstones for success. It taught me that adaptability and a willingness to embrace the unfamiliar are essential traits for building a secure and fulfilling future.

Key Takeaways:

- **Adaptability is non-negotiable for growth.** The ability to face the unknown and persevere opens doors.
- **Financial discipline starts early.** Earning and saving from a young age instils lasting habits that shape the future.

---

4. ***Pharmacy Education - A Turning Point:*** *Attending the National University of Singapore (NUS) for pharmacy was a transformative chapter of my life. The rigorous curriculum wasn't just an academic pursuit; it was a turning point that demanded discipline and focused on preparing me for a meaningful career. My time at NUS reinforced several key*

lessons: the importance of perseverance, the value of education as an investment, and the necessity to adapt to challenges. This experience solidified my belief that education is a powerful tool for building a successful future, and that every challenging step is a vital part of the journey toward achieving your dreams.

Key Takeaways:

- **Education empowers long-term success.** It equips individuals with the skills and mindset necessary for both personal and professional growth.
- **Perseverance turns potential into performance.** Sustained effort, even through difficulties, is what drives progress and carries individuals forward.

The early lessons I learned about resilience and responsibility would later shape my career decisions and ultimately fuel my re-careering journey.

My Journey: From Adversity to Opportunity

New Horizons (Singapore):
- Event: Moved to Singapore, new education system.
- Impact: Language barrier, part-time work.
- Key Lesson: Adaptability and perseverance.

Adversity (1967):
- Event: Monsoon flood in Kelantan.
- Impact: Family business destroyed.
- Key Lesson: Resilience through adversity.

A Turning Point (Pharmacy):
- Event: Studied Pharmacy at NUS.
- Impact: Academic rigor, personal growth.
- Key Lesson: Education as a pathway to impact.

Family Support (Early Years):
- Event: Supported by siblings for education.
- Impact: Financial hardship, shared sacrifices.
- Key Lesson: Power of family and purpose.

"Your Starting Point Doesn't Define Your Future!" ~ YK Png

Why Early Planning Matters More Than Privilege

The path to financial independence is often perceived as a luxury reserved for those born into privilege—individuals with inherited wealth or elite connections. This belief, however, is a profound misconception.

Financial independence isn't sustained by an advantageous starting line; it's built through proactive decision-making, disciplined habits, and a long-term mindset. As numerous studies, including the seminal work *The Millionaire Next Door*, show, the vast majority of millionaires are self-made. Their success is rooted not in generational advantage, but in intentional choices, prudent spending, and steady accumulation over time.

Early planning is the great equalizer. It doesn't require starting with more—it requires making more of what one has. This essential shift in mindset is the real driver on the journey to freedom.

The Mechanism: Time and Habits Outperform Capital

The true power of early planning lies in its harnessing of mathematical principles and behavioural discipline.

1. **Compounding Rewards the Early Planner:** Time is the most crucial variable in the wealth-building equation. Starting early allows compounding to work its magic exponentially, drastically increasing long-term returns.

   Illustration: *An individual who begins investing $500 per month at age 25 with a 7% annual return may accumulate over $1 million by age 65. Starting the same plan just 10 years later at age 35 results in roughly half that amount. The early years make the greatest difference.*

2. **Savings Rate Outperforms High Income:** Financial discipline and consistent habits sustain wealth far more reliably than inheritance. Success is determined less by the size of your paycheck and more by your **savings rate**. A person earning $50,000 and saving 40% will likely reach financial independence faster than a person earning $150,000 who spends 90% of their salary. A mindset rooted in responsibility and continuous learning forms the true foundation of sustainable success.

My Journey - The Lesson: *While the full story is shared earlier, the relevant lesson here is that I did not have financial privilege. Instead, early challenges moving to Singapore for education forced me to learn resourcefulness, manage money carefully, and prioritize long-term skill acquisition. These early, small choices—planning ahead even with limited resources—were the seeds that compounded into future financial independence.*

Strategy: Myths to Break and Pitfalls to Avoid

Unlearning common misconceptions and avoiding typical traps are essential for building a confident and sustainable path to F.I.R(Re-career).E.

Myths to Break on the F.I.R(Re-career).E. Journey

Myth	Reality	Tips/Example
"I must be rich to achieve FIRE."	It's about your **savings discipline**, not your income. A cleaner saving 40% may reach independence faster than a six-figure spender.	Track your savings rate and automate contributions into investments.
"FIRE means I'll never work again."	Most don't stop working; they re-career into meaningful ventures. They gain control over their time and purpose.	***Example:*** *Mr. Loo Cheng Chuan, founder of the 1M65 movement, built substantial CPF wealth and now channels his energy into advocacy work.*
"It's too late to start in my 40s or 50s."	While starting early helps, mid-career shifts can still create freedom. Downsizing, cutting expenses, and building a "bridge fund" allow flexible or part-time work.	Begin by increasing financial literacy. Take courses or consult trusted financial planners to map your accelerated path.

Myth	Reality	Tips/Example
"Financial planning is only for experts."	Ordinary individuals succeed by starting simple: automating savings into low-cost investments and learning along the way. Consistency matters more than expertise.	Use robo-advisors, online guides, or community groups for support.
"Taxes don't matter after retirement."	Tax efficiency is critical when income shifts to dividends, rentals, or pensions. Poorly timed withdrawals can erode savings.	***Example:*** *In Singapore, spreading SRS withdrawals over 10 years keeps retirees in lower tax brackets, avoiding spikes from lump sums.*

Common Pitfalls that Delay Progress

1. **Lifestyle Inflation:** As income rises, expenses (cars, bigger homes, luxury upgrades) often follow. This actively erodes savings. Grow your savings rate with each pay increase, not your spending.
2. **Lack of Clear Goals:** Vague aims like "retire early" are unhelpful. Define your specific vision: e.g., "debt-free home by 55," or "$2,000 monthly passive income." Set measurable milestones and review them quarterly.
3. **Chasing Returns Without Understanding Risk:** FOMO drives many into speculative bets without knowing the risks. Invest in line with your goals and risk tolerance; education precedes execution.
4. **Postponing Action:** The biggest illusion is waiting for the "perfect time"—when you earn more, or when markets stabilize. Start small, start now. Automate savings and let inertia work in your favour.

Key Strategies for Early Planning

1. **Setting Clear Goals:** Success is the result of clear, actionable goals. Whether in finance, career, or personal development, a well-defined vision helps maintain focus and motivation.

   Actionable Steps:
   - Long-term goals should be documented and broken into smaller, achievable milestones.
   - Regular review and adjustment of goals are crucial, based on progress and evolving circumstances.
   - Visualizing future success reinforces motivation and clarity.
   - Guidance from mentors or coaches can provide valuable insights and support accountability.

2. **Building Financial Discipline Early:** Financial independence is determined less by income level and more by effective resource management. The accumulation of wealth is significantly influenced by behavioural patterns, suggesting that sound financial habits are more critical than initial earnings.

   Actionable Steps:
   - A fixed percentage of income should be saved consistently, regardless of the amount.
   - Understanding various investment vehicles and the power of compound interest is essential.
   - Lifestyle inflation should be avoided; increased earnings do not necessitate increased spending. Focus should remain on wealth growth rather than escalating expenses.

3. **Career Planning with Future Trends in Mind:** The job market is undergoing rapid evolution. Automation and artificial intelligence are projected to reshape industries, making adaptability and continuous learning indispensable for career growth. Staying ahead of trends and actively developing in-demand skills are key to future-proofing one's career.

   Actionable Steps:
   - Research into emerging career trends and alignment of skills with future demands are advised.
   - Mentorship from industry professionals who have navigated similar paths can provide valuable insights.

- Investment in continuous learning through courses, certifications, and networking is crucial.

4. **Time Management and Productivity Habits:** While financial resources can often be replenished, wasted time is irretrievable. Prioritizing high-value activities ensures steady progress toward long-term goals.

   Actionable Steps:
   - Time-blocking techniques can be utilized to schedule important tasks.
   - Distractions should be avoided, and clear priorities established for each day.
   - Continuous refinement of productivity strategies is recommended to maximize efficiency.

Success is not dictated by starting points but by the efficacy of planning, adaptability, and decisive action. The earlier thoughtful financial and career decisions are initiated, the greater the likelihood of building a life characterized by financial independence, personal fulfilment, and career satisfaction. While initial advantages may offer a head start, discipline, strategic planning, and resilience ultimately determine outcomes.

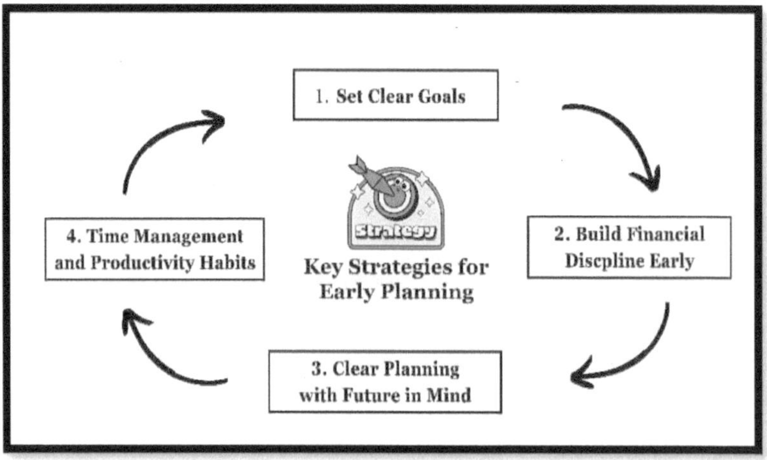

What F.I.R(Re-career).E. Really Means: Redefining Success on Your Terms

F.I.R(Re-career).E. is more than a concept; it's a transformative framework for designing a life of financial independence, career fulfilment, and purposeful living. It is about moving beyond societal expectations and crafting a life that is truly yours. This framework consists of three interconnected pillars:

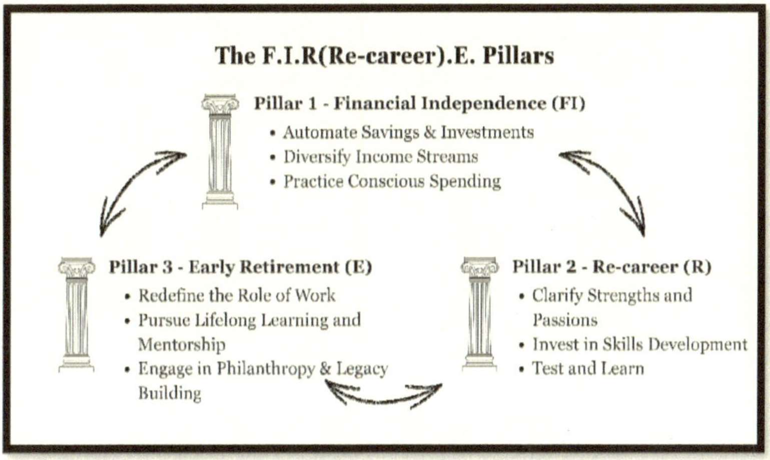

1. **Pillar 1 - Financial Independence (FI):** Financial independence occurs when income from assets or diversified sources covers living expenses. It is not just about wealth accumulation, but about reclaiming control over time and choices. With financial security, career decisions can be made deliberately, and lifestyles aligned with personal values.

   Recommended Actions:
   - **Automate Savings & Investments**: Set up regular contributions to retirement accounts, index funds, and other passive instruments.
   - **Diversify Income Streams**: Build secondary sources such as dividend-generating assets, rental income, or advisory work.
   - **Practice Conscious Spending**: Prioritize investments in experiences, personal development, and long-term security rather than consumption.

2. **Pillar 2 – Re-career (R): Redefining Work and Contribution:** Re-careering is the intentional pivot into a new career path that better reflects evolving interests, values, or life stages. Whether mid-career or post-retirement, re-careering supports continued growth, relevance, and fulfilment.

   Recommended Actions:

   - **Clarify Strengths and Passions Using the Ikigai Framework**: The Ikigai[1] model—originating from Japan—helps identify a fulfilling career path by exploring four dimensions:

     1. *What one loves?*
     2. *What one is good at?*
     3. *What the world needs?*
     4. *What one can be paid for?*

     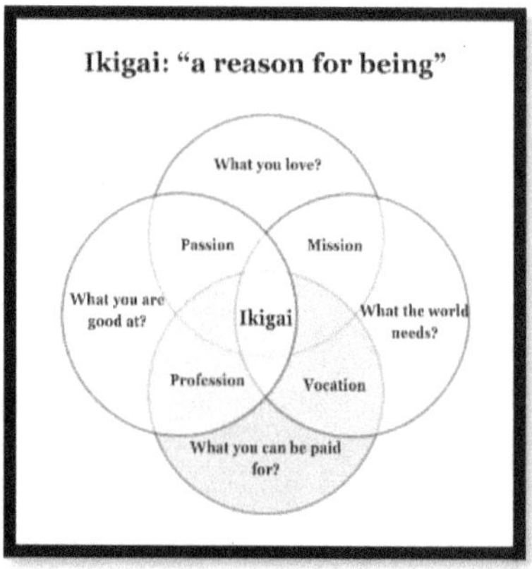

     By mapping overlapping areas among these dimensions, individuals can uncover meaningful professional directions that integrate passion, talent, contribution, and sustainability.
   - **Invest in Skills Development**: Attend professional workshops, online courses, or formal education tailored to the desired field.
   - **Test and Learn**: Pilot new ideas through side projects, consulting, or volunteering to assess interest and fit before full transition.

[1] **Further reading:** The practical application of the Ikigai framework is explored in detail in *Limitless Possibilities ~ YK Png* (available on Amazon).

3. **Pillar 3 – Early Retirement (E): Freedom to Redefine Time and Purpose:** Early retirement within the F.I.R(Re-career).E. framework is not a complete withdrawal from work, but a conscious exit from obligatory employment. It is the freedom to dedicate time to intrinsically motivating pursuits—creative work, travel, contribution, or personal growth—supported by financial stability.

   Recommended Actions:

   - **Redefine the Role of Work**: Shift focus from full-time employment to flexible or impact-driven activities.
   - **Pursue Lifelong Learning and Mentorship**: Many early retirees contribute as mentors, educators, or community leaders, sharing accumulated experience.
   - **Engage in Philanthropy and Legacy Building**: Financial freedom enables efforts that generate lasting social or generational impact.

The Interconnected Pillars: Integrated Design for a Fulfilling Life

These three pillars—Financial Independence, Re-career, and Early Retirement—are mutually reinforcing. Financial independence provides the security to re-career without fear; re-careering sustains relevance and energy; early retirement offers the space to pursue meaning on one's own terms.

Together, they form a holistic life design framework—one that supports personal agency, career fluidity, and purposeful contribution across all life stages.

Reflection Prompt - Define Your Version of Success:

- *What does a meaningful career look like to me?*
- *How do I want to contribute to society when money is no longer a concern?*
- *Which pillar do I need to focus on most right now—and why?*

The Transformative Power of Financial Independence and Re-careering

F.I.R(Re-career).E is more than a financial strategy—it is a philosophy of intentional living. Financial independence empowers individuals to redesign careers and lives around values, purpose, and long-term goals. Here's how this framework can transform an individual's life:

- **Empowerment to Make Purposeful Choices:** With financial freedom, work and activities are driven by conviction, not necessity. Time becomes a currency for teaching, mentoring, writing, entrepreneurship, or community impact.
- **Reduction of Financial Stress and Improved Well-Being:** Financial independence eases chronic stress, a leading contributor to mental strain. While not eliminating all challenges, it allows decisions to be made with clarity and confidence, improving overall quality of life.
- **Enabling Meaningful Risk-Taking:** Security creates space for calculated risks—career transitions, business ventures, or creative projects—without fear of destabilization. Planning, budgeting, and risk assessment turn uncertainty into opportunity and long-term growth.
- **Inspiring Transformation in Others:** Living intentionally sparks curiosity and hope in others. Many have asked how I shifted from a conventional career to a purposeful, flexible life—questions that inspired this book. Witnessing deliberate living can create a ripple effect, encouraging others to redefine success.

F.I.R(Re-career).E reframes success around meaning, freedom, and contribution. It is not reserved for the wealthy—it is for anyone willing to plan strategically, act consistently, and live deliberately. Financial independence and re-careering are tools, not endpoints, enabling a life that truly matters.

Summary

Chapter 1: My Journey Towards Financial Independence and Re-careering explores my personal journey towards financial independence and re-careering, highlighting how early planning, rather than privilege, plays a crucial role in shaping our financial and professional future. Through my experiences—from facing adversity to discovering new opportunities—I share the pivotal moment that reshaped my understanding of money and freedom.

The chapter also redefines what F.I.R(Re-career).E. means and explains why financial independence and re-careering are life-changing beyond conventional financial success. It is a framework for designing a fulfilling, flexible, and purpose-driven life, where financial independence empowers you to pursue meaningful work on your terms.

Key Takeaways:

- **Your Starting Point Doesn't Define Your Destination:** Success comes from resilience and determination.
- **Adversity Can Be a Catalyst for Growth:** Challenges like career setbacks can become opportunities to build strength and discover new paths.
- **Adaptability is Key to Progress:** Stepping outside comfort zone, like overseas jobs, drives growth and future success.
- **Financial independence equals freedom:** It's about options and control, not just money.
- **Plan early, pivot strategically:** Proactive planning and career shifts can reshape your future.
- **Re-careering unlocks passion:** With financial security, you can pursue work that aligns with your values and purpose.

Practical Tips:

- Start tracking your expenses and set financial goals.
- Identify skills and interests that align with re-careering paths.
- Explore passive income opportunities and financial literacy.

In the next chapter, we will delve into **The F.I.R(Re-career).E. Mindset**, exploring the mental shifts needed to break free from traditional career limitations. We will discuss the key differences between financial security and true financial freedom, how to cultivate a growth mindset, and real-life examples of individuals who successfully transitioned into fulfilling re-careers.

Reflection Prompts & Mini Exercises

"Engage with your own journey as you reflect on mine." ~ YK Png

---

1. From Adversity to Opportunity

Prompt:

- *What early life challenges shaped your mindset around money, career, or self-worth?*
- *In hindsight, what hidden strengths did those experiences reveal?*
- *How have those lessons influenced your path to financial independence or re-careering?*

Mini Exercise: Adversity Strength Map

- Draw a circle in the center and label it with a past challenge.
- Around it, write the skills, traits, or values you developed as a result *(e.g., resilience, adaptability)*.
- Reflect: *How can you apply these to your next chapter?*

---

2. Early Planning vs. Privilege

Prompt:

- *Did you grow up with access to financial education or role models?*
- *What proactive planning habits have made the biggest difference in your life so far?*
- *What choices are within your control today, regardless of your background?*

Mini Exercise: Control What You Can Chart

- In two columns, list:
  – Column A: "Circumstances I Couldn't Control" *(e.g., upbringing, economic background)*
- – Column B: "Decisions I Can Control" *(e.g., saving early, lifelong learning)*
- Highlight one decision you can make this week that builds your future.

---

3. Breaking the Myths of Success

Prompt:

- *What common success myths have influenced your career or financial path?*
- *Have you ever felt "behind" due to comparing with others?*

- *Who is someone who defied conventional definitions of success—and how?*

Mini Exercise: Myth Buster Journal

- Write down one success myth you've believed *(e.g., "You must own property to be successful").*
- Counter it with a truth or example that redefines success on your terms.
- What belief will you now replace it with?

---

4. Pitfalls to Avoid on the F.I.R(Re-career).E Journey

Prompt:

- *Looking back, what financial or career decision do you wish you had made differently?*
- *What led to that decision—lack of information, pressure, fear, etc.?*
- *What do you now do differently as a result of that experience?*

Mini Exercise: Decision Debrief

- Choose one past misstep *(e.g., delaying investments, job-hopping without strategy).*
- Reflect: *What mindset or habit would have helped then?*
- Write down a new commitment or behaviour to avoid repeating it.

---

5. Creating Your Re-careered Future

Prompt:

- *What would your ideal life look like 5 years from now—career, lifestyle, health, contribution?*
- *What trade-offs are you willing to make today to create that future?*
- *How would financial freedom change your impact and daily experience?*

Mini Exercise: Future Vision Board (Quick Sketch)

- Sketch or list three things your re-careered life includes *(e.g., flexible work, part-time coaching, location freedom).*
- Write one action for each to begin making it real—starting today.

Chapter 2: The F.I.R(Re-career).E. Mindset

"Financial freedom is not about being rich; it's about having control over your time and choices." ~ YK Png

---

The F.I.R(Re-career).E. journey represents a fundamental shift in mindset—moving beyond the pursuit of wealth accumulation toward designing a life of autonomy, purpose, and alignment. Rather than waiting for conventional retirement to live fully, this mindset empowers individuals to redefine success much earlier.

This chapter explores how embracing this journey requires both psychological and strategic reorientation. It is not solely about disciplined saving or intelligent investing—though those elements are critical—but also about reframing beliefs about money, work, and life satisfaction. The F.I.R(Re-career).E. mindset envisions a world where work becomes optional, time is intentionally allocated, and career choices reflect core values.

The Difference Between Financial Security and Financial Freedom

Many people use the terms financial security and financial freedom interchangeably, but they represent distinct stages of financial well-being.

- **Financial Security - Stability Without Freedom:** Financial security reflects having sufficient savings, insurance, and income to cover basic needs—such as housing, food, and healthcare—without constant financial anxiety. However, employment may still be required to sustain this lifestyle. ***Illustration:*** A professional earning $8,000 monthly may appear secure, with the ability to meet obligations and save. Yet, job loss would quickly reintroduce stress if financial buffers were insufficient.

- **Financial Freedom - Autonomy and Choice:** Financial freedom is achieved when passive income from investments covers living expenses, enabling work to become a choice rather than a necessity.

Feature/Aspect	Financial Security	Financial Freedom
Core Definition	Funds cover basic needs without constant anxiety.	Passive income covers all living expenses.
Key Characteristic	Stability for essential needs.	Autonomy and Choice in life/work.
Relationship to Work	Employment still required.	Work becomes a choice.
Primary Income Source	Active employment income.	Passive income from investments
Example Scenario	Meeting obligations on $8K/month, but job loss creates stress.	Investment income covers all monthly expenses, enabling chosen pursuits.
Outcome/Feeling	Peace of mind for basics, limited flexibility.	Complete control of time/decisions, ultimate flexibility.

Practical Steps Toward Financial Freedom:

1. **Define the Financial Security Number:** Calculate the monthly amount required to meet essential expenses without strain.
2. **Set a Financial Freedom Target**: Identify the passive income needed to maintain a preferred lifestyle.
3. **Build Income Streams:** Establish sustainable sources of passive income, such as dividend-yielding investments, real estate, or digital assets.

Cultivating a Growth Mindset[2] for Career and Financial Resilience

In today's dynamic global environment, career and financial success are no longer dictated solely by credentials, technical skills, or even hard work. Increasingly, the differentiating factor lies in one's mindset—specifically, the cognitive framework through which challenges, setbacks, opportunities, and personal potential are perceived.

Central to this transformative perspective is the shift from a Fixed Mindset to a Growth Mindset, a concept popularized by psychologist Carol Dweck (2006). Those with a fixed mindset see abilities as innate and unchangeable, while growth-minded individuals recognize that skills and potential can be developed through effort, learning, and perseverance.

This mindset distinction is not merely academic; it profoundly influences the navigation of careers, financial endeavours, and processes of personal reinvention.

My Growth Mindset Journey: From Struggle to Reinvention

Success in career and finance isn't just about talent or luck—it's about mindset. My journey has been shaped by resilience, adaptability, and a relentless commitment to growth, even when faced with daunting challenges.

1. ***Early Education - Overcoming Language and Cultural Barriers:*** *Growing up in a Malay-speaking environment in Kelantan, Malaysia, I faced a major transition when I moved to an English-medium secondary school in Singapore. The language barrier was intimidating, and I struggled to keep up. But instead of giving up, I embraced the challenge:*
    - ***Worked harder*** *than my peers to improve my English.*

---

[2] **Further reading:** The "Mindset" is explored in detail in *Limitless Possibilities ~ YK Png* (available on Amazon).

- ***Developed resilience****—understanding that struggle is part of growth.*

This experience taught me that obstacles are temporary if met with persistence.

2. ***Career Setbacks - Job Loss, Failed Business, and Reinvention:*** *Years later, as a professional, I faced a major test: losing my job at UCB due to company restructuring. Instead of self-pitying and living in misery, I decided to explore new paths.*
   - ***Tried entrepreneurship****, launching a generic trading firm. Though it eventually closed, the experience as an entrepreneur and lessons in staying resilient and coping with failures were invaluable.*
   - ***Diversified income streams****, working as a hospital pharmacist, part-time lecturer, course writer, and locum pharmacist in a retail store. This "multi-hat" approach not only restored financial stability but also broadened my professional horizons. It taught me the importance of financial adaptability, resilience mindset and the power of having multiple income streams.*

3. ***Stepping Out of Comfort Zone - Leading in a Cantonese Speaking Environment:*** *One of my biggest leaps of faith was accepting a General Manager role in Hong Kong, despite not speaking Cantonese. Many would have avoided such a challenge, but I saw it as a growth opportunity:*
   - ***Learned key Cantonese dialect*** *to connect with local teams.*
   - ***Focused on leadership and operational skills,*** *ensuring language limitations never overshadowed core competencies.*
   - ***Built trust through competence and adaptability,*** *demonstrating that a proactive mindset consistently trumps perceived barriers*

This experience reinforced that growth happens outside comfort zones. Language was a barrier, but mindset was undeniably the bridge.

Key Lessons from My Journey:

- **Leverage Strengths and Address Gaps:** Maximize proficiencies while strategically improving weaknesses.
- **Embrace Continuous Growth:** See development as an ongoing, lifelong endeavor. Sustained learning, curiosity, and adaptability are key.
- **Reframe Challenges as Opportunities:** View obstacles as starting points for growth, innovation, and resilience.
- **Extract Lessons from Setbacks:** Treat every failure as valuable feedback to learn, adapt, and progress.
- **Cultivate Skills and Relationships:** Competence opens doors; meaningful relationships with mentors, peers, or clients unlock unforeseen opportunities.

Building a Growth Mindset: Practical Strategies

To foster a mindset of growth and adaptability, consider the following practices:

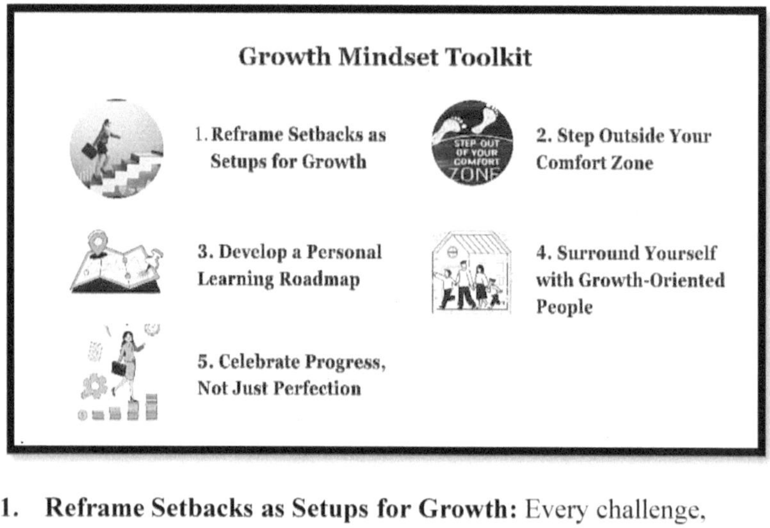

1. **Reframe Setbacks as Setups for Growth:** Every challenge, failure, or disappointment is an invitation to grow. Ask yourself: *"What can I learn from this?"* or *"What is this experience trying to teach me?"*

   Example: *When my business venture didn't succeed, I didn't see it as the end—I saw it as on-the-ground training for my next chapter.*

2. **Step Outside Your Comfort Zone Regularly:** Growth doesn't happen where it's comfortable. Whether it's taking on a new role, learning a new skill, or entering an unfamiliar environment—lean into discomfort.

3. **Develop a Personal Learning Roadmap:** Create a plan for continuous development. Identify one area for career growth and one for financial knowledge every quarter. Read, attend workshops, or find mentors.

   My Practice: *I continued investing in certifications and skills well into my fifties and beyond—including coaching, adult education, and digital entrepreneurship.*

4. **Surround Yourself with Growth-Oriented People:** Environment matters. Seek mentors, peers, and communities who challenge and inspire growth. Avoid echo chambers of negativity or stagnation.

5. **Celebrate Progress, Not Just Perfection:** Focus on consistent progress over time. Acknowledge improvements over perfection.

By intentionally applying these strategies, you'll develop the mental resilience and adaptability required for both professional reinvention and long-term financial independence. The growth mindset isn't a switch you flip—it's a muscle you strengthen. Keep working it, and you'll unlock possibilities you never thought possible.

From Paycheck to Purpose: Reimagining Work

From early on, work is often framed as a transaction—time exchanged for money. This mindset can trap individuals in routines that meet obligations but lack meaning, with fulfilment postponed to retirement.

Work, however, can be more than a paycheck. When aligned with values and passions, it becomes a source of growth, contribution, and purpose. Professional pursuits then shift from necessity to meaningful calling, creating both personal satisfaction and lasting impact.

Two dominant mindsets around work provide contrasting lenses:

1. **The Paycheck Mindset - Survival and Stability:** This mindset views work as primarily transactional. Priorities include income, job security, and external validation. While this phase may be necessary in the early stages of a career, remaining in it indefinitely can come at a cost:
   - **Burnout**: Prolonged emotional output without alignment or fulfilment leads to exhaustion.
   - **Disengagement**: Work becomes routine; presence without purpose.
   - **Midlife Crisis**: Accumulated achievements feel hollow when intrinsic meaning is absent.
   - **Untapped Potential**: Playing safe may prevent the pursuit of more meaningful and impactful contributions.

   Illustration: *Mr. Lim, a banker in Singapore, spent two decades in a lucrative yet unfulfilling role. Despite material comfort, he experienced a lack of direction, prompting a later-life reassessment.*

2. **The Purpose Mindset - Meaning and Contribution:** This mindset redefines success through alignment with values, intrinsic motivation, and impact. Purpose-driven professionals may not always earn more, but they experience:
   - **Deeper Engagement**: A strong connection to the work being done.
   - **Intrinsic Motivation**: Productivity and creativity are powered by passion.
   - **Resilience**: Challenges are embraced as purposeful missions.

   Illustration: *Sim Wong Hoo, the late founder of Creative Technology, pursued innovation over profit, exemplifying a purpose-led career that reshaped an industry.*

A Framework for Shifting from Paycheck to Purpose

Transitioning from a purely income-driven work mindset to one rooted in purpose does not necessitate a dramatic career change overnight. The key lies in intentional exploration and incremental action, starting from one's current position and utilizing existing resources.

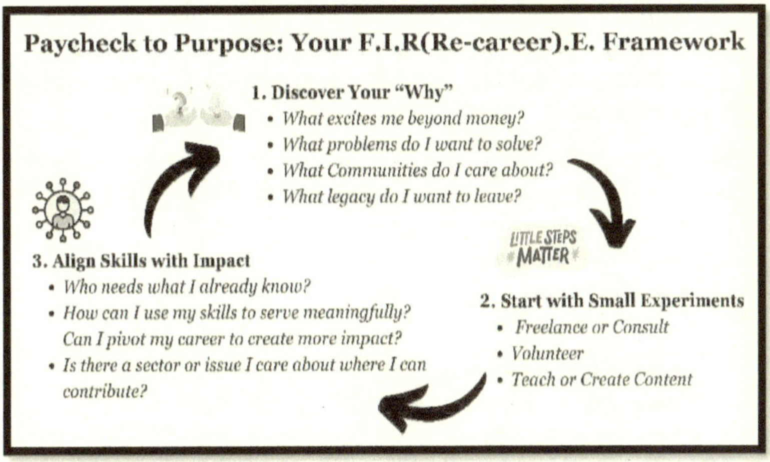

This framework outlines a strategic approach to cultivate meaningful professional engagement:

1. **Discover Your "Why":** Before chasing promotions or higher salaries, reflect on deeper drivers:
   - *What excites me beyond money?*
   - *What problems do I want to solve?*
   - *Which communities matter to me?*
   - *What legacy do I wish to leave?*

   Exercises:
   - Apply the *5 Whys*: ask "Why do I work?" five times to uncover intrinsic motivation—service, creativity, impact, or freedom.
   - List your top three non-financial motivators. If none emerge, consider exploring new directions.

2. **Start with Small Experiments:** Purpose-driven work can begin without leaving your job:
   - **Freelance or consult:** Apply existing skills in areas of interest.
   - **Volunteer:** Support NGOs, social enterprises, or mentoring programs.
   - **Teach or create content:** Launch workshops, blogs, or part-time classes to test interests.

Example: A corporate lawyer in her 40s volunteered with a social enterprise for low-income entrepreneurs, eventually transitioning into full-time advocacy, turning legal expertise into social impact.

3. **Align Skills with Impact:** Your current skills often hold more value than perceived. Seek ways to contribute meaningfully:
   - *Who needs my expertise?*
   - *How can I serve a meaningful cause?*
   - *Can I pivot to create greater impact?*
   - *Which sectors or issues resonate with me?*

   Example: A mid-career marketing executive moved into sustainability, helping green start-ups communicate their mission—work that energizes her more than traditional corporate roles ever did.

Adopting an Abundance Mindset

Purpose-driven work thrives with an abundance mindset:
- Competition inspires, rather than threatens.
- Challenges are learning opportunities.
- Actions arise from confidence, not fear.

Success is no longer defined by title, income, or hours, but by alignment with values, vision, and meaningful contribution. Stagnation is not permanent; it's never too late to begin, and no one is too far behind.

The journey starts with one question: *"What life—and legacy—do I want to create?"* From there, intentional steps guide the path toward a fulfilling, purpose-driven career.

My Journey: From Corporate Leader to Regulatory Service Provider, Business Coach & Writer

After decades in the pharmaceutical industry, I discovered that my true passion lay in empowering individuals—especially fellow pharmacists, mid-career professionals, and young talents—to thrive in their careers. Whether it's advancing in corporate roles, transitioning into entrepreneurship, or finding deeper purpose in their work, I am committed to helping others unlock their potential.

Even during my tenure in senior leadership, I found fulfilment in coaching and developing my teams. While I could have easily delegated training responsibilities, I chose to personally mentor staff, recognizing the lasting impact of growth-driven leadership. That insight sparked a purposeful transition into the next phase of my career.

To re-career with intent, I:

1. *Earned certifications in coaching and adult education, equipping myself as a certified coach and trainer.*
2. *Expanded my capabilities into digital marketing and built a values-aligned professional network.*
3. *Authored Limitless Possibilities to share my experiences and empower others through personal growth.*
4. *Re-engaged with the pharmaceutical field as a regulatory service provider, collaborating with fellow pharmacists to support product registration for both local and overseas companies.*

Today, I wear multiple hats—business coach, trainer, writer, and regulatory consultant. Each role allows me to combine expertise, purpose, and service in ways that energize and inspire me.

Key Takeaways:

- **Evolving Purpose in Career:** Careers are rarely linear. Even after decades in corporate roles, it is possible to realign with passions and discover renewed purpose in new roles.
- **Leadership as Empowerment:** True leadership goes beyond managing teams—it involves mentoring, coaching, and investing in others' growth.

- **Strategic Re-careering Requires Preparation:** Continuous learning, certifications, upskilling, and cultivating a purpose-driven network are essential for meaningful career transitions.
- **Complementary Diverse Roles:** Embracing multiple roles—coaching, writing, consulting—can create a dynamic, fulfilling career that leverages past experience while pursuing passion and impact.
- **Leveraging Industry Experience:** Returning to a familiar field, such as pharmaceutical consulting, demonstrates that re-careering can redeploy existing knowledge toward a new mission.
- **Contribution as Fulfilment:** Aligning professional work with service—through coaching, consulting, or authorship—leads to deeper personal and professional satisfaction.

The Reward: A Career That Feels Like a Calling

Shifting focus from *"What can I get?"* to *"What can I give?"* transforms work and life:

- **Enhanced Resilience:** Challenges become stepping stones rather than roadblocks. Purpose provides the "why" that fuels perseverance and converts setbacks into growth opportunities.
- **Intrinsic Motivation:** When work holds inherent meaning, performance thrives without external pressure. Passion drives energy, focus, and momentum, independent of titles, promotions, or pay.
- **Legacy Beyond Material Wealth:** The true measure of a purposeful career lies in the impact made—mentoring, improving systems, helping clients, or inspiring others. Contribution leaves a lasting imprint beyond financial gain.

When professional activities align with personal values and vision, work becomes a platform for joy, growth, and contribution. True success transcends financial independence; it is waking each day with purpose, knowing actions matter.

Financial stability and personal meaning are not mutually exclusive. It is possible to re-career into work that inspires, elevates others, and fully leverages one's potential. The journey toward a fulfilling, purpose-driven career can—and should—begin today.

Summary

Chapter 2: The F.I.R(Re-career).E. Mindset introduced the foundational mindset behind Financial Independence and Re-careering Early (F.I.R(Re-career).E.). Rather than starting with numbers or financial strategies, the journey begins with a mindset shift—a conscious decision to reclaim ownership of your time, align your work with your values, and redefine success beyond traditional wealth.

The text distinguished between financial security and financial freedom. While security offers stability, freedom gives you choice—the freedom to decide *how, when, and whether* you want to work. This shift requires more than just saving; it involves setting clear financial freedom targets and building diversified income streams that support your ideal lifestyle.

A central pillar of the F.I.R(Re-career).E. mindset is growth. Drawing from my own career transitions—from overcoming early language barriers to re-careering after setbacks—the chapter demonstrated how a growth mindset cultivates resilience, adaptability, and continuous learning.

The summary then examined the shift from a paycheck mindset—working out of necessity—to a purpose mindset—working for meaning. When career aligns with passions and values, it transforms into a source of fulfilment rather than obligation. Practical tools, like identifying your "*why*" and testing purpose-driven projects, help guide this transition.

Drawing from my personal journey—from corporate leadership to regulatory service provider, coach, and writer, I shared how this mindset shift enabled me to re-career with purpose and clarity.

Key Takeaways:

- **Financial freedom is about choice**, not escape—it's the power to decide how your time is spent.
- **A growth mindset is essential** to resilience, reinvention, and long-term success.
- **Reframing your work around purpose** enhances motivation, engagement, and well-being.
- **Your career is not fixed**—it should evolve with your values, passions, and aspirations.

Practical Tips:

- **Define Your Financial Freedom Target:** Know the amount of passive income needed to support your ideal lifestyle.
- **Adopt a Growth Mindset:** Embrace challenges and setbacks as stepping stones. Develop both technical and human skills.
- **Explore Purpose:** Use the "5 Whys" exercise to dig into what truly drives you.
- **Start Small, Experiment Before You Leap:** Test your interests through freelancing, volunteering, or side projects before making a full transition.
- **Reflect Often:** Keep a journal of your progress. Your growth story becomes both a roadmap and a source of motivation.

In the next chapter, **Planning for the Future – Career, Finances, and Life**, we'll move from mindset to strategy. You'll learn how to integrate career planning, financial strategy, and personal well-being into a cohesive roadmap. Drawing from real-life transitions—including my own—you'll discover how to make deliberate choices at each life stage to prepare for your ideal re-career. Whether you're in your 30s, 40s, or 50s, it's never too early—or too late—to start building the future you want.

Reflection Prompts & Mini Exercises

"Engage deeply. Reflect honestly. Apply purposefully". ~ YK Png

---

1. Financial Security vs. Financial Freedom

Prompt:

- *What does "financial security" look like currently?*
- *What would "financial freedom" enable you to do?*
- *Are your current financial habits moving you closer to freedom or just sustaining security?*

Mini Exercise: Draw two circles.

- Label one *Security* and list your current financial commitments.
- Label the other *Freedom* and list the things you would pursue if money weren't a limitation (e.g., starting a business, traveling, contributing to a cause).
- Now identify one habit you can adopt today to begin bridging the gap.

---

2. Cultivating a Growth Mindset

Prompt: Recall a past challenge or failure.

- *What did you learn from it that you still apply today?*
- *In what areas of your life are you operating from a fixed mindset (e.g., "I'm just not good at ___")? How can you reframe that belief?*

Mini Exercise: Growth Audit.

- Write down three skills or areas you feel you're *"not naturally good at."*
- For each, list one action you can take this month to improve—even slightly. *e.g., "Networking" → Attend one industry meet-up or LinkedIn coffee chat.*

---

3. Paycheck vs. Purpose Mindset

Prompt:

- *Why did you choose your current job? B*
- *What energizes you at work beyond your salary?*
- *Have you ever felt "in flow" at work?*

Mini Exercise: Purpose Clarity Journal. Write down answers to:

- *"What do I value most in life and work?"*
- *"What kind of problems do I feel called to solve?"*
- *"Who benefits from my work today—and who could benefit if I aligned more with my purpose?"*

---

4. Shifting from Paycheck to Purpose

Prompt:

- *If you had one day a week to work on anything you wanted—regardless of pay—what would it be?*
- *What skills do you currently possess that can be repurposed to make a greater impact?*

Mini Exercise: Purpose Pilot Project

- Commit to a "purpose experiment" for the next 30 days: Start a blog, consult a non-profit, mentor a junior, or explore a side hustle aligned with your interests.
- Reflect weekly: *What energizes me? What feels like flow?*

---

5. The Re-career Mindset in Action

Prompt:

- *What assumptions are you holding about age, re-careering, or financial risks?*
- *How would your career change if you believed it was never too late to grow or pivot?*

Mini Exercise: Re-career Vision Canvas

- Imagine it's 3–5 years from now. You've re-careered successfully. Describe: *What are you doing? Who are you serving? How does it feel?*
- Now, list three practical steps you can take this year to move in that direction.

Chapter 3: Planning for the Future - Career, Finances, and Health

"Success is where preparation and opportunity meet." ~ Bobby Unser

---

Success is often attributed to hard work, talent, or luck, but one critical factor is frequently overlooked—intentional planning. Without a roadmap, even the most ambitious dreams remain out of reach.

The journey toward F.I.R(Re-career).E. is not about reacting to life's circumstances—it's about proactively building a life that reflects values, priorities, and vision for the future. That kind of life doesn't happen by accident. It requires thoughtful planning across the areas that matter most.

This chapter explores a three-pillar framework that has anchored the F.I.R(Re-career).E. journey: Career, Finances, and Health.

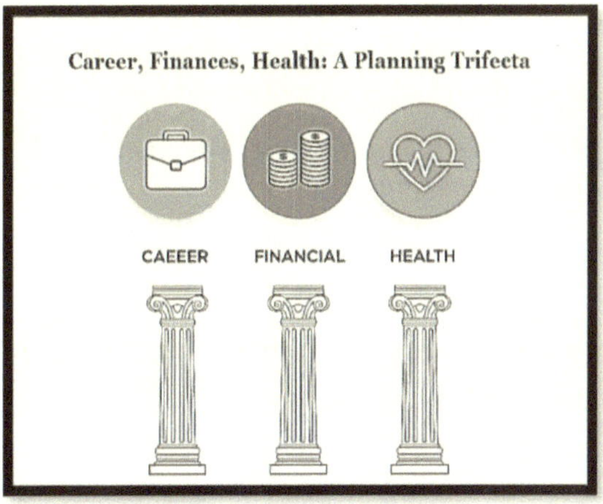

These pillars don't exist in silos—they influence and reinforce each other. A thriving career without financial discipline can still lead to stress. Financial independence without health limits freedom. And chasing health goals without purposeful work may feel hollow.
This isn't about striving for perfection—it's about aligning efforts with purpose. This chapter will help to build a plan that supports not just success—but significance.

Pillar 1: Career planning - Navigating Transitions with Purpose

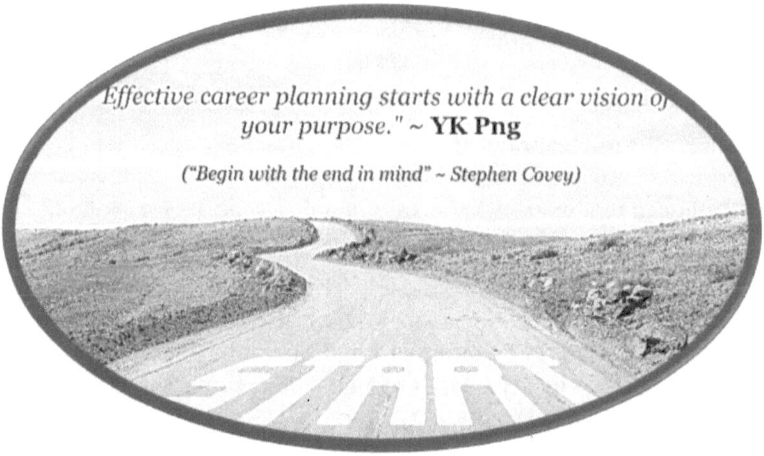

The traditional career ladder —spend 40 years with one company and retire with a gold watch—is no longer relevant. Industries shift, technologies evolve, and job roles transform overnight. Today, career success is less about climbing a set path and more about navigating change with intention, agility, and foresight.

My Journey: Laying the Foundation – Financial Strategy and Career Transitions

My path to re-careering was gradual, grounded in financial discipline, skill development, and deliberate career choices. Re-careering, I realized, is not simply changing jobs—it is creating the conditions to explore what truly matters.

- ***Strategic Industry Pivot:*** *Motivated by financial opportunity and skill growth, I moved into the pharmaceutical industry, exploring roles in sales, marketing, and leadership. Each role broadened my expertise and opened new doors. Financial discipline—saving, investing, and resisting lifestyle inflation—gave me the flexibility to take calculated risks, pursue further education, and relocate for career advancement.*
- ***Deliberate Skill Stacking:*** *Sales honed communication and persuasion. Marketing strengthened strategic thinking.*

Regulatory affairs deepened analytical skills and attention to detail. General management cultivated leadership and a systems perspective. These transferable skills became the foundation for versatile career options.

- ***Financial Preparedness:*** *Tracking expenses and adopting a long-term investment mindset allowed me to live below my means and invest consistently. This discipline created choices—often more valuable than money itself.*
- ***The Crossroads:*** *By my early 50s, having achieved partial financial independence, I faced a decision: continue climbing the corporate ladder or pivot to work with deeper meaning. The financial foundation provided the freedom to choose purpose over obligation.*

Key Takeaways:

- **Strategic Career Pivots:** Early, intentional role changes expand skills and unlock growth opportunities.
- **Prioritizing Financial Health:** Saving, investing, and avoiding lifestyle inflation provide flexibility for calculated career risks.
- **Deliberate Skill Stacking:** Acquiring transferable skills enhances adaptability and opens diverse professional avenues.
- **Financial Discipline:** Consistently living below one's means and investing the difference generates future options.
- **Choice Through Financial Independence:** Even moderate financial independence enables pivoting toward meaningful work rather than being bound by traditional career progression.

Practical Questions to Guide Planning

Some practical questions to ask yourself:

- *What kind of lifestyle do I want to lead in later life?*
- *What does financial freedom look like for me?*
- *How much would I need to sustain it?*
- *What kind of work would bring me purpose as I age?*

While not every goal may be fully realized, early planning provides clarity, confidence, and a roadmap for future pivots. Guidance from mentors or career coaches can offer accountability, insight, and support as values are clarified and informed decisions are made.

Career Planning Across Life Stages

Career planning is a lifelong journey, not a single event. Just like financial planning, it's a continuous process of reflection, reassessment, and realignment. Whether you're a student or a seasoned professional, intentional career planning can lead to a life of purpose, fulfillment, and financial independence.

1. **Undergraduates – Exploration and Learning:** University years are a time for exploration. Don't rush to commit to a single path. Instead, use this time as a testing ground.
    - **Explore Broadly, Commit Deeply:** Explore internships in diverse fields like tech, non-profits, or government. Unexpected passions may be discovered in unforeseen areas.
    - **Engage with Professionals:** Talk to people in roles to be admired. Ask about their daily work, challenges, and what truly motivates them.
    - **Master the Skill of Learning:** In a rapidly changing world, the ability to learn, unlearn, and relearn is the most valuable asset.

> **Tip:** Use tools like MBTI and Holland RIASEC Model to understand your personality traits and natural inclinations—it'll help you choose more aligned paths.

2. **Young Professionals – Building the Foundation:** Early career is all about building a solid foundation of skills and credibility. Be bold, take calculated risks, and maximize every learning opportunity.
    - **Build Foundational Skills:** Focus on developing core competencies like leadership, communication, and project management. These are valuable in any industry.
    - **Identify Energy Patterns:** Pay attention to which tasks energize, and which ones drain. Over time, these patterns will guide career moves.
    - **Seek and Offer Mentorship:** Learn from those ahead and help those just starting. Mentorship is a two-way street that grows both network and perspective.

> **Tip:** Keep a career journal. Reflect monthly on what you've learned, what you enjoyed, and where you struggled. Patterns will emerge that guide your future moves.

3. **Mid-Career Professionals – The Reinvention Imperative:** By the 40s or 50s, many have years of experience and a stable income, but may also feel restless or stuck. This is a pivotal time for reinvention. The goal is no longer just to climb the ladder, but to realign a career with evolving values and priorities. The decisions made now will shape one's professional legacy and personal fulfillment.

   Common Challenges Faced by Mid-Career Professionals:

   - **Career Stagnation:** A feeling of being confined to the same role or function for an extended period.
   - **Job Insecurity:** Disruptions arising from automation, globalization, or economic downturns.
   - **Work-Life Imbalance:** Difficulties in effectively managing professional responsibilities alongside family and personal priorities.
   - **Skill Irrelevance:** The rapid pace of change rendering certain skills outdated without continuous refreshment.

   To effectively navigate this stage, equipping oneself with the **BRIDGE Elements**[3] is recommended:

   - **B – Branding:** Reinventing one's personal brand to accurately reflect current strengths and aspirations.
   - **R - Right Attitude:** Maintaining an open-minded, proactive, and future-oriented disposition.
   - **I - Interpersonal Skills and Networking**: Cultivating authentic relationships that facilitate new opportunities.

---

[3] **Further reading:** The "BRIDGE Elements" is explored in detail in *The BRIDGE Career Handbook* and *Limitless Possibilities ~ YK Png* (available on Amazon).

- **D – Development:** Investing in acquiring new skills, particularly in areas such as digital fluency, coaching, and data literacy.
- **G - Gain Influence:** Demonstrating value and leading with impact, even in informal capacities.
- **E - Emotional Intelligence:** Developing the ability to understand and manage oneself and others, especially in complex situations.

BRIDGE Elements

B - Brand Yourself: Be the Most Interesting Person in the Room.

R - Right Attitude: Foundation for Growth.

I - Interpersonal Skills and Networking: Building Bridges to Success.

D - Development: Your Continuous Journey of Growth.

G - Gain Influence: Become a Leader Worth Following.

E - EQ: The Key to Connection and Transformation

My Personal Journey: A Journey of Resilience and Reinvention

In the early 2000s, I was doing exceptionally well at UCB, a global pharmaceutical company. I led the growth of key products like Zyrtec across several countries in Southeast Asia, and the markets under my leadership were thriving. However, when Zyrtec lost its patent protection, major markets like the U.S., Europe, and Japan saw significant sales decline. Despite the strong performance from my region, I lost my job due to global restructuring.

This unexpected turn was a defining moment in my life. As the main provider for my family, I had no luxury of time or prolonged uncertainty. I took on multiple roles at once—working as a hospital and locum pharmacist, and a part-time marketing lecturer. Leveraging the master's degree I had earned, I also became a course writer for a polytechnic and the Open University. These opportunities kept me professionally active and financially afloat.

This mindset eventually paid off. I was headhunted for an international role as General Manager for a medical equipment company in Hong Kong and China. The move could have been intimidating since I didn't speak Cantonese, but I saw it as an opportunity to learn a new dialect, immerse myself in a new culture, and expand my regional leadership skills.

Key Takeaways:

- **Resilience is Key:** Setbacks are inevitable. Your response and adaptability define you.
- **Financial Agility:** Cultivating multiple income streams provides stability during transitions.
- **Leverage Your Strengths:** Reframe existing skills to unlock new opportunities.
- **Embrace Discomfort:** Growth happens outside your comfort zone. Challenges spark breakthroughs.
- **Continuous Learning:** Reinvention is a mindset. Stay curious and open to possibilities.

Tips:

- **Create a 10-Year Career Map.** Ask yourself:
  - *Where do I want to be in a decade?*
  - *What new competencies do I need?*
  - *What kind of work would give me meaning and momentum?*

Attend relevant conferences, enrol in modular courses, or take up short-term certifications to keep your knowledge fresh and your network active.

- **Reassess your goals:**
  - *Are they still meaningful?*
  - *What does success look like now compared to ten years ago?*
- **Future-proof your skills:** Digital fluency, data literacy, coaching, and cross-cultural communication are fast becoming baseline competencies.
- **Test side gigs or alternative pathways:** Whether it's consulting, teaching, or launching a small business, explore before you leap.

4. **For Aspiring Retirees - Redefine "Work":** Retirement has evolved. For many, it's no longer a complete stop but a new chapter for re-careering—a chance for renewed meaning, greater flexibility, and sustained contribution. This is the perfect

time for an "encore career" that uses a lifetime of experience and aligns with personal passions.

Instead of posing the question, *"What now?"*, a more pertinent inquiry becomes, *"What's next?"* This new chapter can be intentionally shaped with purpose—one that continues to challenge and inspire. Whether through mentoring, teaching, consulting, writing, or community service, numerous avenues exist for re-careering with fulfilment.

This stage of life is also a great time to activate the BRIDGE elements. These principles, which underpinned earlier career success, become even more relevant as one moves toward a contribution-focused lifestyle.

- **B - Branding:** Cultivate a clear personal brand that reflects one's values and expertise. Use platforms like LinkedIn or a personal website to showcase thought leadership. Pro bono work or speaking engagements are excellent ways to stay visible and relevant.
- **R - Right Attitude:** Embrace a growth mindset. See retirement as a dynamic transition, not a withdrawal. A positive attitude can transform uncertainty into opportunity.
- **I - Interpersonal Skills and Networking:** Prioritize maintaining connections. Engaging with professional associations, attending lifelong learning programs, or joining interest groups can lead to unexpected opportunities and renewed energy.
- **D – Development:** Commit to continuous growth. Pursue short courses, workshops, or certifications in areas of genuine passion, both professionally and personally.
- **G - Gain Influence:** Use one's voice to make an impact. Mentoring others, sharing a personal journey, or participating in initiatives that influence an industry or community are powerful avenues for contribution.
- **E - Emotional Intelligence:** Remain attuned to personal motivations, strengths, and interpersonal dynamics in this new phase. Emotional intelligence will serve as a guiding compass for reinvention with empathy and clarity.

My Personal Journey: Re-career for Meaning, Not Just Money

After stepping away from full-time corporate leadership, I didn't "retire" in the traditional sense. Instead, I embarked on a mission-driven career that now includes coaching, training, writing, and contributing to healthcare as a regulatory affairs service provider. These roles allow me to combine both passion and purpose—building on what I know, while still learning and growing every day.

When retirement is perceived as a platform—rather than merely an endpoint—a world of possibilities unfolds, seamlessly blending passion, purpose, and flexibility. The trajectory beyond traditional retirement is not a process of winding down, but rather, one of elevation—an ascent into a life characterized by authenticity, impact, and joy. The requisite tools and wisdom are present. Now is the opportune time to construct that next bridge.

> **Tip**: Reflect on the activities that bring you energy, joy, and purpose. Identify how you can turn one or more of these into meaningful contributions—be it through paid work, volunteering, or legacy-building initiatives.

Career Personality & Strengths Assessment

Choosing a career is about more than just a high salary. It's about finding a role that aligns with your strengths, interests, and personality. Career personality and strengths assessments are powerful tools for gaining clarity. They help you understand your natural inclinations, work preferences, and ideal professional environment, which leads to more informed and fulfilling career choices.

Below are two widely used career assessment tools—the MBTI (Myers-Briggs Type Indicator) and the Holland Codes (RIASEC Model)—and, more importantly, how to apply them to career planning.

1. **MBTI - Understanding Work Style:** The MBTI is a personality assessment that categorizes individuals into 16 personality types based on four key dimensions:
    - **Extraversion (E) vs. Introversion (I)**: *How you gain energy?* (from people vs. solitude).
    - **Sensing (S) vs. Intuition (N)**: *How you process information*? (facts vs. patterns and possibilities).

- **Thinking (T) vs. Feeling (F)**: *How you make decisions*? (logic vs. values and emotions).
- **Judging (J) vs. Perceiving (P)**: *How you approach structure and organization*? (planned vs. spontaneous).

A step-by-step guide to applying the MBTI to career path selection is outlined below:

- **Step 1 - Choose a Work Environment That Suits:** This step considers whether an individual's preference leans towards Extraversion (E) or Introversion (I).

  Are you being Extraverted (E) or Introverted (I)?

Personality Type	Ideal Work Environment	Example Careers
Extravert (E)	Collaborative, social, fast paced	Sales, marketing, consulting, event planning
Introvert (I)	Quiet, independent, focused	Writing, research, programming, accounting

Example: *An Extravert (E) thrives on client interaction and deal negotiation, leading to a career in sales. Conversely, an Introvert (I), who prefers in-depth analysis and independent work, pursues a role as a data analyst.*

- **Step 2 - Choosing How Information Is Processed:** This step examines whether information processing is primarily Sensing (S) or Intuitive (N): *Are you more Sensing (S) or Intuitive (N)?*

Personality Type	Ideal Work Environment	Example Careers
Sensing (S)	Practical, hands-on, structured, detail-focused	Engineering, healthcare, law enforcement, accounting
Intuition (N)	Future-focused, big-picture, creative, innovation-driven	Entrepreneurship, psychology, design, research

Example: *A Sensing (S) type thrives on working with clear data and established procedures, leading to a career as an accountant. Conversely, an Intuition (N) type, who enjoys brainstorming and envisioning future possibilities, thrives in entrepreneurship.*

- **Step 3 - Identifying Careers That Match Strengths:** This step focuses on decision-making styles, distinguishing between Thinking (T) and Feeling (F) preferences: *How do you make decisions?*

Personality Type	Key Traits	Example Careers
Thinking (T)	Logical, data-driven	Engineering, finance, law, IT
Feeling (F)	People-focused, empathetic	Counselling, HR, teaching, nursing

Example: *A Thinking (T) type who is logical and data-driven excels in engineering, leading to a career in IT. Conversely, a Feeling (F) type, who is people-focused and empathetic, thrives in roles like counselling or teaching.*

- **Step 4 - Improving Communication & Teamwork:** This step addresses approaches to tasks and organization, differentiating between Judging (J) and Perceiving (P) preferences.: *How do you approach tasks and organization?*

Personality Type	Work Style	Recommended Career Paths	Development Tip
Judging (J)	Organized, structured	Project management, law, administration	Embrace flexibility and adapt to evolving situations
Perceiving (P)	Flexible, spontaneous	Creative roles, entrepreneurship, journalism	Strengthen time management and planning capabilities

Example: *A Judging (J) type who is organized and prefers structure excels in project management. Conversely, a Perceiving (P) type, who is flexible and spontaneous, thrives in creative roles like journalism.*

This framework supports individuals in aligning their innate preferences with career environments that enhance engagement, performance, and long-term satisfaction. While MBTI is not a definitive career determinant, it serves as a powerful starting point for intentional career design.

How to Apply This Framework to Your Career Path?

1. **Take a personality test** (MBTI or similar).
2. **Identify your type** *(e.g., ENTJ, ISFP).*
3. **Use the tables above** to find work environments that match your strengths.
4. **Test your fit** through side projects, internships, or networking.
5. **Make strategic career moves** based on your personality.

2. **RIASEC Model - Matching Personality with Career:** Developed by John Holland, the RIASEC Model classifies individuals into six personality types that align with different career fields:

The Holland Model (RIASEC): Finding the Interest

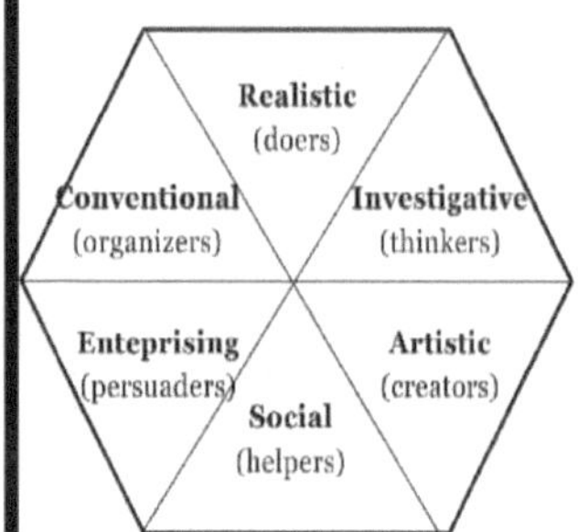

1. **Realistic (R):** Practical, hands-on, and enjoy working with tools and solving physical problems.
2. **Investigative (I):** Analytical, curious, and prefer research and intellectual problem-solving.
3. **Artistic (A):** Creative, imaginative, and drawn to tasks involving self-expression through art.
4. **Social (S):** Compassionate, empathetic, and enjoy helping others through social interaction.
5. **Enterprising (E):** Outgoing, ambitious, and prefer leadership, persuasion, and entrepreneurial tasks.
6. **Conventional (C):** Organized, detail-oriented, and enjoy structured tasks involving data and systems.

- **Realistic (R):** Hands-on, practical, prefers physical work *(e.g., engineers, mechanics, chefs).*
- **Investigative (I):** Analytical, enjoys research and problem-solving *(e.g., scientists, data analysts, medical researchers).*
- **Artistic (A):** Creative, expressive, prefers unstructured environments *(e.g., designers, writers, musicians).*
- **Social (S):** People-oriented, enjoys helping others *(e.g., teachers, counsellors, social workers).*
- **Enterprising (E):** Persuasive, ambitious, thrives in leadership roles *(e.g., entrepreneurs, sales executives, politicians).*
- **Conventional (C):** Detail-oriented, organized, prefers structure *(e.g., accountants, administrative managers, data entry specialists).*

A step-by-step guide to applying the Holland Codes (RIASEC) to career is provided below:

- **Step 1 - Identify the Holland Code Personality Type:** Undertake a Holland Code test (or reflect on personal strengths and interests). The result will be a combination of three letters *(e.g., IRE, ASC, SEC).*
- **Step 2 - Match the Personality Type to Suitable Career Paths:**

Personality Type	Key Traits	Example Careers
Realistic (R)	Practical, hands-on, enjoys working with tools	Engineering, construction, mechanics, agriculture
Investigative (I)	Analytical, curious, research-driven	Scientist, data analyst, medical researcher
Artistic (A)	Creative, expressive, prefers flexible environments	Graphic design, writing, performing arts
Social (S)	Empathetic, people-oriented, enjoys helping others	Counselling, teaching, nursing, HR
Enterprising (E)	Persuasive, energetic, enjoys leadership	Sales, entrepreneurship, management
Conventional (C)	Detail-oriented, organized, enjoys structure	Accounting, administration, finance

Example: *An Investigative (I) type who loves solving complex problems and analyzing data excels as a data scientist. Conversely, an Artistic (A) type who enjoys self-expression and storytelling thrives as a writer.*

- **Step 3 - Find Work Environments That Suit Your Style:**

Personality Type	Preferred Work Setting	Example Work Environments
Realistic (R)	Outdoor, hands-on, action-driven	Construction sites, workshops, nature reserves
Investigative (I)	Quiet, research-based, detail-oriented	Labs, universities, tech firms
Artistic (A)	Open-ended, flexible, expressive	Studios, theatres, marketing agencies
Social (S)	Collaborative, supportive, people-centric	Schools, hospitals, community centres
Enterprising (E)	Competitive, fast-paced, leadership-driven	Corporate offices, startups, politics
Conventional (C)	Structured, rule-based, process-driven	Banks, government offices, accounting firms

Example: *An Enterprising (E) type who thrives in fast-paced environments and enjoys leading teams excels in corporate management. Conversely, a Conventional (C) type who prefers order and stability thrives as a financial analyst.*

- **Step 4 - Use RIASEC to Explore Career Transitions:** For those considering a career pivot, RIASEC can be utilized to identify transferable skills and discover new opportunities that align with existing strengths.

Current Career (Primary Code)	Potential Transition (New Code)
Teacher (S)	Corporate Trainer (E, S)
Accountant (C)	Financial Consultant (E, C)
Engineer (R, I)	Data Scientist (I, C)
Artist (A)	UX Designer (A, I)

Example: *A Realistic and Investigative (R, I) type who started as a mechanical engineer but desired more data-driven work often transitions to AI research. Conversely, a Social and Artistic (S, A) type who was a teacher but enjoyed creating educational materials often becomes an instructional designer.*

How to Apply This Framework to Your Career Path?

1. **Take a Holland Code test** (or analyse your work preferences).
2. **Identify your top three RIASEC letters** (e.g., SEA, IRC).
3. **Use the tables above** to find careers and work environments that match your strengths.
4. **Explore potential career pivots** using the transition table.
5. **Gain relevant skills** (online courses, certifications, side projects) to shift into your ideal role.

Designing a Future-Ready Career: Goal Setting and Skill Building for Long-Term Success

A successful career is not achieved by chance; it demands clear goals, intentional actions, and continuous adaptation. Goal setting extends beyond merely ascending the corporate hierarchy; it involves aligning one's professional journey with personal values, strengths, and aspirations.

The establishment of specific and challenging objectives significantly enhances performance. Without clear direction, professionals often experience stagnation or a lack of fulfilment, even in the presence of financial stability.

My Personal Journey: *When I first entered retail pharmacy, my motivation wasn't purely passion—I was driven by financial security and the long-term goal of owning my own pharmacy at 55. At the time, I believed this was the smartest plan to achieve financial independence. However, as I gained experience, I realized that my strengths and interests extended beyond retail pharmacy. This led me to explore new career paths in sales, leadership, and eventually business coaching.*

This experience taught me that career paths are fluid and adaptable, but only when we take the time to assess, reflect, and set intentional goals.

Note: Your vision may evolve, and that's okay! The key is to start with a direction and adjust as you grow.

A career is a journey, not a destination. Whether an undergraduate exploring options, a mid-career professional re-evaluating a path, or an aspiring retiree seeking reinvention, setting clear and inspiring goals will shape the future. Below are suggested steps for setting meaningful career goals:

- **Step 1 - Define Career Vision:** Before setting goals, it is beneficial to engage in unrestrained ideation. Key questions for consideration include:
    - *What do I want to achieve in the next 5–10 years?*
    - *What does success look like to me? (Is it leadership, financial freedom, or meaningful work?)*
    - *What type of work excites and fulfils me? (Do I love problem-solving, creating, teaching, or leading?)*
    - *How do I want my career to contribute to my personal life and financial goals? (More flexibility, a legacy, financial security?)*
- **Step 2 - Set SMART Career Goals:** A vision, without a roadmap, remains aspirational. SMART goals ensure that aspirations translate into actionable plans. The SMART framework ensures that career goals are Specific, Measurable, Achievable, Relevant, and Time-bound.

Goal Type	Vague Goal	SMART Goal Example
Skill Development	*"I want to get better at public speaking."*	"I will complete a public speaking course and give two presentations within six months."
Career Advancement	*"I want to earn more money."*	"I will apply for a promotion to Senior Manager within 12 months by leading two key projects."
Career Pivot	*"I want to change careers."*	"I will complete an adult learning certification and build a coaching portfolio within 18 months."

- **Step 3 - Break Down Long-Term Goals into Actionable Steps:** Big career goals can feel overwhelming. Breaking them into small, manageable steps prevents procrastination and keeps motivation high.

Example: *If your goal is to become a digital marketing specialist in two years, your roadmap could look like this:*

- *Month 1-3: Take a Google Digital Marketing certification.*
- *Month 4-6: Apply skills to personal projects or start freelancing on small projects.*
- *Month 7-12: Build a portfolio, network, connect with industry mentors or apply for jobs.*
- *Year 2: Apply for mid-level marketing roles.*

Success is achieved not through massive leaps, but through consistent progress. Progress occurs in incremental steps, not overnight transformations.

- **Step 4 - Align Goals with Market Trends and Financial Stability:** While passion is a powerful driver, a career must also be financially sustainable. Aligning goals with market demand is crucial for long-term success.

  Example: *When planning my F.I.R(Re-career).E. journey, I didn't blindly jump into coaching. Instead, I researched coaching industry trends, income potential, and accreditation pathways before making the shift. This step ensured that my new career path was both fulfilling and financially sustainable.*

  For effective market research to inform this alignment, several resources are recommended:

  - **LinkedIn and Job Boards:** These platforms are valuable for identifying current in-demand skills.
  - **Industry Reports:** Reviewing these documents can help ascertain growing sectors and future projections.
  - **Professional Consultations:** Engaging with experienced professionals provides expert opinions on emerging opportunities.
  - **Career Coach or Mentor:** Consideration of a career coach or mentor can offer valuable guidance and strategic insights.

- **Step 5 - Track Progress and Adapt as Needed:** Life is inherently unpredictable. Aspirations held today may evolve in five years. Regular goal review and adjustment, based on new experiences and insights, are key.

Examples of career check-In questions:

- *Am I making progress toward my career goals?*
- *What skills have I developed recently?*
- *Do I still feel passionate and fulfilled in this direction?*
- *Are there new opportunities I should explore?*

A career journey is fluid, not a rigid plan. Embracing adjustments based on new insights and remaining open to opportunities is essential. Continuous growth and strategic adaptability, guided by aspirations, define true career success, rather than adherence to inflexible plans.

Key Takeaways:

- Define a clear career vision to establish a sense of direction.
- Utilize SMART (Specific, Measurable, Achievable, Relevant, Time-bound) goals to develop a clear and actionable plan.
- Break down larger objectives into smaller, manageable steps to facilitate consistent progress.
- Align strategies with prevailing market trends to ensure long-term financial stability.
- Regularly review and adapt goals as personal interests and professional opportunities evolve.

Developing Marketable Skills for Career Growth

The job market is changing at an unprecedented pace, driven by technology and new industry demands. To remain competitive, professionals must continuously cultivate both technical and soft skills that align with these needs. Developing these skills is not just about maintaining employability; it's about unlocking new opportunities. A well-rounded skill set allows a professional to navigate career transitions, take on leadership roles, and build resilience against job market fluctuations. The core principle lies in continuous learning and adaptation.

- **Understanding Technical vs. Soft Skills:** Both technical (hard) and soft skills are crucial for career success. Technical skills are job-specific abilities that can be learned and measured, such as coding, data analysis, or financial modelling. Mastery of these skills enhances one's ability to perform specific tasks efficiently. Soft skills, on the other hand, define interpersonal interactions and workplace navigation. These include communication, emotional intelligence, adaptability, and teamwork. While they are more challenging to quantify, they are essential for collaborating with colleagues, leading teams, and adapting to a dynamic work environment.

My transition: *I started my career with clinical pharmacy knowledge but quickly realized that to advance, I needed to develop soft skills like people management and business acumen. This investment in personal growth helped me successfully pivot into business coaching and entrepreneurship.*

- **Staying Relevant in a Changing Job Market:** The rise of AI, automation, and remote work is fundamentally reshaping industries. Skills considered essential just five years ago may now be obsolete. To maintain relevance, continuous skill upgrading and adaptation to new industry trends are imperative. A key strategy is to embrace technological advancements. For instance, a digital marketer who becomes proficient in AI-powered analytics tools gains a competitive edge. An accountant who upskills in FinTech can offer more innovative solutions. Beyond technical expertise, understanding current and future industry trends is crucial. Following industry reports, attending webinars, and networking with thought leaders helps professionals anticipate changes and stay ahead. Cultivating a growth mindset—one that is open to learning and reinvention—is vital. Professionals who embrace lifelong learning and adaptability are better equipped to navigate transitions and capitalize on emerging opportunities.

- **Applying the BRIDGE Elements for Lasting Success:** In today's competitive job market, success is not solely determined by technical expertise. It requires a combination of personal branding, adaptability, networking, and emotional intelligence. The BRIDGE framework highlights six essential elements for professionals to cultivate for career thriving:
    - **B - Branding:** A strong personal brand enhances credibility and visibility. A well-crafted LinkedIn profile and thought leadership within one's industry can unlock new opportunities.
    - **R - Right Attitude:** A growth mindset, resilience, and adaptability are fundamental to long-term success. Embracing challenges as learning opportunities ensures continuous progress.

- **I - Interpersonal and Networking Skills:** Building meaningful professional relationships, effective communication, and collaboration are vital for career advancement. Networking, both online and offline, facilitates valuable connections.
- **D - Development:** Lifelong learning, upskilling, and continuous self-improvement are critical for maintaining relevance. Investing in professional development leads to long-term career satisfaction.
- **G - Gain Influence:** Leadership and influence extend beyond formal job titles. The ability to inspire, persuade, and guide others is an invaluable skill that enhances professional impact.
- **E - Emotional Intelligence:** Understanding and managing emotions contributes to effective teamwork, leadership, and conflict resolution.

Checklist – Setting Meaningful Career Goals

1. Define your Career Vision

☐ Reflect on your passions, strengths, and aspirations

☐ Ask: "What does success look like for me?"

☐ Use the Ikigai Framework to align vision with purpose

☐ Accept that vision may evolve over time

2. Set SMART Career Goals

☐ Use the SMART Framework (Specific, Measurable, Achievable, Relevant, Time-bound)

☐ Translate vague ambitions into actionable steps

☐ Set goals under different categories (skills, advancement, pivot)

☐ Ensure alignment with long-term vision

3. Break Down Big Goals

☐ Break long-term goals into smaller, achievable tasks

☐ Set timelines for each milestone

☐ Track weekly or monthly progress

☐ Celebrate small wins to stay motivated

4. Align with Market Trends & Stability

☐ Conduct market research

☐ Use LinkedIn, job portals, and industry reports

☐ Talk to mentors, coaches, or industry professionals

☐ Evaluate if goals are financially sustainable

☐ Stay adaptable to evolving job market demands

5. Track Progress & Adapt

☐ Conduct regular career check-ins

☐ Ask: "Am I fulfilled? What's changed?"

☐ Adjust goals as priorities shift

☐ Stay flexible while keeping direction

☐ Commit to lifelong learning and self-awareness

6. Develop Marketable Skills

☐ Build both technical and soft skills

☐ Identify current and future in-demand skills

☐ Commit to upskilling regularly

☐ Blend formal learning with real-world application

☐ Maintain a growth mindset

7. Apply the BRIDGE Elements

☐ Strengthen core areas for long-term success

☐ Branding – Build visibility and professional presence

☐ Right Attitude – Embrace resilience and growth mindset

☐ Interpersonal Skills & Networking – Connect and collaborate effectively

☐ Development – Engage in lifelong learning

☐ Gain Influence – Lead and inspire without a title

☐ Emotional Intelligence – Manage self and relationships effectively

Action Steps:

1. Write one big career goal.
2. Identify one small step to take this week.
3. Review your progress monthly.
4. Refine goals based on insights and opportunities.

[4]

[4] **Further reading:** For deeper insights and actionable strategies, refer to *Limitless Possibilities ~ YK Png* (available on Amazon).

Pillar 2: Financial Planning – Designing Your Freedom

***"Financial freedom is not about being rich, it's about reclaiming your time and choices."* ~ YK Png**

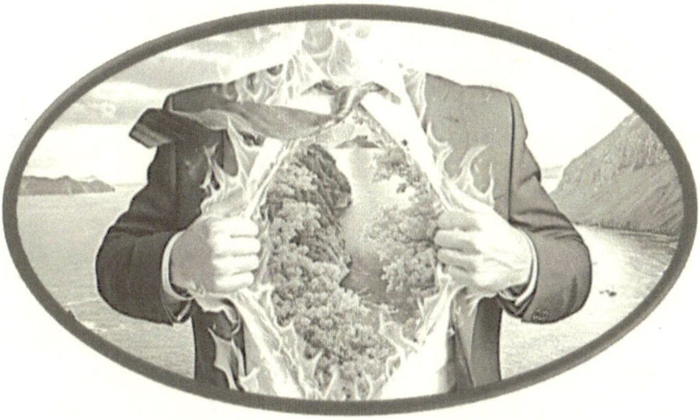

For many, financial security feels like the ultimate goal—a stable job, a comfortable savings buffer, and a retirement plan. Yet, this can be just the beginning. True empowerment emerges when the mindset shifts from financial security to financial freedom—where work becomes optional, time becomes accessible, and choices align with deepest values.

In Singapore, where the cost of living is among the highest in the world, the idea of financial freedom might seem a distant dream. However, individuals from all walks of life—from pharmacists to corporate professionals—have broken free from the paycheck-to-paycheck cycle and designed lives of purpose and autonomy.

Financial Security versus Financial Freedom

While they may seem similar, financial security and financial freedom have vastly different foundations and outcomes.

- **Financial Security - Stability Without Freedom:** Financial security provides peace of mind, ensuring essential needs are covered. It's built on a reliable income, emergency savings, and some protection through insurance and retirement plans. However, this stability often comes at the price of dependence, especially on a single job or employer. The illusion of control can quickly unravel with corporate restructuring or economic downturns. Job security is not life security.

- **Financial Freedom - Choice and Control:** Financial freedom is not just about having more money; it's about having more choices. It's the point where income from multiple sources—investments, side businesses, royalties, or freelance work—covers living expenses, giving complete control over time, energy, and purpose. This represents the difference between reacting to life and designing one's life.

Real-Life Example: The Pharmacist in Transition

Consider David (not his real name), a successful pharmacist in his mid-40s who was a senior executive at a multinational pharmaceutical company. For over two decades, his career was a model of success with a high salary and a luxury lifestyle.

Then, an unexpected corporate restructuring made his position redundant. His entire financial ecosystem was built around one income source—his corporate job. The loss of income quickly turned his financial stability into vulnerability. This is the crux of financial security: it feels safe until it isn't.

In contrast, those who intentionally pursue financial freedom—by investing early, building side businesses, or freelancing—are able to adapt more nimbly to similar disruptions. Their life security, not just job security, comes from having designed independence, not relying on corporate structures alone

---

In Essence:

- **Financial Security** = Peace of Mind, but Stability Without Freedom.
- **Financial Freedom** = Freedom of Choice and Control.

Comparative Table: Financial Security vs Financial Freedom

Aspect	Financial Security	Financial Freedom
Core Focus	Stability and safety	Autonomy and purpose
Main Income Source	Single employer (job-dependent)	Multiple streams (investments, business, re-career)
Risk Exposure	High—dependent on employer, market changes	Low—diversified, adaptable income
Time Control	Limited—dictated by job	High—flexible, self-directed
Life Choices	Constrained by job commitments	Driven by personal values and interests
Career Path	Shaped by organizational structure	Self-designed, passion-aligned
Vulnerability to Change	High—layoffs, restructuring, industry shifts	Low—resilient to external shocks

If an individual is in the security zone, the next step involves building freedom levers—side hustles, investments, or lifestyle shifts. This process begins by defining what freedom means personally. Subsequently, tools like budgeting apps and robo-advisors can be utilized to gradually build passive income.

The F.I.R(Re-career).E. Mindset: Freedom Through Alignment

What if one could live a life where work becomes a choice, not an obligation? A life where daily pursuits reflect deepest values—not merely the needs of a bank account? This is the essence of the F.I.R(Re-career).E. Mindset—aligning financial independence with meaningful re-careering to enable living and working on one's own terms.

My Personal Journey: *For decades, I followed the traditional success path—building a corporate career, rising to leadership, and enjoying financial security. But over time, I realized I was following expectations, not necessarily purpose. That internal tension pushed me to re-evaluate, re-career, and eventually embrace a portfolio career: coach, trainer, author, and regulatory pharmacist. It wasn't an exit from work. It was a re-entry into work that energized and empowered me.*

Rethinking FIRE: From Frugality to Fulfilment

Unlike traditional FIRE movements that focus purely on early retirement through extreme frugality, F.I.R(Re-career).E. stands for Financial Independence and Re-careering Early with Purpose. It represents a shift from a job that merely pays the bills to work that fuels passion and contribution.

This approach acknowledges that for many individuals, especially in countries like Singapore where the cost of living and social expectations are high, "retiring early" may not be realistic or even desirable. However, re-careering early is possible. It means transitioning into work that is meaningful, flexible, and values aligned.

Key Takeaway: The **F.I.R(Re-career).E. Mindset** is a proactive approach to career transitions, especially later in life, emphasizing:

- **F**inancial awareness for flexibility,
- **I**ntentionality in defining purpose,
- **R**eskilling for new opportunities, and
- **E**xperimentation to explore different paths.

Three Anchors of the F.I.R(Re-career).E. Mindset

1. **Clarity of Purpose:** True freedom begins with clarity—knowing what truly matters. Without this, there is a risk of running on someone else's treadmill. Ask:
    - *What does success look like beyond money?*
    - *What kind of work energizes me?*
    - *What legacy do I want to leave behind?*

    Purpose gives direction to financial goals. The aim is not merely to save for retirement but to invest in the freedom to live on one's own terms.

2. **Financial Discipline with a Vision:** Achieving F.I.R(Re-career).E. requires intentional planning. This includes tracking finances, eliminating high-interest debt, automating savings, and building multiple income streams. Equally important, it means aligning spending with core values.

   Example: *When I first envisioned stepping out of the corporate world, I had to make choices: simplifying my lifestyle, reducing liabilities, focusing on long-term investments, and designing a runway that could fund my transition. That discipline became the fuel for my freedom.*

3. **Mindset Shift - From Scarcity to Possibility:** Many professionals delay re-careering out of fear: *What if I fail? What if I can't earn enough? What will people say?* But the F.I.R(Re-career).E. mindset reframes the narrative from fear to opportunity. It says: *I have skills that are valuable beyond my current job. I can learn, adapt, and build a new path. I am not starting over—I am evolving.*

   My Personal Reflection: *"I thought I was leaving stability behind. What I found was a new kind of security—the kind that comes from knowing I can shape my own path."*

The F.I.R(Re-career).E. Mindset isn't about rejecting the past; it's about reimagining the future. It's purposeful reinvention: the choice to pause, reflect, and redesign a path with intention.

Giving permission to explore what matters most—whether that's coaching, entrepreneurship, writing, or service—begins to build a new, empowering relationship with work. It isn't necessary to reach a specific financial milestone before starting to live meaningfully. With thoughtful planning and the courage to act, aligning work with values can begin much earlier than anticipated.

Once the experience of living with autonomy and authenticity is realized, settling for anything less becomes unimaginable. Not every answer may be clear now, and that's acceptable. All that's needed is the clarity to reflect, the courage to begin, and the conviction that a life true to oneself is absolutely within reach.

Start designing freedom today.

Reflective Questions: Use these prompts to explore your own F.I.R(Re-career).E. potential:

- *What would I do if I had full control over my time and energy?*
- *What kind of work would I do—even if I didn't "have" to?*
- *What small step can I take today to bring more alignment into my work and life?*
- *What does "enough" look like—for income, impact, and lifestyle?*

These questions don't have immediate answers. But they are the starting point of a deeper journey—a journey toward a life where your time, talents, and treasures are fully aligned.

Understanding the Financial Landscape

Before diving into the specifics of financial planning at different life stages, it is essential to recognise the key pillars of the Singaporean financial system:

- **Central Provident Fund (CPF):** A compulsory savings plan designed to provide for retirement, healthcare, and housing needs. CPF offers several accounts—Ordinary Account (OA), Special Account (SA), and MediSave Account (MA)—each with its own purpose.
- **Insurance:** Protection against life's uncertainties. This includes life insurance, health insurance, critical illness coverage, disability income, and more.
- **Investment Instruments:** Options range from low-risk government bonds and fixed deposits to higher-risk instruments like unit trusts, ETFs, equities, property investments, and even digital assets such as cryptocurrencies.

These tools form the foundation of financial stability and are central to any effective financial plan. We will delve into these instruments in detail in Part II of this book.

Financial Planning Across Life Stages

Building a purposeful and financially secure future starts with mindful planning. The journey to financial independence and career fulfilment is not a one-size-fits-all approach. It evolves and must be tailored to specific life stages, aspirations, and responsibilities.

- **Stage One: Undergraduates - Building a Financial Foundation:** The undergraduate years are a crucial period to develop a strong understanding of financial principles and cultivate positive habits, regardless of one's current financial situation. The knowledge and mindset built at this stage will be invaluable for the future.
    - **Financial Literacy is Key:** Focus on understanding fundamental concepts like how interest works, the basics of budgeting, and the difference between needs and wants. This knowledge empowers informed decisions later.
    - **Cultivate Mindful Spending Habits:** Develop awareness of spending. Tracking where money goes, using student discounts, and exploring free activities are all part of building good habits that prevent future financial pitfalls.
    - **Understand Financial Aid and Future Resources:** For those with loans (like the CPF Education Loan) or financial aid, it is important to understand the terms and repayment obligations. Begin to learn about CPF, Singapore's national savings plan, and its future role.
    - **Invest in Earning Potential:** The primary focus at this stage should be on education and gaining skills that will enhance future earning capacity. Prioritizing studies and seeking internships is the most significant long-term financial investment one can make.

Practical Tips:
• **For those with the capacity to save:** Start small and early. Even consistent, small savings can benefit from the power of time. Explore high-interest savings accounts or low-risk, beginner-friendly investments like passively managed ETFs if there are surplus funds.

- **For those with limited funds:** Focus on resourcefulness by finding creative ways to meet needs without excessive spending, such as utilizing campus facilities or sharing resources. If time permits, seek out part-time work to build a small income stream.

- **Stage Two: Young Professionals - Laying Strong Financial Foundations:** The early working years, typically in one's 20s and early 30s, are a unique window to lay the building blocks for long-term financial security and career flexibility. This is the time to establish strong habits and plant the seeds for financial independence.
  - **Automate and Grow Savings:** Commit to a "pay yourself first" strategy. Allocate at least 20% of monthly income to savings and investments before spending. Automate transfers into a high-yield savings account and begin with low-cost investments like ETFs or index funds.
  - **Track and Tame Expenses:** Create a realistic monthly budget and use tools to monitor spending. Be mindful of "lifestyle inflation"—as income increases, resist upgrading one's lifestyle proportionally.
  - **Maximize CPF and SRS:** Understand how CPF accounts—Ordinary Account (OA), Special Account (SA), and MediSave—contribute to housing, retirement, and healthcare. Consider voluntary top-ups to the SA for compounding returns and tax relief. The Supplementary Retirement Scheme (SRS) can provide further tax savings while building long-term investment capital.
  - **Begin Investing and Secure Adequate Protection:** Kickstart an investment journey with a diversified portfolio. Complement this with essential insurance policies—such as hospitalization and term plans—for financial protection.
  - **Start an Emergency Fund:** Build up at least 3 to 6 months' worth of essential expenses in an easily accessible account to cushion against job loss or health emergencies.
  - **Invest in Skills and Career Capital:** Continue learning. The return on investment (ROI) on career development is especially high at this stage and opens future options for re-careering or entrepreneurship.

- **Stage Three: Mid-Career Professionals - Accelerating Toward Financial Freedom:** In one's 30s to 40s, responsibilities often increase with children, home loans, and aging parents. This is also when income potential peaks. Smart financial decisions now can accelerate the path to financial independence and provide options later in life.
  - **Track and Review Net Worth Annually:** Regularly assess one's net worth (assets minus liabilities) to gain clarity on progress and identify areas for improvement.
  - **Review and Adjust the Financial Plan Regularly:** Reassess financial goals, timelines, and progress. Monitor the investment portfolio wisely, rebalance as needed, and reinvest gains.
  - **Strategic Property Investment as a Wealth-Building Tool:** Property remains a powerful pillar for wealth-building, offering capital appreciation, steady rental income, and portfolio diversification against inflation. For those with capacity, acquiring a second rental property is an option, but requires thorough due diligence and consideration of regulatory costs like ABSD (Additional Buyer's Stamp Duty).
  - **Optimize CPF and Explore Tax-Efficient Tools:** Maximize CPF-SA and consider voluntary contributions. Leverage SRS for additional tax savings. These instruments can significantly boost retirement readiness.
  - **Build Multiple Income Streams:** Beyond a main salary, explore side hustles, dividend investing, or freelancing. These buffers can reduce dependence on a single job.
  - **Shield Your Wealth:** Ensure adequate insurance coverage. Review coverage regularly as needs evolve.
  - **Commit to Continuous Financial Learning:** Stay informed about financial markets, economic trends, and investment opportunities. Regular learning empowers one to make sound decisions and adapt to changing conditions.
  - **Family Financial Planning:** It is important to discuss money with a partner, align on shared goals, and begin simple money conversations with children.

Key Takeaway: This is the phase to consolidate, protect, and multiply. Stay disciplined, maximize income and tax strategies, and move toward freedom—not just survival.

Recognise and Prepare for Mid-Career Vulnerabilities

Mid-career can be a time of financial stability and career progression, but it also comes with heightened risks. This group is increasingly vulnerable to industry restructuring, job displacement from automation, and age-related hiring biases. Professionals in this stage may also face greater difficulty re-entering the workforce due to higher salary expectations or specialized roles that are harder to replace.

What to Do:

- **Upskill and Reskill Proactively:** Invest in continuous learning to stay current with evolving industry demands. Consider professional certifications, digital literacy, or pivoting into adjacent fields with better growth potential.
- **Strengthen a Professional Brand:** Build visibility through thought leadership, networking, and active engagement on platforms like LinkedIn. Credibility and relevance can open doors beyond a current role.
- **Maintain a Lean Lifestyle and Buffer:** Avoid overextending finances. Build an emergency fund that can sustain 6–12 months of expenses and review insurance coverage to manage unexpected disruptions.
- **Stay Open to Career Pivots or Portfolio Careers:** Be mentally and practically prepared to explore alternative career models such as consulting, freelancing, teaching, or entrepreneurship if traditional employment becomes unstable.
- **Network Strategically:** Cultivate and maintain professional relationships before they are needed. Connections across industries can offer job leads, partnerships, or mentoring support during transitions.

> **Key Insight:** Remaining relevant isn't just about competence—it's about adaptability, visibility, and being ready for what's next. Preparing early puts one in control, even in uncertain times.

- **Stage Four: Aspiring Retirees - Preserving Wealth and Purposeful Re-Careering:** As a professional moves into their 50s and 60s, the focus shifts from **accumulation to** preservation, protection, and purposeful deployment of wealth. It's also a time for deep reflection: What will provide fulfilment beyond a main career?

- **Reassess Lifestyle Needs and Financial Goals:** Define what an ideal retirement or re-careered life looks like—part-time work, a business, mentoring, travel, or volunteering? Translate that vision into a monthly income need.
- **Reassess and Optimize Investments and Financial Products:** Streamline and align a financial portfolio with changing goals, risk appetite, and desired lifestyle. Begin by consolidating investment products where possible. A simplified portfolio is easier to manage, monitor, and rebalance. Review the investment strategy to determine if a shift is needed—from a growth-focused approach to one that prioritizes dividend payouts, which can serve as a supplementary income stream.

Additionally, assess opportunities to maximize CPF returns. For instance, if one has used CPF to finance their housing, consider repaying the loan to CPF to benefit from the attractive interest rates offered, particularly within the Special Account. Review insurance coverage. As needs evolve, some riders or high-premium policies may no longer be necessary. Explore reinvestment into lower-risk instruments that still provide consistent dividend yields to preserve capital while generating passive income.

Finally, take full advantage of the CPF LIFE scheme. Where possible, optimize a Retirement Account (RA) by making voluntary top-ups to secure higher lifelong monthly payouts. This provides a predictable and stable income stream, reinforcing financial peace of mind.

- **Simplify and Streamline Expenses:** Downsize if appropriate. Reduce fixed expenses (e.g., car loans, subscriptions, large homes). Simpler living extends a financial runway.
- **Preserve Capital and Mitigate Risks:** Shift a portion of a portfolio into lower-risk, income-generating assets such as CPF LIFE, annuities, or bonds. Maintain some growth assets to hedge against inflation.
- **Formalize Legacy Planning:** Update a will, CPF nominations, insurance beneficiaries, and consider setting up a lasting power of attorney (LPA). Discuss plans openly with family members.

- **Re-career With Intention:** Consider **portfolio careers** or part-time engagements that bring meaning and supplement income. Examples include consulting, teaching, coaching, or advisory roles. This is where **F.I.R.E.** becomes a lived reality.

Key Takeaway: Retirement doesn't have to mean stopping work. It's about aligning time, energy, and money with what matters most. Financial readiness allows one to retire on their terms and repurpose the next chapter.

The PASS Model: A Foundation for Financial Clarity

*~ By **Martin Toh**, Co-Author (AIA District Director, High Net Worth, CFP, ChFC, ESP.)*

In today's fast-changing and competitive world, the ability to pivot careers in one's 40s or 50s is no longer a luxury—it is increasingly a necessity. Whether driven by structural industry shifts, personal aspirations, or unplanned circumstances such as retrenchment or health issues, mid-life career transitions are becoming more common. The key to navigating these changes without compromising one's quality of life lies in proactive planning and financial preparedness.

My Journey: From Struggle to Abundance

At the start of my career, I had just $163 in my bank account. Each evening, I was confronted by the same persistent question:

"What must I do to break the cycle of having 'not enough' and move toward abundance?"

Conventional wisdom urged me to secure a stable job, save diligently, and spend cautiously. Yet, deep down, I sensed that this formula alone would not create the financial breakthrough I was seeking. I asked myself another pivotal question: "Do I know anyone who became a millionaire simply by saving money in the bank?" The answer was a clear no.

That realization prompted a change in mindset—and a bold decision to take a different path. By challenging traditional assumptions, making deliberate financial choices, and building on a set of guiding principles, I earned my first million before the age of 30. By 40, I had accumulated over $10 million in assets.

This transformation did not happen by chance. It was the result of applying a structured, disciplined approach to wealth-building, risk management, and long-term planning. This same foundation not only helped me achieve financial independence but also gave me the confidence to make multiple career pivots—without the fear of financial instability.

Achieving financial independence and navigating career transitions effectively requires a proactive and resilient approach. Individuals face two primary categories of scenarios that shape their financial lives:

1. **Events beyond one's control** – such as economic downturns, technological disruptions, or health challenges.
2. **Events within one's control** – such as career aspirations, skills upgrading, or lifestyle adjustments.

To tackle these scenarios, a structured framework was developed—the PASS model. This model is a simple, strategic approach to holistic financial planning that helps individuals gain clarity and confidence over their financial life:

- **P – Protect: Safeguard Current Lifestyle**
  - **Tailored Protection:** Customize insurance coverage to suit life stages and family responsibilities, ensuring peace of mind.
  - **Income Continuity:** Ensure income replacement during unexpected events such as illness, disability, or job loss.
  - **Adapt to Life Changes:** Regularly review and restructure protection to align with evolving priorities and avoid duplications.
  - **Foundation First:** A strong protection strategy precedes accumulation to maintain financial stability in any season of life.
- **A – Accumulate & Affordability: Build Wealth and Financial Health**
  - **Understand Commitments:** Know cash flow, lifestyle expenses, and current financial obligations.
  - **Use Financial Ratios:** Assess financial health objectively before making money decisions.
  - **Mindful Habits:** Understand current spending, saving, and investing behaviour to gain clarity and improve decision-making.
  - **Start Early and Grow Steadily:** Leverage time and compounding by beginning with affordable, consistent contributions.
  - **Explore Diversified Tools:** Go beyond traditional strategies with options suited to goals and risk appetite.
- **S – Strategize: Create a Retirement Roadmap**
  - **Define Clear Retirement Goals:** Clarify desired lifestyle, retirement age, and monthly needs.
  - **Leverage Existing Resources:** Include CPF LIFE, company benefits, property, investments, and insurance plans.

- **Blueprint, Not Products:** Focus on building a clear, step-by-step roadmap, not buying more products.
- **Plan Consumption Phase:** Strategically allocate and withdraw from retirement buckets to stretch every dollar.
- **Clarity Brings Confidence:** A clear map makes the journey toward early retirement achievable and less stressful.

- **S – Succession: Plan the Distribution of Wealth**
  - **Clarify Intentions:** Plan early to ensure assets are distributed according to wishes and to minimize conflicts.
  - **Promote Family Harmony:** Utilize tools like a WILL and transparent communication to maintain trust and unity.
  - **Ensure Adequate Resources:** Check for shortfalls and prepare sufficient resources to fulfil legacy.
  - **Bridge the Gaps:** Where necessary, use cost-effective tools to supplement succession plans.

Integrating the PASS Model

Financial independence and career flexibility are not achieved overnight. They are the result of consistent planning and decision-making. The PASS framework provides the foundation to weather life's uncertainties and embrace opportunities with confidence.

True abundance is more than just financial security—it is the freedom to live purposefully, pursue meaningful transitions, and make decisions from a place of strength rather than constraint.

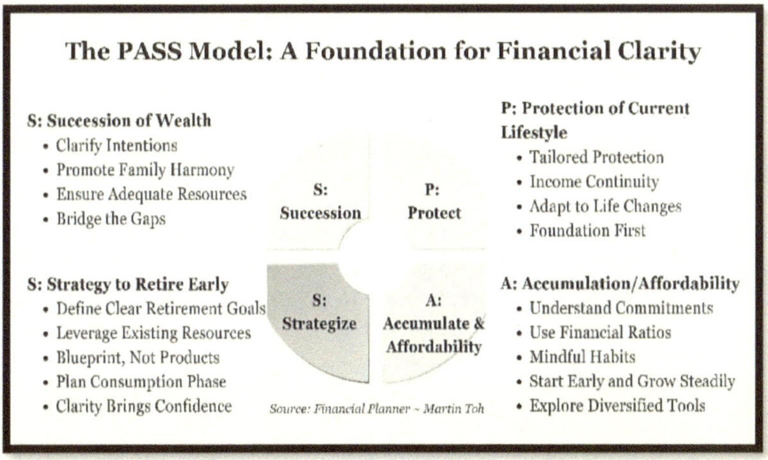

Pillar 3: Health Planning – The Foundation of It All

In the pursuit of career advancement and financial independence, health is often taken for granted—sidelined until a crisis demands attention. Yet, it is health that forms the true foundation upon which all other pillars of a fulfilling life rest. Without physical vitality, mental clarity, and emotional balance, achievements in work and wealth are diminished in value and sustainability.

Health is not merely the absence of illness. It is the enabler of peak performance, meaningful engagement, and the capacity to enjoy life's milestones. Prioritising health is therefore not optional—it is strategic, integral, and non-negotiable in any long-term plan for independence and re-careering.

I learned the hard way that no amount of career success or financial gain is worth the cost of your health.

My Personal Journey: When Health and Values Collide with Career Demands

1. ***When Earning More Wasn't Enough:*** *As I ascended the corporate ladder, working as a Chief Representative and General Manager for a medical equipment company in China, I was often traveling between four different cities in China and the corporate office in Hong Kong. My job demanded long working hours, frequent travel, and weekends on the road. At the time, I didn't realize that my health was silently deteriorating as I prioritized work over sleep, exercise, and personal well-being. I saw my family only once every quarter, and it seemed like the sacrifices I was making were worth it for my career.*

   Thankfully, disciplined changes—healthier eating, regular sleep, daily 10,000 steps, and 150 minutes of activity weekly—helped me reverse the condition. I now prioritize proactive living with regular screenings.

Key Takeaway: Health is the foundation of success. Without it, career gains lose meaning.

---

2. ***Knowing When It's Time to Move On:*** *Another significant turning point in my career came during a senior leadership position. While I enjoyed financial stability and professional success, I felt increasingly unfulfilled because the company culture clashed significantly with my personal values. This was compounded by a toxic work environment and a toxic regional manager whose leadership style was antithetical to mine. My inability to adequately reward and recognize my team due to organizational limitations further added to the strain. The deep misalignment between my role and my core principles ultimately led to severe burnout and frustration.*

   Recognizing this misalignment, I took a bold step: I challenged senior management to remove me from my position, as I felt I could no longer lead effectively within the company's rigid structure. This move reinforced my need for a career that aligned with my values.

   This turning point gave me the clarity to plan my exit. With a new sense of purpose and financial preparedness, I began my F.I.R(Re-career).E. journey, where financial independence and meaningful work could coexist.

Key Takeaway: Alignment between values and career is non-negotiable for long-term fulfillment.

Lesson: True Wealth is Control Over Time.

Health and values provide the bandwidth to live with intention. Time is our most precious resource—and good health extends it.

Reflect on these powerful questions:

- *Am I working for money, or is my money working for me?*
- *How much control do I have over my time?*
- *If I stopped earning today, how long could I sustain my lifestyle?*

Answering these questions requires honesty—and often reveals areas where health and work are misaligned. True wealth lies in the freedom to choose how we spend our time, and that freedom is underpinned by our health.

Career advancement and financial goals are often pursued with intensity, yet the foundational element that sustains them—health—is frequently overlooked. The effects of burnout, chronic stress, sleep deprivation, poor nutrition, and physical inactivity are not always immediate, but over time, they erode capacity for performance, connection, and fulfilment. The consequences extend beyond medical issues to include missed moments, diminished energy, and reduced joy in daily living.

Prioritizing health is not indulgent. It is foundational. When we invest in our well-being, we're not only extending our lifespan—we're enhancing the quality of the years we live. We become more present, more productive, and more resilient to change.

A Strategic Commitment

When planning for F.I.R(Re-career).E., health cannot be an afterthought. It is the first freedom upon which all others are built. Key strategies include:

- Scheduling **regular health screenings** to monitor risks and ensure early intervention
- Setting **physical activity goals** aligned with national health guidelines
- Establishing **daily routines** that prioritise movement, rest, and nutrition
- Cultivating **mental wellness** through mindfulness, adequate sleep, and social connection
- Developing body awareness and responding to physical and emotional signals proactively

When health is protected, the capacity to lead, contribute, and live with intention is significantly enhanced. A well-lived life begins with a well-cared-for body and mind.

Building Resilient Well-Being: Physical, Mental, and Lifestyle Foundations for High Performance

- **Physical Health - Sleep, Movement, and Nutrition:** The foundation of sustainable performance lies in three interrelated pillars: restorative sleep, regular movement, and nourishing food. While sophisticated health strategies exist, these fundamentals remain the most powerful levers for vitality.
    - **Sleep** is essential for cognitive clarity, emotional regulation, and immune function. A consistent sleep

routine—supported by practices such as reduced screen time, cool room temperatures, and dark environments—improves decision-making and resilience.
In my earlier career years, sleep was often sacrificed. Today, it is a non-negotiable element of my routine.

- **Movement**, even in small doses, promotes circulation, energy, and stress reduction. For busy professionals, integrating activity through walking meetings, desk stretches, or active commuting can make a meaningful impact. Consistency outweighs intensity.
- **Nutrition** fuels both body and mind. Whole, nutrient-dense foods—fruits, vegetables, lean proteins, and healthy fats—support sustained energy and focus. Avoiding processed foods and maintaining healthy snacks within reach helps maintain steady productivity throughout the day.

These practices are simple but powerful—critical to both high performance and long-term well-being.

- **Mental Health – Resilience, Stress Regulation, and Mindfulness:** Beyond physical wellness, mental and emotional health are equally vital. Burnout and emotional fatigue are prevalent among high performers and often surface only after prolonged neglect.
    - **Resilience** is developed by reframing challenges, embracing growth, and maintaining a supportive network. Setbacks are viewed not as failures, but as catalysts for learning.
    - **Mindfulness** strengthens emotional balance and stress management. Techniques such as deep breathing, reflective journaling, and structured pauses can be integrated into daily routines. Gratitude practices and mental reframing support a stable internal state, especially during transitions or high-stress periods.

The capacity to adapt, regulate emotion, and remain focused is a core asset in the re-career journey.

- **Work-Life Harmony – Establishing Boundaries That Support Health:** Health is preserved not only through individual habits but also through intentional boundaries. True harmony stems from alignment between professional roles and personal values.
    - Defining **work boundaries**, allocating time for family and personal priorities, and adhering to structured schedules help mitigate overwork and decision fatigue.
    - **Time-blocking**, realistic expectation setting, and clear communication within teams foster a healthier work rhythm.
    - Practicing **digital detachment** outside of work hours reinforces mental clarity, deepens presence, and supports emotional recovery.

  In high-performance environments, sustained success depends on systems that protect health and uphold balance.

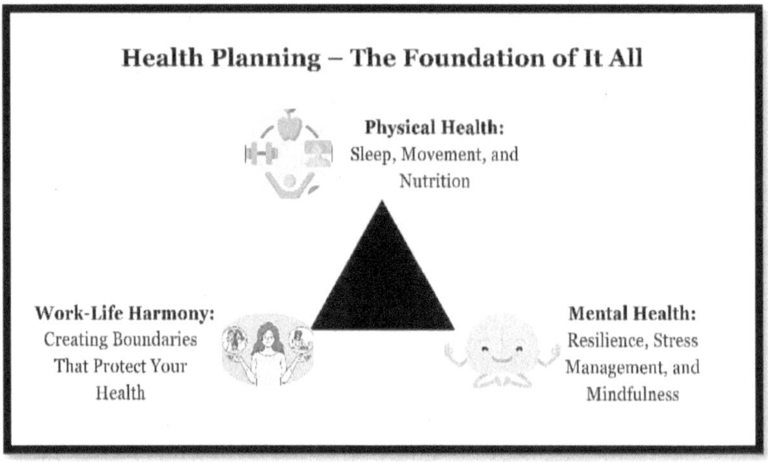

Health is not a soft concept. It is the infrastructure that supports leadership, contribution, and fulfilment. Those who achieve enduring success do so by integrating well-being into their strategy—not as an afterthought, but as a pillar of resilience and purpose.

Health Planning Across Life Stages

Health is dynamic. It evolves with age, career demands, and lifestyle transitions. Long-term well-being requires intentional planning that adapts to changing needs across life stages. Aligning physical and mental health priorities with each phase of life strengthens vitality, prevents burnout, and sustains the capacity to perform—both professionally and personally.

- **In the 30s – Laying the Foundation:** This decade is often marked by career progression, family formation, and expanding responsibilities. Amidst ambition and multitasking, health can be unintentionally sidelined—yet this is precisely when foundational habits must be established.
  - **Key Priorities**: Develop sustainable routines around sleep, physical activity, nutrition, and stress regulation.
  - **Why It Matters**: Habits formed in the 30s shape physical and mental resilience in later decades. For instance, consistent sleep patterns may reduce the risk of burnout or chronic illness in the 40s.
  - **Suggested Practices**:
    - Maintain a regular sleep-wake cycle
    - Integrate simple but consistent strength and cardiovascular exercises
    - Set clear boundaries to prevent overextension from work or caregiving demands

  This is the investment phase—early attention to health compounds benefits over time.

- **In the 40s – Managing Energy and Prevention:** The 40s bring leadership responsibilities, dual caregiving roles, and greater life complexity. As metabolism slows and recovery periods lengthen, a shift toward preventive care and energy optimisation becomes essential.
  - **Key Priorities**: Focus on prevention, hormonal balance, and sustained energy.
  - **Why It Matters**: Health risks such as hypertension, elevated cholesterol, and insulin resistance may develop silently. Proactive monitoring and timely intervention are critical.

- **Suggested Practices**:
    - Schedule regular health screenings (e.g., blood pressure, glucose, colonoscopy)
    - Incorporate mobility and functional strength into fitness routines
    - Transition from reactive healthcare to proactive wellness planning

  This stage calls for intentional recalibration—emphasising quality over quantity in personal and professional commitments.

- **In the 50s and Beyond – Proactive Aging and Longevity:** From the 50s onward, the focus shifts toward preserving independence, enhancing quality of life, and enabling active re-careering or retirement. Health planning must now support both function and purpose.
  - **Key Priorities**: Maintain muscular strength, support cognitive health, and reduce systemic inflammation.
  - **Why It Matters**: Age-related risks—such as sarcopenia, reduced bone density, and cognitive decline—can be managed through preventive action.
  - **Suggested Practices**:
    - Engage in resistance training at least twice weekly
    - Follow an anti-inflammatory diet rich in omega-3s, vegetables, and lean proteins
    - Pursue mentally stimulating activities such as mentoring, reading, or acquiring new skills
    - Remain attentive to emotional well-being, especially during transitions that may trigger stress or isolation

  Health at this stage is the enabler of a purposeful, engaged second career or active retirement.

Designing a Personalized Health Strategy

Health, like career and financial planning, must be customised. A personalised health strategy aligns physical and mental well-being with professional direction and lifestyle vision.

A simple framework for personalised health planning includes:

- **Track Core Metrics**: Monitor key indicators such as sleep duration and quality, daily step count, screen time, hydration levels, and perceived stress. Regular tracking builds awareness, highlights patterns, and facilitates timely adjustments before issues escalate.
- **Leverage Tools**: Utilize systems that support habit consistency and data visibility—such as wearable fitness devices, health apps, journals, or analogue trackers. The goal is to make health routines measurable, visible, and actionable.
- **Establish Non-Negotiables**: Define and commit to essential daily habits that serve as the foundation of well-being. For example:
  - **Sleep**: Aim for 7–8 hours of restorative rest.
  - **Movement**: Incorporate at least 30 minutes of physical activity.
  - **Reflection**: Dedicate 10 minutes to mindfulness, journaling, or quiet reflection.
- **Regularly Assess Alignment**: Conduct periodic self-checks or reflections to ensure continued alignment between health behaviors and broader life priorities. Consider prompts such as:
  - *Am I prioritizing rest, exercise, and nutrition daily?*
  - *Have I set clear boundaries between work and personal life?*
  - *Am I checking in with my mental health proactively?*

Small, consistent actions—the "Minimum Effective Dose"—yield significant long-term results. Examples include 10 minutes of stretching between meetings, swapping sugary snacks with fruit and nuts, or turning off devices 30 minutes before bed. These modest behaviours accumulate to create lasting benefits.

Reminder: Health is the First Freedom
Health is not optional—it's your most essential asset. Without it, wealth, success, and freedom lose their meaning.
So, whether you're climbing the corporate ladder, launching your second act, or planning for early retirement, remember: ***your journey starts—and is sustained—with your health.***

Integrating the Pillars – A Holistic Approach to a Purposeful Life

Future planning extends beyond goal setting or financial projections. It requires the intentional alignment of career direction, financial structure, and health strategy to enable a life anchored in purpose, autonomy, and fulfilment.

These three pillars—career, finances, and health—are interdependent. When integrated cohesively, they generate a reinforcing synergy that enhances overall well-being and long-term sustainability. When one pillar is neglected, the stability of the entire framework is compromised. When all three are nurtured in unison, they form the solid foundation of a resilient and meaningful F.I.R(Re-career).E. journey.

My Journey - When My Pillars Were Misaligned

As shared earlier in the Chapter, in the prime of my corporate career, I had what many would consider success—leadership titles, financial rewards, and regional influence. However, my health began to show signs of strain. I traveled excessively, slept poorly, and lived apart from my family. My finances gave me options, but my career demands consumed my time and energy.

A medical check-up revealed a case of fatty liver. While not serious and since normalized, this diagnosis—often a symptom of a high-stress lifestyle—was a powerful wake-up call. It exposed the imbalance: my career success and financial stability meant little if I lacked the vitality to enjoy them or the presence to be with loved ones. Health—often the silent pillar—was the first to crack.

That moment led me to re-evaluate everything.

As you reflect on your own journey, consider asking yourself:

- *What kind of work energizes me instead of draining me?*
- *How can I use financial independence to gain time freedom—not just more income?*
- *What habits must I install to sustain my physical and mental well-being over decades, not just years?*

These questions could be pivotal in launching your F.I.R(Re-career).E. journey—a path where purpose replaces pressure, and where wealth includes time, health, and meaning.

How the Three Pillars Work Together

1. **Career Anchored in Purpose, Sustained by Health:** A meaningful career is defined not by titles or status, but by alignment with personal values, interests, and long-term vision. However, sustaining purposeful work requires energy, mental clarity, and emotional resilience—capabilities that stem from strong physical and mental health. When well-being is prioritised, performance improves, decision-making sharpens, and presence deepens.
2. **Financial Stability as an Enabler of Career Flexibility:** Sound financial planning—built on emergency reserves, diversified income, and disciplined investing—offers the freedom to pursue career transitions, sabbaticals, or purpose-driven projects without being constrained by financial pressure. Clarity in financial strategy empowers intentional career choices and supports long-term re-careering goals.
3. **Health as the Multiplier of Time and Wealth:** Time and financial resources hold limited value without the vitality to experience them fully. Physical health, mental well-being, and emotional balance enhance one's ability to engage meaningfully with life. Prioritising health amplifies the return on life—enabling deeper connection, greater productivity, and enduring fulfilment.

Micro-Integration in Daily Routines

Holistic integration of career, finance, and health need not begin with sweeping changes. Small, consistent actions create lasting impact. Examples include:

- **Career**: Evaluate new opportunities through the lens of energy sustainability and alignment with long-term direction.
- **Finance**: Automate essential savings and allocate resources toward learning or tools that reinforce health and career development.
- **Health**: Schedule movement, rest, and reflection as essential components of the daily calendar—on par with professional obligations.

Intentional micro-decisions compound over time, forming a resilient and purposeful foundation for the F.I.R(Re-career).E. journey.

My Transition: *When I transitioned to coaching, I deliberately restructured my workweek to align with my values. I scheduled most meetings on weekdays, preferably in the morning or early afternoon—so I could preserve my late afternoons for exercise or quality time with family before evening.*

My calendar wasn't just a tool for productivity; it became a reflection of my priorities, with health and family as fixed, non-negotiable anchors.

Conclusion: The Power of Intentional Design

Sustainable success and personal well-being are not opposing outcomes—they coexist when approached with clarity, alignment, and intention. A fulfilling life is not left to chance; it is consciously shaped through daily decisions that reflect long-term vision and values.

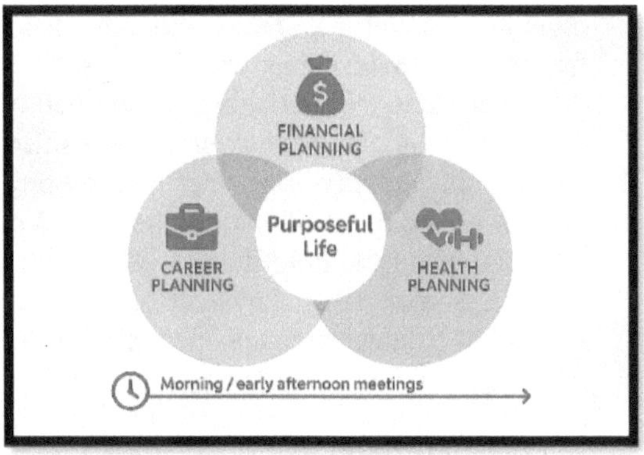

As career transitions unfold, financial frameworks take shape, and health priorities evolve, key reflective prompts remain essential:

- *Am I designing a life I won't need a vacation from?*
- *Do my daily actions reflect my long-term vision?*
- *What does success look like for me—not just on paper, but in how I feel, live, and lead?*

This integrated mindset serves as a compass. Meaningful transitions are not the product of circumstance, but of intentional design—grounded in clarity, guided by purpose, and sustained by well-being. Your future isn't something you wait for. It's something you build—one integrated choice at a time.

Summary

Chapter 3: Planning for the Future – Career, Finances, and Health explored how purposeful planning across three core pillars—career, finances, and health—creates a strong foundation for your F.I.R(Re-career).E journey. A fulfilling and sustainable life is not achieved by accident, but by intentional design across these interconnected areas.

Pillar 1: Career Planning highlighted how career decisions must evolve across life stages. From understanding your strengths and career personality to setting meaningful goals and cultivating marketable skills, this section provided tools for navigating transitions with clarity and purpose.

In **Pillar 2: Financial Planning**, we moved beyond simple budgeting to focus on financial clarity and freedom. With the PASS model as a foundation, we examined how to align financial strategies with personal values and career aspirations, empowering you to make choices from a place of strength rather than survival.

Finally, **Pillar 3: Health Planning** underscored the non-negotiable role of well-being. Drawing from my personal wake-up call, we looked at how sleep, movement, nutrition, mental health, and work-life boundaries serve as the foundation for long-term performance and fulfilment. Health is the enabler of all other goals.

Key Takeaways:

- **Career clarity** is a lifelong process. Your path should evolve with your strengths, passions, and changing life priorities.
- **Financial freedom** is achieved by aligning income, spending, and investment strategies with your long-term goals and values.
- **Health is foundational.** Neglecting well-being can undermine career and financial success. Prioritize it with intentional habits.
- An integrated approach to career, finances, and health creates stability, adaptability, and purpose through all seasons of life.

Practical Tips:

- **Conduct a Career Assessment**: Identify your career personality and values to align your next move with who you are.
- **Set SMART Career Goals**: Break down your long-term career vision into actionable short-term steps.
- **Apply the PASS Model**: Define your financial priorities and track progress toward financial security and freedom.
- **Prioritize Health Non-Negotiables**: Establish routines around sleep, movement, and nutrition—especially during busy periods.
- **Practice Mindful Boundaries**: Use time-blocking and digital detox strategies to protect mental health and personal time.
- **Review Health KPIs**: Track sleep, stress levels, and activity regularly. Adjust your lifestyle and workload to maintain balance.

In the next chapter, **From Mindset to Action - Navigating Career Transitions**, we build upon these principles by exploring how to pivot successfully, leverage coaching and mentorship, and overcome career setbacks with resilience. This chapter provides practical insights on turning challenges into opportunities and creating a career path that aligns with your evolving goals and aspirations.

Reflection Prompts & Mini Exercises

"Reflect, audit, and act. Use these prompts to integrate your career, finances, and health." ~ YK Png

---

1. Career Clarity Across Life Stages

Prompt:

- *How has your definition of career success changed over the past 10 years?*
- *Are your current professional goals aligned with your evolving values and priorities?*
- *What kind of work do you want to be doing 5–10 years from now?*

Mini Exercise: Life Stage Career Map

- Draw a timeline of your career by decade (20s, 30s, 40s, etc.).
- In each stage, list your career focus, key accomplishments, and personal priorities.
- Reflect: *What patterns do you see? What needs to shift for the next stage of your career?*

---

2. Your Financial Freedom Anchor

Prompt:

- *What is your "enough" number—the amount you need to feel financially free?*
- *Are your spending and savings aligned with your long-term priorities or short-term gratification?*
- *What stories or beliefs around money did you inherit, and are they serving you?*

Mini Exercise: The PASS Audit

- Review the four elements of the PASS Model (Plan, Assess, Strategize, Sustain).
- Score yourself from 1 to 10 in each category.
- Choose one area to focus on for improvement over the next quarter and write down 2 action steps.

---

3. **The Cost of Health Neglect**

Prompt:

- *Have you ever experienced a health scare or burnout due to overworking?*
- *What would your health look like today if it had been your top priority the past 5 years?*
- *What's one small but impactful change you could make this week for your well-being?*

Mini Exercise: Wake-Up Call Reflection

- Write about a time your health suffered due to work or stress. *What were the warning signs you ignored? What did you learn?*
- Now, create a list of three "health non-negotiables" you will honour moving forward.

---

4. **Work-Life Harmony Reset**

Prompt:

- *Are you living a life of integration, or are your personal and professional worlds in constant conflict?*
- *What boundaries do you struggle to maintain—and why?*
- *Who or what drains your energy most during the week?*

Mini Exercise: Energy Audit

- Track your energy levels for one week using a simple log (Morning, Midday, Evening).
- Identify what activities or people energize vs. deplete you.
- Decide one boundary you will put in place *(e.g., no emails after 8pm, one screen-free night per week).*

---

5. **Designing Your Personal Health Blueprint**

Prompt:

- *What are your key health metrics? Are you tracking them regularly?*
- *What does optimal well-being look like for you—not by society's standards, but your own?*
- *How can your career and financial plans better support your long-term health?*

Mini Exercise: Health Habit Tracker

- Create a simple table to track daily sleep hours, water intake, steps/movement, and stress levels (1–10). Track for 7 days.
- At the end of the week, reflect: *What's working well? What needs adjusting?* Commit to one change.

Chapter 4: From Mindset to Action - Navigating Transitions

"Success is not about where you start, but how you adapt, learn, and apply your strengths in new ways." ~ Carol Dweck

---

Career progression is rarely linear. It involves evolving mindsets, conscious adaptation, and deliberate action. Whether at the start of a professional journey, navigating a mid-career pivot, or preparing for a purposeful second career, transitions demand clarity, resilience, and alignment with one's evolving identity and values.

This chapter builds upon earlier mindset foundations and moves toward practical application. It introduces personal experiences, guiding frameworks, and actionable strategies to support confident navigation through career transitions—whether by leveraging strengths, reframing challenges, or aligning professional choices with long-term purpose.

Navigating Career Paths at Different Life Stages[5]

Each phase of a professional journey presents distinct considerations. Understanding the unique dynamics of each stage enables more informed, strategic decision-making.

- **Early Career (0–3 Years) - Building Capability and Exposure:** In the early years, the focus lies in developing foundational skills, cultivating adaptability, and expanding professional networks.
    - Internships, volunteer work, and apprenticeships offer real-world exposure and valuable insight into diverse work environments.

---

[5] For a more in-depth look at career planning across life stages, refer to Chapter 3.

- Emphasis should be placed on mastering core competencies such as communication, collaboration, and leadership in varied settings.
- Participation in industry events, active engagement on professional platforms, and seeking mentorship accelerate visibility and opportunity access.

This stage is about building breadth—gaining experiences, exploring interests, and setting the tone for a values-aligned career.

- **Mid-Career (3–15 Years) - Leading, Upskilling, and Strategic Pivoting:** The mid-career phase often brings the opportunity to refine direction, expand leadership capacity, or transition into adjacent industries or functions.
    - Transferable skills become critical assets when considering a pivot. For example, strong analytical or stakeholder management skills may support movement into new domains such as data strategy or operations.
    - Addressing setbacks—such as redundancy, stagnation, or misalignment—requires a combination of self-awareness, resilience, and structured upskilling.
    - Investing in professional development, certifications, and digital competencies enhances relevance and adaptability in an evolving job market.

  This is the phase where depth is developed—honing expertise, embracing leadership, and exploring purpose-aligned transitions.

- **Late Career and Re-Careering (15+ Years) - Transitioning with Purpose:** For professionals entering their later career stages or preparing for retirement, focus often shifts toward legacy, impact, and alignment with personal meaning.
    - Many begin transitioning from structured corporate roles into flexible, purpose-driven pursuits such as consulting, mentoring, teaching, or entrepreneurship.
    - Experience accumulated over decades can be channelled into domains that deliver personal fulfilment and societal contribution.
    - Financial planning plays a central role in supporting autonomy and ensuring the transition is sustainable and aligned with lifestyle goals.

At this stage, career planning becomes less about advancement and more about significance—designing a life and contribution that reflect accumulated wisdom and personal values.

My Journey - The Inner Shift

Having already navigated roles from clinical settings to corporate leadership, what truly changed wasn't just my job—but my intention. Around the age of mid-50s, I began to feel a quiet shift. It was no longer just about success; it was about significance.

As I shared in Chapter 3, financial preparedness gave me the freedom to pivot. But in this chapter, I want to focus on how that freedom enabled me to pursue purpose and meaning.

Re-careering was not simply about changing titles or industries—it was a mindset shift. I had to let go of an identity built over decades and embrace a learner's posture once more. That inner shift was harder than updating my LinkedIn title.

I began to reframe success, seeing it not as climbing a ladder, but as the ability to uplift others through coaching, mentoring, and teaching. This clarity emerged from deep introspection and journaling. I took intentional steps, enrolling in coach certification programs and surrounding myself with growth-minded individuals.

Ultimately, while financial freedom gave me options, it was purpose that gave me direction. I stepped into this new chapter not out of necessity, but out of a deliberate choice to build, serve, and grow in ways that resonated deeply with who I had become.

Key Lessons from My Journey:

- **Purpose Drives the Next Act:** When achievement no longer satisfies, purpose becomes the fuel for sustained impact and fulfilment.
- **Mindset Shift Precedes Career Shift:** The most powerful career transformations begin with internal clarity, not external opportunity.
- **Financial Independence Is the Enabler, Not the Endgame:** Financial preparedness creates optionality, but how that freedom is utilized ultimately defines an individual's legacy.
- **Re-careering Is a Form of Leadership:** Choosing to pivot, grow, and contribute in new ways sets an example for others—it's leadership by design, not default.

Building Resilience: Turning Setbacks into Comebacks

Career setbacks are inevitable. Whether a rejected job application, a missed promotion, or an unexpected layoff occurs, the response defines the trajectory. Resilience isn't about avoiding failure; it's about bouncing back stronger.

My Journey: Navigating Career Setbacks

1. ***Facing Setbacks – Losing My Job:*** *Losing my job at UCB was an unexpected and difficult moment. It forced me to step back and explore new possibilities. My initial venture into entrepreneurship with a generic trading firm eventually proved to be the wrong path, as I realized my strengths were better suited to leadership within an organization. I made the tough decision to close the business and rethink my career direction.*

2. ***Rebuilding – Through Flexibility and Grit:*** *Understanding the need for financial stability, I took a practical and diversified approach. While actively searching for a new corporate role, I supported my family by taking on multiple jobs, including working as a hospital pharmacist, lecturing part-time, and acting as a locum pharmacist. This period taught me the importance of flexibility and leveraging existing skills to stay financially afloat. Eventually, I was offered a General Manager role at a medical equipment company in Hong Kong, which allowed me to rebuild and expand my leadership regionally.*

Key Lessons from My Journey:

- **Entrepreneurship is not for everyone:** I learned my strengths and interests were better suited to leadership within an organization.
- **Financial resilience is critical:** Diversifying income streams through multiple roles provided stability and peace of mind during career transitions.
- **Adaptability opens new doors:** Being open to opportunities outside of Singapore eventually led to a leadership role with broader regional responsibilities.

- **Every setback is a stepping stone:** What seemed like a career derailment ultimately led to a more fulfilling and expansive professional journey.

Building a Resilient Mindset

Resilience is a crucial mindset and practice for navigating career transitions and achieving long-term fulfillment. Here are seven key strategies to build and strengthen your resilience.

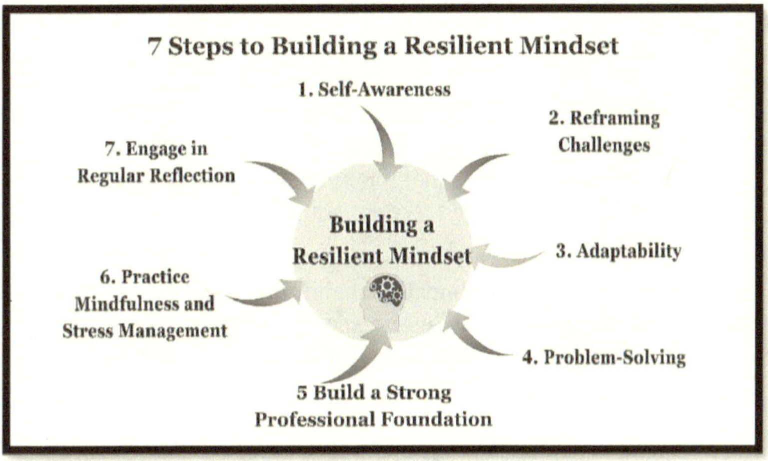

1. **Self-Awareness:** Identify emotional triggers to respond intentionally, not impulsively, maintaining composure during adversity.
2. **Reframing Challenges:** View failures as learning experiences (*"I learned what doesn't work"*) to maintain momentum and stay solution-oriented.
3. **Adaptability:** Adjust to evolving circumstances without losing direction. Cultivating openness to new roles or strategies is essential for long-term career resilience.
4. **Problem-Solving:** Tackle challenges by breaking them into manageable, actionable steps, which restores clarity and reduces overwhelm.
5. **Build a Strong Professional Foundation:** Continuously invest in learning, building relationships, and seeking mentorship to provide a strong platform for recovery and repositioning.

6. **Practice Mindfulness and Stress Management:** Use mindfulness practices to manage internal states and improve emotional clarity during high-pressure situations.
7. **Engage in Regular Reflection:** Regularly assess decisions, outcomes, and thought patterns through journaling or review sessions to convert experience into insight and foster continuous growth.

Leveraging Transferable Skills for Career Pivots

Career transitions introduce uncertainty, but embedded in every professional experience is a valuable reservoir of transferable skills—core competencies that retain relevance across contexts. Recognizing and applying these capabilities is the essence of a strategic pivot.

Transferable skills are foundational abilities applicable across sectors and functions. Unlike role-specific technical skills, these competencies grow in depth and utility over time, forming the bridge between accumulated experience and new purpose-driven pathways.

Core Categories of Transferable Skills

- **Communication:** Expressing ideas clearly to support collaboration, influence, and alignment.
- **Leadership and Influence:** Guiding, inspiring, and mobilizing action, both formally and informally.
- **Critical Thinking and Problem-Solving:** Assessing situations, identifying patterns, and developing sound solutions in dynamic environments.
- **Adaptability and Learning Agility:** The readiness to adjust and acquire new knowledge—a strategic advantage in environments of rapid change.
- **Collaboration and Team Dynamics:** Working effectively within diverse teams, navigating different perspectives, and fostering cohesion.
- **Time and Task Management:** Prioritizing, organizing, and executing efficiently to ensure sustained productivity.

- **Negotiation and Persuasion:** Aligning interests and influencing outcomes through clear reasoning and relationship-building.

My Journey - Leveraging Transferable Skills for Career Pivots

With over 30 years in the pharmaceutical industry across sales, regulatory affairs, and leadership, my corporate chapter ending could have been viewed as a full stop. Instead, I chose to reframe it as a pivot point. By leveraging my communication acumen, problem-solving mindset, and leadership experience, I transitioned into coaching, adult education, and regulatory affairs services. The journey was not about discarding my past; it was about repurposing it. That's the essence of a career pivot: moving forward with your strengths, not in spite of them.

How to Identify and Apply Your Transferable Skills

1. **Conduct a Skills Inventory:** Reflect on your career history. Ask: *"What skills helped me excel?" "What challenges have I overcome?", and "how did I navigate them?"*
2. **Rebrand Your Career Story:** Focus on skills and achievements rather than just job titles. Use action-oriented language, such as, *"Led cross-functional teams to achieve X result."*
3. **Bridge the Gap with Learning and Upskilling:** If a pivot requires additional knowledge, invest in targeted courses, certifications, or mentorship to maintain career agility.
4. **Network Strategically:** Leverage informational interviews and industry events to gain insights into how others successfully transitioned into your target field.
5. **Showcase Transferable Skills in Interviews:** Use the STAR method (Situation, Task, Action, Result) to structure compelling stories that highlight your adaptability and problem-solving abilities in action.

Career transitions are not a departure from past experience, but a reconfiguration of existing strengths. When transferable skills are identified and intentionally applied, they become the foundation for navigating change with clarity and assurance.

Networking for Career and Life Design

Transitions are moments of transformation where sustainable success depends heavily on the relationships and communities you engage with. Networking, when done with intention and authenticity, becomes a life design strategy. In my re-career journey, I learned that doors often open not through cold applications, but through warm conversations.

To navigate purposeful networking with clarity, the **BRIDGE Elements** serve as a practical guide: **B**randing, **R**ight Attitude, **I**nterpersonal Skills, **D**evelopment, **G**ain Influence, and **E**motional Intelligence.

Applying the BRIDGE Elements in Career Transitions

- **B – Brand with Authenticity:** Refine and communicate a clear, purpose-aligned narrative (on LinkedIn or professional bios) that helps others understand your direction ahead.
- **R – Right Attitude and Mindset:** Network genuinely from a mindset of learning and mutual respect, prioritizing thoughtful questions and active listening over transactional exchanges.
- **I – Interpersonal Skills and Relationship Building:** Nurture professional relationships over time with simple follow-ups (thank-you notes, relevant content sharing) to signal care and attentiveness.
- **D – Development through Communities:** Actively involve yourself in professional groups or industry forums (volunteering, moderating) to reinforce credibility and establish visibility.
- **G – Gain Influence by Giving First:** Offer help, recommend others, and share knowledge. This proactive generosity builds trust and reciprocity, positioning you as a collaborator rather than a seeker.
- **E – Emotional Intelligence and Mindful Connection:** Acknowledge others' circumstances and communicate with empathy. Even brief, thoughtful check-ins can turn simple messages into impactful exchanges.

When applied with intention, the BRIDGE elements transform networking from a transactional task into a purposeful practice. Connection is not a final step; it is a continual practice—anchored in who you are and where you are heading.

BRIDGE Elements

B - Brand Yourself: Be the Most Interesting Person in the Room.

R - Right Attitude: Foundation for Growth.

I - Interpersonal Skills and Networking: Building Bridges to Success.

D - Development: Your Continuous Journey of Growth.

G - Gain Influence: Become a Leader Worth Following.

E - EQ: The Key to Connection and Transformation

Empower through Coaching and Mentorship[6]

Career transitions—whether prompted by aspiration, disruption, or a search for renewed purpose—are inflection points that benefit greatly from guided support. Coaches and mentors play distinct yet complementary roles in these periods of change. Each provides structure, insight, and momentum to translate intention into meaningful action.

Coaching and Mentorship in Career Transitions

A coach acts as a strategic facilitator—helping individuals clarify direction, develop relevant capabilities, and stay focused during career shifts. A mentor offers long-term perspective, sharing wisdom born of experience and guiding with contextual understanding. Both roles serve to shorten the learning curve and accelerate purposeful progress.

The Role of a Coach

- **Clarity through Reflection and Goal-Setting:** Coaches support structured self-reflection and help identify goals aligned with values, strengths, and evolving market needs. Frameworks such as purpose-driven models *(e.g. Ikigai)* guide this discovery process.
- **Skill Development for Growth:** Whether transitioning into leadership, adapting to a new industry, or building technical capabilities, coaches offer tailored strategies to close skills gaps and prepare for new challenges.
- **Job Search and Career Strategy:** Practical guidance around CV crafting, interview preparation, and networking enhances positioning. Coaches also help navigate less visible opportunities through targeted outreach and personal branding.

---

[6] "Beyond Solo - The Power of a Coach and Mentor" is explored in greater depth in *Limitless Possibilities ~ YK Png.* (Available on Amazon.Com)

- **Accountability and Progress:** Coaches serve as accountability partners—tracking milestones, reinforcing progress, and helping individuals stay anchored during uncertainty or inertia.

The Role of a Mentor

- **Wisdom through Experience:** Mentors share insights from their personal journeys—offering context, caution, and encouragement drawn from real-life scenarios. Their input often provides perspective that transcends immediate goals.
- **Access to Networks:** Through introductions and informal advocacy, mentors can open doors, make strategic connections, and expand professional visibility.
- **Strategic Career Development:** Mentors help identify advancement opportunities and navigate internal dynamics. Their guidance often addresses unspoken norms and longer-term positioning.
- **Enduring Relationship:** Mentorships frequently evolve into trusted, long-term relationships that support holistic growth—personal, professional, and relational.

Coach vs. Mentor: A Comparative Overview

Aspect	Coach	Mentor
Focus	Specific goals and performance	Career and life trajectory
Approach	Structured and goal-oriented	Conversational and experience-based
Duration	Short to medium term	Often long term
Interaction Style	Facilitates self-discovery	Offers direct advice and perspective
Scope	Defined objectives	Broad developmental support

Key Characteristics of a Coach

- **Time-Bound Engagement**: Coaching relationships are typically short-term and focused on achieving defined objectives.
- **Guided Exploration**: Coaches ask powerful questions, enabling individuals to discover solutions rather than offering direct advice.
- **Skill and Performance Focus**: Coaches help enhance skills, overcome obstacles, and achieve measurable results.

- **Professional Expertise**: Many coaches use structured methodologies, such as the GROW model (Goal, Reality, Options, Will) or ICF guidelines, to drive progress.

Key Characteristics of a Mentor

- **Long-Term Relationship**: Mentorship often spans months or years, allowing for deeper connections and sustained development.
- **Experience-Based Guidance**: Mentors leverage their own experiences to offer practical advice, insights, and lessons.
- **Holistic Support**: Mentors address broader aspects of growth, including career decisions, life balance, and values alignment.
- **Informal Structure**: Mentorship tends to be less structured, evolving naturally based on the mentee's needs.

Selecting between a coach and mentor depends on the individual's immediate context and longer-term goals. The following steps provide a practical approach to identifying a suitable coach or mentor:

1. **Clarify Development Needs:** Define desired outcomes and areas of focus—be it leadership, decision-making, communication, or re-alignment with personal values.

   Examples of reflection questions:
   - *What shifts am I seeking in my professional life?*
   - *What skills or mindset gaps require attention?*
   - *What kind of support would be most helpful at this point?*

2. **Consider Expertise and Style:** The right coach or mentor brings relevant experience and an approach aligned with the individual's learning style. Coaches often ask powerful questions that surface hidden drivers or limiting beliefs. Mentors may share personal stories that offer foresight and inspiration.
   Consider:
   - Comfort with direct advice versus guided discovery.
   - Preference for formal structure versus organic conversation.

3. **Tap into Networks and Communities:** Referrals, professional platforms, and peer recommendations are valuable sources when seeking potential coaches or mentors. Participation in

industry events and community forums often leads to natural, trust-based connections.

4. **Test for Compatibility:** Initial conversations—whether labeled as discovery or chemistry sessions—are essential for assessing mutual fit. Observe the quality of interaction, alignment of values, and clarity of communication.

   Sample exploratory questions:
   - *What is your approach when supporting transitions like mine?*
   - *How do you measure success in a coaching/mentorship relationship?*
   - *Can you share examples of growth you've helped others achieve?*

5. **Evaluate Holistically:** Finding the right coach or mentor goes beyond just ability and compatibility. Here are some other factors to consider for a well-rounded selection process that sets you up for a successful partnership:
   - **Chemistry and Communication Style**: Ensure comfort and open communication.
   - **Availability and Time Commitment**: Align schedules and lifestyle needs.
   - **Cost and Value**: Prioritize value over cost and explore payment structures.
   - **Credentials and References**: Research certifications and seek references or reviews.

Partnerships with a coach or mentor can provide clarity and momentum during transitions. This support isn't about dependence; it's about intentional discovery, focused development, and empowered decisions. A trusted partner helps you enhance your self-awareness, improve your execution, and build a more resilient career path.

Checklist for Finding a Coach or Mentor

Step 1: Define Your Needs

- [ ] **Identify career aspirations:** What are your short-term and long-term goals?
- [ ] **Specify development areas:** Which skills or competencies do you need to improve (e.g., leadership, communication, technical skills)?
- [ ] **Clarify desired outcomes:** What do you hope to achieve from this relationship?

Step 2: Explore Potential Matches

- [ ] **Search professional associations:** Look for experienced coaches and mentors in your industry.
- [ ] **Attend industry events:** Network and meet potential matches in person.
- [ ] **Leverage your network:** Ask colleagues and professional contacts for recommendations.

Step 3: Assess the Fit

- [ ] **Review expertise:** Do they have relevant industry knowledge and experience?
- [ ] **Evaluate coaching style:** Does their approach (e.g., direct, collaborative) align with your preferences?
- [ ] **Verify credentials:** Check for certifications, training, and client testimonials.

Step 4: Conduct a Chemistry Session

- [ ] **Prepare questions:** Have a list of key questions ready to assess their methodology and expertise.
- [ ] **Discuss your challenges:** See how well they understand and propose solutions for your specific needs.
- [ ] **Gauge rapport:** Assess communication style, mutual understanding, and respect.

Step 5: Make Your Final Selection

- [ ] **Confirm logistics:** Ensure their communication style and availability align with yours.
- [ ] **Review cost:** Balance the program's cost against the value they offer.
- [ ] **Make a decision:** Choose the person who best fits your needs, goals, and working style.

Summary

Chapter 4: From Mindset to Action – Navigating Transitions explores how mindset influences successful transitions—whether in careers, life stages, or personal identity. Transitions are often marked by uncertainty, yet they also hold tremendous potential for reinvention and growth. This chapter provides strategies to move from passive contemplation to purposeful action by reframing mindset, leveraging internal strengths, and applying the BRIDGE Elements for career and life design.

We examine the power of a growth mindset and how embracing adaptability, learning agility, and self-awareness can unlock new possibilities. The chapter introduces the BRIDGE Elements—Branding, Right Attitude, Interpersonal Skills and Networking, Development, Gain Influence, Emotional Intelligence—as a practical lens for navigating personal and professional change. Through real-life examples and coaching insights, readers learn how to assess their readiness for change, align values with career direction, and intentionally shape their next steps.

The chapter also clarifies the distinct roles of coaches and mentors during transitions, guiding readers through the process of choosing the right support. It offers actionable guidance on identifying goals, assessing fit, and establishing meaningful developmental relationships.

Key Takeaways:

- **Transitions are not detours but pathways to growth**: Start with the right mindset.
- **The BRIDGE Elements** offer a comprehensive framework to navigate career and life shifts.
- A **coach** supports performance and action; a **mentor** offers experience-based insight.
- Clarity, commitment, and support systems are critical to sustained change.

Practical Tips:

- **Reframe setbacks as feedback;** transitions often involve temporary discomfort.
- **Use reflective questions** *(e.g., "What would I do if I wasn't afraid?")* to uncover deeper motivations.
- Evaluate potential **coaches or mentors** through chemistry sessions and alignment with your values and goals.
- Apply the **BRIDGE framework** to identify areas for growth and repositioning.

In the following section, **Pat II**: **Mastering Financial Planning for F.I.R(Re-career).E.** We explore the fundamentals of financial planning, covering budgeting, saving, investing, and wealth preservation.

In the next chapter, **Financial Foundations for Freedom**, we will guide you in assessing your financial situation, setting SMART goals, managing your money effectively, and laying the groundwork for long-term financial security.

Reflection Prompts & Mini Exercises

"Mindset is the compass; action is the movement. Navigate your transitions with clarity, intention, and courage." ~ YK Png

---

1. Mindset Reframe for Growth

Prompt:

- *What fixed beliefs are holding you back from making a needed change?*
- *When was the last time you took a risk that led to unexpected growth?*
- *How do you typically respond to uncertainty—retreat, react, or reframe?*

Mini Exercise: Limiting Beliefs Audit.

- Write down 3 beliefs that have stopped you from taking action.
- Next to each, write a more empowering alternative *(e.g., "I'm too old to change careers" → "My experience gives me an edge in reinvention").*
- Choose one reframe to focus on and test in the next 30 days through small action.

---

2. Designing Your BRIDGE Plan

Prompt:

- *Which of the BRIDGE elements (Branding, Right Attitude, etc.) is your strongest?*
- *Which element, if strengthened, would most enhance your transition?*
- *How do you want others to perceive your evolving professional identity?*

Mini Exercise: BRIDGE Self-Assessment

- Rate yourself from 1 (low) to 10 (high) on each of the BRIDGE Elements.
- Identify one area to develop over the next 90 days. Create a micro-action plan *(e.g., "Improve Networking – Reach out to 1 new connection each week").*

---

3. **Coaching vs. Mentorship Reflection**

Prompt:

- *Have you ever benefited from coaching or mentorship during a life or career transition?*
- *What support do you need most right now—clarity, accountability, or wisdom?*
- *Are you clear on the kind of guidance that would serve your next chapter?*

Mini Exercise: Support System Map

- Draw three columns: Coaches, Mentors, and Peers. List individuals in your life who fit these roles.
- Now ask: *Where are the gaps? What's missing?*
- Identify one new person to approach for guidance and connection.

---

4. **The Transition Readiness Inventory**

Prompt:

- *What change are you currently resisting, and why?*
- *What does "readiness" look like for you—emotionally, financially, and practically?*
- *What would happen if you waited another year to make this change?*

Mini Exercise: 3-Stage Readiness Model

- Write down your current transition *(e.g., career pivot, retirement planning).*
- Break it down into three stages: Awareness, Preparation, and Action.
- Place yourself in one stage and list 2 things you need to move to the next.

---

5. **Reclaiming Purpose Through Transitions**

Prompt:

- *In moments of change, what values keep you anchored?*
- *What kind of impact do you want your next chapter to have—on yourself, your family, or your community?*
- *Are you pursuing success, or significance?*

Mini Exercise: Purpose Alignment Check-In

- Write your top 3 values and your current top 3 life goals.
- Draw arrows connecting them. *Do they align?*
- If not, rewrite one goal so it better reflects your purpose and priorities.

Part II: Mastering Financial Planning for F.I.R(Re-career).E.

"Financial freedom is available to those who learn about it and work for it."

~ Robert Kiyosaki

Chapter 5: Financial Foundations for Freedom

"Do not save what is left after spending but spend what is left after saving." ~ Warren Buffett

---

Disclaimer: *This chapter provides general financial guidance based on the authors' understanding at the time of writing. It does not constitute financial advice. Readers should consult licensed professionals before making any financial decisions. Regulations and market conditions may change.*

Part I established that Financial Independence and Re-careering Early (F.I.R(Re-career).E.) begins with a mindset of purpose and choice. However, transforming this vision into reality demands disciplined financial mechanics. This chapter is your essential starting point, moving from theoretical alignment to practical execution.

Here, you will establish your financial foundation, starting with the basics: accurately assessing your current situation, setting SMART goals, and implementing a budgeting system anchored in purpose. We'll explore the importance of key security items like emergency funds, and introduce the necessary principles of cash flow, debt management, and basic investing. Only by mastering these foundational elements—and transitioning your financial identity, as emphasized by models like Robert Kiyosaki's Cashflow Quadrant—can you confidently move into the specialized wealth-building chapters ahead.

My Path to F.I.R(Re-career).E.: A Personal Odyssey

For me, financial independence wasn't about stopping work entirely; it was about gaining the flexibility to pursue meaningful projects. A solid financial foundation underpinned this confident transition, enabling a portfolio career where I could work less, live more, and pursue interests like travel and writing books—including Limitless Possibilities, The BRIDGE Career Handbook, The BRIDGE to Career Mastery, and the current one—without financial strain.

In this chapter, we explore the foundational principles that support financial freedom: managing income and expenses, building buffers, investing with purpose, and designing a financial system that empowers career flexibility and long-term fulfillment. Whether the goal is re-careering, semi-retirement, or simply having more time for what matters, financial independence provides the means to live with intention and freedom.

Understanding Financial Situation

Clarity about your financial situation is the foundation for financial freedom. It goes beyond income—it involves a clear picture of assets, liabilities, income, expenses, and savings patterns.

1. **Living Within One's Means:** Spending less than what is earned is a fundamental principle. Research by Lusardi et al. (2017) found that consistent frugality in early adulthood is strongly associated with better financial outcomes later in life.

   My Journey – Frugal Beginnings: *When I started my career, I made intentional decisions to live within my means. For example, instead of a new car, I opted for a second-hand Mitsubishi Colt and learned basic maintenance to save on repair costs. These small, intentional decisions laid the groundwork for my financial stability.*

2. **Cash Flow Awareness - Tracking Income and Expenses:** Awareness of cash flow—the inflow and outflow of money each month—is essential. It enables the identification of spending patterns, control of discretionary expenses, and alignment of spending with priorities.

   My Journey – Budget Discipline: *Early in my career, I used a simple notebook and spreadsheet to track expenses. This practice provided a clear view of where money was going and allowed me to establish realistic savings goals. Today, many free digital tools and apps make tracking easier and more efficient.*

3. **Understanding Net Worth:** Net worth, calculated as total assets minus total liabilities, serves as a snapshot of financial

health. It reflects both wealth accumulation and financial progress over time.

My Journey – Gradual Awareness: *While I didn't formally track my net worth initially, I ensured each month ended with a positive cash balance and no lingering debts. Over time, I began tracking assets like savings, investments, and CPF balances against liabilities such as loans.*

4. **Responsible Debt Management:** Not all debt is detrimental. Differentiating between productive debt (e.g., home loans) and destructive debt (e.g., high-interest credit card balances) is key to maintaining financial control.

   My Journey – Responsible Borrowing: *I took on car loans at different points, but I always ensured the loan amount was within my ability to repay comfortably each month. I chose short repayment periods to avoid long-term interest burdens and made it a point not to stretch my finances just to drive a newer model.*

5. **Building an Emergency Fund:** A robust emergency fund provides a buffer against unexpected events such as job transitions or health emergencies. It is a critical element of financial stability.

   My Journey – Safety Net Planning: *I aimed to build an emergency fund equivalent to at least 6 months' worth of essential living expenses. Achieving this goal early in my career gave me peace of mind during transitions and uncertainties.*

6. **Awareness of Financial Goals and Priorities:** Clarity on short- and long-term financial goals shapes day-to-day financial decisions. Defined goals provide a framework for disciplined action.

   My Journey – Evolving Goals: *My initial goal was basic financial stability. Over time, it shifted to flexibility—having choices—and eventually to independence. Each evolution influenced how I allocated savings, investments, and time.*

Financial Awareness Checklist

Area	Key Questions to Ask Yourself	Action Step
Spending Habits	*Do I spend less than I earn?*	Track all income and expenses monthly
Budgeting	*Do I have a monthly budget and stick to it?*	Create and review a personal budget
Net Worth	*Do I know my current net worth?*	List all assets and liabilities quarterly
Debt Management	*Am I managing debt responsibly and avoiding high-interest loans?*	Consolidate and review all loan repayment plans
Emergency Fund	*Do I have 3–6 months of expenses saved?*	Set up a separate emergency fund
Financial Goals	*Are my short- and long-term goals clear and documented?*	Review and revise goals annually

Understanding your financial situation across these dimensions fosters clarity, which in turn supports better decisions and sustained confidence.

Setting SMART Financial Goals

Financial goals gain traction when framed with clarity and purpose. The SMART framework—Specific, Measurable, Achievable, Relevant, and Time-bound—provides a practical structure to turn aspirations into actionable outcomes.

Financial Goals Across Life Stages:

- **Undergraduates:** Cultivate foundational financial literacy, minimize reliance on student loans, and develop mindful spending habits.
- **Young Professionals:** Prioritize building an emergency fund (3–6 months), optimize CPF and SRS contributions, and begin investing regularly for long-term growth.
- **Mid-Career Professionals:** Focus on income maximization, strategic debt reduction (e.g., mortgage), and portfolio

diversification. Align strategies with future goals like education funding or career transition.

- **Aspiring Retirees:** Shift towards wealth preservation and sustainable income. Rebalance portfolios for risk-appropriate returns, ensure healthcare and insurance are covered, and initiate estate planning.

My Journey - Goal Clarity Before Career Change

My career transition required setting decisive SMART goals to eliminate financial stress. This plan allowed me to take calculated risks confidently. My key measurable objectives were:

- ***Debt Elimination:*** *Fully repay housing and car loans before leaving.*
- ***Retirement Max:*** *Maximize CPF RA contributions to qualify for the highest CPF LIFE payouts.*
- ***Skill Pivot:*** *Obtain my coaching certification while still employed for an immediate transition.*

This level of clarity provided the assurance that my financial base was solid, enabling a confident focus on passion-driven work without the burden of financial uncertainty.

SMART Financial Goals by Life Stage *(Examples)*

Life Stage	Example SMART Goals
Undergraduates	*Save $2,000 by year-end, avoid consumer debt, and complete one personal finance book per semester.*
Young Professionals	*Build an emergency fund covering 6 months' expenses in 18 months. Maximise CPF SA top-ups.*
Mid-Career Professionals	*Clear mortgage within 10 years, invest at least 20% of annual income, and set a target for FI age (e.g., 55).*
Aspiring Retirees	*Convert a portion of assets into income-generating investments. Top up CPF RA to max limits before 55. Prepare estate plans by age 60.*

Aligning financial decisions with SMART goals ensures intentional progress toward long-term financial independence.

Budgeting with Purpose

Budgeting and money management are essential pillars in building long-term financial independence. Budgeting with purpose extends beyond monitoring income and expenses—it is about aligning financial decisions with deeply held values and life aspirations, such as career flexibility or family commitments.

A purpose-driven budget becomes a tool for clarity, discipline, and direction—enabling progress toward F.I.R(Re-career).E. goals with intentionality and confidence.

1. **Begin with a Simple Clear Framework - The 50/30/20 Rule:** This widely recommended method provides a clear structure:
   - **50% Needs:** Essential expenses (housing, food, minimum debt payments).
   - **30% Wants:** Discretionary spending (entertainment, dining, hobbies).
   - **20% Savings & Investments:** Emergency savings, retirement funds, and investment contributions.

   My Experience: *While the 50/30/20 rule provides a helpful framework, my personal approach involved a flexible yet disciplined allocation strategy. I consistently prioritized savings and investments, strategically increasing my savings rate and eliminating outstanding loans—a vital step that provided the confidence to embark on my F.I.R(Re-career).E. journey.*

2. **Apply Zero-Based Budgeting (ZBB) for Intentional Control:** ZBB assigns every dollar a function—ensuring full accountability for all income so that the monthly balance equals zero.
   - **Steps to Implement ZBB:** 1. Start with actual monthly net income. 2. List all expenses. 3. Allocate funds to each category until the total matches your income exactly. 4. Review monthly.

3. **Track to Transform - Visibility Drives Change:** Budgeting creates real impact only when financial activity is consistently tracked.

- **Best Practices:** Use a method that works for you (Excel, apps, or manual logs). Track fixed and variable expenses regularly. Review and adjust to stay aligned with goals.

4. **Choose the Right Tools That Fit Your Style:** A budgeting method is only effective if it's sustainable. Selecting a method that complements your lifestyle is key. Common tools include **Spreadsheets**, **Digital Tools** (apps), and **Manual Systems** (notebooks).

5. **Keep the Budget Dynamic – Regular Review Matters:** Budgets must evolve with changing circumstances.
   - **Monthly:** Review cash flow, spot overspending, and ensure savings targets are met.
   - **Quarterly:** Reflect on any income or lifestyle changes *(e.g., new job, medical expenses)* and adjust categories accordingly.
   - **Annually:** Re-evaluate broader financial goals, update insurance, and assess investment performance.

6. **Align Spending with Life Goals:** A purpose-driven budget reflects what truly matters. It directs financial energy toward meaningful outcomes like a career break, early retirement, or education funding.

   My Journey – Budgeting with Purpose: *Budgeting wasn't just about saving—it was about freedom of choice. By managing my money intentionally, I was able to fund professional certifications, support my children's education, travel purposefully, and step away from financial stress in my 50s.*

When you align your budget with your values, money becomes a tool—not a trap.

Budgeting & Money Management Checklist

Area	Action Step
Know Your Income	Calculate monthly net income (after CPF and tax).
Choose a Budgeting Method	Start with 50/30/20 or try Zero-Based Budgeting.
Track Expenses	Monitor fixed and variable costs monthly.
Set Priorities	Allocate funds for emergency savings, re-careering, and investments.
Cut Wasteful Spending	Identify low-value or impulsive expenses.
Review Regularly	Conduct monthly and quarterly reviews for consistency.
Link to Life Goals	Align budget categories to aspirations like F.I.R(Re-career).E. or sabbaticals.

Starter Kit for Financial Security: Insurance[7], Emergency Funds & Retirement Accounts[8]

Financial independence begins not with accumulation, but with protection. A strong foundation of financial safeguards helps manage risk, maintain stability, and ensure long-term momentum.

1. **Insurance – Safeguarding the Essentials:** Insurance serves as a defensive layer against life's unpredictable events (illness,

---

[7] A detailed discussion on "Insurance: Protecting What Matters Most" will be provided in Chapter 7 by a subject expert.

[8] Topics such as "Maximising CPF for F.I.R(Re-career).E." will be covered in-depth in a Chapter 6.

disability, or premature death). Without adequate protection, savings may be insufficient during emergencies.

- **Key Insurance Essentials:** Term Life Insurance (pure protection), Hospitalisation & Surgical Plans (comprehensive medical), and Personal Accident Insurance.
- **Best Practices:** Start Essential, Scale Up; Review Annually; Seek Guidance.

2. **Emergency Fund:** A financial buffer that absorbs unexpected shocks. It prevents short-term crises from derailing long-term goals.
    - **Building an Effective Emergency Fund:** Target 3–6 months of essential living costs (6–12 months for self-employed). Use a dedicated, accessible high-interest account. Automate monthly transfers.
3. **Retirement Savings:** Early, disciplined planning is key. Time and compounding returns turn even small contributions into a significant fund.
    - **Retirement Strategy Pillars:** Start Early, Grow Gradually; Leverage Tax-Advantaged Platforms *(e.g., CPF, SRS, 401(k)s)*; Portfolio Reviews.
4. **Supplementary Tools – Building on the Core:** Once the fundamentals are secured, products like Endowment Plans, MediSave/HSAs, and Critical Illness/Disability Insurance can enhance protection and discipline.
5. **Life Stage Lens:** Financial tools should evolve with life. Priorities shift from maintaining basic health coverage (Students) to expanding investment and protection (Mid-Career).

Start with Protection, Then Grow with Purpose. Just like a home needs a solid foundation, your financial journey requires a base of security before growth.

Managing Cash Flow, Debt, and Wealth Building

True financial freedom doesn't begin with a bigger paycheck—it begins with clarity, intentionality, and consistent financial habits.

1. **Debt – Tool or Trap?** Debt can be a strategic enabler (productive debt, e.g., home loans) or a limiting burden (**consumptive debt**, e.g., high-interest credit cards). Structured borrowing, supported by a repayment plan, ensures debt serves long-term goals.
2. **Debt Reduction Strategies – Regaining Financial Control:** Two well-established approaches provide structure:
   - **Snowball Method:** Focuses on paying off smallest debts first for psychological momentum.
   - **Avalanche Method:** Targets debts with the highest interest rates first for greater financial efficiency.
3. **Credit Management – Staying in Control:** When managed wisely, credit enables flexibility. Pay balances in full each month, maintain utilization below 30%, and avoid excessive loan tenures.
4. **Redirect Debt Repayment into Wealth Building:** Once repayment obligations reduce, the freed-up cash flow can be redirected toward future-focused goals (investments, emergency reserves, career pivot funds).

   Example: *After paying off my housing and car loans, I reallocated that same cash flow toward investments and professional development—including obtaining my coaching certification and building a runway for my re-career.*
5. **Harnessing Compound Interest:** Compound interest rewards time and consistency. Even modest, regular contributions, sustained over decades, can yield transformative results.

   Illustration: *Saving $500/month from age 25, assuming a 4% annual return, yields ~ $750,000 by age 65. Starting the same plan just 10 years later at age 35 yields ~ $450,000—demonstrating the profound value of time.*
6. **Build Wealth with Consistency and Discipline:** Building wealth is about consistent, intentional actions. Automate

savings, reinvest dividends, review investments periodically, and, crucially, avoid lifestyle inflation.

7. **Financial Clarity Drives Life Choices:** Financial strength is about gaining autonomy. With clarity, you can take calculated risks, pursue meaningful paths, and live proactively, making decisions based on purpose, not pressure.

My Reflection: *The discipline to automate savings, avoid lifestyle inflation, and invest in both my portfolio and personal growth was what gave me the freedom to walk away from the corporate world on my own terms. It wasn't about overnight success—it was about small, smart decisions made consistently over time.*

Ultimately, financial systems and routines—not willpower—create the margin for meaningful life design.

Checklist: From Cash Flow to Wealth Creation

Area	Action Step
1. Know Your Debt Profile	List all debts (amount, rate, purpose). Identify good vs. bad debts.
2. Choose a Debt Reduction Strategy	Select Snowball or Avalanche method. Set up automatic payments.
3. Use Credit Strategically	Pay full credit card balances monthly. Keep utilization below 30%.
4. Redirect Repayments to Wealth	Channel freed-up cash into Investments, CPF, or re-career funds.
5. Harness Compound Interest	Start investing early. Reinvest gains.
6. Practice Financial Discipline	Automate savings. Avoid lifestyle inflation.
7. Plan for Your Financial Future	Set clear financial goals *(e.g., early retirement, career change)*.

Investing for the Future[9]: A Primer

Once solid financial foundations are established, the natural next step is to grow capital through long-term investing. More than just a path to wealth accumulation, investing serves to preserve purchasing power, create income streams, and unlock greater financial autonomy.

At its essence, investing involves allocating resources in pursuit of returns, accepting a degree of risk in exchange for the potential of capital appreciation or income. The effectiveness of this process hinges on understanding the risk-return trade-off and leveraging key principles such as diversification, time horizon, and emotional discipline.

A diversified portfolio often includes a mix of asset classes, each serving different financial roles:

- **Equities (Stocks):** Offer potential for capital growth and long-term wealth accumulation.
- **Fixed Income (Bonds):** Provide stability and predictable income, suitable for conservative allocations.
- **Collective Investment Schemes (ETFs/Unit Trusts):** Deliver cost-effective exposure to broad asset classes.
- **Cash Equivalents:** Offer liquidity and principal protection for short-term needs.

Balanced portfolio construction, tailored to specific goals and risk tolerance, helps manage volatility while targeting steady growth.

My Investment Journey: Discipline Over Impulse

My investment journey began defensively, using insurance and endowment plans for a safety net and blended savings. As my career

---

[9] A detailed discussion on "Investment Strategies for Financial Growth" will be provided in Chapter 8 by a subject expert.

progressed, I started exploring a diverse range of products like fixed deposits, bonds, unit trusts, and stocks.

The path, however, wasn't always smooth. I stumbled upon the harsh realities of the market, experiencing losses due to impulsive decisions fuelled by inexperience. I also felt pressure from certain relationship managers whose sales targets didn't always align with my best interests.

These setbacks became valuable lessons. I learned the importance of independent research and critical thinking. While expert advice is invaluable, over-reliance on advisors can be detrimental if their recommendations are influenced by hidden agendas.

Investment Best Practices

Successful investing hinges on discipline, not simply luck. Keep these principles in mind:

Discipline	Best Practices (Dos)	Caution (Don'ts)
Strategy & Risk	Start with clear **goals** and a defined long-term **investment plan**. **Diversify** investments across different asset types and geographies to minimize risk. Invest according to your **comfort level** with risk.	Avoid making **emotional decisions** based on hype or fear. Don't **chase high returns** or invest impulsively.
Execution	Conduct **thorough research** to understand the risks and potential returns before committing. Regularly **review and rebalance** your portfolio based on evolving needs.	Do not **panic sell** during market downturns if your long-term goals remain unchanged.
Due Diligence	Stay **informed** of market trends and economic news.	Avoid **over-relying on others**; conduct your own due diligence and make informed decisions.

Active vs. Passive Investment Strategies

There are two core investment approaches, each suited to different preferences and resource levels:

- **Active Investing:** Involves selecting specific securities to outperform market benchmarks. This strategy demands regular research, attention to market cycles, and a high tolerance for risk.
- **Passive Investing:** Uses vehicles such as index funds or ETFs to simply track overall market performance. This approach is favoured for its simplicity, low cost, and suitability for long-term investors seeking broad exposure without frequent intervention.

For those with limited time or market expertise, passive strategies often deliver dependable, cost-efficient results.

The Role of Lifelong Learning in Wealth Creation

While investing in markets builds financial capital, investing in personal development compounds human capital—often yielding higher and more sustainable returns.

Example: *Throughout my career, I pursued additional education—degrees in sales, marketing, finance, and business leadership. These investments expanded my career options, empowered my transition into coaching and entrepreneurship, and enriched my life far beyond the numbers in my portfolio.*

Key Takeaway: Smart investments, whether in financial markets or personal growth, accelerate wealth-building and open doors to new possibilities.

Investing is not a single event, but a continuous process of learning, adapting, and aligning capital with vision. Mistakes are inevitable, but they are also instructive. A well-considered, values-based approach creates the platform for long-term financial freedom.

Future chapters will explore deeper strategies for portfolio construction, risk management, and emotional resilience—critical elements for navigating evolving market dynamics.

Summary

Chapter 5: Financial Foundations for Freedom shifts the focus from earning alone to managing, protecting, and growing your money with purpose. Whether you're entering the workforce, planning a transition, or preparing for retirement, this chapter equips you with the financial clarity and structure to pursue life on your own terms.

This chapter provides a holistic roadmap for financial mastery—starting with understanding your current situation and setting SMART financial goals, then progressing into purposeful budgeting, protecting your financial base, managing debt, and taking the first steps toward investing.

We focus on building financial systems aligned with your goals, using frameworks like the 50/30/20 rule and zero-based budgeting. You will gain strategies for debt elimination, and an introduction to wealth-building and investing concepts, emphasizing key protections like insurance, emergency funds, and CPF/SRS.

Key Takeaways:

- **Financial Independence Enables Freedom of Choice:** The goal is not early retirement alone—but the ability to make values-driven decisions without financial pressure.
- **Budgeting Is Purpose-Driven Planning:** Systems like 50/30/20 and zero-based budgeting help align spending with what matters most to you.
- **SMART Financial Goals Provide Focus:** Clear, measurable goals bring structure and intention to your financial journey.
- **Foundational Security Comes First:** Insurance, emergency funds, and retirement accounts are essential buffers.
- **Debt Must Be Managed Strategically:** Recognizing productive vs. consumptive debt, and applying targeted repayment methods, creates momentum toward wealth-building.
- **Compound Interest Rewards Time:** Starting early and staying consistent is the most powerful force for long-term wealth growth.
- **Investing Early Builds Momentum:** Understanding risk, diversification, and time horizons is more important than picking "winners."

- **Personal Growth Is a Wealth Multiplier:** Investing in education, skills, and self-awareness yields returns far beyond dollars and cents.

Practical Tips:

- **Assess Your Financial Position**: Track your net worth and monthly cash flow to establish a clear starting point.
- **Set SMART Financial Goals**: Define short-, mid-, and long-term targets that are Specific, Measurable, Achievable, Relevant, and Time-bound.
- **Implement Purposeful Budgeting**: Apply a framework like the 50/30/20 rule or zero-based budgeting to manage your spending and boost savings.
- **Strengthen Your Financial Safety Net**: Build an emergency fund with 3–6 months of essential expenses and ensure basic insurance coverage is in place.
- **Clear Debt Strategically**: Use the Snowball or Avalanche method to eliminate high-interest liabilities and redirect repayments into investments.
- **Start Investing with a Plan**: Begin with diversified, low-cost options suited to your goals and risk tolerance. Learn to stay invested, not reactive.
- **Automate Good Habits**: From savings to loan repayments, automation reduces decision fatigue and builds financial momentum.
- **Invest in Yourself**: Upskill through courses, certifications, or personal development to expand your career options and earning potential.

In the next chapter, **Maximizing CPF for Financial Freedom**, we will dive deeper into how Singapore's Central Provident Fund (CPF) system acts as a foundational pillar for your long-term security and financial independence.

This chapter will guide you through maximizing your retirement: from understanding the different CPF accounts (Ordinary, Special, MediSave, and Retirement) and optimizing contributions for housing and healthcare, to leveraging the Supplementary Retirement Scheme (SRS) to boost savings and secure tax benefits.

Reflection Prompts & Mini Exercises

"Financial independence begins with financial clarity. You can't move toward freedom until you know where you stand." ~ YK Png

---

1. Financial Self-Awareness

Prompt:

- *What is your current net worth, and how does that align with your life goals?*
- *Where are your biggest financial leaks—spending, debt, or missed opportunities?*
- *Do you feel in control of your financial decisions, or are you reacting to circumstances?*

Mini Exercise: Net Worth Snapshot

- List all your assets *(e.g. cash, CPF, investments, property)* and liabilities *(e.g. loans, credit card debt).*
- Calculate your net worth* (Assets - Liabilities).
- Track income vs. expenses over the past month to assess your cash flow.
- Reflect: *What's one habit or decision that can improve this number in the next 90 days?*

****Note:** Digital tools, such as those offered by banks, can help you synchronize your assets and liabilities to accurately reflect your net worth.*

---

2. SMART Financial Goals

Prompt:

- *What short-term financial goal would bring you the greatest peace of mind?*
- *What long-term financial goal excites you the most?*
- *Are your current financial behaviours aligned with either?*

Mini Exercise: SMART Goal Setup

- Choose one financial goal *(e.g., "save for home deposit," "clear $5,000 in credit card debt").*
- Make it SMART: Specific, Measurable, Achievable, Relevant, Time-bound.
- Write down the first micro-step you can take this week.

---

3. **Budgeting with Purpose**

Prompt:

- *Are you budgeting based on your values and goals—or just reacting to bills?*
- *Which category (needs, wants, savings/investments) has the biggest gap from your ideal ratio?*
- *How well does your current budget support your plans for re-career, retirement, or life transitions?*

Mini Exercise: 50/30/20 Reality Check

- Track your expenses for the past month.
- Categorize them: 50% Needs, 30% Wants, 20% Savings/Investments.
- Reflect: *What one category needs adjusting to move closer to your ideal financial ratio?*

---

4. **Managing Debt Strategically**

Prompt:

- *Are your current debts aligned with productive goals (e.g., education, property), or draining your finances?*
- *How would becoming debt-free impact your confidence, flexibility, or ability to re-career?*
- *What's holding you back from accelerating your debt payoff plan?*

Mini Exercise: Debt Domination Plan

- List all debts, interest rates, and minimum payments.
- Choose a payoff strategy: Snowball (smallest first) or Avalanche (highest interest first).
- Commit to one small action—*e.g., an extra $50 toward the next payment this month.*

---

5. **Investing in Growth (Financial + Personal)**

Prompt:

- *How confident do you feel about your current investment knowledge and strategy?*
- *Are you consistently learning and upskilling to increase your income potential?*
- *What investment—financial or personal—has brought you the highest return so far?*

Mini Exercise: Future-Proof Growth Plan

- Choose one area to invest in this quarter:
  → Financial *(index funds, CPF SA top-up)*
  → Personal *(online course, certification)*
- Set a budget and timeline for that investment.
- Journal the expected ROI—not just in dollars, but in skills, time, or opportunities.

---

6. Investing in the Future

Prompt:

- *How confident are you in your current investment decisions and knowledge?*
- *What's holding you back from investing more consistently?*
- *Are your investments aligned with your risk tolerance and long-term vision?*

Mini Exercise: Personal Investment Review

- List your current investments by type *(stocks, bonds, CPF SA, ETFs, etc.)*.
- Assess diversification, fees, and performance (don't panic—this is just a check-in).
  - Choose one next step: *read a trusted source, attend a webinar, or review your asset allocation.*

Chapter 6: Maximizing CPF for Financial Freedom

"The best time to plant a tree was 20 years ago. The second-best time is now." ~ Chinese Proverb

---

> ***Disclaimer***: *CPF policies are subject to change. The content reflects current understanding and is for informational purposes only. Readers should refer to the official CPF Board website and consult qualified advisors for the latest guidance before making CPF-related decisions.*

Achieving financial independence is not solely a function of income generation—it is equally dependent on prudent financial management and long-term planning. In the Singapore context, the Central Provident Fund (CPF) represents a foundational pillar of financial security, providing structured support for key life needs including housing, healthcare, and retirement.

CPF is more than a compulsory savings scheme; it is a versatile financial mechanism that evolves with each life stage. From early-career accumulation to mid-life asset consolidation and post-career income sustainability, CPF offers tax-advantaged, risk-free, and interest-bearing options that can be strategically aligned with broader financial goals.

This chapter explores how to optimize the CPF system as part of a holistic F.I.R(Re-career).E. strategy. It covers the structure and components of CPF, key milestones across the Member's lifecycle, and practical strategies for maximizing CPF usage—including the Retirement Sum Scheme, CPF LIFE, housing applications, MediSave utilization, and approved investment schemes. When integrated effectively, CPF can serve as a stable anchor for long-term financial independence and career flexibility.

My Personal Journey: Unlocking the Potential of CPF

Early in my career, CPF felt like a distant, compulsory deduction. Like many young professionals, I saw it as a burden, not a tool. However, I soon realized its potential for securing financial stability and supporting major life milestones.

Strategic Use for Major Milestones

My first major financial decision was buying a home. I chose to finance it using my CPF Ordinary Account (OA) to reduce my bank loan. The interest rate on my CPF loan was lower than the bank's, which made it a cost-effective choice. This move preserved my cash for other uses and lowered my monthly burden.

As my financial literacy grew, I began investing my CPF savings through the CPF Investment Schemes (CPFIS). This allowed my money to work for me rather than remain idle. At the same time, I made yearly contributions to the Supplementary Retirement Scheme (SRS), a voluntary scheme that offered tax relief. I invested these SRS funds in unit trusts, which provided diversification and the potential for higher returns.

Optimizing CPF for Retirement and Beyond

Approaching my F.I.R.E. journey, I became even more intentional with my CPF. I prioritized repaying my housing loan to restore funds to my CPF OA. This move allowed me to earn the stable CPF interest rate, which is risk-free and government backed. The OA earns a base rate of 2.5% per annum, while the Special, MediSave, and Retirement Accounts (SA, MA, and RA) earn 4% or more.

I also took advantage of CPF top-ups for both myself and my spouse to ensure higher CPF LIFE annuity payouts in the future. CPF LIFE, Singapore's national annuity scheme, provides a lifelong monthly payout starting at age 65. The more we contribute, the higher our payouts, which helps us maintain a comfortable lifestyle in retirement.

A Strategic Tool for Freedom

Looking back, CPF was not just a compulsory savings system—it was a powerful financial tool that helped me secure a home, grow my savings, reduce taxes, and prepare for a stable retirement. By leveraging it wisely, I built a strong financial foundation that supported my transition into my re-career journey, providing peace of mind as I pursued my passions.

CPF Overview: Ordinary, Special, MediSave and Retirement Accounts

The Central Provident Fund (CPF) is structured around four key accounts, each designed to serve specific financial purposes across different stages of life. A sound understanding of the role and function of these accounts enables strategic financial planning and maximization of CPF's benefits.

1. **Ordinary Account (OA):** The Ordinary Account is the most flexible component of CPF savings, supporting essential expenditures related to housing, education, and selected investments. It accrues a base interest rate of 2.5% per annum.
   - **Housing**: OA savings may be used for the purchase of HDB flats or private properties, including servicing home loans, making down payments, and covering stamp duties.
   - **Education**: The OA supports financing of approved educational programs, facilitating career development and professional advancement.
   - **Investments**: Through the CPF Investment Scheme (CPFIS), OA funds can be deployed into approved financial instruments such as unit trusts, shares, and bonds.
2. **Special Account (SA):** The Special Account is dedicated to long-term retirement savings and accrues a higher interest rate of 4% or more per annum. It is structured to support wealth accumulation through risk-free compounding over time.
   - **Retirement Savings**: The SA serves as a key pillar for retirement adequacy, with funds accumulating steadily to meet future income needs.
   - **Guaranteed Returns**: Government-backed interest rates provide stability, making the SA a preferred vehicle for low-risk, long-term growth.
3. **MediSave Account (MA):** The MediSave Account supports healthcare financing and safeguards against medical inflation. It earns an interest rate of 4% per annum and plays a critical role in ensuring financial resilience in the face of health-related costs.

- **Medical Expenses**: MA savings may be used for hospitalization, outpatient treatments, and approved long-term care services.
- **Insurance Premiums**: It can also fund premiums for MediShield Life, Integrated Shield Plans (IPs), and CareShield Life, providing foundational health coverage.

4. **Retirement Account (RA):** The Retirement Account is automatically established at age 55. It consolidates balances from the OA and SA to form the basis of retirement payouts under the CPF LIFE scheme.
    - **CPF LIFE Payouts**: The RA funds lifelong monthly payouts through CPF LIFE, offering income security throughout retirement.
    - **Plan Options**: Members may select from various CPF LIFE plans—Basic, Standard, or Escalating—to suit their retirement income preferences.

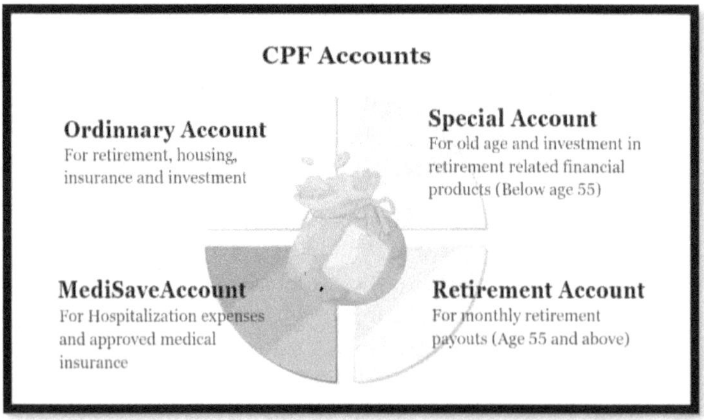

The Importance of CPF Account Integration

Each CPF account serves a distinct role in supporting financial objectives—from home ownership and personal development to healthcare protection and retirement adequacy. When coordinated effectively, they form an integrated system for long-term wealth preservation and financial independence.

CPF optimization should be aligned with life stage and evolving priorities. Earlier in life, focus may be on the OA for housing. In later stages, emphasis typically shifts to building up the SA and MA for retirement and healthcare readiness. The CPF framework offers more than retirement provision—it is a comprehensive financial planning platform supporting diverse life goals.

How CPF Contributions Work

CPF contributions are structured to evolve with an individual's financial needs over their life journey.

The allocation percentages vary by age group. In the earlier stages of one's career, a higher proportion of CPF contributions is directed to the OA to support housing and education goals. As individuals approach midlife and beyond, a greater share is channelled into the SA and MA to prioritise retirement and healthcare needs. This progressive shift encourages long-term financial planning and aligns CPF's structure with evolving life priorities.

For those aiming to optimise CPF for financial independence, recognising these shifts allows for proactive action. For instance, individuals who do not intend to use their OA for housing in the near term may consider transferring part of their OA balance to the SA to benefit from higher interest rates. Although such transfers are irreversible, they can significantly enhance retirement savings over time due to compounding effects.

Understanding the contribution structure enables individuals to make informed decisions about housing, retirement, and healthcare planning at every stage of life.

Using CPF for Housing

Housing is a major life milestone and often the first significant use of CPF savings. While CPF provides a valuable means to fund home ownership—through down payments, monthly loan servicing, and associated legal fees—careful planning is essential to avoid compromising long-term financial goals.

One of the key considerations is the balance between immediate affordability and future retirement adequacy. Excessive use of OA funds for housing can reduce the compounding potential of CPF savings and may lead to a shortfall in retirement reserves. Additionally, when a property is sold, CPF rules require the refund of the principal amount used, along with the accrued interest that would have been earned had the funds remained in the account.

Homebuyers should also be mindful of property type. CPF usage limits differ between HDB flats and private properties. Factors such as the Valuation Limit and Withdrawal Limit can affect how much CPF can be used over time, and whether cash top-ups will be necessary later.

Key Considerations:

- **HDB vs. Private Property**: Different CPF withdrawal limits apply, so choose wisely based on your financial situation.
- **Loan Repayments**: Decide whether to use CPF or cash to service your home loans, considering the impact on your retirement savings.
- **Accrued Interest**: Understand the cost of using CPF for housing, as the accrued interest will need to be returned to your CPF account when you sell your property.

Used strategically, CPF can support home ownership without undermining retirement readiness.

CPF and Healthcare Protection

CPF plays a vital role in providing for healthcare needs through the MediSave Account and associated insurance schemes. As healthcare costs rise with age, having a well-planned approach to medical funding is essential.

MediSave supports a range of medical expenses including hospitalisation, day surgeries, selected outpatient treatments, and insurance premiums. The account accrues interest at attractive rates, making it a reliable reserve for healthcare funding.

In addition to MediSave, CPF supports key national healthcare insurance schemes. MediShield Life offers basic coverage for large hospital bills and selected outpatient treatments. For those seeking enhanced coverage—such as private hospitals or Class A/B1 wards in public hospitals—Integrated Shield Plans (IPs) can be purchased and paid partly from MediSave, subject to withdrawal limits.

CareShield Life, a national long-term care insurance scheme, provides monthly payouts in the event of severe disability. This scheme offers protection not just for the individual, but also peace of mind for families managing caregiving responsibilities.

Practical points to note:

- Regularly review IP coverage to ensure alignment with changing needs.
- Consider voluntary top-ups to MediSave for parents or self-employed individuals, which may also provide tax relief.
- Be aware of withdrawal limits from MediSave when planning for higher-tier insurance premiums or elective procedures.

Taking a structured approach to CPF healthcare planning ensures that medical needs are met without excessive reliance on cash reserves, supporting both financial resilience and well-being.

Growing CPF Savings through Investments

While CPF offers stable, government-guaranteed interest rates, individuals who are comfortable with some degree of risk may explore the CPF Investment Scheme (CPFIS) to potentially enhance long-term returns. CPFIS provides members with the option to invest their Ordinary Account (OA) and, in some cases, Special Account (SA) savings in a range of approved financial instruments.

Crucially, investing through CPFIS is not mandatory, and you bear the risk of losing money. The decision should be guided by your financial goals, investment horizon, and risk appetite. It is important to weigh potential gains against the high guaranteed interest forgone—particularly from the SA, which currently earns up to 4%–5% per annum.

Key Investment Options under CPFIS:

1. **Stocks, ETFs, and Unit Trusts**: Growth-oriented options with higher volatility.
    - **Higher Risk, Higher Returns**: These instruments offer exposure to capital markets and are generally more volatile

than CPF's guaranteed interest rates. While they carry greater risk, they also provide opportunities for superior returns over time.
- **Diversification**: Exchange-Traded Funds (ETFs) and unit trusts enable access to a broad range of sectors and geographies, helping spread risk while capturing market opportunities.
- **Long-Term Growth**: Equities and equity-linked funds are suited for investors with longer time horizons and the capacity to endure short-term market fluctuations. When held over extended periods, they have historically delivered positive real returns.

2. **Bonds and Fixed Deposits**: Conservative options focused on stability and capital protection.
   - **Lower Risk, Stable Growth**: Bonds and fixed deposits offer steady, predictable returns with significantly lower risk compared to equities. These are suitable for capital preservation and income stability.
   - **Capital Preservation**: These instruments prioritize protection of the principal, making them appropriate for risk-averse investors or those approaching retirement.
   - **Short to Medium-Term Investments**: With varying maturity periods, bonds and fixed deposits are ideal for shorter investment horizons or as a stabilizing component in a diversified portfolio.

3. **Endowment Policies**: Structured savings plans with guaranteed elements and insurance protection.
   - **Guaranteed Returns with Participating Bonuses**: Endowment plans typically provide a guaranteed maturity benefit, supplemented by non-guaranteed bonuses depending on the insurer's investment performance. This makes them attractive for those seeking stable, long-term growth.
   - **Structured and Disciplined Saving**: Regular premium commitments foster financial discipline and facilitate systematic wealth accumulation over time.
   - **Insurance Protection**: Many endowment plans include life coverage, offering dual benefits of savings and financial protection for dependents.

While CPFIS introduces potential for enhanced portfolio performance, it also involves exposure to market and credit risks. Strategic use of CPFIS requires careful consideration of financial goals, risk appetite, and investment horizon. A diversified, research-based approach—complemented by ongoing portfolio monitoring—can help optimize long-term outcomes without compromising the security of CPF savings.

SRS: Boosting Retirement Savings

The Supplementary Retirement Scheme (SRS) is a voluntary savings scheme that complements CPF by offering additional tax benefits and investment opportunities. It is designed to encourage individuals to save more for retirement while reducing their taxable income. Below are key features of SRS:

- **Tax Relief:** Contributions to the SRS are eligible for tax relief, which reduces your taxable income.

  Example: *Singapore citizens and Permanent Residents can contribute up to $15,300 annually (foreigners up to $35,700). Contributing to SRS is a win-win: you boost retirement savings while securing valuable tax benefits by lowering your taxable income.*

- **Wide Investment Options:** SRS funds can be invested in a broader array of financial products compared to CPFIS, including equities, bonds, real estate investment trusts (REITs), insurance products, and more.

- **Withdrawal Rules:** SRS withdrawals can be made starting at the prevailing statutory retirement age. If withdraw before this age, a 5% penalty applies, and the entire amount is subject to income tax. Withdrawals after the retirement age are taxed at a concessional rate, with only 50% of the amount subject to tax.

Note for Readers: *As statutory ages are subject to periodic review, please refer to the official CPF Board or Ministry of Manpower website for the latest prevailing statutory retirement and withdrawal ages.*

How SRS Complements CPF:

- **Diversification:** While CPF focuses on risk-free, government-backed returns, SRS allows you to invest in higher-yield products, providing a balanced approach to retirement planning.
- **Tax Efficiency:** SRS contributions reduce your taxable income, while CPF contributions offer tax relief and higher interest rates. Together, they create a powerful combination for maximizing retirement savings.
- **Flexibility:** SRS provides an additional layer of flexibility, allowing you to invest in products that may not be available under CPFIS.

CPF LIFE: Choosing the Right Plan

CPF LIFE (Lifelong Income for the Elderly) is Singapore's national annuity scheme, designed to provide lifelong monthly payouts starting from the payout eligibility age, typically 65. It addresses the longevity risk associated with increasing life expectancy by ensuring a continuous stream of income throughout retirement.

Members with sufficient retirement savings are automatically enrolled into CPF LIFE and can select from three available plans. Each plan is tailored to different income needs, capital priorities, and lifestyle considerations:

CPF LIFE Plan	Starting Payout	Payout Over Time	Bequest to Beneficiaries	Best Suited For...
1. Escalating	Lowest initial payout	Increases by 2% annually for life (inflation protection)	Lowest bequest (as more is paid out over time)	Individuals concerned about rising costs who prioritize long-term purchasing power and are comfortable with a low starting payout.

CPF LIFE Plan	Starting Payout	Payout Over Time	Bequest to Beneficiaries	Best Suited For...
2. Standard	Highest initial payout	**Level** (remains steady throughout retirement)	Moderate bequest	Individuals who prefer a fixed, predictable budget and want the highest starting income possible from the scheme.
3. Basic	Lower initial payout	**Progressively decreases** over time (due to extra interest mechanism)	Highest bequest (as only 10-20% of RA is used initially)	Individuals who have substantial other income sources and prioritize leaving the largest possible legacy to beneficiaries.

Illustrative Examples: Choosing the Right Plan

To understand the practical difference, consider three members, all turning 65 with the same retirement sum:

Persona A: The Inflation Hedger

- **Goal:** Protect purchasing power and maintain lifestyle 20+ years into retirement.
- **Choice: Escalating Plan**
- **Result:** The payout starts lower (e.g., $1,000/month). The 2% annual increment ensures that by age 85, the monthly payout is nearly 50% higher than the starting amount, helping to offset the effects of inflation on daily expenses.

Persona B: The Budget Stabilizer

- **Goal:** Maximize initial stable income and maintain a fixed retirement budget.
- **Choice: Standard Plan**

- **Result:** The payout starts higher than the Escalating Plan (e.g., $1,200/month) and remains level for life. This provides the highest immediate income and simplifies budgeting but requires the member to manage inflation risks using other savings.

Persona C: The Legacy Planner

- **Goal:** Secure a baseline income while prioritizing leaving the maximum residual CPF balance to beneficiaries.
- **Choice: Basic Plan**
- **Result:** The payout starts lower than the Standard Plan (e.g., $950/month) and decreases after age 90. However, because only a fraction of the Retirement Account is used initially, a larger residual sum remains in the account to be paid out to the member's estate upon passing.

Key Considerations:

- **Living Expenses:** Expected monthly needs and whether supplementary income streams are available.
- **Inflation Considerations:** Ability to manage future cost increases through escalating income.
- **Legacy Goals:** Desired amount to be left behind for beneficiaries.

The CPF LIFE Estimator, available on the CPF Board website, allows members to model different plan scenarios based on retirement savings and desired payout ages. CPF LIFE serves as a cornerstone of retirement income planning. By offering flexibility across different plan types, it supports diverse retirement lifestyles while delivering peace of mind through income continuity in the later phases of life.

Retirement Planning with CPF

At age 55, Singaporeans experience a significant transition in their CPF journey with the creation of the Retirement Account (RA). This account is automatically formed using funds transferred from the Special Account (SA) and, if necessary, the Ordinary Account (OA). The RA serves a critical role in building up the Full Retirement Sum (FRS)—a benchmark designed to ensure sufficient monthly payouts for retirement.

Reaching the FRS (or Enhanced Retirement Sum, if one chooses to top up further) is important for securing stable income via CPF LIFE, which begins payouts around age 65. Strategic planning from early working years to mid-life can greatly influence how well-prepared one is at this stage.

Strategies for Maximizing Retirement Savings:

1. **Voluntary CPF Top-Ups**: These top-ups earn attractive, risk-free interest and qualify for personal income tax relief, up to $8,000 per calendar year.
    - **Boost Savings**: Voluntary top-ups to your SA (before 55) or RA (after 55) can significantly enhance your retirement reserves.
    - **Tax Benefits**: Voluntary top-ups earn attractive, risk-free interest and qualify for personal income tax relief, up to $8,000 per calendar year.
    - **Higher Payouts**: Top-ups ensure higher CPF LIFE payouts, providing a more comfortable retirement.

    For individuals with sufficient cash flow, this strategy accelerates CPF balance growth. It is especially effective for self-employed individuals, who do not receive mandatory employer contributions.

2. **CPF Transfers to Family Members**:
    - **Support Loved Ones**: CPF allows members to transfer savings to their loved ones—spouses, parents, or siblings—under specific conditions.
    - **Strengthen Family Security**: This feature can be used to help family members meet their retirement sums or enjoy higher CPF LIFE payouts.

Example: Transferring from a higher-earning spouse's SA or RA to a non-working spouse can enhance household financial security. These transfers can also be a meaningful way to support aging parents who may have insufficient CPF balances.

3. **Understanding Withdrawal Options**: From age 55, members can withdraw any CPF savings above their FRS (or Basic Retirement Sum if they own a property). Strategic withdrawals should consider:
   - Cash flow needs vs. future CPF LIFE payouts.
   - Reserving funds for healthcare emergencies, especially when MediSave limits are reached.
   - Phased withdrawals, particularly for those with multiple income streams, to spread out tax liabilities or manage budgeting more effectively.

CPF Tax Benefits

CPF is not only a secure savings mechanism; it also offers valuable tax planning advantages. For individuals focused on both wealth accumulation and tax efficiency, voluntary CPF contributions present an effective tool. Key benefits of strategic contributions are described below:

- **Reduce Taxable Income**: Contributions to your SA (before 55) or RA (after 55) under the Retirement Sum Topping-Up Scheme are eligible for tax relief, up to $8,000 annually. An additional $8,000 tax relief is available if you top up your loved ones' accounts, such as parents or spouses.
- **Compound Wealth Growth:** These top-ups earn guaranteed interest (up to 4%–5% per annum), leading to substantial growth over time without market risk.
- **Optimize Annual Tax Planning:** CPF top-ups can be timed strategically—e.g., during high-income years—to manage income tax brackets.

Example: *An individual earning $100,000 a year who tops up $8,000 to their RA could reduce their taxable income to $92,000. At a marginal tax rate of 11.5%, this results in tax savings of $920—while simultaneously building retirement income.*

It's important to stay informed of policy changes, annual limits, and income thresholds, as CPF tax benefits evolve over time. Used effectively, they contribute to a well-rounded financial plan.

CPF Nominations and Estate Planning

CPF savings are not automatically distributed through a will. Without a CPF nomination, the funds will be distributed by the Public Trustee's Office in accordance with Singapore's intestacy laws, which may not reflect your personal wishes. As such, making a CPF nomination is a critical component of comprehensive estate planning.

1. **Make a CPF Nomination**: Creating a nomination is a straightforward but essential step to ensure that your CPF savings—comprising your OA, SA, MA, and RA balances—go to your intended beneficiaries.
    - Nominations can be made for specific individuals and in exact proportions.
    - In the event of death, CPF Board will distribute the funds directly to nominees, bypassing probate processes and avoiding legal delays.

    This ensures clarity, efficiency, and alignment with your intentions, especially in families with complex financial dynamics.

2. **Review Estate Plans Regularly**: Estate planning is not a one-time activity. Major life events such as marriage, divorce, the birth of a child, or the passing of a nominee should prompt a review of your CPF nominations.
    - Align nominations with your broader financial and legacy goals.
    - Ensure consistency between CPF nominations, insurance beneficiaries, and trust arrangements.

3. **Consider Trust Structures**: In more complex situations, such as blended families, dependents with special needs, or minor children, CPF funds may be channeled through trust structures (outside of CPF itself) after distribution to nominees.

- **Structured Disbursement**: Trusts allow you to control when and how funds are released to beneficiaries.
- **Protect Beneficiaries**: Trusts can protect assets from mismanagement, especially in cases involving vulnerable dependents.

While CPF funds cannot be willed or directly placed in trusts, post-disbursement estate planning can still incorporate trust-based strategies.

By thoughtfully managing CPF—optimizing contributions, planning withdrawals, and leveraging tax reliefs—it becomes more than a retirement scheme. It becomes a foundation for financial independence, re-careering with confidence, and providing peace of mind for your family.

Summary

Chapter 6: Maximizing CPF for F.I.R(Re-career).E. builds on the principles of financial independence and purposeful living introduced in earlier chapters, focusing on how to leverage Singapore's CPF system and the Supplementary Retirement Scheme (SRS) for long-term financial security and career transitions. This chapter provides a comprehensive guide to understanding and optimizing CPF accounts, from housing and healthcare to retirement planning and estate management, while also highlighting the complementary role of SRS in boosting retirement savings and tax efficiency.

Through practical strategies like voluntary CPF top-ups, smart housing decisions, CPF LIFE planning, and SRS contributions, you'll learn how to use these tools strategically to achieve financial independence and navigate career pivots with confidence.

Key Takeaways:

- CPF is a versatile tool for achieving financial independence, funding major life goals, and securing your legacy.
- Voluntary top-ups and tax relief can accelerate your CPF growth and reduce your taxable income.
- The Supplementary Retirement Scheme (SRS) complements CPF by offering additional tax benefits and investment opportunities for retirement planning.
- Smart housing decisions and CPF LIFE planning ensure long-term financial stability.
- CPF nominations are essential for estate planning and securing your legacy.

Practical Tips:

- **Optimize Your CPF Contributions**: Top up your SA or MA for higher interest and tax relief.
- **Leverage SRS for Tax Efficiency**: Contribute to your SRS account to reduce taxable income and grow your retirement savings through investments.
- **Plan Your Housing Strategy**: Use CPF OA wisely for home purchases without compromising retirement goals.
- **Choose the Right CPF LIFE Plan**: Select a payout plan that aligns with your retirement and re-careering goals.
- **Secure Your Legacy**: Make a CPF nomination to ensure your savings are distributed according to your wishes.

By embracing the lessons and actionable steps from Chapter 7, you'll be equipped to maximize the benefits of CPF and SRS, building a secure financial future that aligns with your values and aspirations.

In the next chapter, **Insurance: Protecting What Matters Most**, we will dive deeper into how insurance plays a critical role in risk management and long-term financial security.

You'll learn the key principles of insurance, evaluate the essential types of personal coverage, understand how insurance needs change across different life stages, and explore strategies for aligning your coverage, avoiding common pitfalls, and building a protection plan that supports your evolving life and financial goals.

Reflection Prompts & Mini Exercises

"CPF: A strategic enabler for financial freedom, purpose, and legacy." ~ YK Png

---

1. Your CPF Mindset Check

Prompt:

- *How do you currently perceive CPF—as a restriction, a safety net, or a financial springboard?*
- *Do you view CPF contributions as "locked-up money" or "future freedom funds"?*
- *How well do you understand the roles of your OA, SA, and MA in your long-term plans?*

Mini Exercise: CPF Perception Reframe

- Write down your top 3 beliefs about CPF.
- For each, ask: *Is this belief empowering or limiting?*
- Reframe one limiting belief *(e.g., "CPF is only for retirement" → "CPF supports multiple life goals—housing, healthcare, and legacy").*

---

2. CPF Alignment with Life Goals

Prompt:

- *What are your top 3 life or career goals for the next 10–20 years?*
- *How can your CPF savings (OA, SA, MA) be strategically used or grown to support these goals?*
- *Are you optimizing your CPF in alignment with your values and timeline for re-careering?*

Mini Exercise: CPF Goal Mapping

- Draw three columns: Goals, CPF Function, Action.
- List 1–2 life goals in the first column *(e.g., homeownership, early retirement).*
- In the second, write which CPF account helps support each.
- In the third, list one action *(e.g., "Top up SA by $5,000 annually for higher returns and tax relief").*

---

3. Unlocking the Value of SRS

Prompt:

- *Have you considered how SRS can supplement your CPF for retirement or semi-retirement?*
- *Are you leveraging its tax benefits and investment flexibility?*

- *What's stopping you from starting, continuing, or maximizing your SRS?*

Mini Exercise: SRS Exploration

- Research one benefit of SRS you didn't know before *(e.g., tax relief, flexible investment options).*
- Identify a monthly or annual contribution amount that fits your budget.
- Set a SMART goal to start or increase your SRS contribution within the next 30 days.

---

4. Securing Peace of Mind Through CPF LIFE

Prompt:

- *• Have you thought about the kind of retirement lifestyle you want and how CPF LIFE can support it?*
- *Are you clear on the different payout options?*
- *How does CPF LIFE fit into your vision of a purpose-driven retirement?*

Mini Exercise: Retirement Simulation

- Visit CPF LIFE Estimator and input your details to explore possible payouts.
- Compare different plans and reflect on which best fits your desired lifestyle and re-careering path.
- Identify one step to move closer to your ideal retirement plan *(e.g., top up SA, review plan with a CPF officer).*

---

5. Legacy Planning with Intention

Prompt:

- *Have you made a CPF nomination? Why or why not?*
- *What values do you want your legacy to reflect—provision, love, responsibility, empowerment?*
- *How can you involve your family in your CPF planning?*

Mini Exercise: CPF Legacy Starter

- If you have not yet, explore the CPF Nomination process online.
- Write down who you would nominate and why—this clarifies your intentions.
- Schedule a discussion with a loved one to share your approach and invite input.

Chapter 7: Insurance: Protecting What Matters Most

~ *By **Martin Toh** (CFP. ChFC. ESP.)*
AIA District Director, High Net Worth | CEO, RTP Organization.

> ***Disclaimer:*** *This chapter offers general insights on insurance planning. It does not replace advice from licensed insurance professionals. Product terms, coverage, and regulations may change. Always review official documentation and consult with a qualified advisor before making decisions.*

Insurance forms a critical pillar in the journey toward financial independence and re-careering. It safeguards the foundations of a well-structured financial plan—protecting income, health, assets, and dependents against life's uncertainties. From medical conditions and disability to accidents and premature death, unforeseen events can derail even the most well-crafted financial strategies.

This chapter explores the essential types of insurance across different life stages, outlines key considerations in coverage adequacy, and positions insurance as a strategic enabler of long-term financial resilience. Rather than viewing insurance solely as a cost, it is best approached as a purposeful risk management tool—designed to preserve wealth, provide continuity, and support the goals of the F.I.R(Re-career).E framework.

Insurance as Risk Management

Uncertainty is an inherent part of life. Events such as illness, accidents, disability, or premature death can occur without warning and have significant financial consequences. Even the most well-structured financial plans can be undermined by such disruptions. Insurance serves as a critical risk management tool, designed to provide financial protection and continuity in the face of unforeseen events.

At its essence, insurance is a contractual arrangement in which a provider agrees to compensate for specified losses in exchange for a premium. The objective is to transfer the financial burden of unexpected risks, enabling greater stability and peace of mind.

While budgeting, saving, and investing focus on building and growing wealth, insurance protects that progress from being reversed by unanticipated setbacks. A well-constructed insurance portfolio functions as a financial safety net—supporting long-term goals by reducing vulnerability to external shocks.

In the context of a F.I.R(Re-career).E strategy, insurance is not merely an expense but a foundational element of long-term financial resilience—preserving optionality, security, and peace of mind throughout one's life journey.

The Concept of Risk Transfer and Financial Protection

Uncertainty is a constant in the journey toward financial independence and re-careering. Health events, accidents, economic downturns, and career disruptions can occur without warning, threatening financial progress and long-term goals. Insurance plays a pivotal role in mitigating these risks by transferring the financial burden from the individual to an insurer.

At the core of insurance is the principle of risk pooling and risk transfer. Rather than bearing the full cost of an adverse event, individuals contribute to a collective pool through regular premium payments. When insured risks materialize—such as critical illness, death, disability, or hospitalization—benefits are paid out from this shared pool, cushioning the financial impact.

Example: *Consider the financial fallout of a major medical emergency costing S$150,000. Without insurance, this could wipe out years of savings. With appropriate health or critical illness coverage, the burden is significantly reduced, or even fully absorbed by the insurer.*

This ability to preserve wealth and ensure cash flow continuity is one of the key reasons why insurance is essential — especially for those working toward F.I.R(Re-career).E. journey. This protective function allows continued progress toward financial independence without derailment from unforeseen setbacks.

Insurance vs. Savings vs. Investments: Know the Difference

A common misconception is the conflation of insurance with investment. Certain insurance products—such as whole life or endowment plans—may include cash value or investment features, but their primary function remains protection, not wealth creation. Attempting to use insurance as a substitute for savings or investments often leads to inefficiencies, including lower returns, limited liquidity, and higher costs.

A clear distinction among the three financial pillars is essential:

Function	Savings	Investments	Insurance
Purpose	Liquidity, emergency funds	Wealth accumulation, passive income	Risk management, protection
Time Horizon	Short to medium-term	Medium to long-term	Variable (based on product type)
Returns	Low, stable	Potentially high, with risk	Not return-focused; based on coverage benefit
Liquidity	High	Medium to low (depends on asset class)	Low (for protection plans)
Risk	Low	Medium to high	Risk-transfer mechanism

Each serves a unique role. Using insurance primarily for investment purposes—especially through high-premium policies—can limit wealth-building potential. Investment-Linked Policies (ILPs), for example, offer market exposure but often include higher costs and complex structures that reduce overall efficiency for those primarily seeking returns.

A Layered Approach to Financial Protection and Growth

A more effective strategy involves building a structured, layered financial foundation:

- **Start with core protection**: Term life, health, and critical illness insurance offer broad coverage at lower cost, forming the foundation of risk management.

- **Establish emergency reserves**: Maintain 3–6 months of essential expenses in readily accessible savings to address short-term financial shocks.
- **Deploy surplus capital for growth**: Direct additional resources into long-term investment vehicles such as CPF (in the Singapore context), ETFs, or diversified portfolios to support capital appreciation and financial independence.

This disciplined approach avoids conflating protection with profit and enables a balanced strategy that addresses both risk mitigation and long-term wealth generation.

Key Takeaways

- **Insurance is foundational** to financial planning—providing security for income, assets, and dependents.
- **Risk transfer** is central to insurance—offering predictability in the face of uncertainty.
- **Insurance is distinct** from savings and investments—each serves a complementary purpose.
- **Begin with protection**—build a strong financial base before expanding into higher-return, higher-risk instruments.

Insurance Checklist: What Should You Have?

Insurance Type	Essential? (Y/N)
Life Insurance	Y
Health Insurance	Y
Critical Illness Insurance	Y
Disability Income Insurance	Y
Personal Accident Insurance	Y
Hospitalisation Shield Plan (Integrated Shield)	Y
Long-Term Care Insurance *(e.g., CareShield Life)*	Y
Home Insurance	Optional
Travel Insurance	Optional
Motor Insurance	Optional

Key Principles of Insurance

Building on the concept of risk transfer, several guiding principles form the foundation of sound insurance planning. These principles shape how insurance operates and how it should be incorporated into a comprehensive financial strategy:

- **Risk Pooling and Shared Responsibility:** Insurance functions as a collective financial buffer. Premiums paid by many are pooled together, enabling payouts to those affected by covered events. This shared responsibility ensures affordability and spreads risk across a larger population.
- **Insurable Interest and Purpose:** A policy must serve a legitimate financial interest—be it protection of income, health, or dependents. Insurance should align with genuine needs, not speculative gain.
- **Utmost Good Faith:** Transparency is essential. Both insurer and policyholder are expected to disclose all relevant information truthfully. Inaccuracies or non-disclosure may affect claims or void coverage.
- **Indemnity and Defined Benefit:** Insurance aims to compensate for loss, not create profit. Policies are designed either to restore financial position (as in health or general insurance) or provide a defined payout (as in life or critical illness coverage).
- **Proportionality and Suitability:** Coverage should be proportional to risk exposure and life stage needs. Over- or under-insuring can result in inefficiencies or financial vulnerability.

Understanding these principles strengthens the ability to evaluate, structure, and maintain appropriate coverage—ensuring insurance remains a tool for protection, not overextension.

Terms to Understand: Decoding the Insurance Language

Understanding insurance requires familiarity with key terms that often determine the scope, cost, and effectiveness of coverage. Clear comprehension of these concepts enhances decision-making and reduces the risk of misinterpretation or underinsurance.

- **Premium:** The premium is the periodic amount paid—monthly, quarterly, or annually—to maintain an active insurance policy.

It represents the cost of transferring financial risk from the individual to the insurer. Premiums vary depending on factors such as age, health status, coverage amount, and policy type.

- **Sum Assured:** The sum assured is the guaranteed benefit amount that the insurer commits to pay upon the occurrence of the insured event—such as death, diagnosis of a critical illness, or permanent disability. It forms the core financial protection offered by life and health insurance plans.
- **Deductible:** A deductible is the initial portion of a claim that the policyholder must bear out-of-pocket before the insurer begins to make payments. It is commonly applied in hospitalization and major medical insurance policies and serves to reduce minor claims while keeping premiums more affordable.
- **Co-insurance:** Co-insurance refers to the cost-sharing arrangement between the insurer and the insured after the deductible has been met. Expressed as a percentage, it indicates the portion of the remaining claim amount payable by the policyholder. For example, with a 10% co-insurance clause, the insured pays 10% of the approved hospital bill, and the insurer covers the balance.
- **Exclusions:** Exclusions are specific conditions, treatments, or circumstances that are not covered under the policy. These may include pre-existing medical conditions, elective procedures, self-inflicted injuries, or high-risk activities. Understanding exclusions is critical to avoid unexpected claim rejections.

Needs-Based vs. Product-Based Insurance: Choose Wisely

There are two common mindsets when it comes to buying insurance: needs-based planning and product-based selling.

1. **Product-based insurance** is when decisions are driven by what's being marketed — flashy brochures, promotional campaigns, or advice that starts with, *"This plan is very popular."*
2. **Needs-based insurance**, on the other hand, begins with life stage, responsibilities, income, and risk exposure. It's about asking:
    - *What happens to my family if I'm no longer around?*
    - *Can I afford medical care if I suffer a major illness?*
    - *Will I be able to continue paying my bills if I'm disabled or hospitalized?*

Here's a simple framework:

Life Stage	Insurance Priority
Young single professional	Hospitalization, basic critical illness, term life (if supporting parents)
Married with dependents	Term life, income protection, critical illness, hospitalization
Mid-life with grown children	Long-term care, hospitalization, critical illness (review existing coverage)
Nearing FIRE / retirement	Hospitalization, long-term care (minimize overlapping investment-linked policies)

Types of Personal Insurance Coverage

Choosing an appropriate mix of insurance coverage depends on life stage, number of dependents, health status, and long-term financial objectives.

1. **Life Insurance - Building a Secure Tomorrow, Today:** Life insurance provides a payout (sum assured) to nominated beneficiaries upon the policyholder's death. It plays a central role in income replacement, debt protection, and securing dependents' financial future.

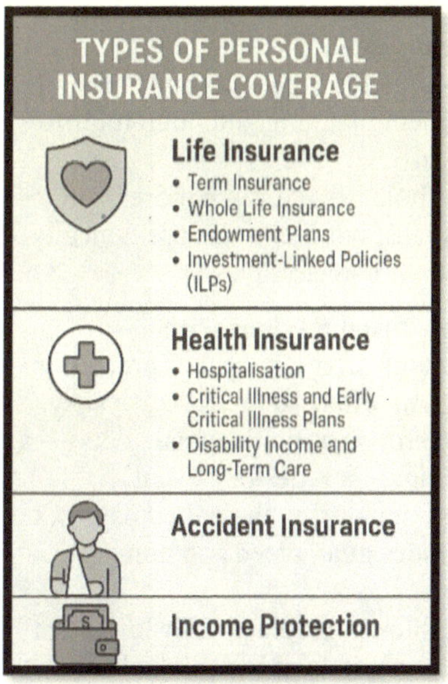

Term vs. Whole Life vs. Endowment vs. Investment-Linked Policies (ILPs)

Each policy type serves distinct purposes and plays a different role in a holistic financial plan.

1.1 Term Insurance - Pure Protection at a Lower Cost: Term insurance is the most straightforward form of life insurance. It offers pure protection — meaning, it pays out a sum assured only if the policyholder passes away (or is diagnosed with a terminal illness) during the policy term. If no claim is made during the covered period *(say, 20 or 30 years)*, the policy expires without any return.

- **Affordability**: Because term insurance is stripped of savings or investment features, it is the most cost-effective way to secure high coverage, making it ideal for young professionals, parents with young children, or those with large financial obligations such as mortgages.
- **Simplicity**: There are no investment risks or surrender charges. What you pay is purely for protection.
- **No cash value**: This can deter some, but if your main concern is income replacement or liability protection, term coverage is a powerful and efficient tool.

1.2 Whole Life Insurance - Protection for Life and Cash Value: Provides lifetime coverage and builds cash value through participating funds.

- **Legacy planning**: Whole life policies are often used for leaving behind a guaranteed sum to beneficiaries, making them suitable for estate planning.
- **Cash value**: The accumulated value can be helpful in emergencies or retirement planning, although returns tend to be conservative.
- **Higher premiums**: Whole life plans are more expensive than term plans, but premiums are typically fixed for life, providing predictability.

1.3 Endowment Plans - Goal-Based Savings with Protection: Endowment plans offer a hybrid of protection and savings over a fixed term, often 10 to 25 years. They are commonly used to save for specific financial goals — a child's education, a wedding, or a milestone event.

- **Maturity benefit**: Upon maturity, the policy pays out a lump sum, which includes guaranteed and non-guaranteed bonuses.
- **Moderate returns**: Endowment plans offer lower but more stable returns compared to market-linked investments, making them attractive for risk-averse savers.

- **Capital guarantee**: Some plans offer partial or full capital protection, which can appeal to conservative investors.

1.4 Investment-Linked Policies (ILPs) - Insurance with Market Exposure: ILPs combine life insurance with investments in unit trusts or managed funds. A portion of premium goes to insurance coverage, while the rest is invested.

- **Flexible coverage and investment choices**: Investment allocations can be adjusted, premiums topped up, or the sum assured changed.
- **Volatility**: Policy value is subject to market performance. In down markets, additional premiums may be required to maintain insurance coverage.
- **High charges**: Investment-linked policies incur multiple layers of fees, including insurance charges, fund management fees, and surrender charges, which can significantly reduce returns.

Determining Adequate Life Coverage

A most common question: *How much coverage is enough?* While there's no one-size-fits-all answer, a widely used rule of thumb is 10 to 15 times annual income. This serves as a useful starting point — but for a more accurate, tailored estimate, a needs-based planning is more accurate. Key questions to ask:

- *How much would my family need to maintain our current lifestyle if I'm no longer around?*
- *Do I have outstanding financial obligations such as a mortgage, car loan, or business liabilities that could burden my dependents?*
- *Would I like to leave behind funds to support my children's education, ageing parents, or charitable causes?*

These considerations form the basis of a needs-based approach to insurance planning. Rather than choosing a number arbitrarily or relying on what a salesperson recommends, use structured needs-based calculators — readily available from the CPF Board or reputable insurers — to determine a realistic sum assured that reflects family's actual needs and financial vulnerabilities.

2. **Health Insurance - First Line of Defense:** Medical emergencies remain one of the most serious threats to financial independence. A single hospitalisation, diagnosis, or course of treatment can derail years of savings and disrupt even the most carefully laid-out plans — especially for those without adequate health coverage.

   Health insurance provides a vital safety net. It not only covers medical bills; it protects long-term financial goals by cushioning the impact of sudden, unpredictable healthcare costs. Without it, individuals are left to choose between draining savings or compromising on care — neither of which is ideal.

   2.1 **Hospitalisation Coverage - Covering the Cost of Hospital Stay Expenses:** In many countries, government-backed healthcare schemes *(such as MediShield Life in Singapore, Medicare in Australia or the US, or NHS in the UK)* provide basic hospitalisation coverage. While these plans are helpful for essential treatments or care in subsidised settings, they often come with limits — such as capped claims, restricted hospital classes, or specific conditions for eligibility.

   To bridge this gap, many people opt for private or supplementary hospitalisation plans, which can offer:

   - **Coverage for private or higher-tier hospital wards**
   - **Higher claim limits** to account for rising healthcare costs
   - **Access to a broader network of specialists**
   - **Optional riders** to reduce deductibles or co-payment obligations

   These enhanced plans can significantly improve the quality and timeliness of care — but they also come with higher premiums that increase with age.

   Singapore Context - Integrated Shield Plans (IPs): *In Singapore, MediShield Life provides universal basic health insurance for Singaporeans and PRs. It covers large hospital bills and expensive outpatient treatments such as dialysis or chemotherapy. However, coverage is limited primarily to B2 or C class wards in public hospitals.*

To expand protection, individuals can purchase Integrated Shield Plans (IPs) from private insurers. These add layers of benefits and give options for:

- ***Private hospital care** or **higher-class wards (A/B1)** in public hospitals.*
- ***Higher claim limits** and broader coverage.*
- ***Optional riders** to reduce co-payments or deductibles.*

2.2 **Critical Illness and Early Critical Illness Plans - Lump-Sum Payout on Diagnosis of Serious Illness:** Critical Illness (CI) plans provide a lump-sum payout upon diagnosis of life-threatening diseases such as cancer, stroke, or heart attack. This payout is not tied to hospital bills — it can be used freely to cover loss of income, alternative treatments, home care, or even a sabbatical to recover.

Early Critical Illness (ECI) plans extend this coverage to earlier stages of disease, enabling early intervention, which can drastically improve recovery outcomes and reduce financial strain.

This is a must-have category of coverage. According to the Life Insurance Association (LIA) Protection Gap Study 2022, the average Singaporean working adult has a CI protection gap of about S$256,000, meaning their existing insurance is insufficient to cover even the most basic needs after a serious illness.

2.3 **Disability Income and Long -Term Care: Protecting Earning Ability:** Disability — whether temporary or permanent — not only affects medical expenses, but it also compromises earning power, often at a time when expenses rise due to care needs.

- **Disability Income Insurance** pays a monthly benefit (usually up to 75% of income). This bridges the income gap and sustains lifestyle and obligations during recovery from illness or injury.
- **Long-term Care Insurance** offers lifelong monthly payouts for severe disability. This can also be supplemented with private add-ons for higher benefits.

***Singapore Context - CareShield Life:** Singapore's compulsory long-term care insurance scheme provides* *monthly payouts for life in cases of severe disability (e.g., when unable to perform 3 or more Activities of Daily Living like walking, feeding, or dressing). The coverage can also be enhanced with private supplements for higher benefits.*

3. **Accident Insurance - For the Unexpected:** Accidents are unpredictable and indiscriminate. They can strike when anytime — at home doing simple chores, commuting to work, exploring a hiking trail overseas, or even during a family weekend activity. Unlike critical illnesses that often develop over time, accidents are immediate and can result in serious physical and financial consequences — especially if they lead to hospitalisation, temporary or permanent disability, or income loss.

   This is where Personal Accident (PA) Insurance becomes a crucial yet often underappreciated component of a holistic protection plan. It serves as a practical and affordable complement to existing health and life coverage, especially for individuals with more active lifestyles, frequent business or leisure travellers, self-employed professionals, or those in physically demanding roles.

   Most PA plans provide a suite of benefits that help to manage both medical costs and financial stability in the aftermath of an accident. Key benefits typically include:
   - **Lump-sum payouts** for accidental death or permanent disability, providing immediate support to loved ones or assisting with necessary living adjustments.
   - **Daily hospital cash benefits** if hospitalized due to an accident, offering financial support during recovery.
   - **Medical reimbursement** for outpatient treatments such as fractures, minor surgeries, or post-injury visits to a general practitioner or specialist.
   - **Optional riders** covering additional needs like burns, mobility aids, physiotherapy, or even child-specific protection for injuries sustained at school or during play.

   These benefits can provide significant relief during unexpected circumstances.

Personal Accident insurance is not meant to replace hospitalization, critical illness, or disability coverage. Instead, it serves as another layer in a financial defence system, offering flexibility and confidence to move forward in life, work, and re-careering with fewer "what if" worries.

Practical Tips for Choosing and Optimizing PA Coverage

- **Start with a needs analysis:** Consider lifestyle, travel frequency, work nature, and physical activity levels. Assess regular movement and any dependents relying on physical ability for work or care.
- **Look for value-added benefits:** Many PA plans now include wellness support, access to physiotherapy, or child-friendly features. For parents, check for family coverage or child riders, often bundled at attractive rates.
- **Mind the overlaps:** Review hospitalization and critical illness plans alongside PA insurance to ensure adequate coverage without paying twice for the same benefit. Each policy serves a specific purpose.
- **Affordability and flexibility:** PA plans are generally affordable and easy to increase. Start with basic coverage and scale up as lifestyle or risk profile changes. Some insurers offer annual renewal without medical underwriting, which proves helpful with age.
- **If self-employed or in transition:** The reliance on physical capacity often goes unrecognized until compromised. Consider coverage beyond death or total permanent disability, focusing on temporary disabilities, fractures, mobility loss, and hospital stays that affect income and daily life.

4. **Income Protection - Safeguarding the Greatest Asset:** An overlooked yet essential truth in financial planning: the ability to earn an income is the most valuable asset, especially during prime working years. Before wealth accumulation through investments, property, or savings, earned income fuels everything: daily living, family needs, loans, insurance premiums, and even retirement contributions.

Few truly consider what would happen if that income stream were to suddenly stop.

Imagine being sidelined by an accident or illness preventing work for several months or longer. Without a safety net, one might be forced to use hard-earned savings, liquidate investments prematurely, or rely on family support to cover basic expenses. This is precisely where income protection insurance steps in—not as a luxury, but as a foundational component of financial resilience.

Income protection insurance—sometimes called disability income insurance—is designed to replace a portion of monthly income if unable to work due to illness or injury. This coverage ensures the ability to continue meeting everyday financial commitments—mortgage, groceries, school fees, utilities, transport, and more—without drawing down long-term savings or retirement funds. It does not cover medical bills, which are handled by hospitalization and critical illness policies.

Key features of these plans typically include:

- **Replacement of 50–75% of monthly income**, paid regularly (e.g., monthly) if medically certified as unable to work.
- **Coverage duration** extending until recovery or a pre-determined age (e.g., 60 or 65), depending on the policy.
- **Flexibility to return to work part-time** or in a reduced capacity, often with partial benefits under some plans.

This coverage is important for anyone with a job or business, becoming especially crucial if:

- Self-employed or a freelancer without employer-provided disability benefits.
- In prime earning years, with family depending on income.
- Committed to early financial independence or a career transition, where every dollar counts.
- Carrying significant financial obligations—loans, dependents, or business overheads.

Income protection is more than just another policy; it's a shield for lifestyle, goals, and dreams. For those on the F.I.R.(Re-career).E. journey, where financial autonomy is the goal, losing the ability to earn can delay or even derail progress.

Taking this one step—protecting income—can make the difference between a temporary health setback and a long-term financial crisis.

Financial independence isn't just about building wealth; it's about protecting the ability to sustain it.
Income protection insurance ensures that even if life presents challenges, goals remain intact, plans stay on course, and family's future isn't compromised.

Practical Tips for Choosing Income Protection Insurance

- **Check existing coverage:** If employer benefits are present, understand what is covered and for how long. Many offer only short-term coverage (e.g., 3-6 months).
- **Match income needs:** Choose a payout amount that covers essential expenses, not necessarily a full salary. This helps keep premiums affordable.
- **Look for long benefit terms:** Opt for plans that provide coverage up to age 60 or 65, if possible, especially with a longer financial runway ahead.
- **Review the definition of disability:** Some policies only pay out if unable to perform any job. Look for plans that cover the inability to perform one's *own occupation*, which provides stronger protection.
- **Factor in waiting periods:** Many policies start paying after 30, 60, or 90 days of disability. Align this with emergency savings buffer.

Insurance Across Life Stages and Life Choices

Insurance is not a one-time decision—it's a lifelong strategy that must evolve alongside your life stages, personal choices, and financial responsibilities. Whether you're a young professional, a parent, a business owner, or preparing for retirement, the right insurance plan is one that aligns with your present needs and anticipated future risks.

This guide outlines how insurance priorities shift across different life circumstances and how thoughtful planning can protect not just wealth, but also health, independence, and legacy.

1. **Young Adults and Singles – Laying a Smart Foundation:** At the start of one's career, it's easy to deprioritise insurance in favour of goals like travel, repaying loans, or saving for a home.

Yet this is the most cost-effective time to secure coverage due to lower premiums and fewer exclusions.

Key Considerations:

- **Hospitalisation Coverage:** Government health systems offer a basic safety net but upgrading to an integrated or private plan improves access and care quality. Timely protection against hospital expenses ensures financial stability.
- **Term Life Insurance (as needed):** For singles supporting ageing parents or carrying joint obligations (e.g., co-signed loans), term insurance provides peace of mind that these responsibilities won't burden others.
- **Personal Accident (PA) Insurance:** Affordable and practical, PA plans cover outpatient treatments and provide lump sums for accidental disability or death—ideal for those with active lifestyles.
- **Disability Income Insurance:** Singles with no backup income source should consider this for income replacement if they're unable to work due to injury or illness. It supports ongoing expenses and preserves financial autonomy.

2. **Dual Income, No Kids (DINKs) – Building and Protecting Lifestyle Goals:** For couples focused on career advancement, lifestyle, and wealth accumulation, insurance plays a crucial role in protecting dual-income dependency.

   Key Considerations:

   - **Hospitalisation and Critical Illness:** Medical issues affecting one partner can disrupt joint financial goals. Both should maintain robust healthcare and CI coverage.
   - **Income Protection:** If either party becomes temporarily or permanently unable to earn, disability income insurance ensures continuity without compromising shared aspirations.
   - **Long-Term Care Planning:** Couples with no children may need to plan for self-funded eldercare. Supplementing national schemes with private plans ensures better support options in later life.

3. **Young Families – Prioritising Dependents and Long-Term Security:** Raising children and supporting a spouse elevates your financial obligations. Insurance at this stage is about protecting the household from income loss, health crises, and future uncertainties.

   Key Considerations:
   - **Term Life Insurance:** Essential to replace income, pay off debts, and fund children's education in the event of death. A general benchmark is 10–15 times one's annual income.
   - **Critical Illness and Early CI Coverage:** A CI diagnosis can pause or derail income. Lump-sum payouts from these policies offer breathing space for treatment and recovery.
   - **Hospitalisation Coverage for Family:** Ensure spouse and children are covered. Family packages or riders often provide cost-effective comprehensive protection.
   - **Education Protection Plans:** These ensure that your children's education continues uninterrupted, even in your absence.

4. **Single Parents – Protecting the Sole Breadwinner:** Single parents shoulder dual roles—caregiver and provider. With no backup income or secondary caregiver, insurance becomes the bedrock of family security.

   Key Considerations:
   - **Life and Critical Illness Insurance:** Ensures your child is financially supported even in your absence or illness.
   - **Hospitalisation and Disability Coverage:** Vital to cover medical expenses and income disruption without impacting your child's well-being.
   - **Clear Beneficiary Nominations:** Ensures claims are paid quickly to the intended recipient—your child or their legal guardian.

Insurance Across Life Stages and Life Choices

Young Adults and Singles: Laying Foundation
- Hospitalisation Coverage
- Term Life Insurance
- Personal Accident (PA) Insurance
- Disability Income Insurance

Young Families: Prioritising Dependents & Long-Term Security
- Term Life Insurance
- Critical Illness and Early CI Coverage
- Hospitalisation Coverage for Family
- Education Protection Plans

Dual Income, No Kids (DINKs): Building & Protecting Lifestyle Goals
- Hospitalisation and Critical Illness
- Income Protection
- Long-Term Care Planning

Single Parents: Protecting the Sole Breadwinner
- Life and Critical Illness Insurance
- Hospitalisation and Disability Coverage
- Clear Beneficiary Nominations

5. **Mid-Career Professionals – The Sandwich Generation Reality:** Mid-life often involves juggling responsibilities for both growing children and ageing parents. Insurance strategies must accommodate this dual-care role.

   Key Considerations:
   - **Comprehensive Life and CI Insurance:** These ensure protection against both death and debilitating illness—supporting dependents and safeguarding lifestyle.
   - **Long-Term Care Planning:** Supporting elderly parents or planning for your own eldercare needs means considering national and private long-term care schemes.
   - **Personal Accident and Disability Insurance:** Provides cash payouts and income continuity in the event of injuries or temporary disability.

   My Reflection (YK Png): *When I was in the thick of my corporate career and raising a family, although my dependents were covered under my employer-sponsored plans, I proactively purchased additional personal plans, knowing employer coverage stops when the job ends. These gave me peace of mind during my re-career transition, ensuring my family remained protected even without corporate benefits.*

6. **Pre-Retirees and Empty Nesters – Preserving Wealth and Dignity:** As children gain independence and career winds down, the focus moves toward sustaining health, lifestyle, and legacy.

Key Considerations:

- **Review Hospitalisation Plans:** Ensure your base plan is sustainable. Consider reducing or removing expensive riders that no longer add value.
- **Reassess Critical Illness Coverage:** Many discover too late that their CI coverage is insufficient. Review while still healthy to secure affordable top-ups.
- **Long-Term Care Insurance:** Supplements like CareShield Life Enhancements offer earlier payouts or higher monthly benefits, providing peace of mind in the face of ageing.
- **Estate and Legacy Planning:** Use life insurance to create liquidity for your estate, equalise inheritance, or cover final expenses. Review nominations, wills, and LPAs for alignment with your wishes.

My Reflection (YK Png): *I once had a hospitalization rider that was covered up to age 70. I reviewed its value and eventually dropped it in favor of maintaining only the base plan—a decision that balanced costs with continued coverage. Reflecting on this, I also underestimated how much Critical Illness (CI) coverage I would need later in life. When I finally realized the gap, the premiums for a top-up were too high to be practical. A timely review years earlier would have made a big difference.*

7. **Self-Employed and Gig Economy Workers – Owning Your Protection:** Without employer-sponsored benefits, freelancers and entrepreneurs must build their own safety nets. This includes both personal and business insurance solutions.

   Key Considerations:

   - **Disability Income Insurance:** Replaces income if you're unable to work. This is critical when your business or freelance work is your sole livelihood.
   - **Hospitalisation and CI Plans:** Without group insurance, you're responsible for all medical costs. Securing coverage early keeps premiums lower.
   - **Business Continuity Coverage:** Solopreneurs may consider keyman or overhead expense insurance to cover fixed costs or business transition support if they're temporarily out of action.

8. **Retirees and Financially Independent Individuals – Securing the Legacy:** At this stage, insurance is less about income replacement and more about healthcare, autonomy, and wealth distribution.

   Key Considerations:
   - **Long-Term Care:** As lifespans increase, so do the chances of requiring extended care. Policies like CareShield Life and private supplements can cover caregiving costs for years.
   - **Hospitalisation Plan:** Health deteriorates with age, so keeping a base hospitalisation plan is essential—even if add-on riders are removed for affordability.
   - **Legacy and Estate Planning:** Whole life or universal life insurance can be a tool for structured wealth transfer. Ensure clear beneficiary nominations and legal documents are in place to avoid disputes and delays.

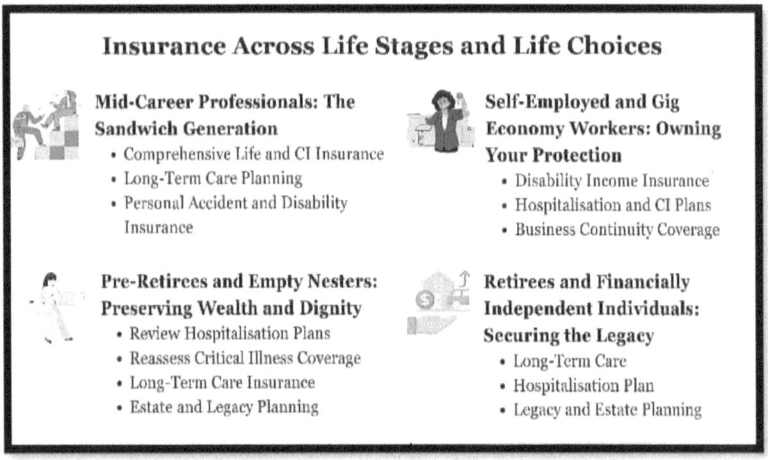

Life Choices that Also Shape Insurance Needs

- **Those Who Choose to Remain Single:** Focus shifts to independent living in old age. Strong CI, hospitalisation, and long-term care plans are essential for sustaining autonomy.
- **Globally Mobile Professionals:** Seek international health plans with cross-border coverage and ensure policies comply with local laws for claims and tax implications.

- **High Net-Worth Individuals (HNWIs):** Insurance becomes a wealth management tool—supporting liquidity, succession planning, and portfolio diversification.

Insurance is a journey, not a product. As life and aspirations evolve, so too should insurance. The goal isn't to hold the most policies—it's to hold the right ones at the right time. Thoughtful insurance planning reinforces resilience, accelerates re-careering confidence, and protects what matters most—health, income, loved ones, and legacy.

Action Step: Map Your Life Stage to Your Protection Plan
Ask yourself:

- *Are my current policies aligned with my life responsibilities and personal goals?*
- *Am I overpaying for outdated or redundant riders?*
- *Do I have sufficient coverage for critical risks—especially CI, disability, and long-term care?*

Schedule a comprehensive review at every major transition—career shift, marriage, parenthood, retirement—to ensure your insurance remains purposeful and future-ready.

Smart Insurance Planning: Aligning Needs, Avoiding Pitfalls

Smart insurance planning involves aligning protection with financial needs and avoiding common pitfalls.

Life presents various uncertainties, such as health crises, accidents, job disruptions, or untimely loss. While many diligently save and invest for the future, insurance is frequently overlooked. It should not be an afterthought but a foundational component of any comprehensive financial plan. However, its purpose is often misunderstood, coverage overestimated, or decisions delayed until it is too late.

Aligning Insurance with Financial Goals

Insurance does not grow wealth in the traditional sense; rather, it safeguards one's ability to accumulate and retain wealth. When chosen wisely, insurance acts as a financial safety net, preventing progress from being derailed by illness, disability, accidents, or death. Conversely, when misunderstood or misaligned, it can become a costly burden or an illusion of security

Some examples of questions to clarify financial goals:

- *Am I working toward early retirement and want to shield my portfolio from unforeseen withdrawals due to medical costs?*
- *What significant life events do I anticipate in the next 5-10 years, and how might they impact my financial stability? (e.g., getting married, buying a home, starting a business, caring for elderly parents, career change)*
- *What are my current debt obligations (e.g., mortgage, student loans), and how would they be managed if my income were to cease due to unforeseen circumstances?*
- *How would a major health crisis (e.g., critical illness, long-term disability) impact my ability to generate income and cover ongoing expenses?*
- *What lifestyle do I wish to maintain for myself and my dependents, even if I'm unable to work? Do I want to ensure my children's education is uninterrupted even if I'm no longer around?*
- *Do I want to avoid being a financial burden to my family if I face a critical illness?*

An insurance strategy should support these goals, not contradict them. For instance, if the goal is early financial independence, committing a large portion of income to bundled insurance products with low liquidity and long lock-in periods may be counterproductive. Instead, consider term insurance for pure protection and allocate surplus funds to more flexible investment vehicles.

When reviewing existing coverage, it is crucial to assess whether each policy continues to serve current goals. Insurance decisions should not be static; they must evolve with life changes such as marriage, parenthood, career transitions, or approaching retirement.

The Dangers of Under-insurance and Over-insurance

Many individuals fall into the trap of being either underinsured or overinsured, both of which have significant consequences.

1. **Under-insurance** is the more prevalent issue. Some believe that youth or good health negates the need for coverage.

However, insurance is most affordable and accessible when one is healthy and young. Once a medical condition is diagnosed, coverage may come with exclusions or high premiums or become unavailable entirely.

Example: *In Singapore, the cost of early-stage cancer treatment—including surgery, chemotherapy, targeted therapy, and hospitalization—can range from $50,000 to over $200,000 (in 2025), depending on the type and stage of cancer. Without adequate critical illness coverage, these costs would necessitate drawing from personal savings, disrupting long-term financial plans, or leading to debt. For self-employed individuals or sole breadwinners, the financial strain can be even more severe due to loss of income during recovery. Early planning ensures that even if a health crisis strikes, the financial foundation remains intact, and loved ones are not burdened.*

2. **Over-insurance**, conversely, typically results from mis-selling or misalignment. Some individuals are persuaded to acquire multiple overlapping policies or expensive investment-linked insurance plans under the impression that they are building wealth. In reality, this often entails high commissions, opaque structures, and inadequate protection. Funds that could have been better utilized for investing, debt repayment, or savings are diverted.

To avoid both extremes, coverage should be purposeful and proportionate. It should address genuine gaps and align with one's stage of life, income, family responsibilities, and aspirations.

A practical exercise is to conduct a personal insurance gap analysis. This helps in assessing existing protection and determining if it matches actual needs.

Here is a step-by-step guide:

- **Inventory Policies:** Document every existing insurance plan, including its type, coverage amount, premium, benefits, riders, exclusions, and beneficiaries.
- **Estimate Protection Needs:** Based on the current life stage, consider key areas such as:
  - Income replacement in case of death or disability.
  - Hospitalization and critical illness expenses.
  - Child education and dependents' support.

    - Retirement healthcare costs.
    - Long-term care and caregiving needs.
- **Identify Gaps or Redundancies:** Compare current coverage with identified needs. Are there shortfalls in critical illness coverage? Are there duplicate hospital plans or riders that are no longer necessary?
- **Take Corrective Action:** Adjust policies accordingly. This might involve acquiring additional term coverage, dropping costly riders, or switching from bundled investment-linked products to more transparent, standalone plans.

This process does not require a financial background, only a willingness to engage with the figures and ask questions. If necessary, consult an independent, licensed adviser who can offer unbiased recommendations based on needs rather than product commissions.

Common Myths and Mistakes to Avoid

Several widespread misconceptions continue to misguide individuals when making insurance decisions. Avoiding these traps can prevent years of regret and significant financial loss.

- ***"I'm healthy, so I don't need insurance."***: This is a dangerous myth. Insurance is not about current health; it is about protecting the future. Illness or injury can strike at any time, and when it does, it may be too late to obtain affordable coverage. Purchasing early not only secures insurability but also ensures lower premiums.
- **Over-reliance on employer coverage**: Many professionals assume their company's group insurance is sufficient. In reality, such coverage is often basic, capped, and non-transferable. It typically terminates upon leaving the job and may not cover dependents. Personal policies ensure consistency and customization.
- **Mixing protection with investment—without understanding the trade-offs**: Bundled products like investment-linked plans or endowment policies are often marketed as offering the best of both worlds. However, they typically provide lower returns than standalone investments and less coverage than standalone protection plans. Unless the structure, fees, and purpose are fully understood, it is generally preferable to keep protection and investment separate.

- **Buying policies without understanding them**: A common mistake is subscribing to policies based on an agent's recommendation without truly comprehending what is covered, what is excluded, and whether it aligns with one's financial plan. Always ask:
    - *What is the purpose of this policy?*
    - *What risks does it cover?*
    - Is *there a more cost-effective alternative?*

Be an informed buyer. Read the policy documents. Seek clarity. Do not allow jargon or pressure to dictate choices that are not fully understood.

Smart insurance planning is not about fear; it is about freedom. With the right protection in place, one gains the freedom to pursue goals with confidence. Whether starting a business, taking a career break, retiring early, or simply experiencing peace of mind, knowing that risks are covered brings significant reassurance.

Government-Backed Insurance Schemes: Foundational Protection, Not Full Coverage

Across the globe, governments have implemented various insurance and social protection schemes to help citizens manage life's uncertainties. These programs, often compulsory or semi-compulsory, serve as essential *safety nets*—offering a baseline of protection in key areas such as healthcare, disability, old age, and death.

While the structure and scope of such schemes differ across countries, their purpose is universal: to provide minimum essential protection so that individuals and families are not left destitute when the unexpected happens. However, these schemes are designed as foundational support, not comprehensive solutions. To build true financial resilience, individuals must assess their own circumstances and take proactive steps to supplement what the government provides.

Typically, state-backed schemes focus on:

- Basic healthcare coverage, often through public hospitals and standardised treatments.
- Limited income replacement due to disability or old age.
- Modest payouts in cases of death or permanent incapacity.
- Housing protection in case of death or disability *(in some countries).*

While these are undeniably helpful, they usually fall short of covering the full cost of treatment, rehabilitation, long-term care, or income replacement.

Example: *A national health insurance plan may cover surgery and hospitalisation but exclude critical illness benefits, outpatient specialist care, or income protection during recovery.*

Such coverage gaps become especially problematic in today's world, where healthcare costs are rising, families are more financially stretched, and longevity means living with chronic conditions for longer. Without adequate personal insurance, even a mild health crisis or temporary disability could derail long-term financial plans.

The Singapore Example: CPF-Linked Insurance Schemes[10] *(accurate as at 2025)*: In Singapore, government-backed insurance is integrated into the Central Provident Fund (CPF) system—an innovative, compulsory savings scheme for retirement, housing, and healthcare. As detailed in Chapter 6, CPF-linked insurance programs form a solid foundation for basic protection. These include:

- **MediShield Life**: A universal health insurance scheme that provides lifelong coverage for large hospital bills and certain costly outpatient treatments. However, it primarily supports

---

[10] For an in-depth explanation of these CPF-linked schemes, how they work, and how to evaluate their adequacy in your financial planning, please refer to Chapter 6 of this book and the official CPF website for the most up-to-date information.

subsidised care in public hospitals (B2/C wards), and higher-tier or private healthcare requires additional coverage.

- **Integrated Shield Plans**: Offered by private insurers and built on top of MediShield Life, these plans enable access to Class A/B1 wards in public hospitals or even private hospitals. Many Singaporeans enhance their protection through these upgrades.
- **CareShield Life (formerly ElderShield)**: A long-term care insurance plan offering monthly payouts if the policyholder becomes severely disabled. It aims to ease the financial burden of long-term care but may not fully cover all care costs, especially with inflation and extended care needs.
- **Dependants' Protection Scheme (DPS)**: A term life insurance plan providing a modest payout upon death, terminal illness, or total permanent disability for CPF members.
- **Home Protection Scheme (HPS)**: Mortgage protection insurance that pays off outstanding HDB loans should the insured pass away or become permanently incapacitated.

These schemes are commendable and have helped many Singaporeans avoid financial ruin during difficult times. But it is critical to understand that these are not meant to be exhaustive or personalised.

Many individuals, particularly those with dependents, private healthcare preferences, or irregular income (like freelancers or business owners), will likely find these baseline coverages inadequate.

Government schemes, regardless of location—be it Singapore, the UK, the US, or elsewhere—usually serve as a foundational layer of protection, not a complete safeguard. They establish a basic level of support but typically do not extend to fully protect individual aspirations, desired lifestyles, or the well-being of dependents.

Personal insurance enables individuals to:

- **Customize protection** based on specific needs and risk profiles.
- **Select higher levels of coverage** for private healthcare, increased income replacement, or larger critical illness payouts.
- **Ensure the financial stability of a family** even in unforeseen circumstances.

- **Preserve long-term financial goals**—such as retirement, children's education, or business continuity—even when facing a crisis.

It is crucial not to confuse basic coverage with comprehensive protection. A common oversight is assuming full protection simply due to enrolment in a national scheme or employer-provided coverage. Only when adversity strikes do individuals often realize the significant shortfalls, sometimes leading to irreversible consequences.

Choosing the Right Insurance Advisor

Insurance planning goes beyond just selecting the right type of coverage—it also involves choosing the right insurance advisor and navigating a marketplace filled with many insurers, each offering a wide range of products with different names and features. With so many providers competing for attention, insurance products today are often marketed with fancy or appealing names, which can be confusing to the average consumer. Despite the branding, most products fall into just a few fundamental categories, as outlined earlier in this chapter—life insurance, health insurance, critical illness, accident coverage, and income protection, among others.

The key is to look past the marketing and understand the actual structure, purpose, and limitations of each plan. Two policies from different companies might sound entirely different but offer nearly identical benefits—or vice versa. This is why it's so important to compare not just the brand or packaging, but the substance: *what risks does it cover? How comprehensive is the coverage? How well does it align with your personal needs and financial goals? and more.*

Equally important is selecting the right insurance advisor. The person who represents the product can influence your understanding, decision-making, and ultimately, your level of protection. A reliable advisor will take the time to understand your needs, explain the details clearly, and help you avoid common pitfalls. Conversely, poor guidance, whether due to lack of experience or a sales-first mindset—can result in underinsurance, unsuitable products, or even financial hardship during critical times.

In an industry where trust and clarity are paramount, choosing both the insurer and the advisor carefully is one of the most impactful steps you can take in securing your financial well-being.

Understanding the Advice Model: Fee-Based vs. Commission-Based

One of the primary distinctions to comprehend when engaging an insurance advisor is their compensation method. This often influences the nature—and potential bias—of the advice provided.

1. **Commission-Based Advisors:** This is the most common model, particularly in Asia. Advisors operating under this framework earn commissions from insurers based on the products they sell. While many demonstrate professionalism and integrity, there is an inherent risk of product-pushing to meet sales quotas or personal income goals. When working with a commission-based agent, it is advisable to ensure they are genuinely conducting a needs-based analysis rather than simply fitting a situation into pre-packaged solutions.
2. **Fee-Based or Fee-Only Advisors:** These advisors charge clients directly for financial planning and advisory services. Because they do not receive commissions, their advice is generally considered more objective. They may also offer a broader, more holistic perspective that encompasses insurance planning, investment advice, retirement planning, and estate matters.

In countries like the U.S., U.K., and Australia, the fee-only model is gaining traction as consumers become more informed and demand greater transparency. In Singapore, this model is still developing, though more professionals are offering hybrid approaches—charging a fee for planning while earning commission on implementation. The key is disclosure and alignment with one's interests.

> **Tip**: Always ask how your advisor is remunerated and whether they are restricted to certain insurers or have access to a wider range of products. This simple question sets the tone for a transparent and open relationship.

Questions to Ask Before Committing to a Policy

When considering an insurance purchase, whether for the first time or during a policy review, it is essential to approach the process with a clear and discerning mindset. Hasty decisions based on fear, guilt, or persuasive sales tactics can lead to policies that do not align with true needs.

To avoid this pitfall, it is crucial to ask the right questions and approach insurance decisions with thoughtful due diligence. By treating insurance as a strategic tool rather than an emotional reaction, one can build a portfolio that provides genuine value and protection. Avoid impulse decisions and use these questions as a personal due diligence checklist:

- ***What specific need or risk does this policy address in my life?*** This is the most fundamental question. Insurance exists to address risks—whether it's the protection of income, the security of a family's financial future, or covering escalating healthcare expenses. For example, a young professional in their 20s or 30s might prioritize health and critical illness coverage as a safeguard against unforeseen medical costs, while someone with dependents may focus on term life insurance or income protection to ensure their family is provided for in the event of a tragedy. It is important to be clear on the risk being mitigated to ensure the policy serves that purpose effectively.
- ***How does this coverage align with my life stage and financial goals?*** Life is constantly evolving, and so are financial priorities. At different stages, different types of coverage may be needed. For instance, early in a career, basic health coverage and a small life policy might suffice. As one ages, marries, or has children, needs shift. The focus might move toward comprehensive health insurance, income protection, and more substantial life insurance to secure a family's future. Understanding how a policy aligns with one's current situation and future financial aspirations is key to ensuring it supports overall goals. For example, a young couple in their early 30s who just bought their first home and are starting to plan for a family may prioritize term life insurance to protect their mortgage and provide for future children's education costs. Meanwhile, someone nearing retirement may focus on long-term care

coverage and annuities to ensure a comfortable post-working life. The key takeaway is that one size does not fit all; insurance should evolve with life stages.

- ***What are the key exclusions and waiting periods?***
  Every insurance policy has exclusions—specific situations or conditions that are not covered. Understanding these exclusions is crucial to avoid unpleasant surprises when coverage is most needed. Ask the advisor directly: "What scenarios are not covered by this policy?" Additionally, waiting periods can significantly impact how quickly insurance benefits are available. For example, with health insurance, some treatments may have a waiting period before they are eligible for a claim. Familiarizing oneself with these terms upfront ensures no unexpected gaps in protection.

- ***What are the policy's limitations and future upgrade options?***
  Insurance is not a static product; it must be able to adapt to changing needs. As life progresses, coverage may need to evolve. Can the policy be adjusted if circumstances change, such as having children or taking on a larger mortgage? Furthermore, inquire whether premiums will increase over time, especially for policies bundling protection and investment elements. Some policies may appear affordable initially but could become significantly more expensive with age or increased coverage requirements. Always check for options to upgrade coverage later without needing another round of health assessments or increased premiums.

- ***How does this policy compare with similar ones in the market?***
  It is essential to ensure value for money. Comparing different insurance policies can be daunting, but it is a necessary step. Ask the advisor how the policy compares with similar ones in the market, specifically in terms of cost, coverage, and flexibility. Conduct independent research as well. While insurers may differentiate products with unique names and marketing strategies, most policies generally offer similar core coverage; what differs are the terms, benefits, and how well they fit individual needs. Take the time to ensure the policy offers a competitive balance of price and protection.

- ***How often will the advisor review my policies with me?*** Insurance should never be considered a "buy and forget" product. Financial and personal situations will change over time, and so will insurance needs. Ideally, an insurance advisor should conduct regular reviews of policies—at least annually or whenever there is a major life event such as marriage, having children, purchasing property, or a career change. A proactive advisor will ensure that coverage remains relevant and continues to provide optimal protection. If an advisor is reluctant to schedule regular check-ins, it can be a red flag.
- ***What are the fees, charges, and surrender penalties?*** This is particularly important for investment-linked or bundled policies, which combine insurance and investment elements. Some policies come with hidden fees, administrative charges, or high surrender penalties if one chooses to cancel or withdraw early. Always ask for a detailed breakdown of fees and charges to fully understand the long-term costs and consequences of purchasing that policy. These additional costs can often erode the value of an investment, so awareness is vital.

The Need for Regular Policy Reviews

Just as life goals evolve, so should insurance coverage. Major life changes such as marriage, childbirth, a new job, a health scare, or buying a new home should prompt a re-evaluation of an insurance portfolio. Regular reviews—ideally at least once a year or when significant milestones occur—are essential to ensuring insurance remains in alignment with current needs.

These reviews allow one to:

- Identify underinsurance or duplicate coverage.
- Cancel outdated or irrelevant policies.
- Optimize premium payments and policy features.
- Stay aligned with new financial goals or risks.

Regular check-ins also help in staying abreast of any policy adjustments that might be needed. Life is dynamic, and so are protection needs. By keeping insurance up to date, it continues to serve its purpose and provide the deserved peace of mind.

Ultimately, choosing the right insurance advisor is about more than credentials. It's about finding someone who genuinely listens, educates clearly, and prioritizes best interests over simply selling a product. The right advisor will help craft a tailored insurance strategy that serves not only immediate concerns but also long-term aspirations, empowering one to live confidently and securely.

As the orchestrator of one's financial future, taking charge of a protection plan means asking the right questions, performing due diligence, and ensuring insurance continues to support the journey through life's inevitable changes.

Reviewing and Optimizing Insurance Portfolio: A Strategic Approach

While regular reviews are essential, the effectiveness lies in the methodology of review and the aspects optimized during the process. As individuals navigate various life stages—marriage, raising children, career shifts, business ventures, or transitioning into retirement—their risk exposure changes. Consequently, their insurance coverage should also adapt.

Therefore, an insurance policy review should not be merely a paperwork check. Instead, it ought to be approached as a strategic opportunity to strengthen one's financial foundation. Consider the following questions during this process:

- *Am I paying for overlapping or unnecessary riders?*
- *Are there better products in the market today that serve the same need at a lower premium?*
- *Can I convert term coverage into a permanent one now that my financial situation has changed?*
- *Am I overinsured in one area but under protected in another (e.g., high life cover but little disability or critical illness)?*

My Journey (YK Png) - Evolving Insurance Planning

When I first started working, my focus was on whole life and health insurance. Disability income protection and regular payout plans like annuities weren't a priority at that point. I could only afford modest coverage due to limited income, but I believed in getting started early. As my career progressed and income improved, I made it a point to scale up my protection—adding riders, upgrading policies, and increasing my sum assured. I also ensured that my spouse had adequate coverage and paid for my children's initial insurance plans before they entered the workforce. Today, they've taken over the premium payments—a proud moment of financial independence for them.

Later in life, I became more conscious of long-term risks like total and permanent disability (TPD) and retirement income sustainability. I adjusted my portfolio accordingly and also maximized my CPF Retirement Account (RA) top-ups to secure a lifelong annuity under CPF LIFE. These decisions gave me peace of mind—knowing my protection strategy was now aligned with my current lifestyle and future needs.

That said, not every part of my journey was perfect. One oversight I now regret was underestimating the importance of critical illness coverage. At the time, I believed my hospitalisation plan and life coverage were sufficient. I postponed upgrading my critical illness protection, and by the time I revisited it seriously, the premiums had become prohibitively high due to age and changing health conditions. It was a hard but important lesson: some forms of insurance are time-sensitive, and delaying action can close the window of affordability or eligibility.

Looking back, I'm grateful I made many right moves, but I also acknowledge the gaps. My experience is a reminder that insurance planning is not just about buying policies—it's about proactive, periodic review and aligning your coverage with your evolving life and goals.

Key Takeaways:

- **Start with What Is Affordable:** Begin with basic and essential coverage, even if it's minimal. Starting early significantly impacts affordability and eligibility.
- **Scale Coverage as Income Grows:** As earning power and responsibilities increase, upgrade and expand insurance protection accordingly.
- **Prioritize Family Coverage:** Ensure spouses and dependents are adequately covered. Supporting children's early insurance can establish a strong financial foundation for them.
- **Review and Adapt Regularly:** Insurance needs evolve with different life stages, such as transitions from employment to self-employment, or from accumulation to retirement.

- **Plan for Disability and Retirement Income:** Do not overlook Total and Permanent Disability (TPD) coverage or regular retirement payouts. Options like CPF Retirement Account (RA) top-ups and annuities can offer long-term peace of mind in Singapore.
- **Act Early on Critical Illness Coverage:** Delaying critical illness insurance can lead to substantially higher premiums or disqualification later. Prioritize this early, while still insurable.
- **Periodic Reviews Save Money and Reduce Waste:** Conduct regular insurance reviews. This can reveal outdated or redundant policies and opportunities to optimize coverage and cost.

Practical Steps for Optimization

Insurance is not a "set and forget" asset. It should evolve as life circumstances change—career shifts, marriage, children, aging parents, or new financial goals. Optimizing an insurance portfolio means ensuring every premium dollar is working efficiently to protect what matters most. Below are practical steps to strengthen a coverage strategy:

1. **Utilize a Coverage Matrix:** Map out existing policies against key risks—death, disability, critical illness, hospitalization, and long-term care—to identify any gaps or overlaps. By visually presenting this information, one can:
    - **Identify gaps** where underinsurance exists *(e.g., missing critical illness or Total and Permanent Disability coverage).*
    - **Spot overlaps** that may result in wasted premiums.
    - **Clarify** whether coverage is individual, family-wide, or duplicated across dependents. This tool proves especially useful during annual reviews or when collaborating with a financial advisor.

2. **Align Deductibles with Emergency Funds:** If sufficient emergency savings are available, opting for higher deductibles can reduce premiums.
    - Generally, higher deductibles lead to lower monthly or annual premiums.

Example: If your hospitalisation plan allows you to adjust deductible tiers, you can save on premiums while relying on your emergency fund for minor or infrequent claims. This strategy is most effective for individuals who are financially stable and aim to optimize cash flow.

3. **Bundle Where Practical:** While not always the least expensive on paper, bundling policies with the same insurer can offer hidden efficiencies:
   - **Multi-policy discounts** are often offered, directly reducing the total premium paid across different plans like home, auto, or life insurance.
   - **Consolidated statements and claims processes** simplify financial management, making it easier to track premiums, understand coverage, and navigate the claims process through a single point of contact.
   - **Better underwriting terms** on new purchases may be available due to an existing relationship with the insurer, potentially leading to more favourable rates or easier approval for additional coverage.

   Some insurers even provide holistic planning options, integrating various policies *(e.g., life, health, accident)* under one comprehensive umbrella. However, it's crucial to compare the specific terms and benefits across different providers to ensure that any bundled plan truly offers value and avoids locking one into suboptimal coverage.

4. **Evaluate Riders Annually:** Insurance riders, which are optional add-ons to a main policy, frequently go unreviewed but can significantly influence premium costs. It's prudent to review these annually and remove any that are no longer relevant to one's current circumstances. Common examples include:
   - A Waiver of Premium rider, which pays future premiums if the policyholder becomes disabled.
   - Early-stage critical illness cover, providing a payout upon diagnosis of specific early-stage conditions.
   - Hospital cash benefits, which offer a daily cash sum for each day of hospitalization.
   - Accidental death riders, providing an additional payout if death occurs due to an accident.

   Consider:

- *Is this rider still relevant to my life stage or financial position?*
- *Am I paying for duplicate protection elsewhere?*

Removing outdated or redundant riders can effectively reduce the overall premium burden without compromising essential core protection.

5. **Review Beneficiaries and Nominees:** Life circumstances are dynamic, and insurance nominations should reflect these changes.
   - **Marriage, divorce, births, or deaths** in the family are clear triggers to update beneficiaries.
   - Regular reviews prevent unintended outcomes *(e.g., payouts going to an ex-spouse or bypassing a new dependent)*. Maintain a record of all nominations and ensure loved ones know where to find them.

Collaborate with, Don't Delegate to, Your Advisor. Treat an insurance advisor as a financial partner. While they possess technical expertise, individuals bring context—their evolving goals, family plans, risk appetite, and financial realities. Work together to ensure that every dollar spent on premiums contributes to long-term security and aspirations.

When both parties communicate effectively, the result is a tailored, cost-effective insurance portfolio that serves long-term aspirations. Ask questions, request annual reviews, and do not hesitate to decline a policy that does not align with needs.

Ultimately, insurance is not just about protection; it's about peace of mind. And true peace of mind is only possible when policies are genuinely working for the individual, rather than merely existing as dormant paperwork.

11

[11] In Singapore, formal nominations are required for policies under the Insurance Act (e.g., whole life or endowment). Be sure these are properly registered.

Insurance Needs Assessment Matrix

Coverage Area	Do You Have Coverage? (Y/N)	Do You Need It? (Y/N/Maybe)	Priority Level (High / Med / Low)
Medical Expenses			
Loss of Income (Disability)			
Death			
Critical Illness			
Accidents			
Long-Term Care			
Property/Assets			
Travel Risks			

Insurance as a Foundation for Peace of Mind

Insurance is more than just a financial product; it serves as a cornerstone of a resilient life strategy. While savings and investments fuel aspirations, insurance functions as the essential safety net, ensuring those dreams do not unravel in the face of unforeseen challenges. It offers peace of mind—not stemming from an expectation of the worst, but from meticulous planning for contingencies.

A well-structured insurance portfolio provides the financial cushioning necessary to weather health setbacks, income disruptions, and life-altering events. Whether confronting a hospitalization bill, a critical illness diagnosis, or a long-term disability, appropriate coverage ensures the preservation of a family's standard of living and keeps long-term goals on track. Rather than being derailed by crisis, one remains anchored and steady, free to focus on recovery and recalibration.

Integrating Insurance into a F.I.R(Re-career).E. Plan

Within the broader Financial Independence, Retire Early (F.I.R.E.) framework, insurance plays a silent yet powerful role. It safeguards the financial foundation that enables confident career pivots and life transitions.

- **In early career stages**, insurance empowers the taking of professional risks—whether exploring a startup idea or investing in further education—without the fear that a health emergency could lead to financial distress for oneself or one's family.
- **During mid-career**, as responsibilities increase, insurance is critical for protecting assets, income, and dependents. This stage is vital for establishing the protection pillars that will support future re-careering decisions.
- **In later years or during a re-career phase**, insurance—particularly long-term care and annuity income—offers stability and continuity. As active income potentially tapers off, greater reliance is placed on passive income and a carefully curated safety net to ensure dignity and choice in how one lives and works.

Integrating insurance into a financial independence roadmap means not merely preparing to live life on one's own terms but actively protecting that freedom.

Peace of mind does not derive from possessing the largest policy or the most expensive riders. Instead, it comes from knowing that risks have been thoughtfully considered, informed decisions have been made, and insurance coverage has been aligned with personal values, lifestyle, and long-term goals.

It is prudent to use insurance strategically—not fearfully—to protect what has been built, support loved ones and empower desired career and lifestyle transitions.

Insurance Planning Across the F.I.R(Re-career).E. Journey

Life Stage	Key Risks	Insurance Focus	Strategy
Early Career	Income loss, hospital bills, early CI	- Term Life (basic) - Health Plan - Starter CI - Personal Accident	- Low-cost plans - Start early for lower premiums
Mid-Career / Family	Dependents, loans, health shocks	- Higher Life Cover - Full CI - Disability Income - Mortgage Term	- Increase coverage - Add riders - Cover spouse & kids
Peak Career	Asset loss, lifestyle, retirement prep	- Private Health - Long-Term Care - Annuity/ILP (selective)	- Review costs - Use deductibles - Build for retirement
Re-career / Pre-Retire	Income drop, medical inflation, longevity	- TPD / CI top-up - CareShield Life - CPF RA Top-Up	- Align with new income - Secure annuity streams
Post-Retire / Legacy	Health costs, estate planning	- Health Plan - Long-Term Care - Legacy Life Plan	- Simplify - Ensure nominations - Plan for care & legacy

Summary

Chapter 7: Insurance – Protecting What Matters Most provides a practical and mindset-shifting guide to understanding insurance as a cornerstone of your F.I.R(*Re-career*).E. journey. Rather than viewing insurance as a cost or obligation, this chapter reframes it as a strategic tool for risk management, financial resilience, and peace of mind.

You will learn how insurance works—from the concept of risk transfer and pooling to the key differences between insurance, savings, and investments. We dive deep into the various types of insurance: life, health, accident, income protection, and how they serve different needs across life stages. The chapter also discusses the importance of aligning insurance choices with your life goals, avoiding common pitfalls, and collaborating—not just delegating—to your advisor.

Drawing from my personal journey, I share lessons on adjusting coverage as income and responsibilities change, identifying gaps (like critical illness coverage), and how government-backed schemes fit into, but don't replace, a robust plan. With worksheets, practical tips, and planning tools, you'll be empowered to make intentional decisions that protect your family, income, and future aspirations.

Key Takeaways:

- **Insurance is Financial Défense:** It protects your income, assets, and dependents from unexpected risks that could derail your financial goals.
- **Know the Purpose:** Insurance is not for wealth accumulation—it is for risk transfer and financial continuity.
- **One Size Doesn't Fit All:** Coverage must evolve with your life stage, responsibilities, and income.
- **Underinsurance is Risky:** Gaps in protection—especially for critical illness or income loss—can have long-term consequences.
- **Government Schemes Are Baselines:** CPF schemes provide foundational coverage, but additional protection is usually needed.
- **Collaborate with Advisors:** You bring the context; they bring the expertise. Don't outsource decisions blindly.

- **Peace of Mind Has Value:** The right insurance strategy frees you to pursue purpose, passion, and re-career confidently.

Practical Tips:

- Use a coverage matrix to map your needs and avoid overlaps or blind spots.
- Adjust deductibles based on your emergency fund capacity to lower premiums.
- Regularly review riders, beneficiaries, and policy relevance.
- Reassess your portfolio with each major life or career transition.
- Don't delay protection—premiums rise with age and health conditions.

In the next chapter, **Investment Strategies for Financial Growth,** we'll transit from protection to growth. We'll guide you through building wealth with purpose. We'll explore different asset classes, risk-return profiles, and how to invest wisely at each stage of your F.I.R(*Re-career*).E. journey.

Reflection Prompts & Mini Exercises

"Insurance doesn't prevent misfortune, but it empowers you to face life's uncertainties with confidence and control." ~ YK Png

---

1. Understanding Your Protection Mindset

Prompt:

- *Do you see insurance as a cost, a safeguard, or a peace-of-mind investment?*
- *What personal experience (yours or others') shaped your attitude towards insurance?*
- *How do you balance optimism about the future with preparedness for the unexpected?*

Mini Exercise: Insurance Belief Check

- Write down 3 beliefs you hold about insurance.
- Ask yourself: *Are these beliefs empowering or limiting your planning?*
- Reframe one limiting belief into a proactive mindset *(e.g., "I'm too young to need insurance" → "Starting early helps lock in lower premiums").*

---

2. Mapping Your Insurance Gaps

Prompt:

- *Which areas of your life are well protected, and which remain vulnerable?*
- *Are your current policies aligned with your life stage and responsibilities?*
- *Have you reviewed coverage for life changes?*

Mini Exercise: Coverage Snapshot

- List the 5 core risk areas: Death, Disability, Critical Illness, Hospitalization, Long-Term Care.
- For each, rate your current coverage level: None, Basic, Adequate, Excessive.
- Identify one area to review within the next 30 days.

---

3. From Delegation to Ownership

Prompt:

- *How involved are you in understanding the terms and details of your insurance plans?*
- *Do you rely solely on your advisor, or do you make informed, collaborative decisions?*

- *What information would make you feel more confident about your portfolio?*

Mini Exercise: Advisor Conversation Prep

- Write down 3 questions to ask your insurance advisor.
- Choose one policy to review in detail—understand its terms, exclusions, and riders.
- Schedule a review meeting within the next 60 days.

---

4. Aligning Insurance with Your *F.I.R(Re-career).E* Goals

Prompt:

- *How does your insurance support your journey toward financial independence and re-careering?*
- *• Are you insured in ways that protect your ability to pursue passion-driven work without fear?*
- *Does your protection plan adaptable to the flexibility and risks of a re-careered life?*

Mini Exercise: Protection Alignment Audit

- List your top 3 career/life goals for the next 5–10 years.
- Now match each goal with the type of protection that would ensure peace of mind along the way.
- Identify one gap and explore options to realign.

---

5. Learning from Your Insurance Journey

Prompt:

- *What would you have done differently if you could re-plan your insurance path?*
- *What key lessons from your experience can you pass on to the next generation?*
- *What is one step you can take today to future-proof your insurance planning?*

Mini Exercise: Legacy Reflection

- Write a short note (real or imaginary) to your younger self about what you've learned.
- Include one regret, one success, and one piece of advice for someone starting out.
- Optional: Share this exercise with a loved one to spark a meaningful conversation.

Chapter 8: Investment Strategies for Financial Growth

~ *By* ***CW Tan*** *(ACCA). Financial Planner.*

> ***Disclaimer:*** *This chapter shares general investment concepts and strategies. It is not financial or investment advice. Markets, products, and regulations change. Readers should do their own due diligence and consult licensed professionals before investing.*

A strong foundation of financial wellness, built on disciplined saving and a clear understanding of net worth, is the prerequisite for sustainable wealth creation. While earning and saving form this critical base, it is through strategic investment that capital begins to work harder, compounding over time to generate income, preserve value, and create long-term financial security. Investment transforms passive capital into a dynamic engine for future growth.

This chapter builds on the principles of financial health to unpack the fundamentals of investment risk, return, and time. It explores key asset classes—from fixed deposits and equities to ETFs, unit trusts, and REITs—and provides practical guidance on aligning investment choices with life stages and financial goals. Whether the aim is wealth accumulation, income generation, or capital preservation, understanding how to construct a resilient, purpose-driven investment portfolio is essential to achieving financial independence and a sustainable re-career.

Financial Wellness and Net Worth: The Foundation of Investment

In an age where social media platforms often showcase lavish lifestyles, from luxury automobiles and high-end properties to designer goods and exotic travel, the outward appearance of wealth can be a source of aspiration or, for many, financial insecurity. However, a lifestyle of luxury does not always equate to true wealth. In numerous cases, individuals may rely on financing and credit facilities to project an image of affluence, while their underlying financial health tells a different story.

This distinction highlights the importance of proper wealth management, which begins with a fundamental understanding of net worth. Rather than focusing on perceived wealth, a more accurate measure of financial security is an individual's net worth. This concept provides a clear, objective snapshot of one's financial position.

Defining and Calculating Net Worth

Net worth is the difference between an individual's total assets and total liabilities. The formula is as follows:

Assets−Liabilities=Net Worth

- **Assets** are any resources, whether tangible or intangible, that hold monetary value. Examples include cash, savings, investments, real estate, and other valuable possessions.
- **Liabilities** are financial obligations or debts owed to others. Common liabilities include mortgages, personal loans, credit card balances, and student loans.

Type of Assets	Type of Liabilities
☑ Cash/Bank account balance/Fixed deposit	☑ Mortgage loan
☑ Market value property	☑ Car loan
☑ CPF balances	☑ Credit card outstanding balance
☑ Insurance with cach value	☑ Buy now, pay later
☑ Cach investment (Stocks / Unit trust)	☑ Personal loan / renovation loan
☑ Other convertible with realizable value	☑ Income tax statement

A positive net worth signifies that assets exceed liabilities, indicating a strong foundation for building wealth. Conversely, a negative net worth suggests that liabilities outweigh assets, signalling a need for more diligent financial planning and management.

Regularly tracking net worth is a crucial practice for monitoring financial progress and making informed decisions on the path toward financial goals. For those in the early stages of their careers and asset accumulation, adopting a disciplined savings habit is one of the most effective strategies for growing net worth. This approach aligns with a fundamental principle of personal finance:

Income−Savings=Expenses

This formula prioritizes savings as a non-negotiable component of one's financial plan, rather than treating expenses as the primary allocation of income. This disciplined approach establishes the foundation for long-term financial wellness.

Practical Notes for Financial Wellness

Achieving financial control and building wealth requires mindful habits. Before making any significant purchase, a critical assessment of whether the item is a genuine necessity or simply a want is essential. This conscious approach to spending is the first step toward better financial control.

Furthermore, when considering loans or financing, it is imperative to look beyond seemingly low flat interest rates (e.g., 2.8%) and instead focus on the effective interest rate, which can be significantly higher (often 5% or more). Understanding the true cost of borrowing enables smarter financial decisions and helps in avoiding potential debt traps. Continuous monitoring of asset value and a commitment to spending within one's means are key habits that contribute to steady, long-term wealth accumulation.

Investment Fundamentals: Risk, Return & Time

Investing is the deliberate choice to put money to work today in pursuit of a greater financial benefit tomorrow. Unlike spending—which offers immediate gratification but no enduring value—investing defers reward in exchange for the possibility of growth, income, or security over time. Whether directed toward financial markets, real estate, or even personal development such as education or acquiring new skills, a sound investment has one defining trait: the expectation of future return.

At the core of all investing are three interconnected principles—risk, return, and time. Understanding how they interact is essential for designing a purposeful, resilient investment strategy.

1. **Risk - No Reward Without Uncertainty:** All investments carry risk. The key is not to avoid risk altogether, but to understand and manage it. The types of investment risks:
   - **Financial Risk:** The potential loss of part or all of the capital invested. Stocks, for example, are subject to price volatility driven by company performance, market sentiment, and broader economic conditions. A well-performing company today may underperform tomorrow due to unexpected events.
   - **Market Risk:** Broader systemic factors—such as recessions, interest rate changes, or geopolitical tensions—can affect entire asset classes. Even a diversified equity portfolio can decline sharply during market downturns.
   - **Inflation Risk:** Often underestimated, inflation risk erodes the real value of money over time. If an investment yields 3% annually but inflation runs at 4%, the investor is effectively losing purchasing power. Over the years, this silent drag can significantly undermine financial goals.
   - **Liquidity Risk:** Some investments, such as property or private equity, may be difficult to convert into cash quickly without significant loss of value. Liquidity becomes especially important when capital needs arise unexpectedly.
   - **Credit Risk:** Particularly relevant for bond investors, this is the risk that an issuer (such as a company or government) may default on its obligations.

   Risk cannot be eliminated—but it can be diversified, mitigated, and matched to appropriate investment goals. For instance:
   - Long-term retirement savings may tolerate equity risk.
   - Short-term goals may be better served with cash or fixed-income instruments.
   - A diversified portfolio helps smooth out the effects of any one asset's underperformance.

2. **Return - What Are You Investing For?** Return is the financial reward received from an investment—measured either as income *(e.g. dividends, interest)* or capital appreciation (increase in value). Returns are typically expressed as a percentage gain or loss over a given period.

But return is more than a number—it reflects an investment's effectiveness in meeting its intended purpose. A return must be evaluated in context.

Key Questions for Evaluating Return:

- ***What rate of return is necessary to meet your financial goals?***
  E.g. If retiring at 55 requires a portfolio worth $1 million, how much return must your investments generate annually to reach that target?
- ***What is the time horizon?*** Longer timelines may allow for more aggressive (and volatile) investments; shorter horizons require stability and liquidity.
- ***What level of risk are you willing and able to accept?*** Risk tolerance varies based on personality, income stability, and life circumstances.
- ***What are the opportunity costs?*** Allocating capital to one investment may mean forgoing another with potentially higher returns or lower risk.

Understanding return in relation to risk and time is vital—chasing high returns without considering volatility or drawdown potential can derail financial plans.

3. **Time - The Great Amplifier of Returns:** Time is one of the most powerful tools available to investors. The longer money is allowed to grow, the more effective compounding becomes. Compounding refers to the process where earnings are reinvested to generate additional earnings—a virtuous cycle that accelerates wealth creation.

   The Power of Compounding:
   An initial investment of $10,000 earning 6% annually will grow to approximately:

   - $13,382 in 5 years
   - $17,908 in 10 years
   - $32,071 in 20 years
   - $57,435 in 30 years

   This growth doesn't happen in a straight line. It accelerates over time—the later years account for much more of the final value than the early ones. That's why starting early is often more impactful than trying to "catch up" with larger sums later in life.

Time and Investment Strategy:

- **Short-term horizon (0–3 years)**: Prioritise capital preservation and liquidity. Use instruments like fixed deposits, money market funds, or short-term bonds.
- **Medium-term horizon (3–10 years)**: Blend growth and stability. Consider a mix of bonds, equities, and REITs.
- **Long-term horizon (10+ years)**: Embrace compounding and tolerate volatility. Equities, ETFs, and growth-oriented funds can play a key role here.

Case Study: Business as an Investment

Launching a food and beverage (F&B) venture can serve as a practical analogy for understanding investment fundamentals. Suppose an individual invests a fixed sum of capital to start a cafe-style restaurant, with the goal of recovering the initial investment within six months.

To achieve this, the business must generate consistent daily sales, maintain tight cost controls, and implement proactive risk management. Success depends not only on culinary quality, but also on strategic decision-making across several key investment dimensions:

- ***Risk**: The business is exposed to multiple risks—operational (supply disruptions, staffing), compliance (licensing, hygiene standards), reputational (online reviews, food quality), and financial (cost overruns, cash flow challenges). Identifying and mitigating these risks upfront is critical, much like managing volatility in an investment portfolio.*
- ***Return**: The return is measured by the speed and magnitude of profit generation. A well-managed cafe might yield $3,000–$5,000 per month in net income. If the business scales or gains customer loyalty, the investor could exceed the break-even point within six months, achieving a positive return on investment (ROI).*
- ***Time**: The six-month target introduces a defined investment horizon. Time affects not only recovery of capital but also the ability to reinvest profits, absorb fluctuations, and build long-term sustainability. A longer horizon would allow greater flexibility but increases exposure to cumulative risks.*
- ***Goal Clarity and Alignment**: Just like in financial planning, having a clearly defined objective (e.g., break even in six*

months) shapes decisions on pricing, marketing, and operations. Without this clarity, resources may be misallocated, reducing the chances of meeting expected returns.

- ***Risk-Return Trade-Off***: *Faster returns often require higher upfront investment, more aggressive promotion, or operational intensity—all of which increase risk. This mirrors the trade-off in investing: higher return potential comes with greater uncertainty.*

This case underscores that whether one invests in a business or a financial instrument, the principles remain consistent—clear goals, disciplined risk management, and alignment between risk appetite, return expectations, and time horizon are fundamental to long-term success.

Successful investing is not about chasing the highest return or avoiding all risk—it's about clarity of purpose, disciplined execution, and aligning financial resources with life goals. The trio of risk, return, and time offers a simple yet powerful framework for making informed investment decisions.

When this foundation is well understood, other investment tools—such as stocks, bonds, REITs, and ETFs—can be evaluated and integrated meaningfully into a coherent portfolio.

Asset Classes & Their Risk-Return Profiles

A well-constructed investment portfolio fundamentally relies on a judicious mix of asset classes. This diversification is crucial for balancing the potential for returns with an investor's individual risk tolerance. Each distinct asset class possesses unique characteristics concerning income generation, capital appreciation, liquidity, and volatility. A thorough understanding of these differences empowers investors to align their

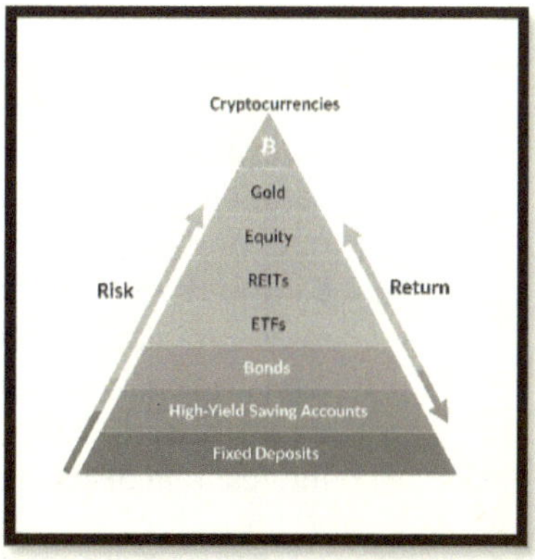

investment decisions precisely with their specific financial goals, prevailing life stages, and personal risk appetite.

We can generally categorize asset classes by their inherent risk-return profiles, from lowest to highest:

1. **Capital Preservation & Liquidity - Fixed Deposits and High-Yield Savings Accounts**

   Risk Profile: Very Low.
   These instruments are primarily focused on robust capital preservation and high liquidity. Returns are generally modest but highly predictable, making them ideal for safeguarding funds.

   For investors prioritizing safety and immediate access to funds, Fixed Deposits (FDs) and High-Yield Savings Accounts serve as foundational components for liquidity management.

   1.1. **Fixed Deposits (FDs):** These are low-risk term instruments offered by banks and finance companies. An investor places a lump sum with the institution for a predetermined tenure, earning a fixed interest rate for the entire duration. FDs are highly favored for their strong capital protection and predictable returns, as they are generally insulated from broader market volatility. In the hierarchy of a bank's capital structure, FDs typically rank just below secured creditors, indicating a high priority in repayment should the financial institution face distress. While their safety is undeniable, their returns are generally modest and may struggle to keep pace with inflation over extended periods.

   The interest rates offered on FDs are dynamic and influenced by several interconnected factors:

   - **Internal Liquidity and Funding Requirements:** A bank's immediate need for funds directly impacts the rates it offers to attract deposits.
   - **Competitive Positioning:** Banks constantly adjust rates to remain competitive within the financial landscape and attract a larger share of depositors.
   - **Central Bank Monetary Policy:** Guidance and interest rate decisions from the Monetary Authority of

Singapore (MAS) significantly shape the prevailing interest rate environment.

- **Prevailing Demand and Supply:** The overall demand for and supply of retail deposits within the market also plays a crucial role.

1.2. High-Yield Saving Accounts: These accounts are specifically designed to offer superior interest rates compared to conventional savings accounts, while simultaneously providing impressive flexibility and daily liquidity. Banks often incentivize enhanced rates by linking them to specific customer behaviors, such as:

- Direct salary crediting.
- Consistent monthly card usage.
- Setting up GIRO bill payments.
- Linking to insurance or investment products.

The recent emergence of digital banks in Singapore has further democratized access to better returns, with many now offering high-yield accounts with minimal or no qualifying conditions, simplifying the process for depositors to earn more on their savings.

In Singapore, eligible deposits held in fixed deposits and savings accounts are safeguarded by the Singapore Deposit Insurance Corporation (SDIC), providing coverage up to S$100,000 per depositor per member bank. This statutory protection makes Fixed Deposits (FDs) and high-yield accounts exceptionally suitable vehicles for establishing emergency funds to address unforeseen circumstances. They are also ideal for saving towards short-term financial goals with a defined timeframe, offering both security and accessible growth. Furthermore, these accounts serve a crucial role in maintaining liquidity buffers, acting as a strategic and stable component within a well-diversified investment portfolio.

2. Income & Stability: Bonds and Bond Funds

Risk Profile: Low to Medium.
Bonds offer regular income through interest payments (coupons) and typically display lower volatility than equities. They play a vital role in portfolio diversification and are particularly appealing to conservative investors or those nearing retirement.

Bonds are fixed-income securities issued by either governments or corporations to raise capital. Investors lend money to the issuer in exchange for periodic interest payments and the return of principal at maturity. In Singapore, investors can broadly access corporate bonds, government bonds, and bond funds.

2.1 Corporate Bonds: Corporate bonds are issued by private companies to finance operations, acquisitions, or expansion. These bonds carry a fixed coupon rate and maturity date, typically indicated in the bond's name. There are two main formats of corporate bonds:

- **Wholesale Bonds:** Traded over the counter (OTC), these require a high minimum investment (typically S$250,000 or more). They are generally accessible to accredited or institutional investors.
- **Retail Bonds:** Listed on the Singapore Exchange (SGX), these cater to individual investors with lower entry points (usually from S$1,000 per lot). Retail bonds in Singapore commonly offer coupon rates between 3% and 6%.

While coupon payments are fixed, the bond's market price fluctuates based on interest rate movements, issuer credit ratings, and macroeconomic conditions. Bond prices generally move inversely to market interest rates—rising rates tend to lower bond prices, and vice versa.

2.2 Government Bonds: Government bonds are debt instruments issued by the state to finance infrastructure and public services. In Singapore, these are considered among the safest investment options due to the nation's strong fiscal position and stable regulatory environment.

Key categories include:

- **Singapore Government Securities (SGS):** These include Treasury Bills (T-bills), SGS Bonds, and SGS Infrastructure Bonds, issued through regular auctions and traded on the secondary market. SGS instruments suit investors seeking safety and predictable returns over varying durations.
- **Singapore Savings Bonds (SSB):** Designed for individual investors, SSBs offer flexible tenures of up to 10 years, with interest that "steps up" over time.

They can be redeemed without penalty after the first month, providing both capital protection and liquidity. As of 2025, the Monetary Authority of Singapore (MAS) confirms that proceeds from SSBs are invested separately from government expenditure, reinforcing their credibility and low-risk profile.

2.3 Bond ETFs *(e.g., Bond ETFs, Bond Unit Trusts)*: Bond funds are collective investment schemes that pool capital from investors to purchase a diversified portfolio of bonds. These funds cater to investors seeking fixed-income exposure without the complexity of analyzing and selecting individual bond issues.

Bond funds can be broadly classified into Bond Exchange-Traded Funds (ETFs) and Bond Unit Trusts, each offering distinct advantages in terms of cost, flexibility, and management style.

- **Bond ETFs:** Bond ETFs are passively managed funds designed to replicate the performance of specific bond indices. They are traded on stock exchanges, providing real-time liquidity, price transparency, and cost efficiency. Unlike traditional bond purchases, which often require substantial capital and direct access to OTC markets, Bond ETFs offer investors fractional access to a diversified basket of bonds with relatively low investment thresholds. Key features of Bond ETFs include:
    - **Low Fees:** As passively managed instruments, they typically charge lower management fees compared to actively managed funds.
    - **Diversification:** Exposure spans multiple issuers, sectors, or geographies, reducing concentration risk.
    - **Liquidity:** Investors can buy and sell units on the stock exchange throughout the trading day, similar to equities.
    - **Transparency:** Holdings and index composition are usually disclosed regularly, offering clarity to investors.

- **Bond Unit Trusts:** Bond Unit Trusts are actively managed funds where professional fund managers make discretionary investment decisions based on market conditions, economic trends, and credit analysis. These funds aim to generate optimal income and manage interest rate or duration risk through active rebalancing of bond holdings. Key features of Bond Unit Trusts include:
    - **Active Management:** Fund managers assess interest rate forecasts, credit spreads, and issuer fundamentals to tactically adjust portfolios.
    - **Customisable Mandates:** Depending on the fund's objective, portfolios may focus on high-yield bonds, investment-grade credits, emerging market debt, or short-duration securities.
    - **Income Focus:** Many bond unit trusts aim to deliver regular distributions, appealing to income-seeking investors.
    - **Currency Hedging Options:** Some funds offer hedged classes to reduce currency risk for international bond exposure.

  These actively managed funds suit investors who prefer a hands-off approach but want a professional manager to navigate interest rate cycles, credit developments, and global macroeconomic shifts.

Bond ETFs are suitable for cost-conscious investors seeking transparent, broad-market exposure with easy liquidity. Bond Unit Trusts are ideal for those who value active management and are comfortable with the associated fund-level risks and fees in exchange for potentially enhanced returns or targeted strategies.

3. **Passive Real Estate Income: Real Estate Investment Trusts (REITs)**

   Risk Profile: Medium.
   REITs offer exposure to real estate income and potential capital appreciation, but their value is influenced by property market cycles, interest rates, and economic conditions. They tend to be more volatile than bonds but generally less volatile than individual stocks.

REITs are publicly listed vehicles that invest in and operate income-producing properties. They offer retail investors an accessible pathway to participate in the real estate market without requiring the substantial capital outlay or the operational responsibilities associated with direct property ownership.

Key Characteristics of REITs include:

- **Income Distribution:** A defining feature of REITs is their legal obligation to distribute a significant portion (typically 90% or more) of their taxable income to unitholders. This makes them highly attractive to income-seeking investors.
- **Liquidity:** Unlike direct property investments, REITs are traded on stock exchanges (such as the SGX in Singapore) like conventional stocks, providing investors with daily liquidity.
- **Yield Potential:** REITs often deliver higher dividend yields compared to traditional fixed-income instruments like bonds, making them appealing for steady income generation.
- **Inflation Protection:** Many rental contracts within REIT portfolios include escalation clauses tied to inflation or periodic market rent reviews. This feature can provide a degree of protection against inflationary pressures, as rental income may rise in tandem with general price levels.

Investors can gain exposure to REITs in a few ways:

- **Individual REITs:** This allows for targeted strategies, focusing on specific property sectors such as healthcare, industrial, retail, or hospitality.
- **REIT ETFs:** For broad exposure to multiple REITs through a single instrument, REIT ETFs are an excellent option.

  Key Considerations include:

  - **Interest Rate Sensitivity:** Rising interest rates can make REITs less attractive relative to fixed-income instruments, as their borrowing costs increase, potentially impacting distributions.
  - **Leverage Risk:** REITs typically utilize debt to fund property acquisitions and developments. Higher gearing (leverage) can amplify both returns and risks.

- **Sector-Specific Risks:** The performance of a REIT is heavily dependent on the specific property sector it operates in. For example, hospitality REITs faced significant challenges during the COVID-19 pandemic, while retail REITs constantly adapt to the disruption caused by e-commerce.
- **Regulatory Limits:** In Singapore, the MAS imposes regulatory limits on REIT leverage, capping it at 50% of total assets (as of 2020), although certain exceptions and temporary adjustments may apply. This helps to
- mitigate excessive debt levels within the sector.

4. **Diversified Growth: Diversified Equity Funds (Equity ETFs, Equity Unit Trusts)**

Risk Profile: Medium to High.
While offering diversification across many stocks, these funds are still primarily exposed to equity market volatility. Their risk level depends on the specific sectors, geographies, and investment strategies of the underlying fund. They aim for capital growth.

Diversified Equity Funds are professionally managed investment vehicles (like Equity ETFs and Equity Unit Trusts) that pool money from investors to invest in a broad portfolio of stocks. They offer a convenient way to gain exposure to equity markets with built-in diversification.

4.1 Equity ETFs: Equity Exchange-Traded Funds (ETFs) are passively managed investment vehicles that aim to replicate the performance of a specific stock market index. They provide broad market exposure, built-in diversification, and lower management fees compared to actively managed equity funds. Equity ETFs are traded on stock exchanges, allowing investors to buy or sell units throughout the trading day at market prices, similar to individual stocks.

Examples:

- *SPDR STI ETF: Provides exposure to the top 30 companies listed on the Singapore Exchange (SGX), replicating the performance of the Straits Times Index.*

- *iShares MSCI World ETF: Offers broad global developed market equity exposure, providing diversification across major economies.*

4.2 Equity Unit Trusts: Equity Unit Trusts are actively managed investment funds that pool capital from investors to build and manage a diversified portfolio of listed equities. Unlike passive ETFs, these funds are overseen by professional fund managers who conduct in-depth research, perform market analysis, and make active decisions on stock selection, asset allocation, and portfolio rebalancing to achieve specific growth objectives. Key Benefits of Diversified Equity Funds include:

- **Built-in Diversification:** By investing in a single fund, investors gain exposure to multiple underlying securities within one product, significantly spreading risk compared to individual stocks.
- **Professional Management:** For actively managed funds, investors benefit from the expertise of dedicated fund managers who conduct extensive research and perform ongoing market analysis.
- **Cost Efficiency (ETFs):** Equity ETFs generally boast lower management fees compared to actively managed funds, as their strategy often involves simply tracking an index.
- **Accessibility:** These funds are highly accessible, with relatively low minimum entry points, making professional asset management available to a broad investor base.

5. **High Growth Potential: Individual Equities (Stocks)**

Risk Profile: High.
Investing in individual company stocks carries the highest level of specific company risk (idiosyncratic risk) and market volatility. While offering the highest potential for capital appreciation, they also have the highest potential for significant losses.

Equities, commonly known as stocks, represent fractional ownership in publicly listed companies. Investors gain exposure to the underlying company's profitability and growth potential primarily through two mechanisms:

- **Capital Appreciation (rising share prices):** This occurs when the market price of the shares rises, reflecting an increase in the company's perceived value or future earnings prospects.
- **Dividend Income (when declared):** When a company declares dividends, a portion of its profits is distributed to shareholders, providing a regular income stream.
  Unlike the relative stability of savings instruments, individual equities offer a significantly higher return potential but inherently carry a substantially higher degree of volatility. Market movements are influenced by a complex interplay of factors, including:
  - **Corporate Performance:** A company's earnings, innovation, and management decisions directly impact its share price.
  - **Economic Cycles:** Broader economic growth or contraction significantly affects corporate profits and investor sentiment.
  - **Global Trends:** Geopolitical events, technological advancements, and shifts in consumer behaviour on a global scale can profoundly influence stock markets.
  - **Investor Sentiment:** Collective optimism or pessimism among investors can drive market swings, sometimes independently of fundamental company performance. Risks to Note:
  - **Market Sensitivity:** Equities are highly sensitive to market downturns. For instance, DBS shares experienced a significant decline of approximately 35% during the initial stages of the COVID-19 crisis.
  - **Volatility Management:** Navigating this inherent volatility effectively requires a long-term perspective, strategic diversification across various stocks and sectors, and a resilient mindset to withstand market fluctuations.

6. **Alternative Investments: Gold, Cryptocurrency, and Private Equity**

   Risk Profile: Medium to Very High.
   Alternative investments represent non-traditional asset classes that do not fall into the standard categories of equities, bonds, or cash. These assets offer portfolio diversification through

exposure to different return drivers and risk characteristics. While they may offer higher potential returns, they are typically less liquid, more complex, and carry higher volatility or risk compared to traditional investments.

Alternative investments are most suitable for experienced investors with a higher risk appetite, longer investment horizon, and a strategic interest in diversifying beyond conventional markets.

6.1 Gold: Gold has long served as a store of value and a hedge against inflation, currency debasement, and geopolitical uncertainty. It is not income-generating but is valued for its ability to preserve purchasing power during economic downturns or market stress. Key Characteristics include:

- **Inflation Hedge:** Gold historically maintains its value during periods of high inflation and fiat currency weakness.
- **Crisis Protection:** Demand tends to increase in times of financial instability or geopolitical tension.
- **No Yield:** Unlike bonds or equities, gold does not provide regular income, and holding costs may apply *(e.g., storage or insurance for physical gold).*
- **Modes of Exposure:** Investors may access gold through physical bullion, gold ETFs, mining stocks, or gold savings accounts.

6.2 Cryptocurrency: Cryptocurrency is a form of digital or virtual currency secured by cryptographic methods and decentralized through blockchain technology. The most prominent example, Bitcoin, has pioneered a decentralized financial system not reliant on traditional intermediaries. Key Characteristics include:

- **Decentralisation and Transparency:** Blockchain infrastructure allows for peer-to-peer transactions that are verifiable, immutable, and independent of central authorities.
- **Innovation Potential:** Cryptocurrencies serve as the foundation for decentralised finance (DeFi), digital asset ownership (via NFTs), and programmable contracts (smart contracts).

- **Volatility and Speculation:** Prices can be highly volatile, driven by speculative trading, regulatory developments, and adoption dynamics.
- **Limited Practical Use:** While adoption is growing, cryptocurrencies are not yet widely accepted as a mainstream medium of exchange

Risks to Note:

- **Regulatory uncertainty across jurisdictions:** The legal status of cryptocurrencies varies widely across countries, and regulations are still evolving. Sudden policy changes—such as bans on trading, restrictions on exchanges, or taxation changes—can significantly impact the market and investor confidence.
- **Cybersecurity threats and loss of private keys:** Digital assets are stored in wallets secured by private cryptographic keys. If these keys are lost, stolen, or compromised (e.g., through hacking or phishing attacks), investors may permanently lose access to their funds. Security remains a critical vulnerability, particularly for self-custodied assets.
- **Market manipulation due to fragmented trading venues:** The global cryptocurrency market operates across numerous unregulated or lightly regulated exchanges, making it susceptible to price manipulation, wash trading, and sudden liquidity shocks. This can lead to distorted price signals and increased risk for retail investors.
- **Extreme volatility that can lead to substantial gains or losses:** Cryptocurrency prices can fluctuate dramatically within short periods, often driven by sentiment, social media influence, or macroeconomic speculation. While this volatility creates opportunities for high returns, it also exposes investors to sharp and unexpected losses.

6.3 **Private Equity:** Private equity involves investing in non-publicly traded companies, either directly or via private equity funds. These investments are typically long-term and illiquid, but can deliver substantial returns through business growth, operational improvements, or strategic exits (e.g., IPO or acquisition). Key Characteristics include:

- **High Return Potential:** Private equity investments target high capital gains through strategic interventions such as improving operational efficiency, scaling the business, introducing new management, or expanding into new markets. Because these businesses are often in early or transformational stages, the return potential can significantly exceed that of public equities—though so can the risk.
- **Limited Liquidity:** Private equity is inherently illiquid. Capital is typically committed for a multi-year period (often 5 to 10 years), during which investors cannot redeem their investment. Exit opportunities are event-driven and depend on successful outcomes such as a sale or public listing. This lock-up period requires patience and long-term financial commitment.
- **Accredited Investor Access:** Due to regulatory requirements and the complex nature of private equity structures, most opportunities are restricted to accredited or institutional investors. These investors are expected to have sufficient financial means, investment experience, and risk tolerance to participate in such offerings. Entry thresholds are usually high, and transparency can be limited compared to public markets.
- **Active Management:** Private equity fund managers play a direct and hands-on role in driving business performance. This may include strategic planning, capital restructuring, recruiting key executives, implementing best operational practices, or providing industry connections. The goal is to enhance company value for a profitable exit.

Integrating Asset Classes Into a Balanced Portfolio

Constructing a truly durable and effective investment portfolio extends beyond merely selecting individual assets; it necessitates a sophisticated approach to integrating diverse asset classes in a manner that meticulously matches investments to an investor's specific objectives. This strategic allocation is the cornerstone of a resilient financial plan, designed to navigate market fluctuations while consistently advancing towards both immediate and long-term financial goals.

Matching Investments to Objectives: A Strategic Allocation Framework

A portfolio's composition should reflect its intended purpose. Different asset classes, with their distinct risk-return profiles, naturally align with varying financial goals and time horizons. The following framework outlines how to align assets with specific objectives:

- **Emergency & Short-Term Goals:** For funds designated for unexpected expenses or short-term objectives *(e.g., a down payment)*, the priority is liquidity and capital preservation. Assets like Fixed Deposits and High-Yield Savings Accounts are ideal for this purpose, providing stability and easy access. Their SDIC protection in Singapore makes them excellent liquidity buffers.
- **Growth & Appreciation:** When the primary objective is long-term wealth accumulation, growth-oriented assets are essential. Individual Equities and Equity ETFs offer the highest potential for capital appreciation over extended periods. Direct stock investments allow for targeted growth in specific companies, while ETFs provide diversified exposure to broad markets, reducing individual company risk.
- **Income & Stability:** For investors seeking regular income streams and a moderating force against equity market volatility, a portfolio should include assets like Bonds, Bond ETFs, Dividend-Paying Stocks, and REITs. These assets provide predictable cash flow and act as a stabilizing component, particularly for those in or nearing retirement.
- **Diversification & Professional Management:** For investors who prefer a hands-off approach or seek sophisticated

strategies, Mutual Funds or Unit Trusts offer significant advantages. They provide instant diversification across numerous securities, sectors, and geographies, all under the management of experienced professionals.

Goal / Horizon	Suitable Assets
Emergency & short-term	FDs, high-yield savings accounts
Growth & appreciation	Stocks, equity ETFs
Income & stability	Bond ETFs, dividend stocks, REITs
Diversification	Mutual funds/unit trusts

The Benefits of Balanced Allocation

By strategically allocating capital across these diverse categories, investors can achieve multiple objectives simultaneously:

- **Mitigate Volatility:** Diversification across assets with differing risk-return profiles can help smooth out portfolio returns. When one asset class underperforms, another may be performing well, reducing the overall impact of market swings.
- **Enhance Risk-Adjusted Returns:** A balanced approach aims to achieve the best possible returns for a given level of risk, or conversely, to minimize risk for a target return. This optimization is key to sustainable wealth building.
- **Support Both Lifestyle and Legacy Goals:** A well-integrated portfolio can generate income for current lifestyle needs while simultaneously growing capital for long-term objectives like retirement, funding significant life events, or ensuring an efficient transfer of wealth to future generations.

Ultimately, successful investing hinges on effectively balancing risk, return, and time horizon. Different asset classes inherently serve distinct functional roles within a comprehensive financial plan. Therefore, a robust investment strategy must dynamically evolve with personal and financial stages. A truly well-rounded portfolio masterfully integrates these diverse elements, creating a cohesive and adaptable framework for lifelong financial resilience.

Portfolio Construction and Asset Allocation

Building on the foundation of asset class understanding and integration, portfolio construction focuses on how these instruments come together in a structured, strategic manner. Asset allocation is the deliberate process of distributing capital across asset categories to achieve optimal balance between growth, income, and risk. This allocation must remain responsive to individual goals, life stages, and market conditions, forming the core of a resilient and adaptive investment strategy.

Principles of Asset Allocation

Asset allocation begins with clarity around personal financial objectives, risk appetite, and investment horizon. These parameters influence the proportion of capital assigned to different asset classes such as equities, fixed income, property, and cash.

- **Risk Tolerance:** This refers to the capacity to endure market volatility without compromising long-term commitment. A higher risk tolerance supports a greater allocation to equities or growth assets, while a conservative risk profile leans toward income-generating or capital-preserving instruments.
- **Investment Horizon:** The length of time before the capital is needed for specific goals—such as retirement, children's education, or major life events—guides asset mix decisions. Longer horizons allow for higher equity exposure due to the capacity to ride out short-term market fluctuations.
- **Financial Objectives:** Whether the goal is capital accumulation, passive income, wealth preservation, or legacy building, each objective requires a tailored asset mix. For instance, a retiree seeking regular income would prioritise yield-bearing instruments over growth stocks.

A frequently referenced rule of thumb is the "100 minus age" approach to equity allocation. While this offers a starting point, actual allocation should be personalised, considering other factors such as liquidity needs, market experience, and income stability.

Strategic vs. Tactical Asset Allocation

Portfolio design can follow either a strategic or tactical approach, depending on the level of investor involvement and the desired degree of flexibility.

- **Strategic Asset Allocation** is a long-term, structured framework where a fixed target allocation is set based on the investor's profile. For example, a strategic allocation might comprise 60% equities, 30% bonds, and 10% cash equivalents. This mix remains relatively stable over time, with periodic rebalancing to maintain the original proportions. The strength of this approach lies in its discipline and alignment with long-term objectives.
- **Tactical Asset Allocation** involves temporary adjustments to the portfolio mix in response to perceived market opportunities or economic shifts. For example, increasing equity exposure during a market downturn or reducing bond allocation during interest rate hikes. While tactical shifts can enhance returns, they also carry higher risk if driven by speculation or emotion rather than informed analysis.

Strategic allocation ensures long-term consistency, while limited tactical adjustments may complement it when implemented based on clear frameworks rather than market timing instincts.

The Role of Diversification

Diversification is a foundational principle in risk management. By spreading investments across different asset classes, sectors, and geographies, portfolio volatility can be reduced without necessarily sacrificing return potential.

- **Asset Class Diversification:** Combining equities, fixed income, REITs, and cash allows the portfolio to benefit from different economic conditions. While equities offer growth, bonds provide stability, and real estate contributes income and inflation hedging.
- **Sector and Geographic Diversification:** Exposure to various industries (e.g., technology, healthcare, financials) and regions (e.g., developed markets, emerging economies) protects the portfolio from country-specific or sector-specific downturns.
- **Currency and Liquidity Diversification:** Investing in multiple currencies can reduce foreign exchange risk, while maintaining

a blend of liquid and illiquid assets ensures that capital can be accessed when needed without disrupting long-term holdings.

Diversification does not eliminate risk entirely, but it smoothens the investment journey and enhances the ability to stay the course during turbulent periods.

Rebalancing Strategies

Over time, market movements can cause the actual asset allocation to deviate from the intended mix. Rebalancing is the process of realigning the portfolio to its original or updated target allocation, ensuring that risk exposure remains appropriate and in line with the overall investment strategy.

- **Calendar-Based Rebalancing:** This method involves reviewing and adjusting the portfolio at fixed intervals—commonly quarterly, semi-annually, or annually. It ensures regular discipline, regardless of market conditions.
- **Threshold-Based Rebalancing:** Rebalancing is triggered when any asset class deviates from its target allocation beyond a pre-defined threshold—typically 5% or more. For example, if equities exceed 65% in a portfolio targeting 60%, partial trimming may be required.
- **Hybrid Approach:** This combines both time-based and threshold-based methods, offering greater flexibility. The portfolio is reviewed at regular intervals, but adjustments are only made if deviations exceed acceptable limits.

Rebalancing may involve selling outperforming assets and reinvesting in underweighted categories—effectively buying low and selling high. It also reduces emotional investing and aligns the portfolio with the intended risk-return profile, especially during periods of high volatility or economic transition.

Investment Strategies Across Life Stages

Investment decisions are not static—they evolve in tandem with life circumstances, priorities, and financial capacity. A portfolio that is well-suited for an individual in the early accumulation phase may be misaligned with the needs of someone approaching retirement. Aligning investment strategies with life stages enhances portfolio relevance, optimises risk exposure, and supports the broader objectives of financial independence and re-careering transitions.

Each life stage presents distinct opportunities and constraints. Understanding these shifts enables more intentional allocation and decision-making throughout the investment journey.

- **Early Career - Focus on Growth and Risk-Taking:** The early-career phase typically spans the 20s to early 30s, a period marked by a longer investment horizon and fewer financial commitments. This stage provides a unique opportunity to capitalise on the compounding effect of time.
  - **Asset Allocation Tilt:** Portfolios at this stage are often equity-heavy, with significant exposure to growth-oriented assets such as global stocks, ETFs, and equity unit trusts. Volatility is less of a concern given the extended runway before retirement.
  - **Priority Actions:** Building investing discipline, automating regular contributions (e.g., dollar-cost averaging), and avoiding emotional reactions to short-term market movements.
  - **Risk Posture:** Higher risk tolerance allows for embracing short-term fluctuations in exchange for long-term growth potential. There is also room to learn from early missteps with minimal long-term impact.

- **Mid-Career - Balancing Growth with Capital Preservation:** During the mid-career phase—typically from mid-30s to late 40s—financial responsibilities often increase, including home ownership, children's education, and elderly care. Investment strategies must now balance continued growth with increasing emphasis on capital protection and income generation.
  - **Asset Allocation Tilt:** A more balanced approach emerges, with gradual inclusion of lower-risk assets such as bonds,

REITs, and dividend-paying stocks to complement core equity holdings.

    - **Priority Actions:** Reviewing financial goals regularly, increasing investment size in line with income growth, and managing debt responsibly to maintain financial flexibility.
    - **Risk Posture:** Moderate risk tolerance. Greater importance is placed on portfolio stability and the ability to absorb financial shocks without derailing long-term plans.

- **Pre-Retirement - Risk Management and Income Planning:** The pre-retirement stage—generally in the 50s to early 60s—marks a crucial transition from accumulation to preservation and income preparation. The margin for error narrows, and the focus shifts to securing existing gains and preparing for drawdown needs.
    - **Asset Allocation Tilt:** Continued diversification with increased exposure to income-generating assets (e.g., REITs, bonds, annuities) and capital stability instruments (e.g., fixed deposits, short-duration bond funds).
    - **Priority Actions:** Conducting retirement income projections, consolidating accounts, and adjusting investment strategy to reduce exposure to high-volatility instruments.
    - **Risk Posture:** Lower tolerance for capital loss. Sequence-of-return risk becomes a key consideration, as market downturns close to retirement can impact the sustainability of withdrawal strategies.

- **Post-Retirement - Drawdown Strategies and Portfolio Decumulation:** Post-retirement investment strategies focus on generating sustainable income, managing withdrawals, and preserving capital to support longevity and potential legacy goals.
    - **Asset Allocation Tilt:** A defensive posture with reduced equity exposure, emphasising liquidity, income stability, and downside protection. Allocations may include annuities, dividend stocks, and cash reserves.
    - **Priority Actions:** Implementing a withdrawal plan—such as the 4% rule or a bucket strategy—to balance income needs and portfolio longevity. Monitoring inflation impact on purchasing power and adjusting drawdowns accordingly.

- **Risk Posture:** Conservative. Portfolio decisions aim to protect against outliving one's assets while retaining sufficient growth potential to support rising healthcare and living costs.

Tailoring investment strategies to life stages enhances alignment with the broader F.I.R(Re-career).E. vision. It ensures that each phase of life is supported by a portfolio that reflects current needs, anticipates future transitions, and upholds long-term financial resilience.

EARLY CAREER (20s-30s)	MID-CAREER (40s-50s)	PRE-RETIREMENT (50s-earely 60s)	POST-RETIREMENT (60s+)
Focus: Growth & Risk-Taking • Asset Allocation: Equity-heavy (stocks, ETFs) • Key Actions: Build discipline, automate investments, ignore short-term market noise. • Risk Posture: High —time allows for mistakes and long-term growth.	**Focus: Balance Growth & Preservation** • Asset Allocation: Balanced (stocks, bonds, REITs) • Key Actions: Review goals, increase investment size, manage debt. • Risk Posture: Moderate—prioritise stability over high volatility.	**Focus: Risk Management & Income Planning** • Asset Allocation: Diversified (income assets, bonds, fixed deposits) • Key Actions: Plan for retirement income, reduce high-volatility assets. • Risk Posture: Low —protect existing gains, avoid major losses.	**Focus: Sustainable Income & Drawdowns** • Asset Allocation: Defensive (annuities, cash, dividend stocks) • Key Actions: Implement a withdrawal plan, monitor inflation. • Risk Posture: Conservative—preserve capital to last a lifetime.

Passive vs. Active Investing

Choosing how to implement an investment strategy is as important as selecting the underlying assets. Investors can broadly approach portfolio execution through passive or active strategies—each with distinct characteristics, cost implications, and behavioural demands. The choice depends on individual preferences, available time, confidence in market research, and belief in market efficiency.

Understanding the differences between passive and active investing empowers more informed and intentional execution, especially within the broader context of achieving financial independence and navigating re-careering transitions.

- **Passive Investing - Simplicity, Cost-Efficiency, and Long-Term Focus:** Passive investing involves tracking a market index or benchmark with minimal intervention. It is rooted in the belief that markets are generally efficient over the long term, making it difficult to consistently outperform through active trading.
    - **Key Instruments:** Index funds, Exchange-Traded Funds (ETFs), and robo-advisors that automatically replicate benchmark portfolios (e.g., S&P 500, MSCI World, STI Index).
    - **Advantages:**
        - **Low costs:** Expense ratios are generally lower due to minimal trading and management fees.
        - **Transparency:** Holdings are typically well-defined and predictable.
        - **Time-efficiency:** Ideal for investors who prefer a "set and review" approach rather than active monitoring.
    - **Limitations:** Passive portfolios track market performance and do not seek to outperform. In certain market downturns, passive investors may experience full downside exposure without defensive action.

- **Active Investing - Flexibility, Tactical Decisions, and Targeted Opportunities:** Active investing involves attempting to outperform the market through tactical asset selection, market timing, or thematic positioning. This approach assumes that skilled investors or managers can identify mispriced assets and capitalise on short-term inefficiencies.
    - **Key Instruments:** Actively managed funds, discretionary portfolios, direct stock selection, and thematic strategies led by fund managers or individual investors.
    - **Advantages:**
        - **Potential for outperformance:** Skilled managers may outperform benchmarks in certain conditions.
        - **Downside mitigation:** Active strategies can use defensive positions or asset rotation to reduce losses in volatile markets.
        - **Customisation:** Greater flexibility to align investments with personal convictions or market views.

- **Limitations:** Higher management fees, trading costs, and tax implications. Consistent outperformance is difficult to achieve, and results are often subject to manager skill and timing accuracy.

Evaluating Costs, Returns, and Personal Alignment

- **Fees and Expenses:** Active funds typically charge higher management fees and may incur additional transaction costs. Passive products, by contrast, are designed to minimise expenses and turnover.
- **Performance Evidence:** Research indicates that over long horizons, many actively managed funds underperform their passive counterparts after fees. However, performance can vary by asset class, market cycle, and region.
- **Volatility and Behavioural Discipline:** Passive strategies demand patience and discipline, especially during downturns. Active strategies require constant attention, deeper knowledge, and the ability to manage emotional decision-making.

The decision between passive and active investing is not binary. Many investors adopt a core-satellite strategy, using passive instruments for core holdings and layering active positions for specific themes or tactical opportunities.

Selection depends on:

- Comfort with market monitoring and decision-making
- Time availability and investment knowledge
- Willingness to pay higher fees for potential outperformance
- Confidence in long-term market efficiency

Both passive and active approaches have a role in a well-rounded investment plan. When applied with clarity, discipline, and alignment to individual goals, either strategy—or a blend of both—can support sustainable wealth building throughout the F.I.R(E). journey.

Tax Considerations for Investments

While investment strategy is often focused on risk and return, tax efficiency plays a critical—yet sometimes overlooked—role in optimising long-term outcomes. Tax treatment can influence net returns, especially for income-generating assets or internationally diversified portfolios. Even in jurisdictions with relatively low personal income tax rates, strategic structuring can enhance after-tax performance.

This section introduces key tax considerations relevant to investing, with detailed planning strategies explored in **Chapter 10: Tax Planning and Wealth Preservation**.

Taxation of Dividends and Capital Gains

The tax treatment of investment income varies considerably across international borders, necessitating a global perspective for investors with diversified portfolios:

- **Dividends:** Some jurisdictions do not impose tax on local dividends, while others may apply withholding tax on foreign-sourced dividends. For example, investors receiving dividends from U.S. stocks may face a 30% withholding tax, subject to treaty relief.
- **Capital Gains:** Gains from the sale of assets may be tax-exempt in certain regions, while others impose capital gains tax based on holding periods, asset type, or residency status.

These factors influence decisions around asset class selection, portfolio structuring, and market allocation—particularly for investors with international exposure.

Singapore Context and Broader Tax Considerations

Singapore does not impose capital gains tax on the sale of investments such as equities or properties under normal circumstances. This provides a structurally favorable environment for growth-focused investors. However, exceptions may arise if the gains are deemed to be revenue in nature—for example, in cases involving frequent trading or business-like activity. Likewise, Singapore-sourced dividends are generally tax-exempt in the hands of individual investors, while foreign-sourced dividends may be subject to withholding tax in the country of origin but are typically not taxed upon remittance to Singapore.

Tax-Deferred Accounts and Schemes

Investment within tax-advantaged accounts can defer or reduce tax liability, providing structural benefits for long-term investors.

- **Supplementary Retirement Scheme (SRS):** In Singapore, SRS offers tax-deductible contributions and tax-deferred growth until withdrawal at retirement. Only 50% of withdrawals after the prescribed age are taxable, supporting long-term wealth accumulation.
- **Pension-linked or retirement-specific products:** Similar benefits exist in other jurisdictions via plans like U.S. 401(k)s and IRAs. Each has specific rules on contributions, tax deductibility, and withdrawals, so globally mobile individuals must understand local implications.

These schemes are helpful in supporting the F.I.R(Re-career).E. objective by enabling retirement-focused capital to grow more efficiently.

Withholding Taxes on Foreign Income

For globally diversified portfolios, foreign-source income such as interest, dividends, or real estate distributions may be subject to withholding tax in the source country. This impacts net returns, especially for REITs or dividend-heavy equity portfolios. Investors holding foreign assets must be acutely aware of cross-border tax implications to prevent unnecessary leakage:

- **Withholding taxes** are commonly applied at source on interest payments, dividends, or Real Estate Investment Trust (REIT) distributions originating from overseas sources. These taxes are often deducted before the income reaches the investor.
- The **availability of double taxation treaties (DTAs)** between countries is paramount, as these bilateral agreements aim to reduce or eliminate withholding tax, thereby preventing income from being taxed twice. These treaties provide clarity and often preferential rates for residents of signatory countries.
- Beyond DTAs, the **potential for foreign tax credits** can offer further relief. Where applicable, these credits allow investors to offset taxes paid to foreign governments against their domestic tax liability, further avoiding double taxation. The applicability

and calculation of such credits are subject to specific local tax policies and the investor's classification.

Asset Location for After-Tax Efficiency

Beyond traditional asset allocation, sophisticated asset location strategies can further optimise after-tax returns by strategically placing different asset types within appropriate account structures:

- Income-generating assets, such as REITs or fixed income instruments, which typically produce regular taxable income, may be best placed within tax-deferred or tax-exempt structures like SRS accounts. This strategy shields the annual income from immediate taxation, allowing it to compound more effectively.
- Conversely, growth-oriented assets, such as equities, can often be advantageously allocated to taxable accounts, particularly in jurisdictions like Singapore where capital gains on their sale are not taxed under normal circumstances. This allows the appreciation of these assets to remain tax-free upon realisation, maximizing net gains.

This interplay between asset type, account structure, and jurisdiction underscores the profound importance of integrated tax planning as a core component of a sound investment strategy.

Tax considerations are not ancillary to investment performance—they are integral to it. Effective tax awareness complements sound portfolio construction and strengthens overall financial outcomes, allowing more of one's hard-earned returns to contribute directly to life goals and aspirations.

For a detailed discussion on personal income tax systems, cross-border implications for wealth, retirement tax strategies, and legacy planning, individuals are encouraged to refer to **Chapter 10: Tax Planning and Wealth Preservation**.

Behavioural Finance and Common Investor Biases

While technical knowledge and sound strategy are fundamental to successful investing, human behaviour often proves to be the deciding factor in long-term outcomes. Behavioural finance explores how cognitive biases, and emotional responses can lead investors to make irrational or suboptimal decisions—particularly under stress, uncertainty, or market volatility. Understanding these inherent tendencies is essential for building psychological resilience and maintaining disciplined execution, especially for long-term investors aligned with Financial Independence and Re-careering (F.I.R.E.) goals, where consistent action over decades is paramount.

Key Cognitive Biases That Affect Investment Decisions

Certain behavioural patterns recur across investor profiles, often leading to costly mistakes that erode potential returns. Recognizing these predispositions is the first step towards mitigating their impact:

- **Loss Aversion:** Investors tend to feel the pain of losses far more acutely than the joy of equivalent gains. This deep-seated aversion may result in prematurely selling winning investments to "lock in" profits, or conversely, holding on to losing positions well past their rational recovery point in the hope of merely breaking even, preventing capital reallocation to more promising ventures.
- **Overconfidence:** Many investors overestimate their knowledge, timing ability, or forecasting skill, often believing they possess superior insights. This can lead to excessive trading, taking on disproportionately concentrated bets, or ignoring fundamental diversification principles, thereby increasing portfolio risk unnecessarily.
- **Herd Mentality:** The powerful urge to follow market trends or the actions of the majority without independent critical analysis can drive irrational exuberance during speculative bubbles or excessive fear during sharp market downturns. The inherent desire for social validation or to avoid being "left out" may override sound rational judgement and a well-defined investment plan.
- **Recency Bias:** Investors often give disproportionate weight to recent events, extrapolating short-term trends into long-term

expectations. For example, a prolonged market rally might lead to an aggressive overexposure to equities, while a recent downturn might push investors to abandon well-considered long-term plans prematurely, missing subsequent recoveries.

- **Anchoring:** This bias involves fixating on a specific, often arbitrary, reference point—such as a stock's previous high price, its purchase price, or an initial valuation estimate. Such rigid adherence to an anchor can cloud objective judgement and hinder a necessary reassessment of current fundamentals or true valuation, leading to missed buying opportunities or prolonged holding of underperforming assets.
- **Confirmation Bias:** The inherent tendency to seek out, interpret, and remember information that confirms existing beliefs, while actively discounting or ignoring contradictory data, can reinforce flawed strategies or delay necessary course corrections. This selective filtering of information prevents objective self-assessment and adaptive portfolio management.
- **Sunk Cost Fallacy:** This bias describes the tendency to continue investing resources (time, money, effort) in an endeavour simply because one has already invested heavily in it, even when current evidence suggests it is a poor decision. In investing, this often manifests as holding onto a declining stock, not because its future prospects are strong, but because of the significant amount initially paid for it, hindering a rational decision to cut losses and redeploy capital.

Practical Strategies to Mitigate Biases

Awareness alone is insufficient without structured responses and disciplined execution. Practical approaches can serve as vital safeguards against the pitfalls of behavioural biases:

- **Establishing and committing to a long-term investment plan:** A clearly articulated plan, aligned with specific F.I.R.E. goals and documented during periods of calm, acts as a critical psychological anchor, providing a rational framework to revert to during times of market turbulence or emotional temptation.
- **Automating investments:** Implementing regular contributions through strategies like dollar-cost averaging mechanically removes emotional timing decisions from the investment process. This ensures consistent investing regardless of market highs or lows, mitigating the impact of fear or greed.

- **Rebalancing portfolios based on predefined thresholds rather than market noise:** Periodically adjusting asset allocations back to target percentages, triggered by pre-set deviations rather than market fluctuations, enforces a disciplined approach. This naturally involves selling high and buying low, countering recency bias and loss aversion.
- **Documenting investment decisions and rationales to review objectively over time:** Maintaining a journal of investment choices, including the reasoning behind them and the expected outcomes, fosters self-reflection. Reviewing this record later allows for objective learning from both successes and mistakes, reducing the impact of overconfidence and confirmation bias.
- **Using an Investment Checklist or Framework:** Developing and consistently applying a predefined checklist or structured decision-making framework for every investment consideration can significantly reduce impulsive or emotionally driven choices. This forces a systematic evaluation of fundamentals, risks, and alignment with the overall strategy, promoting objectivity and discipline.
- **Engaging professional advisors or using robo-advisory platforms to enforce discipline:** An objective third party, whether a human advisor or an algorithmic platform, can provide an invaluable external perspective, challenge biased thinking, and help maintain adherence to a long-term plan, especially during periods of stress when emotions run high.

Investor Psychology as a Competitive Edge

Developing behavioural awareness is not merely defensive—it offers a potential competitive advantage in the investment landscape. Investors who cultivate self-discipline, emotional regulation, and patience are often better positioned to ride out volatility and, crucially, capitalise on market inefficiencies created by others' misjudgements and irrational decisions. When others panic, the disciplined investor may find opportunities.

Integrating behavioural finance into one's investment approach reinforces the broader mindset pillar of the F.I.R.E. framework. It fosters calm, consistent decision-making aligned with long-term goals rather than reactive responses to short-term market noise, ultimately paving a more stable and predictable path towards financial independence.

Investment Scams and Red Flags

In the pursuit of financial independence, it is not uncommon for investors—especially those early in their journey or actively seeking higher returns—to encounter seemingly attractive but fraudulent investment schemes. These scams often exploit the psychological triggers of greed, fear of missing out (FOMO), and urgency, preying on even the most educated individuals. Awareness and due diligence are critical components of a sound investment strategy.

The following are common red flags and warning signs that investors must vigilantly watch for:

- **Unrealistic Promises & Unverifiable Performance:** Any investment claiming to deliver consistently high returns with little to no risk warrants immediate suspicion. Genuine investment opportunities inherently carry a degree of risk-return trade-off, and the absence of volatility should prompt further investigation. Coupled with this, be wary of schemes that publish impressive-looking performance charts lacking independent verification, consistent methodologies, or long-term verifiable data. Historical returns without proper disclosures or disclaimers should always be treated with profound scepticism.
- **Lack of Transparency & Vague Structures:** Legitimate investment opportunities are characterized by clarity and openness. Be highly cautious of schemes that cannot clearly explain their underlying business model, how returns are genuinely generated, or where the capital is being invested. This often extends to overly sophisticated jargon or "tech-washing"—using complex financial or technological terms (like "AI-driven arbitrage," "quantum yield," or "blockchain multipliers") to impress and confuse, masking a fundamental lack of substance or transparency in the actual offering. Additionally, legitimate funds and platforms typically undergo regular third-party audits and hold client assets with independent custodians; a lack of these safeguards, or refusal to disclose such arrangements, is a significant red flag.

- **Regulatory & Legal Red Flags:** Investment providers who are not licensed or regulated by the appropriate financial authorities should be treated with the utmost caution. In Singapore, for instance, the Monetary Authority of Singapore (MAS) maintains a Financial Institutions Directory and an Investor Alert List to help individuals verify credentials. Globally, similar regulatory bodies serve to protect retail investors. Always verify credentials directly with official regulatory websites. Furthermore, be suspicious of investments marketed through offshore jurisdictions or unregulated platforms, as these often fall outside the protection of local laws, creating significant legal and practical challenges in recourse or fund recovery if the investment fails. Some scams even fabricate or misuse regulatory logos, legal statements, or endorsements to create a false sense of legitimacy; cross-checking directly with official regulatory websites is paramount.
- **High-Pressure & Emotionally Manipulative Tactics:** Scammers frequently use high-pressure tactics, such as exclusive "limited time offers" or artificial deadlines, to force hurried decisions and bypass rational analysis. Sound investment decisions require time for thorough research, comparison, and reflection—never urgency. Beyond time pressure, fraudsters often target emotional pain points like job dissatisfaction, fear of inflation, or dreams of early retirement. Overly emotive language, rags-to-riches stories, or aspirational imagery should be examined critically, especially when used to bypass rational due diligence. Lastly, receiving unsolicited investment offers via cold calls, emails, or social media channels, particularly from unknown individuals or overseas numbers, is a common tactic used in scams; legitimate financial institutions rarely operate this way.
- **Difficulty Withdrawing Funds:** One of the most critical warning signs is experiencing delays, restrictions, or excuses when attempting to withdraw invested funds. Legitimate investment platforms provide clear, transparent terms for liquidity and redemption; any sudden or persistent hurdles in accessing your capital can be a strong indicator of a fraudulent or collapsing scheme.
- **Recruitment-Based Schemes (Ponzi & Pyramid):** Be extremely cautious of schemes that primarily reward participants for recruiting new investors, especially when

promised returns seem to depend more on new joiners' capital than on genuine underlying investment performance. These are often classic hallmarks of Ponzi or pyramid schemes, even when disguised as legitimate "affiliate," "multi-level marketing," or "community growth" models.

- **Social Media Pump-and-Dump Groups:** Online forums and chat groups, particularly those on messaging apps or social platforms, may coordinate to artificially inflate the price of niche investments, notably cryptocurrencies or micro-cap stocks, through collective buying hype. Participants are then encouraged to sell at the inflated price, leaving new or unaware investors with substantial losses as the price inevitably plummets. Participation in such groups carries extremely high risk and offers little recourse.

An educated and discerning investor must not only focus on financial returns but also, crucially, on capital preservation and fraud prevention. Incorporating critical thinking, independent research, and professional advice into one’s investment decisions is an essential layer of defence in today’s evolving financial landscape. Being prudent is not about missing out—it is about safeguarding the foundation of long-term wealth and autonomy.

Investment Scam Red Flags: A Quick Reference Checklist

1. Promises & Performance:
[ ] Promises **unrealistically high returns** with low or no risk? *(e.g., "guaranteed 20% monthly")*
[ ] Claimed performance is **inconsistent or unverifiable** by third parties?
[ ] Lacks a **clear, logical explanation** of how returns are generated?

2. Transparency & Structure:
[ ] Investment structure is **vague, overly complex, or uses confusing jargon**?
[ ] No independent audits or **refusal to disclose custodian arrangements** for assets?
[ ] Relies excessively on **testimonials, influencers, or social media hype** without evidence?

3. Regulatory & Legal Status:
[ ] Provider is **not licensed or regulated** by a reputable financial authority *(e.g., MAS in Singapore)*?
[ ] Promoted through **unregistered products or offshore entities** outside legal protection?
[ ] Uses **fake or misused regulatory logos or credentials**? (Always cross-check with official regulators.)

4. Pressure & Manipulation Tactics:
[ ] Subjected to **high-pressure sales tactics**, artificial deadlines, or "limited time offers"?
[ ] Marketing uses **overly emotional language** or rags-to-riches stories to bypass due diligence?
[ ] Received offer via **unsolicited cold calls, emails, or messages** from unknown sources?

5. Access to Funds:
[ ] **Delays, restrictions, or excuses** when attempting to withdraw or redeem funds? (Legitimate platforms offer clear liquidity terms.)

6. Specific Scheme Types:
[ ] Heavily emphasizes **recruiting new investors** for returns (Ponzi/pyramid)?
[ ] Encouraged to join social media/chat groups for "pump-and-dump" schemes?

Working with Financial Professionals

While many individuals pursuing Financial Independence and Re-careering prefer a self-directed approach, others value the guidance, structure, and objectivity that professional advisers can provide. Engaging the right financial professionals can be especially helpful in navigating complex life transitions, optimising intricate tax strategies, and ensuring disciplined implementation of long-term plans. However, the decision to work with an adviser should always be made thoughtfully, with a clear understanding of one's specific needs, expectations, and the value proposition offered.

Key Considerations When Choosing a Financial Professional

- **Clarity of Role, Scope and Expertise:** Determine whether the engagement is for one-off, specific advice (e.g., an investment portfolio review, insurance planning, or a retirement projection) or for ongoing, comprehensive support (e.g., full financial planning, continuous portfolio management, or wealth transfer strategies). Professionals vary significantly in their specialisation—some focus predominantly on investment strategies, while others specialise in estate, tax, or retirement planning. It is crucial to seek those with relevant expertise aligned with one's current life stage and financial complexity, particularly if cross-border considerations, unique re-career income structures, or entrepreneurial ventures are involved.
- **Alignment with Personal Values and Planning Philosophy:** Financial planning is far from a one-size-fits-all endeavour. It is paramount to choose professionals who genuinely understand and respect your fundamental life goals and planning philosophy—be it the accelerated path of F.I.R.E., a focus on sustainable and impactful investing, ensuring a lasting family legacy, or achieving entrepreneurial freedom. A significant misalignment in core philosophy (e.g., an adviser promoting aggressive trading when your preference is passive, long-term investing) can lead to friction, mistrust, and ultimately undermine the successful execution of your long-term financial outcomes.

- **Professional Credentials, Experience, and Character:** This pivotal consideration encompasses three distinct yet interconnected pillars.
    - **Credentials:** Look for advisers with reputable designations such as CFP® (Certified Financial Planner), CFA® (Chartered Financial Analyst), CPA (Certified Public Accountant), or equivalent. These internationally recognized credentials signal a professional's mastery of a standardized body of knowledge, adherence to stringent ethical standards (often including a fiduciary duty to act in your best interest), and a verifiable commitment to continuous professional development through ongoing education. Affiliations with recognized industry bodies also provide an essential layer of accountability and a clear recourse mechanism in the event of disputes or ethical breaches.
    - **Experience:** While credentials provide foundational knowledge, practical experience offers invaluable wisdom. Seek professionals who have navigated various market cycles (bull, bear, volatile), dealt with diverse client situations similar to yours, and demonstrably adapted to evolving financial landscapes. Experience cultivates intuition, refines problem-solving abilities, and builds resilience that coursework alone cannot impart.
    - **Character:** Beyond technical competence, an adviser's character is paramount. Look for qualities such as unwavering integrity, genuine empathy, and clear, consistent communication. An adviser with high integrity will always prioritize your best interests and communicate transparently, even when discussions are challenging. Empathy allows them to truly grasp your aspirations and concerns, while strong communication ensures complex concepts are explained clearly, fostering a robust, trusting relationship. The ideal professional embodies a client-first mindset, backed by a history of reliability and consistent follow-through.

- **Fee Transparency and Incentive Structure:** A clear understanding of how your financial professional is compensated is non-negotiable. Compensation models typically fall into fee-only, commission-based, or hybrid structures. Fee-only advisers, who are paid directly by you for their advice *(e.g., flat fee, hourly rate, or percentage of assets)*, are generally considered to have fewer conflicts of interest, as their recommendations are not incentivised by product sales. Commission-based advisers earn from products they sell, which can create a conflict if a higher commission product is recommended over a more suitable, lower-commission alternative. Always request and thoroughly review a full disclosure of all fees, charges, and any potential commissions to assess for any conflicts of interest that might influence advice.

- **Communication Style, Accessibility, and Digital Tools:** The effectiveness of an advisory relationship often hinges on seamless communication. A good adviser listens attentively, explains complex concepts clearly and patiently, and maintains regular, proactive communication. In today's digital age, consider their accessibility and the digital tools they offer. Some professionals provide secure client portals or interactive dashboards for real-time access to financial plans, portfolio performance data, and secure document sharing. For those who value transparency, convenience, and responsiveness, strong digital integration can significantly enhance the overall advisory experience.
- **Trust, Chemistry, and Long-Term Fit:** Beyond all technical and structural considerations, the intangible elements of trust and personal chemistry are essential. A sound advisory relationship is built on a foundation of openness, mutual respect, and consistent follow-through on commitments. It is a partnership. Consider starting with a limited-scope engagement—such as a one-time financial review or a specific planning session—to evaluate compatibility, communication effectiveness, and overall fit before committing to a comprehensive, long-term advisory mandate.

Engaging a financial professional is a strategic decision that can significantly impact your financial trajectory. The right adviser, with the necessary credentials, experience, and character, acts as a catalyst for clarity, confidence, and disciplined execution of your F.I.R(Re-career).E. journey. However, the ultimate responsibility for the vision and direction remains firmly with you. An effective adviser is a partner, but the process must always be client-led.

Summary

Chapter 8: Investment Strategies for Financial Growth provides a comprehensive, practical, and mindset-shifting guide to investing as a key pillar in your F.I.R(Re-career).E. journey. This chapter moves beyond basic financial literacy to equip readers with the knowledge and frameworks necessary to build long-term wealth, grow passive income, and achieve financial independence with intention.

We begin by breaking down investment fundamentals—risk, return, compounding, and the role of time—before exploring the characteristics of major asset classes including equities, ETFs, bonds, unit trusts, REITs, and cash equivalents. Each class is assessed through a risk-return lens to help readers make informed, purpose-aligned decisions.

Readers are introduced to portfolio construction principles, asset allocation strategies, and the importance of diversification. We highlight how investment strategies should evolve across life stages—from accumulation to preservation—and discuss the pros and cons of passive vs. active investing. Tax implications, often overlooked, are addressed as an integral part of maximizing net returns and long-term sustainability.

A special section explores common behavioural biases and emotional pitfalls that derail investors, while practical tools are offered to cultivate disciplined, long-term thinking. We also shine a light on investment scams and red flags, equipping readers with a due diligence checklist to protect against fraud and misinformation.

Finally, we guide those who prefer advice-driven planning through how to evaluate and work with financial professionals—recognizing that there is no one-size-fits-all path to building wealth.

Key Takeaways:

- **Investing is a Long-Term Engine:** It is essential for preserving purchasing power, generating income, and achieving financial freedom.
- **Risk and Return Go Hand-in-Hand:** Understanding personal risk tolerance is critical when selecting investments or structuring portfolios.

- **Diversification Protects and Optimizes:** A well-balanced portfolio helps manage volatility and improve consistency in returns.
- **Strategy Must Align with Life Stage:** Investment goals and risk appetite shift over time; portfolios should be reviewed and adjusted accordingly.
- **Tax Efficiency Matters:** Smart tax planning enhances net investment returns and extends portfolio longevity.
- **Emotions Can Undermine Logic:** Behavioural discipline is as vital as financial knowledge in achieving investment success.
- **Scams are Sophisticated:** High returns, pressure tactics, and lack of transparency are warning signs—always verify before you invest.
- **Professional Support Has a Role:** Trusted advisors can add value through expertise, perspective, and accountability—provided the relationship is transparent and aligned.

Practical Tips:

- Use a risk-return matrix to map your preferred asset classes.
- Rebalance portfolios periodically to maintain your desired asset allocation.
- Automate investments to build consistency and reduce emotional decisions.
- Conduct regular due diligence on investment products and platforms.
- When engaging financial professionals, assess licensing, compensation models, and advisory philosophy.

In the next chapter, **Property: Wealth-Building Strategy**, we will explore how real estate can serve as a powerful tool for wealth creation, passive income, and portfolio diversification—particularly when integrated thoughtfully into your broader F.I.R(Re-career).E. plan.

Reflection Prompts & Mini Exercises

"Tax planning is not about avoidance—it's about alignment. Aligning your goals, values, and strategy across time and borders."
~ YK Png

---

1. Tax Awareness and Mindset

Prompt:

- *What are your current beliefs about taxes—are they a burden, a neutral necessity, or a planning opportunity?*
- *Do you see tax planning as relevant only for the wealthy or as a strategic tool for all income levels?*
- *How confident are you in your understanding of your country's tax system and benefits?*

Mini Exercise: Reframing Your Tax Mindset

- List your top 3 beliefs about taxes.
- Identify whether each belief is empowering, neutral, or limiting.
- Reframe one limiting belief into a proactive opportunity *(e.g., "Taxes take away my income" → "Strategic tax planning helps me preserve and grow my wealth").*

---

2. Aligning Tax Strategy with Life Stage and Career Goals

Prompt:

- *Which life stage are you currently in: early career, mid-career, or semi/retirement?*
- *Are your income sources (e.g., employment, investments, side income) structured tax-efficiently?*
- *How do you factor taxes into major decisions such as property purchase, re-careering, or retirement planning?*

Mini Exercise: Tax-Life Alignment Map

- Draw three columns: Life Goal, Tax Opportunity, Next Step.
- List 2–3 goals *(e.g., international relocation, early retirement).*
- Identify one tax strategy or structure for each *(e.g., SRS contribution, tax residency planning).*
- Write a next step to explore or act on the strategy.

---

3. Understanding SRS and Tax-Smart Investing

Prompt:

- *Are you contributing to SRS or a similar tax-deferred retirement scheme?*

- *Have you explored the types of investments available through SRS?*
- *How might tax benefits improve your net investment returns over time?*

Mini Exercise: SRS Value Discovery

- Use a tax calculator to simulate how an SRS contribution would reduce your taxable income.
- Research 2–3 asset classes you could invest in via SRS.
- Set a SMART goal for your next SRS contribution or portfolio review.

---

4. Estate and Legacy Planning Essentials

Prompt:

- *Do you have a valid will, trust, or nomination for your financial accounts and property?*
- *What values or intentions do you want your legacy to reflect?*
- *Have you had conversations with your family or beneficiaries about your plans?*

Mini Exercise: Legacy Planning Starter Checklist

- Tick off items: Will drafted? Trust created (if applicable)? CPF/insurance/property nominations made?
- Reflect: What's one area of your estate plan that needs updating or initiation?
- Write down one action step for the next 30 days *(e.g., "Schedule a consultation with an estate lawyer").*

---

5. Spotting Red Flags and Avoiding Tax Scams

Prompt:

- *Are you aware of the common red flags associated with fraudulent tax schemes or "too-good-to-be-true" investments?*
- *Have you been approached by agents promising unrealistic tax savings or offshore investments?*
- *What's your personal threshold for verifying credibility before making a financial move?*

Mini Exercise: Scam-Proof Your Plan

- Write down 3 questions to ask before engaging any tax-related service *(e.g., "Is the advisor licensed?", "Can they provide official documentation?", "Is the structure legal in my jurisdiction?").*
- Note one resource to consult *(e.g., tax authority website, financial professional directory).*

6. Choosing the Right Financial Professionals

Prompt:

- *Do you understand the differences between fee-only, commission-based, and hybrid financial professionals?*
- *What matters most to you in a professional: independence, experience, ethical standards, or alignment with your values?*
- *How do you verify a professional's credibility and track record?*

Mini Exercise: Advisor Evaluation Matrix

- Create a 3-column table: Criteria, Why It Matters, Evaluation *(e.g., "Licensed CFP®", "Ensures credible advice", "Yes/No").*
- Rate at least 3 financial professionals or firms based on these criteria.
- Identify the top 1–2 you might consult and write down your reason for choosing them.

Chapter 9: Property: Wealth-Building Strategy

~ *By* ***Anna Png****. Certified Real Estate Consultant | Property Wealth Strategist | Founder, Churros Factory.*

Disclaimer: *This chapter provides general principles and Singapore-based examples of property investing. Laws, taxes, and policies differ by country and may change. Readers should consult licensed real estate or legal professionals in their local context before acting.*

Property ownership represents different things at different stages of life. For some, it fulfils a fundamental need for security and shelter. For others, it is a strategic investment vehicle—one that enables wealth accumulation, passive income, and financial optionality. Between these extremes lies a wide spectrum of motivations and outcomes, shaped by personal values, financial circumstances, and market dynamics.

When planned and executed with discipline, informed decision-making, and a long-term perspective, property can be a powerful component of a financial independence and re-careering strategy. While it does not offer guaranteed returns and carries inherent risks, property has consistently demonstrated its potential to deliver capital appreciation and recurring income, particularly in stable markets like Singapore.

This chapter examines how property can be integrated into a well-structured financial plan across different life stages—from early homeownership to legacy planning. It outlines the evolving objectives behind property decisions, highlights the financial and regulatory considerations involved, and provides practical insights on leveraging real estate for wealth creation, lifestyle flexibility, and long-term financial security.

The Role of Property in Financial Independence Plan

Property ownership remains one of the most enduring pillars in long-term financial planning. Beyond providing shelter, it functions as a versatile asset—offering potential capital appreciation, rental income, and leverage that can accelerate wealth accumulation. For those pursuing financial independence and exploring re-careering options, real estate offers both stability and optionality at different stages of life.

When selected prudently and managed with foresight, property can support a dual objective: meeting personal housing needs while simultaneously serving as a vehicle for income generation. In the context of F.I.R.(Re-career).E., property is not just a financial instrument but a strategic enabler that supports transitions, sustains lifestyle flexibility, and underpins long-term security.

Real Estate: A Reliable Vehicle for Wealth and Income

Unlike more volatile asset classes, real estate offers relative stability over time, particularly in well-regulated markets. In Singapore, the private residential property index tracked by the Urban Redevelopment Authority (URA) has demonstrated long-term resilience, with prices generally trending upward over multiple economic cycles.

This long-term appreciation potential, combined with the ability to derive recurring income through rental yields, positions property as a valuable asset for individuals seeking to reduce reliance on active income. A well-located and well-maintained investment property can deliver consistent cash flow—supporting lifestyle choices such as reduced working hours, entrepreneurship, or partial retirement.

One of the most distinct advantages of real estate lies in leverage. Regulatory frameworks such as the Total Debt Servicing Ratio (TDSR) and Mortgage Servicing Ratio (MSR) ensure responsible borrowing, while enabling buyers to gain control of a high-value asset with a relatively modest capital outlay. When leveraged prudently, this amplifies returns and accelerates capital growth.

While each property market has its unique dynamics—governed by local tax policies, financing rules, and rental demand—the fundamentals remain consistent: well-selected properties tend to appreciate in value, generate income, and create long-term financial value when aligned with personal strategy.

More Than Just Numbers: Optionality and Lifestyle Flexibility

Property also provides non-financial benefits that are especially relevant during life transitions. A second property might support children's overseas education, serve as a transitional base during a career pivot, or provide peace of mind during uncertain times. The ability to hold, lease, sell, or repurpose an asset offers a level of flexibility that is difficult to replicate with other asset classes.

This optionality—being able to choose how and when to utilise a property asset—contributes significantly to the autonomy required in a re-career journey. Whether funding a sabbatical, backing a new venture, or enabling location flexibility, real estate plays a quiet but significant role in supporting these life choices.

Globally, these fundamentals still hold. From London to Melbourne, Kuala Lumpur to New York, real estate has been a cornerstone in many F.I.R.E. (Financial Independence, Retire Early) journeys. Each market has its nuances, of course—tax laws, financing rules, rental regulations, and demand patterns differ—but the core principles remain: well-chosen properties tend to grow in value, can generate rental income, and can be leveraged to build your asset base faster.

Personal Reflection (YK Png) – A Quiet Enabler

For my financial independence journey, property wasn't the main focus, but it quietly enabled key life transitions.

I bought my first home, a subsidized HDB flat. After the mandatory five-year period, I sold it for nearly five times the original price. This move unlocked enough capital to upgrade to a private condominium for my family.

Years later, with a more stable financial position, I ventured into property investment. I bought a second property, rented it out for a year, and then sold it for a profit to buy a new launch project.

That seemed like a smart move until I ran the numbers. The new property, still under construction, provided no rental income for several years. I also had to pay a higher price and new Additional

Buyer's Stamp Duty (ABSD), which didn't exist for my previous purchase.

A full calculation revealed the profit from this sell-and-repurchase strategy was only marginally higher than if I had simply kept my original investment property. The paper gain was diluted by missed rental income, higher prices, and other hidden costs.

Takeaway: Always do the math. It's easy to be drawn into what seems like a lucrative exit or upgrade strategy, but the real return is only clear when you consider all costs—not just visible profits, but also transaction fees, stamp duties, loan interest, and opportunity costs.

Clarifying Purpose: Homeownership vs. Investment

A critical distinction in any property strategy lies in purpose. A property built for lifestyle is not the same as one chosen for rental yield or capital growth.

So, before diving into property, pause and ask: *Is this a home or an investment?*

1. **Homeownership** provides emotional security, stability, and a hedge against rising housing costs. It's typically not a cash-flow generating asset *(especially when you live in it)*, but it can be a good store of value.
2. **Investment properties** are chosen based on yield, growth potential, and cash flow. The goal here is income generation, capital appreciation, or both—often detached from emotional considerations.

Trying to combine the two often leads to disappointment. The best approach is to be clear from the outset about the intended goals—because clarity leads to better decisions.

Property as an Enabler of Re-career Choices

As part of a broader financial independence plan, property can serve as a buffer that allows for reinvention. For individuals seeking purpose-aligned work, entrepreneurship, or semi-retirement, the passive income generated from real estate can ease financial pressures and provide greater control over career choices.

Property may also serve as collateral for business loans or provide capital for personal development or relocation. In these instances, the role of property is not to replace active income entirely, but to expand the range of possibilities available.

My Reflection (YK Png): *Looking back, I don't credit property with transforming my life. But I do credit it with creating the stability, flexibility, and optionality that enabled me to make bold choices—choices that led me to the purposeful work I do today.*

Property, in itself, may not be a catalyst for reinvention—but it can quietly create the conditions for it. When selected and managed with intentionality, it offers more than just financial returns. It provides a foundation of stability, a buffer of liquidity, and the flexibility to navigate life transitions with greater confidence.

For individuals planning to pivot, re-career, or align work with purpose, these attributes matter deeply. Property can fund sabbaticals, reduce dependency on active income, or unlock capital for new ventures. It may also serve as a hedge against future uncertainty, or as a legacy for future generations.

The most empowering role of real estate lies not in market timing or speculative gain, but in its ability to support decisions that are grounded in values, aligned with long-term goals, and resilient across life stages.

As with all elements of the F.I.R.(Re-career).E. journey, clarity of purpose and disciplined execution remain essential. With the right strategy, property can be more than an investment—it can be a quiet enabler of freedom, fulfilment, and choice.

Building Foundations: First Home and Early-Stage Planning[12]

In the early stages of adulthood, property acquisition typically centered on affordability and access to government-subsidized housing. Entry-level income levels and limited savings present challenges, but the availability of public housing schemes such as Build-To-Order (BTO) flats helps bridge the gap for eligible buyers.

Key Considerations for BTO Eligibility and Planning

For aspiring homeowners in Singapore, especially young adults and newlyweds, the government's public housing scheme provides one of the most accessible entry points into the property market. The most common route is through the Build-To-Order (BTO) system—government-subsidised housing units developed by the Housing & Development Board (HDB), Singapore's national housing authority. These flats are offered at below-market prices and cater primarily to Singapore citizens with moderate incomes.

Securing a BTO flat requires careful financial preparation and meeting specific eligibility criteria, which include:

- **Citizenship**: At least one applicant must be a Singaporean Citizen. If applying as a couple, the second applicant may be a Singapore Permanent Resident (SPR), though additional conditions or costs may apply.
- **Age Requirements**: The minimum age for most schemes is 21 years old. Singles may apply from age 35 under designated schemes.
- **Household Income Ceilings**: Eligibility also depends on income:

---

[12] Singapore's housing policies, income limits, and eligibility schemes are subject to periodic review. Readers are to refer to the latest information from the Housing & Development Board (https://www.hdb.gov.sg/cs/infoweb/homepage) or CPF Board (https://www.cpf.gov.sg/member) for the most current guidelines and requirements.

- 2-room units: Up to S$7,000
- 3- to 4-room units: Typically capped at S$14,000, or S$21,000 for extended families

Applicants must first obtain an HDB Flat Eligibility (HFE) letter, which confirms their eligibility for housing loans and applicable grants. Once obtained, the application can be submitted via the official HDB portal. While policy details may change, the typical upfront costs as of writing include:

- **Administrative Fee**: S$10 (non-refundable)
- **Option Fee**: S$500 to S$2,000 depending on unit size
- **Downpayment**: Usually 20–25% of the purchase price, payable via Central Provident Fund (CPF) Ordinary Account savings and/or cash
- **Buyer's Stamp Duty (BSD)**: A tiered tax on property purchases, ranging from 1% to 4% based on property value

For many first-time buyers, these homes represent both a practical place to live and a stepping stone toward financial security. When chosen carefully and financed prudently, public housing can be an effective starting point for building long-term equity.

Early-Stage Exit Strategy and Capital Appreciation

The significance of a first property extends beyond ownership—it becomes an opportunity for capital growth. In Singapore, BTO flats are typically priced below market value, providing a strong entry point. Once the Minimum Occupation Period (MOP) of five years is met, homeowners gain the flexibility to sell their flats in the open market, often realising substantial capital appreciation due to pent-up demand, location advantages, and general market appreciation.

My Journey (YK Png): Unlocking Value Through Intentional Property Planning

My first matrimonial home was a government-subsidised flat under the public housing scheme in Singapore (HDB). After completing the Minimum Occupation Period (MOP), the property was sold at a price that was more than five times the original purchase price. This substantial capital gain, combined with available CPF housing funds, enabled a significant next step—purchasing my first private property, a freehold condominium.

This transition marked a strategic milestone. By taking advantage of subsidised housing as a young couple and planning for an eventual upgrade, the initial purchase laid the financial foundation for private home ownership. The outcome was not accidental, but the result of deliberate planning—buying with a view to unlocking value post-MOP and positioning for long-term asset growth.

Key Takeaways:

- **Leverage Policy Support Wisely**: Government-subsidised housing schemes can provide an affordable entry point into the property market. When selected with long-term planning in mind, they can serve as powerful springboards for future property upgrades.
- **Plan with an Exit in Mind**: Having a clear intention—such as selling after the Minimum Occupation Period (MOP) to unlock capital—can help guide decisions on property type, location, and financing structure.
- **Reinvest Strategically**: Capital gains from a first property can be reinvested to upgrade to a private property, allowing for long-term appreciation potential, enhanced lifestyle, and asset diversification.
- **Think Beyond Shelter**: While a first home meets basic housing needs, it can also be the foundation for wealth accumulation when approached with clarity, discipline, and purpose.

Fundamentals of Smart Property Investing

Property investing can serve as a powerful vehicle for wealth accumulation and financial independence—when approached with clarity, strategy, and prudence. While real estate offers tangible value, recurring income, and long-term capital growth, it also involves complexity and risk. Sustainable success in property investing is rarely the result of chance; it stems from a deep understanding of foundational principles that hold true across market cycles and geographic contexts.

Across diverse property landscapes—whether in Singapore, London, Melbourne, or beyond—effective decision-making is anchored in core investment criteria: location, value, yield, growth potential, tenure, and financing. Each of these elements contributes to a property's financial viability and its role in supporting broader life objectives, such as generating income, diversifying assets, or enabling a purposeful career transition.

What follows are key considerations and insights drawn from practical experience—serving as a framework for approaching property investment with long-term discipline, rather than short-term speculation.

- **Location, Value, Yield, Growth Potential, and Tenure**
    - **Location:** The real estate mantra "location, location, location" is more than a cliché—it remains the single most important factor in determining a property's success, regardless of country. A well-located property—near transport links, business hubs, schools, or lifestyle amenities—tends to attract stable demand, strong rental returns, and long-term value appreciation.
    - **Value:** Beyond location, a thorough evaluation of value is essential. This includes examining whether the property is fairly priced relative to nearby units and assessing prevailing market sentiment. Strategic investors often rely on publicly available transaction data, historical trends, and comparative market analyses to ensure that the purchase is grounded in value, not hype.
    - **Yield:** Rental yield, typically expressed as a percentage of rental income relative to the property's cost, is especially important for income-focused investors. In developed cities, gross yields of 3% to 6% are common, though yields can vary significantly by location and asset type. In emerging markets, yields may be higher but accompanied by elevated risks such as political instability, volatile currencies, or legal uncertainties in tenancy enforcement.
    - **Growth Potential:** Capital appreciation is influenced by various macro and micro factors—urban planning initiatives, population growth, infrastructure development, and shifts in employment patterns. Investors who perform due diligence by analyzing master plans, economic development strategies, and demographic shifts are better positioned to select properties that benefit from long-term demand growth.

- **Tenure:** Ownership structure—freehold versus leasehold—is often misunderstood or oversimplified. Freehold properties generally command higher prices due to their perpetual ownership status, making them attractive for long-term capital preservation and generational wealth transfer. In contrast, leasehold properties may offer better entry prices and yields, especially when located in high-demand areas.
  From a tenant's perspective, the property's tenure typically holds little relevance. Rental decisions are more commonly influenced by factors such as proximity to work, schools, transport, and lifestyle offerings. Hence, well-positioned leasehold units can outperform freehold counterparts in terms of rental yield and cost-efficiency.
  As lease tenure shortens, however, complexities emerge. Properties with fewer than 60 years remaining may face financing constraints, reduced eligibility for government pension use (e.g., CPF in Singapore), and diminished resale demand. Nevertheless, properties in growth corridors or urban renewal zones—even if leasehold—can deliver robust returns when entry costs are low and demand fundamentals remain strong.
  In summary, tenure selection should be intentional. It must reflect the investor's objectives—whether focused on yield, capital growth, or legacy—and be grounded in local market realities.

- **Understanding Financing: LTV, Debt Servicing, Leverage, and Mortgage Strategy:** In property investment, how an asset is financed often matters as much as the asset itself. Sound financing strategy enhances portfolio resilience, protects cash flow, and enables long-term sustainability—especially in uncertain or rising interest rate environments.
  - **Loan-to-Value (LTV)** ratios, while varying across jurisdictions and financial institutions, follow a consistent principle: the lower the leverage, the stronger the buffer against market volatility.
    For first-time property purchasers, lenders typically offer financing of up to 70%–80% of the property's value. However, as property portfolios expand, financial institutions tend to reduce LTV allowances in response to increasing borrower risk.

- **Debt servicing** is another crucial consideration. Regulatory frameworks such as Singapore's Total Debt Servicing Ratio (TDSR), the Debt-to-Income (DTI) ratio in the United States, or the UK's Mortgage Affordability Test are designed to ensure borrowers remain within sustainable limits. These mechanisms protect both investors and lenders from overexposure, particularly in fluctuating interest environments.
- **Funding sources** also shape the overall financial strategy. Some jurisdictions permit the use of retirement savings or tax-advantaged funds for property purchases *(e.g. CPF in Singapore, SMSFs in Australia)*. While this can provide easier access to capital, it may also impact long-term retirement adequacy. Such options must be weighed carefully, taking into account withdrawal conditions, opportunity costs, and the investor's broader financial horizon.
- **Mortgage types:** Fixed rate vs. variable (floating) rates. Choosing the right mortgage type is a key decision in any property investment strategy, and it can significantly affect cash flow and risk exposure. One of the most common choices globally is between fixed-rate and variable-rate (or floating-rate) mortgages.
    - A **fixed-rate mortgage** locks in interest rate for a predetermined period—typically two to five years, depending on the country and lender. This provides predictability and stability, as monthly repayments remain constant regardless of interest rate movements in the broader economy. For individuals who value financial certainty—such as those nearing retirement, transitioning to a lower-income phase of life, or managing tight cash flow—fixed rates can offer peace of mind. While fixed rates shield against rising interest costs, they may forego potential savings during periods of falling rates.
    - In contrast, a **variable-rate mortgage** fluctuates in tandem with benchmark rates, such as central bank policy rates or bank board rates. These loans provide upside potential during periods of declining rates but carry the risk of increased repayments in a tightening environment. Investors with higher risk tolerance or

shorter holding periods may favour this approach, provided adequate financial buffers are in place. Some financial institutions offer hybrid mortgage packages, combining fixed and floating components to balance predictability with flexibility.
Ultimately, the choice of financing structure should align with one's investment goals, income stability, holding timeline, and risk profile. Comparing packages across lenders and seeking independent, professional advice—particularly in complex or cross-border transactions—can help tailor a mortgage strategy that supports both financial independence and long-term wealth creation.

Fixed vs. Variable Rate Mortgage: Pros and Cons

Mortgage Type	Pros	Cons
Fixed-Rate	• Predictable monthly repayments• Protection against interest rate hikes• Good for long-term financial planning	• Typically, higher initial interest rates• No benefit if interest rates fall• Penalty fees for early repayment in some cases
Variable-Rate	• Potential for lower payments when interest rates fall• Often lower initial rates• Greater flexibility in some loan structures	• Exposed to interest rate volatility• Harder to budget long-term• Financial stress if rates rise significantly
Hybrid (Fixed + Variable)	• Balance of stability and flexibility• Some protection with potential for savings	• May be complex to manage• Requires understanding of both structures• Still partially exposed to rate movements

- **Evaluating Strategies - Buy-to-Let, Buy-and-Hold, and REITs:** Real estate investment offers multiple pathways toward financial independence, each with its own risk-return profile, level of involvement, and capital requirements. Selecting the right strategy requires not only an understanding of market fundamentals but also alignment with one's financial goals, time horizon, and personal bandwidth. Three commonly adopted approaches are Buy-to-Let, Buy-and-Hold, and Real Estate Investment Trusts (REITs).

1. **Buy-to-Let - Earning Income Through Rental Properties:** Buy-to-let refers to the practice of purchasing a property specifically to rent it out for regular income. This model is particularly attractive to investors who want semi-passive income while retaining ownership of a tangible asset that could appreciate over time.

   Advantages:
   - Generates consistent rental income, which can support cash flow or partially fund loan repayments.
   - Leverage through tenant contributions—rental income often offsets mortgage payments, maintenance, and other operating costs.
   - Potential capital appreciation over time enhances total return on investment.
   - Tax deductions may apply for expenses like interest, maintenance, and property management *(depending on your country's tax laws).*

   Challenges:
   - Requires active involvement—tenant sourcing, lease administration, maintenance, and compliance with landlord-tenant laws.
   - Rental income may fluctuate with market conditions or vacancy rates.
   - Property values can decline in downturns, affecting both asset value and rental yield.
   - Unexpected costs *(e.g., repairs, legal fees)* may reduce profitability.

2. **Buy-and-Hold - Playing the Long Game:** The buy-and-hold strategy focuses primarily on capital appreciation rather than immediate rental income. Investors purchase properties in promising locations and hold onto them for years, sometimes decades, with the expectation that values will rise due to urban development, infrastructure upgrades, or land scarcity.

Advantages:

- Real estate has historically appreciated over the long term, particularly in land-constrained, urbanized markets.
- Less pressure to manage tenants or rental fluctuations if not leased out.
- Can be used as a hedge against inflation, preserving purchasing power of capital invested.

Challenges:

- Requires significant capital outlay and financial holding power to sustain ongoing costs.
- May yield little to no cash flow in the short term, especially if vacant or under-rented.
- Illiquidity—selling a property takes time and may incur legal, valuation, and transaction costs.
- Costs such as property taxes, maintenance, insurance, and interest continue to accrue regardless of occupancy.

3. **Real Estate Investment Trusts (REITs): Passive, Diversified Exposure:** REITs offer a way to invest in real estate without owning physical properties. These are companies that own, operate, or finance income-producing real estate—such as office buildings, malls, industrial parks, or healthcare facilities. Investors buy shares of the REIT, just like stocks.

   Advantages:

   - **Low barrier to entry**: REITs can be purchased through stock exchanges, often with minimal capital.
   - **Highly liquid**: Units can be bought or sold quickly, unlike physical property.
   - **Diversification**: REITs often hold portfolios of properties across different sectors and geographies, spreading risk.
   - **Passive Investment:** No direct involvement in operations, leasing, or regulatory compliance.
   - **Regular Income:** Many REITs deliver stable dividends, appealing to income-focused investors.

Challenges:

- Lack of control over asset selection or management decisions.
- Exposure to market sentiment—REIT prices can fluctuate based on broader equity market volatility, not just real estate fundamentals.
- Dividend yields may vary based on underlying property performance or economic conditions.
- Tax treatment of REIT income may differ by jurisdiction and investor profile.

There is no single "best" approach to property investment. Each strategy offers distinct benefits and limitations depending on the investor's objectives, resources, and investment horizon. In practice, many investors adopt a blended strategy—holding physical assets for income and appreciation while allocating a portion to REITs for liquidity and diversification.

Goals should be carefully considered:

- If the objective is regular income and there is an ability to manage property, a Buy-to-Let strategy may be appropriate.
- If long-term growth is preferred and strong holding power is available, a Buy-and-Hold strategy warrants consideration.
- For requirements of liquidity, flexibility, and diversification, investment in REITs is recommended.

Ultimately, the right strategy is one that complements the broader financial plan, supports lifestyle goals, and reflects both current capabilities and future aspirations. Property can play a powerful role in the journey toward financial independence—but success lies not in chasing trends, but in disciplined planning, informed execution, and aligning each investment with purpose and clarity.

Comparison Table: Property Investment Strategies

Strategy	Description	Pros	Cons	Best Suited For
Buy-to-Let	Purchase a property to rent out for income.	• Steady rental income• Asset appreciation • Leverage potential	• Active manageme nt• Tenant risks• Maintenan ce & legal issues	Income-seekers who can handle property manageme nt or engage agents
Buy-and-Hold	Buy property and hold long-term for capital gains.	• Long-term wealth growth• Compounds with time• Lower turnover = fewer taxes (in some markets)	• Ties up capital• No immediate income• Market cycle exposure	Patient investors aiming for future value with holding power
REITs	Invest in a fund that owns and manages properties.	• Low capital entry• High liquidity• No managemen t hassle• Regular dividends	• No control over assets• Subject to stock market volatility	Beginners, retirees, or those wanting real estate exposure without owning property

Exploring Housing Options Beyond the First Home

As financial capacity grows and life priorities evolve, many individuals begin to explore residential property options beyond their first home. This next phase of property planning often involves reassessing goals—be it for upgrading lifestyle, building a passive income stream, diversifying assets, or preparing for legacy and retirement. A range of housing types exist to meet different needs and strategies, each offering distinct benefits, risks, and timelines.

In Singapore, this may include various forms of public and private housing—from resale flats and executive condominiums (ECs) to private condominiums and new launch projects. For global readers, similar categories may exist under different frameworks, but the principles of due diligence, affordability, investment return, and timing remain universally relevant.

The following outline common property types, along with practical considerations to guide informed decision-making aligned with broader financial and re-career goals.

Property Type	Characteristics
Resale HDB	Immediate occupancy, potential to use contra facility, but subject to MOP for resale.
New EC	Deferred payment schemes, no ABSD for first property, longer holding period (~8–10 years).
Resale/MOP EC	Competitive pricing compared to private condos, immediate rental potential.
Resale Private Condo	Capital gain potential depends on condition, surrounding developments, and pricing gap with upcoming launches.
New Launch Condo	Lower initial outlay due to construction period, suitable for investors targeting capital gains within 4–5 years.

1. **Resale Public Housing (HDB Flats):** Resale flats under Singapore's public housing scheme offer immediate occupancy, making them attractive for buyers with urgent housing needs. These flats may also qualify for contra facilities, which allow simultaneous sale and purchase transactions using CPF savings, reducing cash outlay.

   However, buyers should be mindful of the Minimum Occupation Period (MOP)—typically five years—before the flat can be sold or rented out. Additionally, the potential for capital appreciation in mature estates may be modest compared to private alternatives, though newer resale flats in emerging towns may still offer upside.

2. **New Executive Condominiums (ECs):** New ECs are a hybrid between public and private housing, developed by private developers but initially sold at subsidised prices to eligible buyers. They offer a deferred payment scheme—where loan

repayments begin only upon project completion—which can ease short-term cash flow pressure.

For eligible first-time buyers, ECs are exempt from Additional Buyer's Stamp Duty (ABSD), making them more cost-effective compared to private condominiums. However, they are subject to a longer holding period—a five-year MOP before they can be sold to Singaporeans and Permanent Residents, and ten years before they become fully privatised and available to foreigners.

3. **Resale or Newly MOP Executive Condominiums:** Once ECs complete their MOP, they may be resold in the open market to Singaporeans and Permanent Residents. These resale ECs often offer a price advantage compared to fully private condominiums of similar size and location yet retain comparable amenities.

   Moreover, their tenure is typically 99 years, and units are generally well-maintained due to the shorter age of the property. Investors may benefit from immediate rental potential and capital upside, especially in districts where the pricing gap between ECs and private condos continues to widen.

4. **Resale Private Condominiums:** Resale private condominiums offer the flexibility of immediate ownership, without MOP or resale restrictions. However, buyers need to exercise due diligence to ensure the unit presents true investment value. Key evaluation factors include:
   - **Price per square foot (psf) gap** compared to new launches in the vicinity.
   - **Building condition** and maintenance level.
   - **Renovation Requirements and Tenant Readiness.**
   - **Surrounding developments**, such as new MRT stations, shopping malls, or schools.
   - The strength of the **management council and sinking fund** for ongoing maintenance.

   Units in older developments may require significant renovations, affecting the overall return on investment. In contrast, newer resale units often demand minimal upfront costs and are more attractive to potential tenants.

5. **New Launch Private Condominiums:** New launches appeal to investors due to progressive payment schemes that reduce financial pressure during the construction period. Since the full purchase price is not immediately payable, buyers can align their cash flow planning over several years.

   These properties typically incur lower renovation costs upon completion, as they come with new fixtures and finishes. In strong markets, investors may target capital appreciation within a 4–5-year holding horizon, especially when buying at early phases of the launch.

   However, the lack of immediate rental income and the risk of delayed construction should be considered. Furthermore, developers may price future launches aggressively, potentially narrowing resale profit margins.

The post–first-home stage presents a wide spectrum of property choices, each with different implications on liquidity, yield, holding period, and growth trajectory. Selecting the right asset depends on the buyer's financial goals, life stage, and appetite for risk.

Whether upgrading to a larger home, entering the private market, or investing for rental income, clarity of purpose remains the anchor. By assessing both tangible (costs, location, condition) and intangible (lifestyle, timeline, flexibility) factors, property decisions can be aligned to support long-term financial independence and re-career readiness.

13

[13] As housing policies and regulations may change, readers are encouraged to consult the Housing & Development Board (HDB): https://www.hdb.gov.sg/cs/infoweb/homepage and Urban Redevelopment Authority (URA): https://www.ura.gov.sg, or professional real estate advisors for the most up-to-date guidance on eligibility, loan limits, and investment trends.

Comparison of Residential Property Types

Property Type	Key Characteristics	Pros	Considerations / Cons	Suitable For
Resale Public Housing *(e.g., HDB flats – Singapore)*	Immediate availability; sold in the open market; subject to MOP rules	•Lower entry cost •Government grants (for eligible buyers) •Contra facility usable	•Limited capital appreciation in mature estates •MOP restricts sale/rental	First-time buyers prioritising affordability and stability
New Executive Condominium (EC)	Hybrid public-private housing; initial subsidies; 5-year MOP, privatises after 10 years	•Priced below private condos •Deferred payment scheme• No ABSD (for 1st-timers)	•Long holding period •Limited liquidity during MOP	Young couples and families planning long-term upgrade path
Resale / MOP EC	EC that has met MOP and is available for resale; often 5–10 years old	•Competitive pricing •Immediate rental potential •Comparable to private condo	•99-year leasehold\•Limited foreign buyer pool (until after 10 years)	Investors seeking yield and capital upside at accessible pricing
Resale Private Condo	Completed private units sold in the open market	•No MOP •Immediate rental and occupancy •Flexible exit options	•Higher upfront costs •Potential renovation needed •May face ABSD	Upgraders and investors focused on near-term flexibility
New Launch Condo	Units sold off-plan by developers; progressive payment during construction	•Lower initial outlay •New fixtures = lower renovation cost• Growth potential	•No immediate rental income •Price may include future value expectations	Investors with medium-term horizon seeking capital gains

Investing in the Family Formation and Pre-Retirement Stages

As individuals progress into the family formation stage, greater income stability and increasing financial capacity open the door to more strategic property decisions. Priorities begin to shift beyond basic shelter toward enhancing lifestyle quality, choosing child-friendly environments, and exploring the possibility of owning multiple properties to meet both personal and investment goals.

In this phase, housing decisions are influenced not only by immediate family needs but also by long-term aspirations—such as building generational wealth, supporting children's education, or preparing for early retirement. With stronger financial footing, buyers may consider tools like decoupling or trusts to optimise tax positions, enable future flexibility, or facilitate legacy planning.

Residential property choices now reflect nuanced priorities. A home for owner-occupation may focus on tenure security *(e.g., freehold)*, liveability, proximity to good schools, and minimal renovation needs. In contrast, an investment property is typically assessed based on yield potential, tenant demand, nearby infrastructure, and resale prospects. The selection criteria and investment thesis must align with specific intentions, whether for personal use, passive income, or capital appreciation.

My Property Ownership and Investment (YK Png): A Tale of Two Properties

My first property purchase, a freehold condominium for my family, was guided by practical factors like price and condition. I overlooked a crucial element: convenience. Despite its excellent price, the lack of proximity to an MRT station and amenities became a more apparent inconvenience over time.

For my second property, a pure investment, the strategy was entirely different. The emphasis was on accessibility, tenant demand, and future appreciation potential. I chose a unit near both an MRT station and an international school to enhance its rental appeal. I even researched Singapore's Urban Redevelopment Authority (URA) Master Plan to identify areas with future growth.

I also made a deliberate choice on unit size. While a one-bedroom had the highest ROI, its absolute rental income was low. A two-bedroom unit offered a better balance of manageable price, decent rental value, and a competitive ROI percentage. This experience highlighted the importance of matching an asset's characteristics to your investment goals.

Key Takeaways:

- **Clarify Objectives** – Differentiate between properties purchased for own stay versus those for investment. Each purpose demands distinct selection criteria.
- **Consider Location Holistically** – Accessibility to transport, schools, and amenities significantly affects long-term satisfaction and rental desirability.
- **Do the Research** – Use resources such as the URA Master Plan to evaluate future development potential and infrastructure upgrades.
- **Evaluate ROI Strategically** – Balance rental yield, capital appreciation, and entry price when selecting investment properties. Two-bedroom units often provide a good equilibrium.
- **Learn from Experience** – Missteps can be valuable. Reflecting on what was overlooked or underestimated provides important insights for future decisions.

Second Property for Investment: Evaluating ROI and Cost Dynamics

Acquiring a second residential property introduces additional financial complexity. Beyond purchase price and mortgage planning, buyers must factor in ABSD, prevailing interest rates, rental yield expectations, renovation costs, property taxes, and holding periods. Understanding the total cost of ownership is critical to evaluating the true return on investment (ROI).

A simplified comparison between a new launch (BUC) property and a resale private property—each valued at approximately S$2 million—offers clarity on how expenses can significantly impact net returns.

Expense Category	New Launch (BUC)	Resale Property
Renovation	~S$15,000	~S$50,000
Management Fees (4 yrs)	~S$4,800	~S$19,200
Interest Incurred (3% p.a.)	~S$36,078	~S$172,455
Property Tax	~S$13,000	~S$52,000
Rental Income	~S$264,000	~S$72,875
Net Cost	~S$105,645	(After all expenses)

This comparison illustrates that while resale properties can generate immediate rental income, the higher initial costs, renovation needs, and ongoing maintenance obligations can erode profit margins. In contrast, a BUC property offers deferred payments and lower initial outlay, although it lacks rental income during the construction phase. Strategic selection, therefore, depends on time horizon, cash flow requirements, and market timing.

Pre-Retirement Stage: Accelerating Wealth Accumulation

As individuals approach the pre-retirement phase, property strategy tends to shift towards consolidation, preservation, and income generation. For many, this stage is an opportunity to leverage accumulated equity or savings to enhance wealth through property, either by upgrading to a higher-value asset or diversifying into multiple holdings.

Property ownership during this stage often serves three strategic functions:

1. **Wealth Creation** – Scaling up from one property to two, either through upgrading or splitting ownership between residential and investment assets.
2. **Wealth Accumulation** – Generating rental income from additional residential properties or high-yielding non-residential assets.
3. **Wealth Preservation** – Investing in freehold or legacy-grade properties with the intention of passing them on to future generations.

Beyond residential real estate, many investors begin exploring commercial or industrial properties. These asset classes do not attract ABSD and may have fewer holding restrictions, making them attractive for portfolio diversification. However, commercial and industrial properties typically face narrower demand and may be harder to exit quickly during market downturns.

Typical Holding Periods by Property Type

Property Type	Typical Holding Period
Build-To-Order (BTO)	8–10 years (including MOP)
Resale HDB	5 years (MOP before sale/rent)
Resale Private Condo	4 years (SSD applies if sold earlier)
Industrial Property	3 years (SSD applies; limited demand)
Commercial Property	No mandated holding period

Each property type carries specific regulatory timelines and liquidity considerations. These holding periods should be incorporated into financial planning, especially if near-term cash flow or portfolio rebalancing is anticipated.

Tip: Align Property Type with Financial Goals

- **Seeking capital growth?** Consider freehold private or new launch properties in growth regions.
- **Prioritising rental income?** Opt for MOP ECs or resale condos in mature estates with high rental demand.
- **Looking for tax efficiency?** Explore commercial units or decoupling strategies, where appropriate and lawful.
- **Planning for legacy?** Evaluate trust structures and freehold options to ensure seamless generational transfer.

This stage of life offers a unique opportunity to accelerate wealth accumulation while establishing longer-term financial safeguards. When property is integrated with clarity and foresight into a broader strategy—whether for passive income, capital growth, or legacy—it becomes more than a dwelling; it becomes a foundational pillar for sustainable financial independence.

Risks, Pitfalls, and Mistakes to Avoid

While property can be a powerful vehicle for building wealth and supporting your path to financial independence, it is not without risks. Many investors—especially first-timers—are often drawn in by glossy brochures, sales hype, or optimistic projections, without fully understanding the underlying commitments and pitfalls. Here are some of the most common missteps to be aware of, and a personal lesson that reinforces the importance of clarity, timing, and action:

- **Over-Leveraging and the Illusion of Affordability:** Excessive reliance on debt—particularly under the assumption that *"property prices always go up."*—remains one of the most dangerous pitfalls in real estate investing. While leverage can accelerate returns in a rising market, it also amplifies losses during downturns or interest rate hikes. The illusion of affordability often emerges when buyers evaluate only surface-level costs and neglect to account for changes in income, interest obligations, and economic cycles.

  True affordability must factor in the full financial implications: monthly mortgage repayments, potential spikes in interest rates, property taxes, insurance, maintenance, and the possibility of vacancies. During career transitions or economic contractions, holding a highly leveraged asset without adequate cash flow buffers can become financially suffocating.

- **Misreading the Market and Underestimating Ownership Costs:** Focusing solely on purchase price without accounting for the total cost of ownership is a frequent oversight. Beyond the headline price, investors must include stamp duties, legal fees, renovation budgets, ongoing maintenance, property taxes, and agent commissions. These cumulative expenses can materially affect investment returns and holding power.

  Additionally, poor market timing or investing in properties based on emotional appeal or speculative hype—rather than data-driven fundamentals—can lead to disappointing capital appreciation or rental income. Local oversupply, weak transport links, or underwhelming neighbourhood transformation plans may dampen a property's potential, despite attractive brochures or marketing narratives.

- **Hidden Property Investment Mistakes:** While over-leveraging and ignoring total ownership costs are well-known traps, many investors—especially first-timers or those re-careering—fall into more nuanced pitfalls. These may not seem critical at first glance but can significantly impact financial outcomes and flexibility.
  - **Misjudging Cash Flow Reality:** Many focus on gross rental yield without accounting for ongoing costs—mortgage repayments, property taxes, maintenance, insurance, vacancies, and agent fees. The result: shortfalls that eat into savings or emergency funds. Always assess net cash flow with conservative assumptions and buffer for contingencies.
  - **Underestimating Renovation and Maintenance Costs:** Older or resale properties may carry hidden issues—plumbing, electricals, or structural wear—that escalate renovation costs. Investors should get professional inspections, detailed quotes, and include a 10–20% renovation buffer in planning.
  - **Over-Reliance on Capital Appreciation:** Buying solely for future price growth—without rental yield or holding power—can be risky, especially during market corrections or policy tightening. A resilient portfolio focuses first on income generation, with appreciation as a bonus.
  - **Weak Tenant Due Diligence:** Tenant-related risks are often underestimated. Late payments, unit damage, or legal disputes can turn an asset into a liability. Screening tenants carefully or using trusted agents can protect income and peace of mind.
  - **Overlooking Exit Costs and Holding Restrictions:** Stamp duties *(e.g. SSD or ABSD in Singapore)* and capital gains taxes (in many countries) can erode profits. Early exit penalties or regulatory caps may limit flexibility. Understand all exit rules before purchase.
  - **Investing Jointly Without Clarity:** Buying with friends or family without formal agreements can lead to disputes on refinancing, selling, or usage. Always have a written

co-ownership or joint venture agreement covering key decision points.

- **Letting Emotions or FOMO Drive Decisions:** Hot market sentiment often leads to hasty decisions. Emotional buying or fear of missing out (FOMO) increases the risk of overpaying or misjudging suitability. Always let strategy and numbers guide investment decision.
- **Misalignment with Life and Career Strategy:** A property that looks good on paper may not support the desired lifestyle or re-career plan. Tying up too much capital in illiquid assets can reduce freedom to transition or pursue other aspirations. Consider broader life goals.

A Personal Reflection (YK Png): The Cost of Inaction

Clarity of intention is crucial—but so is timely execution.

At the peak of my career and with accumulated funds, I had the opportunity to upgrade from a condominium to a freehold landed property. The plan was clear: sell the condominium at a strong profit, purchase an older single-storey landed home in a growth area, and rebuild it into a two- or three-storey residence to maximize long-term value.

I even identified suitable properties—freehold, underutilized land, near transport nodes, and with development potential. The plan was solid, the financing was viable, and the timing was favourable. But I hesitated. I procrastinated.

Fast forward to today—some of those very areas have flourished. Several peers, including my brother and friends who acted on similar strategies, have seen substantial appreciation in their landed homes, outpacing the growth of my current condo by a significant margin.

This episode reminded me of two key takeaways:

1. ***In markets like Singapore**, flipping property every 8–10 years can be a viable way to compound returns—provided one navigates cooling measures, seller stamp duties (SSD), and selects the right asset in the right location. However, it's not without risk and requires calculated decision-making.*
2. ***Clarity is not enough—action matters**. A well-researched plan means little without follow-through. Procrastination, especially in a rising market, often comes at a high opportunity cost.*

Key Takeaways:

- Leverage wisely; avoid debt levels that compromise long-term flexibility.
- Evaluate properties based on fundamentals, not hype or sentiment.
- Calculate total cost of ownership, including hidden and recurring expenses.
- Align property strategy with broader life and career goals.
- Focus on income generation first; treat capital appreciation as an upside.
- Maintain objectivity with regular performance reviews every 5–8 years.
- Take informed action when opportunity aligns with goals—clarity without execution is still a missed chance.

In the pursuit of financial independence and re-career freedom, property investing must be approached with discipline, discernment, and foresight. The market rewards those who are prepared, intentional, and willing to act—not just those who plan.

Property Investment Risk & Readiness Checklist

Before committing to your next property purchase, ask yourself:

Financial Prudence

- *Have I calculated* ***net rental yield****, not just gross yield?*
- *Am I confident that I'm* ***not over-leveraged*** *and can manage the loan during interest rate fluctuations?*
- *Do I have at least* ***6–12 months of buffer funds*** *for vacancies, emergencies, or market downturns?*

True Cost Awareness

- *Have I included* ***all ownership costs*** *(property taxes, maintenance, agent fees, insurance)?*
- *Have I obtained* ***realistic renovation estimates*** *and included a buffer for unexpected costs?*
- *Do I understand the* ***exit costs*** *(stamp duties, early loan penalties, potential taxes)?*

Strategic Fit

- *Does this investment align with my* ***long-term financial and life goals*** *(e.g., re-career flexibility)?*
- *Am I clear whether this is a* ***cash flow play****, a* ***capital appreciation play****, or both?*
- *Have I considered the* ***tenure (freehold vs. leasehold)*** *based on my strategy and risk appetite?*

Market and Risk Awareness

- *Have I done proper research on* ***location fundamentals*** *(infrastructure, schools, transport, future growth)?*
- *Am I making decisions based on data or emotional?*
- *Am I prepared to hold through* ***market downturns****?*

Operational Readiness

- *Do I have a plan to* ***manage tenants****, or have I appointed a reliable agent?*
- *Have I conducted proper* ***tenant screening processes****?*
- *If investing with others, do we have a* ***clear legal agreement*** *outlining responsibilities and exit terms?*

Property as Part of a Balanced Portfolio

As attractive as property investment may be, it is essential to place it within the broader context of a diversified and sustainable financial strategy. Real estate can serve as a powerful vehicle for long-term wealth creation, passive income, and inflation protection — but like all asset classes, it carries risks and limitations. A well-balanced portfolio provides the resilience needed to navigate market cycles and supports long-term goals such as financial independence, early retirement, and legacy planning.

Avoiding Over-Concentration in Real Estate

Many individuals are naturally drawn to property due to its tangible nature and historical performance. In certain markets, real estate has become the de facto investment vehicle, sometimes leading to over-concentration. However, relying too heavily on a single asset class introduces significant risk. Property markets, like any other, are subject to macroeconomic trends, policy changes, demographic shifts, and liquidity constraints.

Unlike equities or unit trusts, real estate is illiquid. Transactions involve substantial costs—including stamp duties, legal fees, and agent commissions—and are typically time-consuming. Moreover, residential property often comes with holding restrictions and financing limitations, particularly for multiple-property owners. Diversifying across asset classes mitigates these risks and ensures flexibility when market conditions shift.

Property Complements CPF, SRS, Stocks, and Other Asset Classes

Real estate investment is most effective when integrated with other financial instruments. A multi-asset approach balances growth, income, liquidity, and stability, offering more comprehensive financial protection and upside.

- **CPF (Central Provident Fund)**: In Singapore, CPF savings can be used to finance property purchases. However, over-utilising the Ordinary Account (OA) for housing may compromise retirement readiness. It is important to ensure that sufficient funds are left untouched to meet CPF Retirement Sum requirements. From age 55 onwards, individuals must set aside at least the Basic Retirement Sum (BRS) in their Retirement Account before using additional CPF savings for housing. At age 65, CPF usage for further property purchases is subject to meeting the Full Retirement Sum (FRS). Balancing CPF usage between housing and retirement needs is essential for long-term financial security.

- **SRS (Supplementary Retirement Scheme)**: A voluntary scheme that allows tax-deferred contributions, SRS complements CPF by offering more investment flexibility. Funds can be channelled into unit trusts, REITs, equities, or fixed income instruments. It enables diversification while enhancing retirement adequacy and tax efficiency.
- **Stocks and ETFs**: Public equities offer liquidity, capital growth potential, and sectoral/geographical diversification. A well-constructed portfolio of global ETFs and quality dividend-paying stocks can provide both income and agility, especially when property markets slow.
- **REITs (Real Estate Investment Trusts)**: For those seeking property exposure without the responsibilities of direct ownership, REITs offer a viable alternative. They provide access to income-producing commercial and retail assets and can be included in CPF Investment Scheme (CPFIS) and SRS portfolios.
- **Cash and Bonds**: Liquidity is a crucial component of any portfolio. Cash reserves, fixed deposits, and high-grade bonds offer capital preservation and flexibility, particularly during market downturns or life transitions.

When these components are thoughtfully integrated, the portfolio becomes more robust and responsive, better supporting varied life goals—from career pivots to phased retirement.

CPF Retirement Sum and Housing Usage[14]

At age 55, the CPF system in Singapore sets aside a portion of members' savings into the Retirement Account (RA) to provide lifelong monthly payouts. The required amount depends on the desired payout level:

- **Basic Retirement Sum (BRS)**: Provides basic monthly income, assuming property ownership.
- **Full Retirement Sum (FRS)**: Offers higher payouts, typically double the BRS.
- **Enhanced Retirement Sum (ERS)**: Allows voluntary top-ups for even higher payouts.

To use CPF for housing at or after age 55, individuals must retain at least the BRS in their RA. After age 65, the FRS becomes the benchmark before CPF funds can be used again for new property acquisitions. This framework highlights the importance of forward planning—ensuring sufficient CPF balances are preserved for retirement while also using CPF prudently for property.

Freehold vs Leasehold: Cost Efficiency in Entry

Freehold properties are often seen as superior due to perpetual ownership and perceived prestige. However, leasehold (typically 99-year) properties may offer a more cost-efficient entry point. On average, leasehold units are priced 15% to 25% lower than their freehold counterparts in comparable locations.

Assuming both property types appreciate at similar percentage rates, leasehold units yield higher capital efficiency—freeing up funds for other investments or reducing overall leverage. In real terms, the capital saved from choosing a leasehold property can be redirected into equities, CPF top-ups, or a second property. This strategy enhances portfolio diversification and liquidity.

Still, buyers should consider the remaining lease and resale demand, particularly as properties age. Properties with less than 60 years of

---

[14] For current CPF Retirement Sum figures and housing usage policies, refer to the official CPF Board website: www.cpf.gov.sg

lease may face financing restrictions or lower buyer interest, which can impact exit value.

When to Hold, Sell, or Wait

Timing decisions are among the most challenging aspects of property ownership. A disciplined review process—every 5 to 8 years—can provide objectivity and guide rational action.

- **Hold**: When rental yields remain healthy, maintenance costs are manageable, and the asset aligns with long-term goals. Properties near future developments or in maturing neighbourhoods may warrant continued holding despite market lulls.
- **Sell**: When the asset no longer serves financial objectives, or when capital can be better deployed elsewhere. This could include reallocating into more liquid or higher-yielding assets.
- **Wait**: When the market is soft and selling would lock in losses. A deferred strategy may preserve long-term value.

Decisions should be grounded in data—considering capital appreciation, rental income trends, maintenance expenditure, and macroeconomic indicators—rather than emotional attachment or sunk cost bias.

Real estate is a meaningful pillar in the pursuit of financial independence and career flexibility. However, its full potential is realised only when it is integrated with a broader, diversified portfolio. By aligning property investments with CPF planning, exploring cost-efficient options like leasehold assets, and maintaining exposure to liquid and growth-oriented instruments, individuals gain the freedom to make empowered life choices—whether to re-career, retire early, or leave a lasting legacy.

Strategic property ownership, in this context, is not about chasing the highest return. It is about building optionality, preserving financial resilience, and enabling a life designed with purpose and control.

Exploring Overseas Property – Opportunity or Overreach?

The prospect of owning property abroad often conjures visions of lifestyle upgrades, portfolio diversification, or a future retirement sanctuary. Emerging markets, attractive exchange rates, and rising tourism economies may appear to offer high-yield opportunities and low entry barriers. However, international property investments demand far more than an appealing price tag or glossy marketing brochure. They require a rigorous, fact-based evaluation of legal, financial, and operational realities.

There are typically four main drivers behind the pursuit of overseas property:

1. **Diversification** – Overseas assets provide a hedge against domestic market cycles, offering exposure to different geographies, economies, and real estate trends.
2. **Yield Enhancement** – In some emerging markets, lower purchase prices may result in higher gross rental yields, especially in fast-urbanising regions with housing demand.
3. **Lifestyle and Retirement Planning** – A foreign property can offer holiday flexibility or serve as a long-term retirement base with a slower pace of life or lower living costs.
4. **Currency and Market Arbitrage** – Investing in undervalued foreign currencies or lower-cost markets can stretch capital and potentially create dual returns from both appreciation and exchange rate movements.

These advantages, however, must be weighed against substantial risks. Cross-border property investments introduce complexity in legal compliance, property management, liquidity, and regulatory uncertainty—particularly in jurisdictions with less transparent frameworks or lower institutional safeguards.

Key Due Diligence Areas for Overseas Property Investment

- **Legal Framework and Ownership Rights**
  Foreign ownership restrictions vary significantly by country. Some markets limit land or freehold ownership to citizens, requiring foreigners to purchase leasehold assets or use

nominee structures. Legal clarity is essential to avoid long-term disputes or invalid transactions.

- **Taxation and Regulatory Compliance**
  Understanding income tax on rentals, capital gains tax, annual property levies, and how these interact with home-country tax obligations is critical. Tax treaties may mitigate or compound liabilities. Failure to comply can result in legal consequences and financial penalties.
- **Currency Risk**
  Foreign exchange volatility can enhance or erode returns. A weakening foreign currency relative to the domestic currency can significantly diminish income or capital gains.
- **Developer and Project Quality**
  Verifying the developer's track record, project financing, and historical delivery is a non-negotiable step. Site visits and engagement with past buyers offer important insights beyond promotional material.
- **Property Management and Maintenance**
  Overseas properties require dependable, professional management to maintain asset value and resolve tenant or maintenance issues. Inadequate oversight can lead to deterioration, income loss, or security concerns.
- **Exit Liquidity and Restrictions**
  Some markets impose capital controls, ownership limits for resale, or restrict sales to local buyers. Assessing exit options and demand is critical before committing capital.
- **Macro Risks and Political Stability**
  Changes in local government policies, rising nationalism, or political unrest can significantly affect property rights, investment flows, and resale prospects.

A Personal Reflection (YK Png): A Pricey Lesson from Port Dickson

At the peak of my career, my brothers and I bought two overseas properties in Port Dickson, Malaysia. The decision was based on attractive prices and an impressive sales pitch that promised upcoming tourism developments and high returns. However, our due diligence was shockingly inadequate. We took the salesperson's word at face value, buying without independently checking the developer's credentials, speaking to locals, or even thoroughly inspecting the site.

Years later, reality painted a very different picture. The properties were poorly managed and showed signs of neglect, with malfunctioning lifts and damaged facilities. To our dismay, we discovered drug addicts had broken into the units and were living there illegally, causing damage and even a termite infestation.

Despite continuing to pay our mortgage, we eventually offloaded both units to a local agent for less than 20% of the original price. The financial loss was significant, but the lesson was far more valuable: never invest without proper due diligence.

Key Lessons from My Overseas Investment Experience

- **Never Buy Without Independent Research:** A convincing salesperson is not a substitute for professional advice and thorough research. Always consult independent sources.
- **Visit the Site and Check the Surroundings:** Physical inspection reveals a lot — not just about the unit, but about surrounding infrastructure, amenities, and local demand.
- **Understand the Local Legal Landscape:** Foreigners may not have the same protections or rights. Engage a lawyer who knows both local and international law.
- **Evaluate the True Cost of Ownership:** Taxes, maintenance, and hidden fees can add up. A low upfront price does not mean a low long-term cost.
- **Consider Management and Security Risks:** Without proper on-site management, even new properties can deteriorate rapidly — especially in low-traffic areas.
- **Have an Exit Strategy Before You Buy:** If resale liquidity is poor, your capital could be stuck for years. Always ask: *"Can I sell this when I want to?"*
- **Don't Be Swayed by Hype or Emotion:** Investment should be driven by data, not desire. Ask yourself if the returns justify the risks — in objective terms.

Overseas property can be a valuable part of a diversified portfolio, but it requires heightened diligence and robust financial planning. The appeal of potential yield should be carefully weighed against inherent market and legal risks. When approached with prudence, these assets can offer strategic benefits; when driven by emotion, they can become costly distractions.

Checklist for Overseas Property Investment

Tip: *If unable to confidently meet 80% of these criteria, pause the decision to gather more information or withdraw.*

1. Legal & Ownership Considerations

- ☐ *Is foreign ownership allowed in this country?*
- ☐ *What are the restrictions (e.g., leasehold vs freehold, quota limits, local partner requirements)?*
- ☐ *Are there any restrictions on repatriating profits/sale proceeds?*
- ☐ *Have I engaged a qualified local lawyer (independent of the developer/seller)?*
- ☐ *Is the title deed clear of encumbrances, liens, or ownership disputes?*

2. Developer and Project Due Diligence

- ☐ *Have I verified the developer's track record/reputation?*
- ☐ *Is the developer financially sound?*
- ☐ *Have I reviewed project approvals and licenses from local authorities?*
- ☐ *Have I spoken to existing buyers/investors (forums, reviews, or site visits)?*
- ☐ *Are there buyer protection mechanisms in place?*

3. Site and Market Research

- ☐ *Have I visited the site physically (or sent a trusted representative)?*
- ☐ *Is the property in a high-demand location with realistic rental or resale potential?*
- ☐ *What are the local market fundamentals (population growth, employment, tourism)?*
- ☐ *Are promised nearby developments already underway or speculative?*
- ☐ *What is the vacancy rate or rental demand in the area?*

4. Financial and Tax Considerations

- ☐ *Have I understood all upfront and recurring costs (legal fees, taxes, insurance, maintenance)?*
- ☐ *What are the applicable property, income, and capital gains taxes — both local and in Singapore?*
- ☐ *Is there a double tax treaty between the country and Singapore?*
- ☐ *Have I considered currency risks (volatility, repatriation, forex conversion costs)?*

- ☐ *Have I accounted for loan availability, interest rates, and financing terms?*

5. Property Management & Maintenance

- ☐ *Is there a reliable and transparent property manager (fees, scope, and standards)?*
- ☐ *What is the condition and build quality of the property (pre- and post-TOP)?*
- ☐ *Who is responsible for maintenance — and what's the track record?*
- ☐ *Are there owners' associations or sinking funds in place?*
- ☐ *Is the property secure and free from illegal occupation or vandalism risks?*

6. Exit Strategy & Liquidity

- ☐ *Is there an active resale market for this property type?*
- ☐ *Are there any restrictions on selling to locals or foreigners?*
- ☐ *Have I considered the potential holding period and liquidity risks?*
- ☐ *What are the exit costs (agent commission, legal, capital gains tax)?*
- ☐ *Do I have a Plan B if the property cannot be rented or sold easily?*

7. Regulatory and Political Environment

- ☐ *Is the country politically stable with investor-friendly property laws?*
- ☐ *Are there sudden or frequent changes in land, tax, or foreign ownership policies?*
- ☐ *Do I understand how the legal system works in the event of disputes?*

8. Personal Readiness

- ☐ *Am I investing based on solid research or emotion?*
- ☐ *Have I allocated only a portion of my total portfolio to this overseas property (i.e., not over-concentrated)?*
- ☐ *Am I prepared for delays, vacancies, or write-downs — without affecting my financial stability?*
- ☐ *Have I involved my family or co-owners in the decision transparently?*

Practical Steps for Aspiring Property Investors

With a strategic foundation laid and key risks and opportunities examined, the next critical phase in property investment is execution. Property remains one of the most consequential financial decisions undertaken. When managed with clarity, discipline, and foresight, it becomes a foundational pillar in achieving financial independence and supporting re-career transitions. Conversely, a poorly timed or misaligned property decision can constrain liquidity and introduce long-term financial strain.

The following lifecycle-based guidelines are designed to support aspiring investors in making sound, purpose-driven decisions from acquisition through to reinvestment—anchoring real estate within a broader financial and personal strategy.

1. **Clarify Investment Purpose:** Every sound investment begins with a clear objective. Properties may serve different roles—capital appreciation, rental income, lifestyle use, or legacy transfer. Without clarity of purpose, choices around location, type, tenure, and financing can become inconsistent.

   Key reflection points:
   - *Is this property meant to generate rental income or for long-term capital appreciation?*
   - *Will it serve as a future retirement home or be passed to the next generation?*
   - *Does it align with broader goals such as financial independence, semi-retirement, or a re-careering timeline?*

   When purpose is clearly defined, the selection process becomes more focused and congruent with long-term personal and financial objectives.

2. **Understand Financing and Total Cost of Ownership:** Sustainable property investing is anchored in prudent financing. Affordability is not solely about the purchase price but encompasses long-term ability to service debt, maintain the asset, and manage regulatory obligations.

   In Singapore, frameworks such as the Total Debt Servicing Ratio (TDSR) and Mortgage Servicing Ratio (MSR) help prevent over-leverage by capping debt exposure based on income.

Key cost components include:

- **Upfront Costs**: Down payment, Option Fee, Buyer's Stamp Duty (BSD), Additional Buyer's Stamp Duty (ABSD), legal fees, valuation, and renovation costs.
- **Recurring Costs**: Mortgage repayments, property taxes, management fees, insurance, and maintenance.
- **Exit Costs**: Seller's Stamp Duty (SSD), agent commissions, and capital gains tax (for overseas properties).

Freehold properties typically command a premium of 15%–20% over leasehold equivalents. However, leasehold properties may offer greater capital efficiency, especially when held over shorter durations or leveraged effectively.

3. **Factor in CPF[15] and Liquidity Considerations:** CPF plays a central role in property financing for Singaporean buyers. However, its use is subject to age-related milestones that affect liquidity and reinvestment flexibility.

Key considerations:

- **At age 55**: The Basic Retirement Sum (BRS) must be set aside in the Retirement Account before CPF OA balances can be used or withdrawn.
- **At age 65**: The Full Retirement Sum (FRS) applies, further restricting CPF usage for property.

Investors nearing these milestones should plan CPF liquidity ahead of refinancing, upgrades, or new purchases to avoid unanticipated funding gaps.

---

[15] CPF policies and thresholds such as the Basic Retirement Sum (BRS) and Full Retirement Sum (FRS) are subject to periodic updates. Readers are advised to refer to the official CPF Board website (www.cpf.gov.sg) for the most up-to-date information.

4. **Anticipate Lifecycle Maintenance and Renovation Costs:** Properties require ongoing upkeep, and maintenance needs evolve with age. These costs can materially affect rental yield, asset value, and cash flow projections.

   Typical lifecycle costs:
   - **0–1 Year**: Typically covered by developer's defect liability period.
   - **1–5 Years**: Minor touch-ups and fittings.
   - **6–15 Years**: Systems replacement—air-conditioning, flooring, carpentry, and bathroom upgrades.
   - **15+ Years**: Structural and infrastructure work—re-piping, rewiring, waterproofing, and layout changes.

   Older resale properties may seem attractively priced but often require significant capital for renovation and carry higher vacancy risk. A renovation buffer of 10%–20% of the purchase price is advisable.

5. **Conduct Rigorous Research Before Purchase:** Investment success is underpinned by informed decisions, not market noise or sales tactics. Evaluate both macro and micro factors:

   Macro-Level Analysis
   - **Economic conditions**: *Is the country or region experiencing growth, stagnation, or contraction?* Economic expansion typically supports rising property values, while downturns may weaken demand.
   - **Demographic shifts**: Look at population growth, household formation rates, and migration trends. These affect housing demand and rental viability.
   - **Government policies**: Monitor regulatory measures such as foreign ownership restrictions, housing subsidies, zoning changes, and cooling measures. Policies can impact affordability, transaction costs, and resale options.
   - **Infrastructure developments**: Planned transport hubs, business parks, or educational institutions often increase property desirability and value over time.

Micro-Level Factors

- **Neighbourhood attributes**: Evaluate accessibility to public transport, schools, healthcare, retail, and employment centres. Local crime rates, noise levels, and urban planning also affect liveability and rental demand.
- **Supply and demand balance**: *Is there an oversupply of similar units in the area?* High vacancy rates or aggressive discounts may signal underlying issues.
- **Rental potential**: Research current rental yields, tenant demand, and occupancy rates to assess income-generating potential.

Property and Developer Due Diligence

- **Developer reputation**: Examine their track record in delivering past projects on time, within quality expectations, and with compliance to local regulations.
- **Project specifics**: Consider the property's age, layout efficiency, build quality, and maintenance history. These impact both resale value and operational costs.
- **Legal checks**: Verify land titles, tenure (freehold vs. leasehold), and any encumbrances or building restrictions.

6. **Evaluate Timing and Market Conditions:** Attempting to time the market perfectly is difficult and often counterproductive. Instead, assess whether the property fits your current financial capacity, long-term goals, and regulatory context.
    - **Financial and life readiness**: *Are you stable in income and clear on your long-term goals?*
    - **Interest rate environment**: *Are you locking in a manageable fixed rate, or are rates volatile?*
    - **Local policies**: *Are there new taxes, restrictions, or subsidies affecting purchases?*
    - **Supply-demand dynamics**: *Is the market oversaturated, or is demand outpacing supply?*

The right time to buy is when the property aligns with your goals and can be sustained comfortably—not just when prices dip.

7. **Integrate Property into Your FIR(Re-career)E Strategy:** Property investing should support, not derail, broader financial independence and re-career goals. If the dream is to semi-retire early, start a passion business, or take a mid-career sabbatical, make sure property decisions are compatible. Reflect on:
   - **Liquidity needs**: *Will this investment tie up capital I may need to start a business, change careers, or take a sabbatical?*
   - **Cash flow consistency**: *Can the property generate reliable income that supports my partial retirement or lifestyle flexibility?*
   - **Time and energy demands**: *Will managing the property distract from my next phase, or can it be outsourced effectively?*
   - **Exit strategy**: *Is there a clear path to sell, refinance, or repurpose the property in future?*

   Aligning real estate with life aspirations ensures the investment enhances rather than restricts future options.

8. **Plan Exit and Reinvestment Strategies Early:** Successful property investment extends beyond acquisition. A well-timed and strategic exit enables capital to be unlocked and redeployed for higher-yielding or more purpose-aligned opportunities. Planning in advance—especially around holding requirements like MOP or SSD—avoids penalties and enables agile reinvestment. Consider the following:

   - **Holding period considerations**: *Have mandatory periods such as MOP or SSD been fulfilled to avoid penalties and optimise returns?*
   - **Capital gains optimisation**: *Is the market condition favourable for exit? Are gains substantial enough to justify the sale?*
   - **Reinvestment readiness**: *Are there suitable reinvestment opportunities aligned with evolving goals—e.g., upgrading, downsizing, or diversifying?*
   - **Cash flow and liquidity impact**: *Will the net proceeds support near-term liquidity needs, such as funding a new property, starting a business, or enhancing income streams?*

   Before any exit, compute net sale proceeds carefully:

- Outstanding mortgage balance
- CPF principal and accrued interest refunds
- Legal and agent fees
- Applicable taxes (e.g., SSD or overseas capital gains tax)

The best exits are not reactive—they are planned with foresight, in alignment with broader financial goals and the next phase of the investor's journey.

Key Guidelines for Sustainable Property Success

- ☑ Define Investment Purpose Clearly
- ☑ Assess Financing and Loan Capacity Prudently
- ☑ Understand Tax Implications (Local and Overseas)
- ☑ Verify Legal Documents and Ownership Structures
- ☑ Conduct Independent Market and Property Research
- ☑ Budget for Lifecycle Maintenance and Renovations
- ☑ Maintain Liquidity and Emergency Buffers
- ☑ Calculate Net Proceeds Before Exit
- ☑ Align with Broader Financial and Career Goals
- ☑ Review Investment Performance Every 5–8 Years

When approached with clarity, foresight, and discipline, property investing becomes more than a financial transaction—it becomes a strategic enabler of long-term wealth, freedom, and re-career potential. It is not about chasing trends or speculative gains but about aligning tangible assets with personal vision and purpose. For the aspiring investor, success lies not in timing the market but in mastering intention, preparation, and execution.

Property Investment Readiness Checklist

Use the following checklist to assess your preparedness before making a property investment decision:

Area	Key Considerations	Checked?
Purpose	*Is the investment goal clearly defined (e.g., income generation, capital growth, own-stay, legacy planning)?*	☐
Budget	*Have all upfront and recurring costs been accounted for, including a contingency buffer (10–20%)?*	☐
Financing	*Are loan eligibility, repayment obligations, CPF usage, and interest rate risks fully understood?*	☐
Research	*Have macro/micro market trends, developer reputation, and location-specific factors been thoroughly assessed?*	☐
Legal Compliance	*Are local and foreign ownership rules, tax obligations, and regulatory requirements clearly understood?*	☐
Property Management	*Will the property be self-managed or outsourced? Are operational responsibilities clearly assigned?*	☐
Exit Strategy	*Is there a defined plan for exit—resale, rental repurposing, or holding? Are MOP/SSD periods factored in?*	☐
FIR(Re-career)E Fit	*Does this investment support broader goals of financial independence and career flexibility?*	☐

Summary

Chapter 9: Property – A Wealth-Building Strategy provides a comprehensive and lifecycle-aligned exploration of how property can serve as both a foundational asset and a strategic enabler in the journey toward Financial Independence and Re-careering (F.I.R(Re-career).E.). Far beyond bricks and mortar, property is reframed as a versatile financial instrument—capable of generating income, preserving capital, and supporting transitions across life stages.

The chapter begins by examining the role of property within a broader financial plan, addressing how it offers capital appreciation, income potential, and long-term utility when acquired and managed with clarity. The distinction between homeownership versus investment property is emphasised, encouraging readers to define intent early in the decision-making process.

Property is also positioned as an enabler of re-career flexibility—whether by unlocking capital from a first home, generating rental income for semi-retirement, or reducing financial pressure during entrepreneurial ventures. Readers are guided through early-stage considerations such as BTO eligibility, first-home planning, and early capital appreciation strategies.

The core of the chapter outlines the fundamentals of smart property investing, including valuation, tenure, financing strategies, and cost-efficiency. Important distinctions are drawn between freehold and leasehold properties, and practical trade-offs in entry cost and return potential are explained. CPF usage is explored in detail, especially in light of retirement account requirements at age 55 and 65, and how these may affect liquidity planning.

At various life stages—from family formation to pre-retirement—the chapter provides tailored guidance on portfolio scaling, evaluating ROI for a second property, and assessing the risks and benefits of accelerated property investment. This includes insights on renovation cycles, maintenance costs by property age, and how these impact cash flow and returns.

Readers are also warned against common pitfalls such as over-concentration in real estate, ignoring exit planning, or falling prey to emotionally driven purchases. The chapter encourages diversification and offers a clear view of how property fits into a balanced investment portfolio, complementing instruments such as CPF, SRS, equities, and insurance.

Special sections address when to hold, sell, or wait, and the potential and pitfalls of overseas property investing. The chapter closes with practical steps for aspiring property investors, including a readiness checklist and a structured framework to align each property decision with the reader's financial vision and re-career aspirations.

Key Takeaways:

- **Purpose Before Purchase:** Clarify whether a property serves lifestyle needs, income generation, capital growth, or legacy planning.
- **Lifecycle Planning Matters:** Property decisions should align with evolving priorities across different life stages—first home, family expansion, or retirement readiness.
- **CPF Strategy Is Integral:** Understand how CPF usage rules change over time and their impact on liquidity and affordability.
- **Financing Must Be Prudent:** Leverage enhances returns but also raises risks. Always plan within sustainable debt thresholds.
- **Total Cost of Ownership:** Consider upfront, recurring, and exit costs—including renovation, maintenance, taxes, and CPF refunds.
- **Portfolio Balance Is Key:** Property should complement—not dominate—your financial portfolio. Consider asset mix, liquidity, and risk.
- **Exit Planning Is Essential:** Always plan your exit and reinvestment strategy early—account for MOP, SSD, and market timing.
- **Overseas Property Caution:** Perform rigorous due diligence when considering global markets. Understand legal systems, taxes, and currency risk.
- **Avoid Emotional Decisions:** Stay grounded in data, research, and long-term objectives—not market noise or peer pressure.

Practical Tips:

- Use a **property readiness checklist** covering purpose, financing, research, legal compliance, and FIR(Re-career)E alignment.

- Review **CPF policies and property affordability limits**, especially near milestone ages (55 and 65).
- Understand **housing options beyond the first home** and evaluate cost-efficiency of upgrading versus investing.
- Regularly assess the **role of real estate in your broader asset portfolio** and rebalance if needed to maintain diversification.
- Factor in **maintenance cycles** and reserve funds for older properties to avoid cash flow strain.
- Revisit your **exit strategy every 5–8 years**, considering life stage, market conditions, and liquidity needs.

In the next chapter, **Tax Planning and Wealth Preservation**, we shift focus from wealth accumulation to wealth structuring. You'll learn how to manage your assets tax-efficiently, protect intergenerational wealth, and make informed decisions around legacy planning—ensuring your FIR(Re-career)E plan remains sustainable across time and borders.

Reflection Prompts & Mini Exercises

"Property isn't just about ownership—it's about optionality, stability, and the freedom to live, work, and re-career on your terms." ~ YK Png

---

1. Clarifying Your Property Purpose

Prompt:

- *Is your next property for income, growth, lifestyle, or legacy?*
- *How does this property align with your long-term life and financial aspirations?*
- *Are you purchasing based on strategy or influenced by emotion, trends, or peer pressure?*

Mini Exercise: Property Intent Statement

- Write a one-sentence purpose statement for your next property.
- Add two supporting goals *(e.g., "To fund partial retirement by generating $3,000/month passive income.")*
- Ask: *Does this purpose align with my FIR(Re-career)E timeline and current financial state?*

---

2. Assessing Property Readiness Across Life Stages

Prompt:

- *Are your finances, CPF usage, and loan eligibility aligned with the scale of investment?*
- *Have you factored in total costs—upfront, ongoing, and exit?*
- *Are you accounting for CPF liquidity restrictions at age 55 and 65?*

Mini Exercise: Life-Stage Readiness Check

- List your current life stage *(e.g., single professional, young family, pre-retiree).*
- Note key financial readiness areas: Budget, CPF access, Debt servicing, Maintenance cost expectations.
- Identify one critical action to strengthen your readiness *(e.g., "Review CPF RA balance before age 55 for refinancing flexibility.")*

---

3. **Planning for Reinvestment and Exit**

Prompt:

- *Do you have an exit strategy for each property—sell, refinance, rent, repurpose?*
- *How are you timing exits with key regulatory milestones like MOP or SSD expiry?*
- *Are you proactively planning how to redeploy gains?*

Mini Exercise: Exit & Reinvestment Mapping

- Choose one property (owned or planned).
- Map out the estimated holding period, regulatory timelines *(e.g., MOP, SSD)*, and exit options.
- Identify one reinvestment scenario aligned with your FIR(Re-career)E goals.

---

4. **Avoiding Over-Concentration in Real Estate**

Prompt:

- *What percentage of your total net worth is in property?*
- *Are you overly dependent on rental income or unrealised capital gains?*
- *Could this limit your agility in a career shift?*

Mini Exercise: Asset Allocation Snapshot

- List your assets across categories: Property, CPF/SRS, Stocks, Bonds, Cash, Business Interests.
- Estimate the percentage allocation.
- Highlight one diversification opportunity *(e.g., reallocating from property into a REIT, equities, or SRS contribution)*.

---

5. **Evaluating Overseas Property Aspirations**

Prompt:

- *What draws you to overseas real estate—yield, lifestyle, diversification, status?*
- *Have you considered the legal, tax, currency, and management implications?*
- *Are you prepared for the complexity and distance involved?*

Mini Exercise: Overseas Investment Readiness Quiz

- Score yourself (1–5) on the following:
  - Local legal & tax knowledge.
  - Currency and financing exposure.
  - Management plan (local agent, property manager).
  - Exit options and timeline.
  - Comfort with geopolitical and market risk.
- Reflect on which areas need strengthening before proceeding.

---

6. Aligning Property Strategy with Re-career Vision

Prompt:

- *Does your current or future property portfolio give you financial and lifestyle flexibility?*
- *Are you planning for liquidity and cash flow to support transitions such as sabbaticals, entrepreneurship, or reduced work hours?*
- *Are your properties assets or obligations during re-career phases?*

Mini Exercise: Property-Life Integration Map

- Write down three career or lifestyle goals *(e.g., "Take 6-month break at 45," "Start a consultancy by 50," "Live abroad for 2 years").*
- For each, assess how your property holdings support, hinder, or are neutral to that goal.
- Identify one change to improve alignment *(e.g., "Sell underutilised unit to unlock capital for business pivot.")*

Chapter 10: Tax Planning and Wealth Preservation

"Tax planning isn't about avoidance, it's about awareness, alignment, and taking control of your financial destiny." ~ *YK Png*

> ***Disclaimer:*** *This chapter discusses general tax planning concepts and may reference Singapore's framework. Tax laws vary across jurisdictions and change over time. Readers should consult qualified tax advisors for accurate, up-to-date, and personalized guidance.*

When contemplating financial planning, the common focus often lies on increasing income, diligent saving, or astute investing. However, one of the most overlooked—and underestimated—instruments in building and preserving wealth is strategic tax planning. This isn't solely for the affluent or the self-employed. Whether an individual is a salaried employee, a freelancer, a business owner, or someone mapping out a re-career transition, comprehending how taxes affect income, investments, and legacy can be the pivotal factor between merely managing finances and attaining genuine financial independence.

In Singapore, there is the advantage of a relatively straightforward and attractive tax system, characterized by no capital gains tax, no estate duties, and competitive personal income tax rates. Despite this tax-friendly environment, many still incur higher tax liabilities than necessary due to a lack of awareness regarding available reliefs, schemes, or intelligent structuring opportunities. For an international audience, the tax landscape may present greater complexity, involving capital gains, inheritance taxes, or cross-border reporting obligations that demand meticulous navigation. Irrespective of jurisdiction, insufficient tax awareness frequently leads to funds unnecessarily diminishing one's long-term financial plan.

This chapter will delve into how tax planning transcends mere liability reduction. It involves aligning financial decisions with established regulations, ensuring that more earned income is retained, investments are made with greater purpose, and wealth is preserved for individuals and causes of significance. Beyond tax considerations, the discussion will extend to wealth preservation and legacy planning—areas often deferred, yet crucial for a holistic F.I.R(Re-career).E journey.

Whether based in Singapore or planning to live, work, or invest internationally, this chapter aims to provide the principles, practical tools, and key considerations necessary to integrate tax and estate planning into one's life strategy—transforming it from a sporadic, once-a-year thought into a continuous, fundamental element.

The Role of Tax Planning in Financial Independence

While wealth accumulation often takes centre stage in financial planning, how much of that wealth you retain ultimately hinges on tax efficiency. Taxes—though often viewed as a compliance necessity—can significantly influence investment returns, cash flow, and the pace at which financial goals are achieved.

Strategic tax planning, when integrated into broader life and career transitions, becomes a powerful enabler for financial independence. It is not merely about reducing liabilities but about structuring income, investments, and assets in ways that preserve capital, enhance flexibility, and support long-term aspirations.

My Journey: The Role of Tax Planning

For much of my career, like many Singaporeans, I took a passive approach to tax. I contributed to the Supplementary Retirement Scheme (SRS), claimed applicable reliefs during tax filing, and made occasional donations to benefit from tax deductions, but I didn't think of tax planning as a strategic lever in my financial journey. Only later did I realize that while Singapore's tax regime is relatively straightforward and low compared to many other countries, there is still room to optimize, especially as one accumulate assets, transition careers, or diversify income streams.

Key Takeaways:

- **Tax Is a Strategic Pillar, Not Just a Compliance Exercise:** Adopting a proactive mindset unlocks long-term savings and wealth optimization.
- **Even in Low-Tax Jurisdictions, Planning Matters:** Singapore's tax regime offers meaningful opportunities for optimization—through reliefs, deductions, and structuring income and assets smartly.
- **Strategic Tax Planning Evolves with Life Stages:** As income sources diversify and career transitions occur, tax strategies should be reviewed and realigned accordingly.
- **SRS and Donations Are Entry Points—Not the Endgame:** Holistic planning involves integrating tax decisions with investment, estate, and retirement strategies.
- **Small Tax Decisions Compound Over Time:** Consistent optimization—even in modest amounts—can significantly enhance wealth accumulation and accelerate the path to financial independence.

Tax planning isn't about evasion — it's about intention. It's the art of aligning financial decisions with legally available structures, reliefs, and allowances so that more hard-earned money can be retained. For someone working towards Financial Independence and Re-careering Early, every percentage point saved in taxes can compound over time, accelerating the journey.

In Singapore, there is the benefit of a relatively low and progressive income tax regime, and tax tools like the Supplementary Retirement Scheme (SRS) and Central Provident Fund (CPF) offer meaningful reliefs. Yet, many still leave tax advantages untapped. For global readers, tax systems may be more complex and punitive. The principle, however, remains universal: Tax planning should be treated as an essential layer in a wealth-building strategy.

The Silent Cost of Tax Inefficiency

To understand why tax planning matters, consider this simple example: *If $10,000 is invested a year earning an average return of 6%, but 1.5% of that return is lost to taxes annually, the portfolio after 30 years would be worth about $70,000 less than if it were invested tax-efficiently.*

That's the power, and cost, of tax drag.

Even without being wealthy, small inefficiencies compounded across salary, rental income, dividends, or side-hustle earnings can delay financial independence or limit re-career choices. This "tax drag" often goes unnoticed. Even small wins — such as deferring tax via SRS *(Singapore only)* contributions, claiming allowable deductions, or restructuring income — can have a cumulative impact on net worth.

Common Myths About Tax Planning

Despite its importance, tax planning is often misunderstood or overlooked. Let's debunk some common myths that may be holding individuals back:

Myth 1: ***"I don't earn enough to worry about tax planning."***

- **Truth:** Tax planning yields the most meaningful long-term benefits for those with modest or growing incomes due to the incredible power of compounding. Every dollar saved is a dollar reinvested, accelerating wealth growth. For freelancers, understanding deductible business expenses can lower tax liability significantly, redirecting capital toward investments.

Myth 2: ***"Tax planning is only for the wealthy."***

- **Truth:** Tax efficiency is often far more critical during the wealth-building phase than it is in the preservation phase. When actively accumulating assets, tax savings directly boost cash flow and compounding power. Even in the distribution phase (e.g., semi-retirees), structuring income from dividends, rental, or freelance work efficiently extends the longevity of assets.

Myth 3: ***"Tax planning is a once-a-year exercise."***

- **Truth:** While illegal schemes are risky, legitimate tax-saving strategies are often simple and accessible. These include making contributions to recognized retirement plans (CPF/SRS in Singapore), claiming available credits, or employing simple investment techniques like tax-loss harvesting. The key lies in understanding and diligently applying what is legal and demonstrably beneficial.

Myth 5: ***"I'm retired (or semi-retired)—taxes don't affect me anymore."***

- **Truth:** Even after retirement, tax efficiency matters—perhaps more than ever. How income streams (dividends, rental, consulting) are timed and structured can significantly influence tax liability and asset longevity.

By breaking free from these common myths, individuals can begin to see tax planning not as a burden, but as a strategic tool for wealth preservation and financial independence.

How Tax Strategies Evolve Across Life Stages

Tax planning is not a static, one-time exercise. It should evolve with income sources, family situation, and financial goals.

- **Early Career (Wealth Accumulation)**: Learning to claim available reliefs, file accurately, and make use of SRS or CPF top-ups. If single, deductions may still qualify via donations or course fee reliefs.
- **Mid-Career / Peak Earning Years**: Beginning to evaluate whether income structure can be optimized *(e.g., salary vs. bonus timing)*, exploring allowable reliefs for dependents, and considering investments that provide tax-efficiency.
- **Transition / Re-career Phase**: As income becomes more flexible — from consulting, freelancing, or investment income — understanding how different income streams are taxed becomes crucial. Business expenses, GST registration, and income timing now matter more.

- **Financial Independence / Legacy Phase**: At At this stage, tax planning focuses on wealth preservation, estate planning, and efficient distribution. Even in Singapore, where estate duty has been abolished, nomination structures for CPF and insurance need to be reviewed, and for global investors, cross-border tax issues should be considered.

<u>Tax Planning Readiness Checklist</u>

Item	Description	Status
Do you know your current tax bracket?	Understand how your income is taxed based on your residency and earnings.	☑ / ✗
Are you fully utilising available tax reliefs and rebates?	*E.g., earned income relief, spouse/parent relief, course fees, NSman relief, etc.*	☑ / ✗
Have you considered CPF top-ups or SRS contributions for tax relief?	These schemes offer immediate tax savings and long-term retirement benefits.	☑ / ✗
Do you claim allowable deductions for insurance, donations, or medical expenses (if applicable)?	These can reduce your taxable income.	☑ / ✗
Do you maintain proper documentation for deductible expenses (especially if self-employed)?	Required in case of audits or reviews.	☑ / ✗
Do you understand how taxes affect different income types (e.g., employment, rental, dividends)?	Different sources may be taxed differently.	☑ / ✗
Do you have any overseas income or assets that may have tax implications?	Be aware of reporting and double taxation agreements.	☑ / ✗
Are you preparing for how taxes will impact your re-career income and retirement drawdown?	Planning now can reduce tax drag later.	☑ / ✗

Navigating the Tax Landscape

A well-informed tax strategy is an essential component of any long-term financial independence and re-career plan. While tax laws and rates differ across jurisdictions, several universal principles apply: optimizing efficiency, minimizing tax leakage, and aligning decisions with one's financial and life transitions. The following overview highlights key considerations that help investors and professionals make better-informed, forward-looking decisions *(applicable mainly to Singapore).*

- **Tax Residency Status:** Tax residency status directly influences tax rates, available reliefs, and reporting obligations. Tax residents often enjoy progressive tax rates and eligibility for various personal reliefs, whereas non-residents may be subject to flat rates with limited reliefs. This is especially relevant for mobile professionals and those navigating career transitions across borders.

- **Personal Income Tax:** Most personal income tax systems adopt a progressive structure, making them favourable for early-stage professionals or those with fluctuating incomes. Annual filing deadlines must be strictly observed to avoid penalties.

- **Allowable Reliefs, Rebates, and Deductions:** Systematic use of available reliefs can materially reduce taxable income. Common categories include:
    - Family-related reliefs (dependents, spouses, parents).
    - Education and upskilling *(e.g., course fee relief)*.
    - Approved charitable donations (often eligible for enhanced deductions).

- **Retirement Accounts and Voluntary Top-Ups:** Structured retirement savings schemes offer valuable opportunities for tax efficiency through mandatory contributions and strategic voluntary top-ups *(e.g., CPF)*. Strategic top-ups, particularly near year-end, can provide both compounding benefits and tax savings.

- **Supplementary Retirement Scheme (SRS) and Tax Deferral:** Voluntary schemes such as the SRS (Singapore) allow participants to defer tax on contributed income up to an annual limit. Investments made using SRS funds grow tax-deferred, and withdrawals post-retirement are often taxed at a concessionary rate *(e.g., 50%)*.

- **Tax-Advantaged Environment for Investments and Legacy Planning:** Certain jurisdictions *(like Singapore)* offer tax-friendly features:
  - **No capital gains tax:** Gains from the sale of shares, properties, or privately held businesses are not taxed in some jurisdictions. This allows investors to retain the full value of appreciation, encouraging long-term investment and strategic portfolio rebalancing without triggering tax liabilities.
  - **No inheritance or estate duty:** The absence of estate taxes enables smoother and more efficient intergenerational wealth transfer. Families can preserve more of their accumulated assets for future generations without needing complex tax-avoidance structures or trusts.
  - **Favourable dividend tax treatment:** Dividend income, particularly from listed securities such as equities or Real Estate Investment Trusts (REITs), may be tax-exempt or subject to lower rates. This improves the net yield for income-focused investors and supports passive cash flow strategies during semi-retirement or re-careering phases.

- **Property-Related Taxes and Considerations:** While capital gains from real estate sales may not be taxed in some jurisdictions, property ownership and transactions are typically subject to various levies that impact acquisition cost, holding costs, and net proceeds upon sale. These include:
  - **Buyer's Stamp Duty (BSD):** A tiered, progressive tax applied to the purchase price or market value of the property, whichever is higher. BSD increases with higher property values and must be factored into the total upfront cost of acquisition.
  - **Additional Buyer's Stamp Duty (ABSD):** Levied on buyers acquiring multiple residential properties or on foreign purchasers, ABSD aims to moderate demand and speculative activity. It can substantially increase the cost of purchase and affect investment viability for subsequent acquisitions.

    - **Seller's Stamp Duty (SSD):** Imposed if the property is sold within a specified short holding period *(e.g., 1–3 years)*, SSD is designed to discourage short-term flipping. Failure to observe SSD holding timelines can erode capital gains and distort return expectations.
    - **Annual Property Tax:** Based on the property's annual value—typically its estimated rental potential—this recurring tax applies to both owner-occupied and investment properties. Rates vary depending on property type and usage.

- **Cross-Border Considerations and Benchmarking:** For individuals with international financial exposure, understanding cross-border tax implications is essential:
    - **Double Taxation Agreements (DTAs):** Bilateral treaties designed to prevent income from being taxed twice in different countries. DTAs help define taxing rights and provide relief mechanisms such as tax credits or exemptions.
    - **Reporting Obligations on Foreign Assets or Income:** Some jurisdictions require residents to declare overseas income, bank accounts, or property holdings. Non-compliance may result in penalties, particularly under automatic exchange of information (AEOI) frameworks like the Common Reporting Standard (CRS).
    - **Currency Risk and Repatriation Limitations:** Cross-border income and asset values are subject to exchange rate fluctuations, which may affect real returns. Additionally, some countries impose restrictions on capital movement or require regulatory approvals for repatriation.
    - **Capital Control Regulations:** In jurisdictions with currency or investment controls, transferring profits or proceeds out of the country may be subject to limits, delays, or foreign investment approval processes.
    - **Withholding Taxes:** Dividends, interest, royalties, or rental income paid to foreign investors may be subject to withholding tax at source, often ranging from 10% to 30%. Understanding treaty rates and whether tax credits are available in the home country is critical.

Tax policies are subject to periodic updates. Always refer to official tax authority websites or certified tax advisors for the most current and jurisdiction-specific information. What remains constant is the principle that smart tax planning is not merely about minimizing liability—but about structuring one's finances in alignment with long-term goals and transitions.

Tax-Efficient Income and Expense Strategies for Employees, Freelancers, and Business Owners

Earning income is only part of the equation. How that income is received, managed, and reported can significantly impact the net retention. Whether an individual is an employee, self-employed professional, or business owner, adopting tax-efficient strategies helps reduce liabilities legally and improve long-term financial position.

- **Maximising Tax Savings Through Legitimate Reliefs and Expense Claims:** Tax efficiency begins with fully utilising available reliefs and deductible expenses. These vary by jurisdiction but often include provisions for family support, continuing education, charitable giving, and health-related costs.
  - **For Employees:** Ensure all eligible personal reliefs are claimed during tax filing. These may include earned income relief, support for dependents (spouse, parents, caregivers), course fee relief for skill upgrades, life insurance premiums (within allowable limits), and approved charitable donations.
  - **For the self-employed and business owners**: Understanding what qualifies as a legitimate business expense is essential. Deductible expenses typically include office rental (or home office allocation), utility and mobile bills, professional development, and business-related travel. Proper documentation—clear records, invoices, and receipts—is critical for compliance and audit readiness.

- **Structuring Income Smartly:** For business owners or directors, the method of drawing income matters. A balanced remuneration structure can optimise both retirement contributions and tax efficiency.
    - **Salary:** Provides stable income, CPF contributions (or equivalent retirement savings), and supports loan eligibility.
    - **Dividends:** May be exempt from further taxation if paid from post-tax corporate profits (as in Singapore), allowing for efficient profit distribution.
    - **Profit-Sharing or Director Fees:** Useful in partnership structures or where flexible compensation is desired.

- **Tax-Smart Expense Tracking and Financial Segregation:** Maintaining discipline in tracking income and expenses is foundational to tax efficiency.
    - Separate personal and business accounts to streamline reconciliation and audit readiness.
    - Use accounting software or digital tools to categorise expenses *(e.g., operations, client acquisition, training)*.
    - Retain e-invoices and bank statements to substantiate all deductible claims.

- **Self-Employed Considerations:** For self-employed individuals, contributions to statutory retirement accounts *(e.g., Medisave or equivalents)* are mandatory and should be budgeted for based on Net Trade Income.
    - **Medisave:** Required contributions help build healthcare reserves and ensure compliance.
    - **Voluntary CPF Top-Ups:** Contributing to one's own or family members' CPF Special or Retirement Accounts can provide dual benefits of tax relief and long-term growth.
    - **Grants and Incentives:** Explore government schemes supporting digitalization, training, or productivity enhancement—such as the Productivity Solutions Grant (PSG) or SkillsFuture Enterprise Credit (SFEC). These tools enhance resilience and sustainability for small business owners and freelancers.

- **Freelancers and Remote Workers:** With location-independent work on the rise, individuals earning across borders must navigate more complex tax obligations. Key strategies include:
    - **Understanding Double Taxation Agreements (DTAs):** DTAs define taxing rights between countries and may reduce or eliminate dual taxation.
    - **Clarifying Tax Residency:** Residency status determines where income is taxed and what reliefs apply. This is usually based on time spent in-country, employment ties, or domicile tests.
    - **Avoiding Permanent Establishment Risk:** Regularly conducting business from a foreign jurisdiction may trigger corporate tax exposure or compliance obligations.
    - **Tracking Source of Income:** Keep records of where services were rendered and where income was derived

Tax efficiency is not a one-time effort—it is a deliberate practice woven into daily business and personal financial decisions. By managing income tax thoughtfully and aligning strategies with personal and professional goals, individuals retain more capital for reinvestment, retirement, or lifestyle transitions.

Tax-Smart Investing and Retirement Planning

Investment returns are only as good as what is kept after taxes. Whether investing for growth, income, or retirement, understanding how investments are taxed—and how to structure them smartly—is essential for building and preserving wealth.

Investment Taxation and Optimization

Tax efficiency plays a critical role in maximizing investment outcomes. Each jurisdiction has unique rules governing how income, dividends, and capital gains are taxed, making it imperative to understand the local context while also planning for potential global mobility.

- **Tax Treatment in Singapore**: Singapore offers a relatively simple and investor-friendly tax environment. For individuals investing domestically, several features contribute to tax efficiency:

- **Local dividends** from tax-resident companies may be exempt from further tax, particularly if profits have already been taxed at the corporate level.
- **Interest income** from approved savings or fixed deposits may enjoy tax exemptions, while returns from non-approved instruments may be taxable.
- **Rental income** is generally taxable, but related costs—such as agent fees, maintenance, and property tax—can often be claimed as deductions.

Globally, tax treatment varies significantly. Some countries offer preferential rates for qualified dividends and long-term capital gains, while others apply withholding taxes. Understanding local and cross-border implications is essential for efficient portfolio structuring.

- **Investing via Supplementary Retirement Scheme (SRS)[16]:** The SRS is a tax-deferred savings scheme in Singapore designed to supplement retirement income. Contributions to SRS accounts are eligible for personal income tax relief, subject to annual caps and individual relief limits. These funds can be deployed into a wide range of investments, including equities, unit trusts, and fixed income products.
    - Contributions are eligible for tax relief, subject to annual limits.
    - Withdrawals made after the statutory retirement age are only 50% taxable.
    - Premature withdrawals are fully taxable and may incur penalties unless exempted *(e.g., medical grounds or death).*

- **Cross-Border Investments and Withholding Taxes:** Global investing opens up diversification but introduces complexity. Investors should be aware of:
    - Foreign-listed ETFs and REITs often impose withholding taxes on distributions *(e.g., a 30% U.S. withholding tax on dividends).*

[16] For a deeper dive on SRS strategies, refer to Chapter 6

    - Strategic selection of investment platforms and jurisdictions *(e.g., Ireland-domiciled ETFs for some investors)* can improve post-tax yields by leveraging DTAs.

- **Using DTAs (Double Taxation Agreements) to Avoid Tax Duplication:** DTAs provide safeguards against the same income being taxed twice. They reduce withholding tax rates and clarify which country has taxing rights, provided correct forms *(e.g., IRS Form W-8BEN)* are filed.

- **Simplified Tax-Efficient Investment Practices:** Even in jurisdictions with low or no capital gains tax, adopting globally recognized strategies can be valuable:
    - **Tax-loss harvesting**: Offset realized gains by disposing of underperforming assets.
    - **Capital gains deferral**: Delay selling appreciating assets until tax conditions are more favourable.
    - **Asset location strategy**: Allocate tax-inefficient investments (e.g., bonds, REITs) into tax-advantaged accounts like SRS or retirement funds.

Retirement Planning with Tax Efficiency

A well-structured retirement strategy considers income distribution in a tax-efficient manner.

- **CPF Shielding[17]:** The CPF shielding technique enables members to maximize the interest accrued on Special Account (SA) funds:
    - Prior to age 55, funds in the Ordinary Account (OA) can be temporarily deployed into approved investments.
    - At 55, the Retirement Account (RA) is formed primarily using funds from the SA. By shielding the OA from transfer, more capital remains in the SA, which accrues higher interest.
    - Post-RA formation, OA funds may be returned, preserving the higher-yielding SA balance.

---

[17] For a deeper dive on CPF strategies, refer to Chapter 6.

- **Creating Diversified Income Streams for Re-career:** In the re-career phase, income is likely to come from multiple sources—including consulting, property, dividends, or intellectual property. Each stream has distinct tax considerations.
  - **Consulting income** (self-employed) is subject to income tax, but business-related expenses can be deducted.
  - **Rental income** is taxable, though expenses incurred in generating that income can reduce the tax burden.
  - **Dividends** from Singapore-listed firms are typically tax-exempt. Foreign-sourced dividends may be taxable depending on the country and whether they are remitted.
  - **Royalties and intellectual property income** may attract withholding tax abroad and personal income tax domestically

Tax-smart investing and retirement planning are about optimizing financial decisions through informed foresight. They extend the longevity of retirement assets, reduce unnecessary tax drag, and enhance the efficiency of income generation in later life.

Wealth Preservation, Estate Planning & Legacy

Financial independence marks a significant milestone in a person's journey, but sustaining and passing on that wealth demands a deeper layer of foresight. Beyond accumulating assets, true peace of mind stems from protecting and transferring wealth effectively—across life stages and generations.

Essential Wealth Preservation and Estate Planning

The focus must shift toward safeguarding what has been built. Wealth preservation entails:

- **Risk Mitigation**: Protecting assets from inflation, mismanagement, legal liabilities, or unexpected events.
- **Tax Efficiency**: Minimizing tax leakage across jurisdictions and investment vehicles.
- **Continuity Planning**: Ensuring assets are accessible, transferrable, and legally secured in the event of incapacity or death.

This shift mirrors the transition from playing offense to integrating defence—ensuring both growth and protection across economic cycles.

- **Foundational Estate Planning Instruments:** Anyone with dependents, assets, or personal preferences benefits from a clearly structured plan. The key tools include:
    - **Will:** A will is a legal document that defines how assets should be distributed, appoints executors, and may include guardianship instructions for minor children. *(In Singapore, the will must be signed in the presence of two witnesses who are not beneficiaries).*
    - **CPF Nomination** *(Singapore only)***:** Ensures Central Provident Fund balances are distributed according to the member's instructions, bypassing intestacy laws. CPF savings do not form part of the estate and are excluded from the will.
    - **Insurance Nomination:** Provides clarity and expedites disbursement of insurance proceeds. *(Singapore offers both revocable and trust nominations under the Insurance Act).*
    - **SRS Nomination** *(Singapore only)***:** Ensures efficient distribution of Supplementary Retirement Scheme funds. Without a nomination, disbursement may be delayed by legal processes.
    - **Lasting Power of Attorney (LPA):** Empowers a chosen individual to make financial or welfare decisions in the event of mental incapacity. Certification by a licensed issuer is required.
    - **Advance Medical Directive (AMD):** Communicates a person's decision to decline extraordinary life-sustaining treatment under terminal conditions, relieving families from difficult decisions.

Together, these instruments form the foundation of an estate strategy that supports autonomy, reduces family disputes, and facilitates timely access to funds when most needed.

- **Strategic Use of Trusts:** A trust is a legal arrangement where assets are held by one party (the trustee) for the benefit of another (the beneficiary). Trusts serve as powerful tools for wealth control, protection, and conditional distribution. Although often associated with the ultra-wealthy, they are relevant for individuals with specific estate planning needs, including:

- Providing for minors, elderly parents, or dependents with special needs.
- Controlling disbursement timing and conditions *(e.g., age-based payouts).*
- Protecting assets from creditors, lawsuits, or marital claims.
- Managing cross-border estate complexities.
- Enabling long-term philanthropic initiatives.

Trusts may be revocable or irrevocable, depending on legal jurisdiction and objectives. Legal guidance is recommended when establishing a trust structure.

- **Inter Vivos Gifting:** Transferring assets during one's lifetime—commonly known as inter vivos gifting—can serve both emotional and strategic objectives. It facilitates tax planning, provides timely support to beneficiaries, and allows the donor to witness the impact of their wealth.

  Gradual, well-documented gifting strategies can balance generosity with prudence and mitigate unintended consequences.

  Singapore Spotlight - Local Considerations: While Singapore has a relatively simple tax system and no inheritance tax, there are local nuances to be aware of:

  - **No Estate Duty:** Estate duty was abolished in 2008. This simplifies estate administration but does not eliminate the need for nominations or wills. Assets may still be tied up in probate or distributed in unintended ways if not plan properly.
  - **Legal Supremacy of Nominations:** CPF, insurance, and SRS follow nomination rules, not the will.
  - **Intestate Succession Act:** If one passes away without a valid Will, the estate is distributed according to a fixed formula, which may not align with personal wishes *(e.g., dividing assets between a spouse and children).*

Generational Wealth Planning and Legacy Building

Sustaining wealth across generations requires more than transferring assets. It's about transmitting values, responsibilities, and decision-making frameworks.

- **Life Insurance as a Legacy Equalization Tool:** Life insurance is a versatile and often underutilized instrument in generational wealth planning. It can be strategically used to:
  - **Equalise inheritances**: When tangible assets like a business or property cannot be easily divided, insurance proceeds can be used to "balance out" distributions among heirs.
  - **Provide liquidity**: Immediate access to funds for funeral costs, outstanding debts, or estate taxes (in countries where applicable) can avoid forced sales of valuable assets.
  - **Create a lasting legacy**: Policies can be directed to fund philanthropic goals or support long-term institutional partnerships *(e.g., education, healthcare, religious organisations).*

  With valid nominations, insurance proceeds can bypass probate and reach beneficiaries quickly, which is particularly useful for cross-border families.

- **Creating Structures for Dependents with Special Needs:** Families with special needs dependents face a unique set of planning responsibilities to ensure continuity of care, financial stability, and legal guardianship.

  Key considerations include:
  - **Special Needs Trusts (SNTs)**: These are dedicated trusts established to provide financial support without disqualifying the dependent from means-tested government benefits.
  - **Guardianship appointments**: Clear nomination of trusted guardians in both your will and legal documents is crucial to avoid disputes or state intervention.
  - **Accessing national support schemes**: In Singapore, the Special Needs Trust Company (SNTC)—a non-profit supported by the Ministry of Social and Family Development—provides subsidised trust services tailored for such families.

This is a moral and emotional commitment to ensure dignity, care, and independence for loved ones.

- **Family Conversations Around Money and Inheritance:** A well-crafted estate plan can be undone by poor communication. Misunderstandings and unspoken expectations often lead to conflict. To avoid this, adopt a proactive approach to family dialogue:
    - **Host structured family meetings** to explain intentions and estate structure.
    - Share the *"why"* behind key decisions—whether it's unequal distributions, charitable bequests, or asset allocations.
    - Encourage open questions and set the tone for respectful, values-based discussion.

Transparency today reduces tension tomorrow, strengthening trust and honoring your legacy more meaningfully than silence ever could.

- **Educating the Next Generation in Stewardship, Not Entitlement:** Passing on wealth without responsibility is a risky proposition. Equip the next generation with the tools to steward wealth wisely:
    - **Teach financial literacy** early—cover budgeting, investing, compounding, and charitable giving.
    - Share personal **entrepreneurial or career journey** to instil appreciation for effort.
    - Joint **family business decisions** *(where applicable)* or introduce investing through joint accounts or mock portfolios.
    - Set up **family mission statements** that define the role of wealth in your collective vision.

Encourage them to see wealth as a tool for impact—to build, create, and serve—rather than a means for consumption or comparison.

- **Leaving a Living Legacy Beyond Assets:** Wealth preservation and estate planning go beyond legal documents; they reflect values, foresight, and care. A well-executed legacy strategy should:
  - Protects loved ones across scenarios.
  - Embeds values and vision across generations.
  - Fosters continuity and unity.
  - Extends financial empowerment beyond one lifetime.

Ultimately, legacy is not just what is left behind—it is how life is lived, guided, and remembered.

Checklist: Generational Wealth & Legacy Planning

Mindset & Preparation
- Shift focus from wealth transfer to value transfer
- Begin family conversations around money early
- Define a family wealth mission or vision

Legal & Structural Tools
- Prepare/update your will
- Make CPF, SRS, and insurance nominations
- Set up life insurance for equalisation or liquidity
- Consider trusts for special needs or controlled disbursements
- Appoint guardians and trustees appropriately

Family Engagement
- Involve heirs in budgeting and giving
- Host family meetings to explain estate intentions
- Share personal stories and values behind decisions

Education & Stewardship
- Teach financial literacy and responsible investing
- Encourage contribution over consumption
- Create opportunities for heirs to earn, manage, and give

Special Circumstances
- Plan ahead for dependents with special needs
- Explore government schemes and SNTC (Singapore)
- Use inter vivos gifting strategically

Global Considerations, Pitfalls & Professional Guidance

As financial independence and re-careering increasingly span borders, a clear understanding of international tax and legal implications becomes essential. Relocation, global investment, or retirement abroad demands evolving tax strategies. Failing to anticipate cross-border regulations or seeking timely professional guidance may result in costly missteps. When preserving wealth and ensuring compliance across jurisdictions, it's crucial to consider key international factors, common pitfalls, and strategies for effective collaboration with advisors to protect assets across jurisdictions.

Global Tax & Re-career Planning

The allure of working remotely for an international firm or tapping into the growth potential of overseas markets is undeniable. However, without a well-informed approach to the tax environment, individuals risk significant financial exposure.

- **Working Overseas or Investing Internationally:** Income generated outside Singapore or investments held internationally may trigger tax liabilities in foreign jurisdictions. These include income tax, capital gains tax, wealth tax, and inheritance tax, depending on the nature and source of income, asset location, and residency status.

  Example: *A Singaporean who works remotely for a US-based company while living in Portugal under the Non-Habitual Resident (NHR) scheme may enjoy a 10-year tax holiday on foreign income. However, However, the crucial detail lies in how that income is received and perceived by the Portuguese tax authorities. If the income is structured or received in a manner that the Portuguese government deems to have a local source, those anticipated tax exemptions might not materialize, leading to unexpected tax liabilities.*

  Key Actions:

  - **Understand Tax Residency Rules of Both Countries:** Defining tax residency is the foundational step. Each country has its own criteria, often based on factors like the number of days spent in the country, the location of primary home, and economic interests. It's possible to be considered a tax resident in more than one country, which can lead to complex tax situations and potential double taxation if not managed correctly.

- **Stay Compliant with Reporting Obligations:** Many countries have stringent reporting requirements for foreign income and assets. For Singaporeans with international financial activities, familiarizing with obligations such as the US Foreign Account Tax Compliance Act (FATCA) and the global Common Reporting Standard (CRS) is paramount. Failure to comply can result in significant penalties.
- **Utilize Legal Structures (e.g., Holding Companies, Trusts) to Manage Tax Impact:** For more complex global financial arrangements, exploring appropriate legal structures can be a strategic move. Depending on circumstances and objectives, establishing holding companies or trusts in suitable jurisdictions can help optimize tax efficiency and manage wealth across borders. However, it's crucial to ensure these structures are legally sound and comply with all relevant regulations in all involved countries.

- **Maintaining Singapore Tax Residency: When It Makes Sense:** Despite attractive incentives abroad, there are compelling reasons to maintain Singapore tax residency while pursuing re-career goals:
  - **Singapore's Progressive Yet Low Tax Regime:** The absence of capital gains tax and the territorial basis of taxation make Singapore advantageous for managing investments and receiving overseas income not sourced within the country.
  - **Preservation of Local Income Streams:** Rental income or local business revenue can benefit from Singapore's favourable tax treatment.
  - **Eligibility for CPF Reliefs and Social Security Benefits:** Continued CPF contributions provide tax deductions and compound growth through retirement savings schemes.
  - **Desire to Retain Ties with Singapore:** Many opt to maintain residency due to ongoing family, property, or social commitments.

- **Planning the "Exit Strategy":** Proactive planning before a permanent move can significantly mitigate tax exposure. Certain countries impose exit or expatriation taxes, particularly on high-net-worth individuals or where pension withdrawals are taxable.

  Example: *a Singaporean retiree who decides to move to Australia to be closer to family. Australia taxes its residents on their worldwide income, which could include foreign pensions, dividends from international investments, and other income sources. In such a scenario, strategically liquidating certain investments while still a tax resident of Singapore (where capital gains are generally not taxed) could potentially reduce future tax exposure in Australia.*

  Similarly, understanding the tax implications of withdrawing funds from your Singapore-based retirement accounts (like the CPF and Supplementary Retirement Scheme - SRS) before or after becoming an Australian tax resident is vital.

  Recommended Strategies:

  - **Use Tax-Deferred Accounts *(e.g., SRS)* Strategically:** Singapore's Supplementary Retirement Scheme (SRS) offers tax advantages for contributions. Carefully consider the timing of withdrawals from SRS, especially if planning to become a tax resident in a country with different tax rules on retirement income. Consulting a tax advisor in both Singapore and destination country can help optimize withdrawal strategy.
  - **Time Your Asset Liquidation Appropriately:** As illustrated in the Australia example, the timing of selling assets can have significant tax implications when moving between countries with different tax regimes on capital gains. A pre-move consultation can help to determine the most tax-efficient timing for any planned asset disposals.
  - **Get a Pre-Move Tax Consultation to Avoid Surprises:** Before making any significant moves, engaging with tax professionals who have expertise in both Singaporean and international tax laws is an invaluable investment. They can provide tailored advice based on specific circumstances, helping to understand the potential tax consequences of relocation and develop strategies to mitigate any adverse

impacts. This proactive step can save significant time, money, and stress in the long run.

Common Tax and Wealth Planning Pitfalls

Even with the best intentions, individuals often fall into traps that can derail their financial plans. These aren't always grand, complex errors, but rather often subtle oversights that, over time, can accumulate into significant challenges.

- **Delayed Planning:** Procrastination, in personal finance, is arguably one of the most insidious enemies. Waiting too long to make crucial financial decisions means actively choosing to miss out on valuable reliefs, growth opportunities, and optimized tax positions. Consider the various mechanisms Singapore offers to encourage prudent financial habits, such as CPF top-ups or tax-efficient Supplementary Retirement Scheme (SRS) contributions. These avenues come with specific annual limits and benefits that are lost forever if not utilized within the calendar year.
- **Incomplete or Outdated Estate Documents:** This pitfall often stems from a combination of discomfort with discussing mortality and a misconception that once a will or Lasting Power of Attorney (LPA) is done, it's done for good.
  However, life is dynamic, and your legal documents must evolve with it. Failure to update critical estate documents like wills, CPF nominations, insurance nominations, or LPAs can lead to significant and often emotionally charged unintended consequences for your loved ones.
- **Overreliance on DIY Without Context or Updates:** In the age of abundant online information, it's tempting to take a do-it-yourself (DIY) approach to various legal and financial matters. While the internet offers incredible resources, an overreliance on generic online templates or outdated advice without understanding your specific context or the current legal landscape is a significant pitfall. Laws change, regulations evolve, and what might have been perfectly valid a few years ago, or in another jurisdiction, may no longer apply or be effective.
- **Failing to Track or Document Business or Investment Income:** As more of us embrace flexible work arrangements, engage in freelance projects, or actively manage investment portfolios, the lines between personal and business income can

blur. A common pitfall is inadequate record-keeping for such income streams, particularly rental income from properties or earnings from freelance consultancy. This oversight can lead to severe consequences, including tax underreporting, significant penalties from tax authorities, or the rejection of legitimate deductions.

- **Underestimating Longevity and Healthcare Costs:** Perhaps the most significant long-term pitfall for those planning for financial independence and early retirement is the tendency to underestimate two critical factors: how long you might live and the ever-increasing cost of healthcare.
  Retirement is no longer a short period; with advances in medicine and healthier lifestyles, it can easily span 30 years or more. While this is wonderful news, it means your financial runway needs to be considerably longer than previous generations might have planned for.
  Furthermore, healthcare inflation consistently outpaces general inflation. What seems affordable today may be prohibitively expensive in a decade or two, especially as we age and potentially require more medical attention.

Collaborating with the Right Professionals

Navigating the complexities of cross-border regulations, optimizing wealth accumulation, and ensuring a seamless transfer of legacy demands more than a general understanding. It requires the precise knowledge and experience of dedicated professionals. Knowing when and why to engage these experts can be the difference between a smooth transition and unforeseen hurdles.

Key Professionals and Their Roles:

- **Tax Advisors:** For individuals embarking on global ventures – be it working overseas, investing internationally, or considering a relocation – a specialized tax advisor becomes indispensable. Their expertise lies in structuring international income to be tax-efficient, advising on potential estate taxes in various jurisdictions, and most importantly, navigating the complexities of international tax treaties that can prevent double taxation and ensure compliance across borders. Their insights are crucial for anyone whose financial footprint extends beyond Singapore.
- **Financial Planners:** While tax advisors focus on optimization and compliance, financial planners provide a holistic

perspective. Their role is to meticulously align savings strategies, insurance coverage, and investment portfolios with precise long-term goals. Whether the objective is early retirement, funding a significant re-career venture, or building a multi-generational legacy, a skilled financial planner helps craft a comprehensive roadmap that ensures every financial decision serves the overarching vision.

- **Estate Lawyers:** The final piece of this professional puzzle, particularly for those with complex global assets or family structures, is an estate lawyer. Their specialization involves drafting robust, legally sound cross-border estate plans, wills, and trusts. They ensure that assets are distributed according to intentions, minimizing potential disputes and navigating the varying legal requirements of different countries. An estate lawyer's expertise is vital in transforming one's intentions into legally binding directives that protect a legacy.

Choosing Ethical, Competent, and Fiduciary Professionals

The market is abundant with individuals offering financial advice. However, selecting the right professional is paramount. The distinction lies not just in their qualifications, but in their ethical framework and commitment to a client's best interests.

- **Ensure they hold recognised qualifications:** Look for credentials that signify rigorous training and adherence to professional standards. For instance, a Certified Financial Planner (CFP) indicates comprehensive financial planning expertise, while a Certified Public Accountant (CPA) points to accounting and tax proficiency. For estate planning, particularly across borders, accreditations like those from the Society of Trust and Estate Practitioners (STEP) are highly regarded. These qualifications are not mere titles; they represent a commitment to ongoing education and a standard of competence.
- **Look for fiduciary duty – advisors who prioritise your best interests:** This is arguably the most crucial criterion. A fiduciary advisor is legally and ethically bound to act solely in a client's best interest, putting their financial well-being above their own. This contrasts with suitability standards, where an advisor only needs to recommend something that is suitable for a client, even if a better option exists that might not benefit

them as much. Always clarify if the professional operates under a fiduciary standard.

- **Evaluate their independence from product sales or commissions:** Understand their compensation model. Are they fee-only, meaning they are paid directly by the client for their advice? Or are they commission-based, earning money from the products they sell? While commission-based advisors are not inherently unethical, it's vital to be aware of potential conflicts of interest that might influence their recommendations. Transparency in compensation is non-negotiable.

Checklist for Engagement: When interviewing potential professionals, ask direct questions to gauge their suitability and ethical standing:

- ***How are you compensated?*** (This clarifies their business model and potential conflicts.)
- ***What's your experience with cross-border clients (if applicable to your situation)?*** (This assesses their specialized knowledge for global financial planning.)
- ***Can you collaborate effectively with my other advisors (e.g., my Singapore tax advisor, my US financial planner)?*** (This is crucial for integrated planning, ensuring all your professional advisors work in concert, rather than in silos.)

To maximize the value of time with professionals and ensure they can provide the most accurate and tailored advice, proactive preparation is key. Having essential documents organized and readily accessible before a consultation can significantly streamline the process and lead to more effective outcomes.

Gather the following comprehensive set of documents:

- **Personal ID and tax numbers:** National ID, passport copies, and tax identification numbers for all relevant jurisdictions.
- **CPF and SRS statements:** Latest statements for a clear picture of your retirement savings and contributions.
- **Recent tax returns (last 2–3 years):** These provide a snapshot of income, deductions, and tax history.
- **Insurance summaries:** Details of all life, health, disability, and critical illness policies.
- **Asset and liability breakdown:** A comprehensive list of all assets *(e.g. property, investments, cash)* and liabilities *(e.g. loans, mortgages)*.

- **Wills, trusts, nominations, LPAs, and AMDs:** All existing estate planning and advance care directive documents.

Integrated, intentional planning is not merely beneficial; it is absolutely essential for financial resilience. Whether aspirations involve re-careering in a new country, diversifying investments on a global scale, or diligently planning for the seamless transfer of a legacy to the next generation, a comprehensive and forward-looking approach ensures robustness in an ever-changing world.

Understanding the laws that govern one's financial life, both locally and internationally, is paramount. Vigilance is required to avoid the common traps that can derail even the best-laid plans. And critically, a commitment to working with trustworthy, ethical, and competent professionals who align with one's best interests is vital. The future self – enjoying the fruits of labour and living a life of purpose – and family, who will benefit from foresight, will undoubtedly acknowledge the diligence and intentionality invested today. Embrace the journey with knowledge, prepare with purpose, and live with the freedom that well-considered planning affords.

Integrating Tax & Wealth Planning into F.I.R(Re-career).E. Plan

Tax and wealth planning must be viewed as essential, integrated components of a well-rounded F.I.R(Re-career).E. strategy. When embedded thoughtfully into the broader planning ecosystem, tax efficiency significantly strengthens financial resilience.

Tax Planning as a Strategic Lever
Strategic tax planning can enhance various aspects of a F.I.R(Re-career).E. plan:

- **Budgeting and Contributions:** Integrating tax considerations into budgeting can unlock immediate benefits. For instance:
  - Allocating funds to tax-advantaged schemes, such as Singapore's Supplementary Retirement Scheme (SRS), can reduce taxable income while simultaneously supporting retirement goals.
  - Making donations to registered charities not only advances philanthropic causes but may offer significant tax relief. As

an example, donations to approved Institutions of a Public Character (IPC) in Singapore attract a 250% tax deduction, making them an efficient tool for both social impact and tax reduction.

- **Tax-Efficient Investing:** Investment instruments can be structured with tax efficiency in mind to influence long-term compounding. My experience has shown that:
    - Choosing tax-efficient vehicles such as Exchange-Traded Funds (ETFs) domiciled in Ireland (for non-U.S. residents) may reduce withholding taxes on dividends.
    - Certain countries offer incentives for specific asset classes. Real Estate Investment Trusts (REITs) in Singapore, for example, enjoy tax transparency, with distributions generally exempt from personal income tax for individual investors.

- **Insurance as a Planning Tool:** Insurance serves as a strategic tax and estate planning tool beyond its traditional risk protection role.
    - Life insurance products—particularly whole life or universal life policies—can be structured to serve as wealth transfer mechanisms.
    - In many jurisdictions, insurance payouts bypass probate and may not be subject to estate duties, providing timely liquidity to beneficiaries.
    - Some policies also include riders or trusts to support special needs planning or multi-generational legacy goals.

- **Income Structuring for Re-careering:** For individuals navigating re-career transitions, the nature and structure of income often change, presenting new tax considerations:
    - Business income may allow for deductible expenses that reduce taxable profits.
    - Passive income—such as dividends, royalties, or licensing fees—may be taxed differently depending on the source country and double taxation agreements in place.
    - Understanding how different income streams are classified and taxed is key to effective financial modelling and cash flow management during re-careering.

Redirected tax savings accelerate progress toward financial independence, fund lifestyle flexibility, or enable higher impact giving. The F.I.R(Re-career).E. plan is strengthened when every dollar saved from tax leakage is reallocated to purposeful goals.

Diversifying Income for Stability and Efficiency

A sustainable F.I.R(Re-career).E. plan hinges on multiple, tax-efficient income streams. This diversification enhances financial flexibility, stabilizes cash flow across economic cycles, and protects wealth from tax inefficiencies or policy shifts.

My journey underscores the importance of a resilient, tax-efficient income portfolio, typically comprising:

- **Active Income:** For re-careering professionals, active income remains vital but redefined. This may take the shape of: consulting, freelance work, part-time employment, or side ventures.
  - ***Tax Note:*** Tax treatment varies, but sole proprietors in Singapore can deduct legitimate business expenses (e.g., home office costs) from their taxable income.

- **Passive Income:** Sources like dividends, interest, rental income, or royalties provide regular cash flow without a corresponding time or energy exchange.
  - ***Tax Note:*** Rental income from overseas properties may be taxed in the host country, and dividend income from foreign-listed stocks may be subject to withholding tax (e.g., 30% U.S. withholding, potentially reduced to 15% under treaty).

- **Deferred Income:** unds accumulated in tax-advantaged vehicles during working years and drawn upon later. Examples include SRS withdrawals, annuity payouts, and insurance-linked savings.
  - ***Tax Note:*** SRS contributions offer immediate tax relief, with only 50% of withdrawals taxable after the statutory retirement age. My personal tip is to sequence income withdrawals smartly: draw down non-taxable capital gains or dividend income first, before tapping into taxable SRS or annuity payouts.

Tax is one of the most significant and consistent costs in an individual's financial life. Conversely, a thoughtfully diversified and tax-aware income plan provides considerable control over the timing, method, and source of income draws, fostering a robust platform for enhanced freedom and flexibility.

Embedding Resilience through Periodic Review

Tax and estate planning form an ongoing, dynamic component of the broader F.I.R(Re-career).E. strategy. Without regular updates, changes in personal circumstances or regulatory frameworks can result in unintended tax consequences or legal complications.

Several life events and policy shifts should prompt a structured reassessment (typically every two to three years):

- **Marriage or Divorce:** Changes in marital status can alter tax filing classifications, asset ownership rights, and the validity of existing beneficiary designations. In some jurisdictions, designations such as CPF nominations or insurance beneficiaries do not update automatically, potentially leading to unintended distributions.
- **Birth of a Child or New Dependent:** The arrival of a new dependent introduces fresh planning considerations—from education funding and life insurance coverage to guardianship arrangements and inheritance provisions. Trusts may be established to provide structured, long-term financial support aligned with evolving family needs.
- **Relocation or Change in Tax Residency:** Moving across borders often redefines tax obligations. Tax residency status affects the treatment of global income, the applicability of tax treaties, and the necessity for foreign asset reporting. Income previously exempt in one jurisdiction may become taxable in another.
- **Acquisition or Sale of Major Assets:** Transactions involving major assets—such as real estate, businesses, or inherited wealth—may trigger capital gains tax, stamp duties, estate taxes, or reporting obligations. These events may also prompt a reassessment of asset allocation, liquidity planning, and the appropriateness of existing legal structures.
- **Changes in Government Policies or Tax Treaties:** Evolving legislation, both domestic and international, can significantly alter the tax landscape. These include changes to CPF withdrawal conditions, revisions in personal relief thresholds, or shifts in bilateral tax treaty benefits. For example, in 2023, some Singapore investors discovered that changes in tax treaties

meant their previously tax-exempt dividends from foreign REITs were now subject to a 15% withholding tax. Without regular monitoring, such changes can significantly reduce net returns if not proactively managed through reallocation or re-domiciling of assets.

- **Retirement or Early Withdrawal:** The decision to transition into retirement, or even to make early withdrawals from retirement schemes, carries significant tax implications.
    - For instance, in Singapore, withdrawals from the Supplementary Retirement Scheme (SRS) after the prescribed retirement age benefit from a 50% tax concession, meaning only half the withdrawn amount is taxable. Spreading these withdrawals over a 10-year period can further optimise tax exposure by keeping annual taxable income within lower brackets.
    - Conversely, early withdrawals from SRS (before the prescribed retirement age) are generally subject to a 5% penalty and the full amount becomes taxable, unless under specific exceptional circumstances like death, medical grounds, or bankruptcy.
    - It is crucial to understand that CPF savings withdrawn are generally not taxable in Singapore. However, any outstanding taxes or MediShield Life/CareShield Life premiums may be recovered from CPF withdrawals.

- Proper planning for retirement income streams, considering both the timing and the source of funds, can greatly influence the overall tax burden and the longevity of one's accumulated wealth.

To maintain alignment, conduct a comprehensive review of tax and estate planning at regular intervals or following any material life or legislative change. Key focus areas should include:

- **Current tax residency and international income exposure:** Assess whether tax residency status has changed and evaluate the tax implications of income earned across multiple jurisdictions. This is particularly important for globally mobile individuals or those with cross-border investments.
- **Asset ownership structures (personal, joint, trust, company):** Review how assets are held to optimise for tax efficiency, liability protection, and succession planning. Different structures may have varying tax treatments and implications for control and distribution.
- **Validity and relevance of wills, CPF nominations, and insurance beneficiaries:** Ensure that legal documents and beneficiary designations reflect current intentions, life circumstances, and family structures. Outdated designations may lead to unintended outcomes or legal complications.
- **Currency exposure and country-specific tax risks:** Evaluate the impact of foreign exchange volatility on asset values and income, and assess exposure to tax regimes that may affect holdings or income abroad. Consider strategies to mitigate these risks.
- **Liquidity to meet future obligations or legacy goals:** Determine whether sufficient liquid assets are available to meet near-term needs, such as healthcare or education, as well as longer-term objectives like estate settlement, philanthropy, or intergenerational transfers.

From Preservation to Purposeful Legacy

At its essence, the F.I.R(Re-career).E. journey is a framework for intentional living—one that prioritizes purpose and meaningful contribution. The final phase is thoughtful wealth preservation and transfer, transitioning from securing individual well-being to enabling generational impact.

- **Maximising Net Outcomes Through Strategic Efficiency:** Careful planning minimises leakages from taxation, fees, or misaligned investment vehicles. Structured properly, wealth remains intact and continues to serve its intended objectives rather than being eroded unnecessarily.
- **Prolonging Wealth Sustainability Over Generations:** Intelligent structuring—via trusts, business succession planning, and tailored withdrawal strategies—extends the utility of assets beyond a single lifetime. It enables wealth to support future generations or long-term causes without compromising financial stability.
- **Ensuring Alignment Between Capital and Core Values:** Financial assets can be directed toward meaningful purposes—be it philanthropic giving, intergenerational education, or community-building initiatives. When values are clearly articulated and integrated into estate and financial planning, capital becomes a vehicle for living out those values in perpetuity.
- **Preventing Disputes and Reducing Complexity in Wealth Transfer:** A well-structured legacy plan prevents unnecessary legal entanglements, delays, or family conflict. By clearly articulating intentions and utilising legal instruments such as wills, trusts, and nominations, wealth transfer becomes a constructive, empowering experience rather than a contentious one.

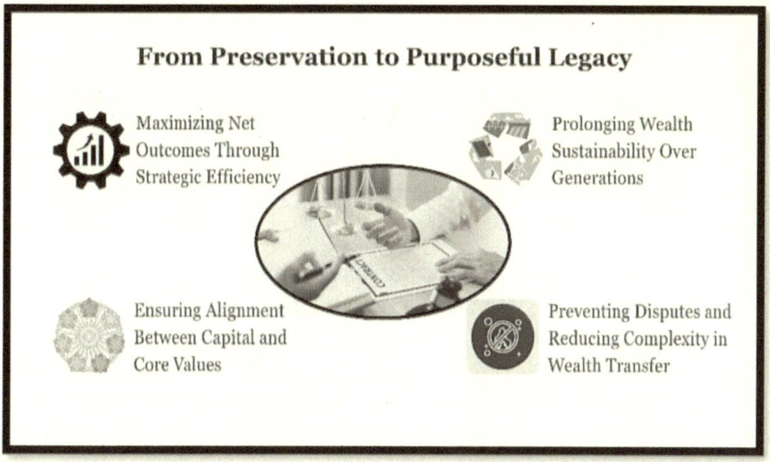

Integrating tax and wealth planning into a F.I.R(Re-career).E. plan is a strategic mindset, not just a technical exercise. When aligned with your income, investment, protection, and re-careering goals, tax-aware decisions help preserve wealth and amplify purpose, unlocking a future of limitless possibilities for you and the communities you touch.

Summary

Chapter 10: Tax Planning and Wealth Preservation underscores the critical role of tax and estate strategies in sustaining financial independence and supporting a meaningful re-career journey. While earning, saving, and investing build wealth, it is tax efficiency and prudent preservation that determine how much is retained, grown, and passed on.

The chapter begins by clarifying tax planning as a legitimate, values-aligned approach to maximising net returns—not tax avoidance. It outlines key principles and structures in Singapore and globally, showing how employees, freelancers, and business owners can benefit from strategies such as deductions, income structuring, and effective use of CPF and SRS.

Tax-efficient investing is explored through asset location, product selection, and capital gains management. The chapter illustrates how different income types—active, passive, and deferred—are taxed across jurisdictions, and how strategic structuring can minimise tax burdens and surprises.

The chapter also focuses on wealth preservation and estate planning. Topics include wills, trusts, nominations, and legacy tools that protect assets, reduce legal complications, and align with long-term intent. Global considerations—such as foreign estate taxes, tax treaties, and the impact of life events or legal changes—highlight the need for regular reviews.

The chapter concludes by emphasising the importance of integrating tax and wealth planning into the broader F.I.R(Re-career).E. strategy—not just for efficiency, but for peace of mind, multigenerational continuity, and purposeful living.

Key Takeaways:

- **Tax planning is a critical enabler of financial independence**—not just a technical exercise but a strategic one.
- **Every income source carries tax implications**; aligning your income mix with tax efficiency increases sustainability.
- **Periodic reviews of your tax and estate plans** are essential to adapt to changing laws and life events.
- **Estate and legacy planning ensure that wealth is preserved, transferred wisely, and aligned with your values.**

- **Collaborating with qualified professionals** (e.g., tax advisors, estate planners, financial coaches) brings objectivity and clarity.

Practical Tips:

- Schedule a **comprehensive tax and estate review every 2–3 years**, or upon major life changes.
- Use **available tax deductions and reliefs** (e.g., SRS, CPF top-ups, business expenses) strategically.
- Consider **deferred or passive income structures** like annuities or REITs for tax efficiency.
- Create or update your **will, CPF nominations, and trust arrangements** as your situation evolves.
- Stay updated on **international tax laws and treaties** if you hold global assets or plan to live abroad.

In the next section, **Part III: Transitioning into the Re-career Journey**, we shift our focus from financial mastery to the mental, strategic, and emotional readiness required to step into your next chapter.

In the next chapter, **Preparing for the Leap**, we explore how to de-risk your transition, assess your readiness, and lay a solid foundation for a life of purpose and freedom beyond traditional employment.

Reflection Prompts & Mini Exercises

"Smart tax and wealth planning is not just about saving money—it's about designing freedom, protecting your legacy, and aligning your finances with your life's mission." ~ YK Png

---

1. Understanding Your Tax Planning Readiness

Prompt:

- *How proactive have you been with your personal tax planning in recent years?*
- *Do you know which deductions, reliefs, or incentives you're eligible for in your country?*
- *Have you considered how taxes affect your investment returns and re-career income?*

Mini Exercise: Tax Clarity Snapshot

- List your top 3 income sources *(e.g., salary, dividends, rental income).*
- For each, write down: *What taxes apply? Are there any exemptions or reliefs?*
- Set one action goal: *(e.g., "Schedule time this month to review available deductions for self-employed income.")*

---

2. Designing a Tax-Efficient Re-career Strategy

Prompt:

- *If you plan to shift from employment to freelancing, business, or semi-retirement, how will your tax position change?*
- *Are you familiar with the tax implications of different income streams (e.g., royalties, consultancy, dividends)?*
- *Are there structures (e.g., private limited companies, trusts, retirement accounts) that can support your transition?*

Mini Exercise: Future Income Mapping

- Sketch a pie chart showing your ideal re-career income mix.
- Note the possible tax rates or benefits tied to each type of income.
- Identify one area to learn more about *(e.g., how dividends are taxed or how to optimize SRS contributions).*

---

3. Integrating Estate Planning with Your Life Vision
Prompt:

- *Do your current estate plans reflect your values, family needs, and financial goals?*
- *Who depends on your wealth today—and who might in the future?*
- *What kind of legacy—financial, emotional, or social—do you want to leave?*

Mini Exercise: Legacy Letter Draft

- Write a short "legacy letter" to your future beneficiaries. *What do you want them to understand about your values, your journey, and the meaning behind your wealth?*
- List 3 concrete steps you'll take to align your estate plans with that intention *(e.g., update your will, create a family trust, initiate open conversations with loved ones).*

---

4. Navigating Global Tax and Wealth Planning
Prompt:

- *Are you working across borders, holding international assets, or considering overseas relocation?*
- *What tax treaties, reporting obligations, or residency issues might affect your financial plans?*
- *Have you consulted a qualified advisor for cross-border guidance?*

Mini Exercise: Global Risk Check

- Create a list of countries where you earn income or hold investments.
- For each, note one potential risk *(e.g., estate tax exposure, reporting requirement)* and one planning opportunity *(e.g., tax treaty, dual residency benefit).*
- Circle one priority to investigate further with professional advice.

---

5. **Aligning Wealth Preservation with Your F.I.R(Re-career).E. Goals**

Prompt:

- *Is your current financial plan designed to protect your wealth from inflation, taxation, or life uncertainties?*
- *Are your risk management strategies (e.g., insurance, diversification, trusts) aligned with your future lifestyle and values?*
- *How can wealth preservation empower, not constrain, your re-career and lifestyle freedom?*

Mini Exercise: Preservation Scorecard

- Rate yourself (1–5) on the following: Asset Protection, Tax Planning, Estate Readiness, Succession Planning, and Legacy Clarity.
- Highlight the lowest-rated area.
- Set one improvement goal *(e.g., "Review my insurance adequacy and asset protection structures by next quarter.")*

Part III: Transitioning into the Re-career Journey

"Don't be afraid to give up the good to go for the great."

~ ***John D. Rockefeller.***"

Chapter 11: Preparing for the Leap – Mental, Strategic, and Practical Readiness

"Retirement is not the end of the road; it is the beginning of a new journey." ~ YK Png

---

Having laid the groundwork for mindset, career alignment, and financial resilience in earlier chapters, this phase marks a transition from vision to execution.

Chapter 11 focuses on the integrated readiness required to make the F.I.R(Re-career).E. leap both sustainable and purposeful. This includes strengthening emotional confidence, refining financial buffers, and designing a transition plan grounded in reality. Whether the next step involves re-careering, early retirement, or a portfolio lifestyle, clarity and preparedness are essential. The chapter offers frameworks, reflection tools, and practical checklists to support a confident and intentional shift into the next chapter of work and life.

Laying the Groundwork

My Journey: A Journey Rooted in Reflection and Relationships

My decision to re-career wasn't a sudden leap, but a measured pivot built over years. It was rooted in deep self-reflection, strategic conversations, and deliberate action.

While still in my corporate role, I sought out individuals who had already re-careered. Their stories offered invaluable insights, helping me foresee potential challenges and envision what success could look like in a new chapter.

At the same time, I strengthened my existing networks, including those from the Pharmaceutical Society of Singapore (PSS) and NUS. These connections kept me rooted in my profession while allowing me to explore new opportunities in coaching, training, and consultancy.

Personal development was also key. I became a certified coach and adult educator not just for the credentials, but to deepen my understanding of how people thrive. This learning journey became the foundation of my new life, where purpose and passion now guide my work.

Recognizing the need for financial stability, I worked with trusted financial planners. We reviewed my readiness, projected cash flow, and assessed my risk appetite. These data-driven discussions turned my vague aspirations into a concrete, sustainable plan.

Looking back, the most transformative part was integrating this mindset shift with practical planning. By aligning my values with a realistic strategy, I created not just a new career, but a new way of living with purpose.

Key Takeaways:

- **Start the conversation early:** Engage with those who have made similar transitions to gain insights and avoid pitfalls.
- **Invest in yourself:** Prioritize continuous learning and credentials to open doors to a more fulfilling career.
- **Strengthen your network:** Leverage existing affiliations and seek collaborations to stay connected and relevant.
- **Plan with professionals:** Collaborate with financial planners to ensure aspirations are grounded in economic reality.
- **Clarity comes with action:** Every step taken, no matter how small, brings one closer to their envisioned future.

De-risking the Leap: Financial Strategies

Transitioning into early retirement or a re-careered path requires more than a milestone net worth—it demands a thoughtfully constructed financial ecosystem that mitigates risk and ensures sustainability. While mindset and strategic planning lay the psychological and logistical groundwork, financial readiness provides the practical foundation for a confident leap.

Here are the essential strategies to reduce financial risks and boost peace of mind:

- **Establishing Financial Resilience:** Create a robust emergency fund with 6-12 months of essential expenses in a high-yield savings or money market account. This reserve protects against unexpected disruptions like medical emergencies or economic downturns without jeopardizing long-term plans.
- **Eliminate High-Interest Debt:** Prioritize paying off high-interest debt like credit card balances and personal loans to improve cash flow and reduce dependency on active income. Clearing long-term obligations like housing and car loans further enhances financial freedom.

  Personal Reflection: *I cleared all outstanding loans, including my housing loan, before re-careering. This allowed me to benefit from the stable, higher interest rates of the CPF Ordinary Account, an efficient way to generate passive income safely.*
- **Aligning Investment Strategy with Income Needs:** Shift portfolio to prioritize income generation and capital preservation. This may involve moving assets to dividend-yielding equities, REITs, bonds, or private annuities to create a stable income stream. In Singapore, CPF LIFE provides a lifelong monthly payout. Additionally, can also re-evaluate cash-based investments to generate immediate passive income.

  My Approach: *I shifted my cash-based unit trust investments from reinvesting earnings to receiving them as dividend payouts, generating a consistent monthly passive income. My CPF and SRS investments, however, continue to reinvest for long-term retirement.*

- **Strategic Drawdowns and Tax Optimization:** Develop a drawdown strategy to optimize for taxes and sustainability. Start by using non-taxable sources before tapping into taxable investments.

  My Approach: *I plan to draw down my SRS funds gradually over 10 years to keep my taxable income in a lower bracket and potentially reduce my overall tax bill.*

- **Cash Flow Management for Re-career Living:** A re-career phase often has irregular income streams. Use a personal cash flow dashboard to maintain oversight of inflows, expenses, and reserves. This allows for proactive planning for large expenses and enhances financial control and confidence.

Sound financial strategy during the transition phase is not merely about defence—it creates room for exploration, creativity, and mission-driven pursuits. By reducing exposure to financial shocks and ensuring stable income, individuals are better positioned to embrace their second act with clarity, security, and purpose.

Financial Readiness Checklist for Re-Career or Early Retirement

Emergency Preparedness

- ☐ I have saved 6–12 months of living expenses in an emergency fund.
- ☐ My emergency fund is kept in a liquid and low-risk account *(e.g., high-yield savings, money market fund).*
- ☐ I have health insurance and/or medical coverage that remains effective post-transition.

Debt Elimination

- ☐ I have cleared all high-interest debts *(e.g., credit cards, personal loans).*
- ☐ I have repaid major loans *(e.g., mortgage, car loan)* or have a manageable repayment plan.
- ☐ I am not taking on new debt to fund my transition.

Income Continuity

- ☐ I have reviewed and rebalanced my investment portfolio from growth to income focus.
- ☐ My portfolio includes dividend-paying stocks, REITs, annuities, or bond funds for regular income.
- ☐ I have a plan to generate passive income monthly without relying on selling principal assets.
- ☐ I have stopped reinvesting dividends and started receiving cash payouts where appropriate.

Tax and Drawdown Planning

- ☐ I understand the tax implications of withdrawing from my retirement or investment accounts.
- ☐ I have a drawdown strategy aligned with income needs and tax efficiency.
- ☐ I've reviewed or optimized my participation in:
    - SRS (Singapore)
    - Roth IRA / 401(k) (US)
    - RRSP / TFSA (Canada)
    - Other country-specific retirement schemes
- ☐ I've consulted a qualified tax or financial advisor.

Cash Flow Planning

- ☐ I've created a monthly cash flow dashboard to track all income and expenses.
- ☐ I've accounted for:

- Passive income (e.g., dividends, rental)
- Active/portfolio income (e.g., consulting, freelance)
- Fixed expenses (e.g., insurance, subscriptions)
- Variable expenses (e.g., travel, dining)

☐ I have a savings buffer to fund any passion projects, business ventures, or travel plans.

Psychological Confidence

☐ I feel confident and emotionally ready for a change in income structure.

☐ I've discussed the financial plan with my partner or family.

☐ I understand that freedom may come with fluctuations, but I have contingencies in place.

Final Check:

☐ If you've checked at least 80–90% of these items, you are in a strong position to pursue a re-career or early retirement with peace of mind.

Emotional Readiness – Navigating Identity and Perception

In most transitions toward early retirement or re-careering, financial preparation typically receives the most attention. However, an equally critical dimension is often overlooked: emotional readiness. Long after financial spreadsheets have been balanced, the more complex and enduring challenge often lies in navigating shifts in identity, self-worth, and perception.

For many professionals, decades of work have deeply intertwined personal identity with job titles, organisational roles, and career achievements. Stepping away from this structured environment can feel less like a break—and more like a quiet identity disruption. Questions may surface, not about resources, but about relevance and self-definition:

- *"Who am I without the role I once held?"*
- *"How will others perceive this transition?"*
- *"Does contribution still matter if it no longer takes place within a formal workplace?"*

These reflections do not signal weakness; they reflect a life lived with deep engagement. They are invitations to redefine contribution, reframe success, and restore inner alignment.

Coping with Identity Shifts and Social Perceptions

Adjusting to a re-careered or post-career phase often requires more than logistical planning—it calls for a thoughtful reorientation of identity and role. The transition may surface internal doubts and be shaped by external perceptions, both of which can influence how change is processed and integrated. Addressing these dynamics proactively is essential to maintaining clarity, confidence, and emotional wellbeing throughout the journey.

1. **Acknowledge and Normalize Emotional Variability:** Emotional transitions often come in waves—ranging from enthusiasm to anxiety, pride to uncertainty. Feelings of loss or guilt may arise, particularly when departing from traditional norms around professional continuity or societal expectations. Recognizing these emotions as valid—and expected—can be a first step toward greater clarity and acceptance.

2. **Practice Self-Compassion:** Shifting away from an established professional identity is not an ending but a redefinition. This period of unlearning, exploration, and renewal can be an opportunity to embrace growth without the constraints of former labels. The absence of a title is not the absence of purpose—it is a gateway to recalibration.

   My Journey: From Corporate Titles to True Purpose
   When I transitioned out of my senior executive role in the pharmaceutical industry, it felt much like stepping out of a well-lit spotlight into the vast, open sky. At first, the space was unfamiliar and even a little intimidating—after decades of being defined by titles, targets, and performance metrics, I was now navigating without a corporate compass.

   But as I leaned into pro bono work, coaching, and mentoring, I discovered a renewed sense of purpose. It was no longer about organizational KPIs, but about empowering individuals and making meaningful contributions to their growth. This shift brought a depth of fulfilment I had never quite experienced in the boardroom.

3. **Reframe the Transition as an Evolution, Not a Departure:** Re-careering is better viewed as progression, not withdrawal. Data supports this. A 2019 study by the Centre for Ageing Research and Education (CARE) at the National University of Singapore revealed that individuals who remained intellectually, socially, or professionally engaged post-retirement reported significantly higher emotional wellbeing and smoother transitions in identity.

The Power of Opening Up: Engaging the Support System

Major life transitions—like re-careering or semi-retirement—are often perceived as personal journeys. And while the decision is deeply individual, the emotional experience doesn't have to be isolating. The presence of a trusted inner circle—family, friends, mentors—can be instrumental in easing emotional friction, especially when engaged openly and intentionally.

My Personal Story: From Silence to Support

As an introvert, I've never been one to openly share personal matters, even with family. When I left my corporate role and stepped into a new phase of semi-retirement and re-careering, I threw myself into the process—building my websites, enrolling in courses, expanding my network, and shaping a new professional identity.

In the midst of this busy period, I started feeling a creeping sense of guilt and unease. I wasn't earning a salary like before, yet I wasn't spending much time with my loved ones. My mind started filling in the blanks, imagining what my family might be thinking. These were not conversations—they were assumptions, often unfounded. And the stress? Mostly self-inflicted.

What I learned from this experience is that silence can become a breeding ground for unnecessary worry. When I finally opened up and shared what I was working on and how I was feeling, I found nothing but understanding and support. It reminded me that sometimes, we just need to take the first step to invite others into our journey.

My experience taught me that re-careering isn't just a professional shift—it's an emotional one. And the path becomes lighter when we stop walking alone:

- **Clarity leads to confidence**: Verbalizing plans and emotions helps articulate intentions, reduces ambiguity, and clarifies direction.
- **Inclusion reduces resistance**: When family and partners are brought into the conversation early, their involvement strengthens mutual understanding and alignment, shifting their role from passive observers to active supporters.
- **Diverse perspectives broaden your strategy**: Input from others—peers, mentors, even past colleagues—can surface insights that refine or accelerate the transition—perhaps even next opportunity.

> **Tip**: Host a "Transition Dialogue" over a relaxed meal or coffee. Share what you're planning, what excites you, what worries you, and what kind of support you'd appreciate. You may be surprised at how open and affirming the responses are—and how much lighter the journey feels afterwards.

Reframing the Mental Noise: Managing Self-Inflicted Stress

In times of transition, the most significant resistance often stems not from external constraints, but from internal narratives. These are the quiet, persistent thoughts that cast doubt and cultivate hesitation:

- *"You're too old to start again."*
- *"What if you fail?"*
- *"What will people think?"*

Such thoughts, though convincing, are frequently assumptions cloaked as truths—beliefs shaped by social conditioning rather than objective reality.

My Reflection: When Silence Fuels Doubt

In the early stages of my re-career transition, I found myself wrestling with these very questions. Not because anyone told me I was making a mistake, but because I never gave them the chance to respond. My stress was rooted in what I thought others might think. It wasn't until I opened up that I realized much of this mental noise was self-created. In truth, my family and peers were far more understanding and encouraging than I had assumed.

This reinforced an important lesson: unchecked internal narratives can sabotage progress. But when we challenge them, we reclaim ownership of our story.

In fact, a 2021 study by the Institute of Mental Health (IMH) and Duke-NUS Medical School found that older adults in Singapore who maintained strong social connections and a sense of purpose reported significantly lower stress levels and higher life satisfaction. This underscores the value of communication and the mental clarity it brings—especially during major transitions.

Reframing Internal Barriers with the ABCDE Model[18]

One effective way to confront these internal barriers is by systematically challenging the beliefs that fuel them. The ABCDE Model, originally developed in cognitive behavioral therapy, offers a structured method to dissect and dispute unhelpful thoughts. It provides a practical framework for identifying the source of fear-based thinking, questioning its validity, and reframing it with more constructive, empowering beliefs.

For anyone navigating transition, this approach can be a game-changer in regaining clarity and confidence.

1. **Identify Fear-Based Thinking:** When feel stuck or overwhelmed, pause and ask: *"Is this a fact, or just a fear?"* Reflective practices like journaling or coaching conversations can help uncover the difference.

2. **Reframe Limiting Beliefs with the ABCDE Model**
   A proven method for shifting mindset is the ABCDE Model:

- **A – Activating Event**: Identify what triggered the thought *(e.g., leaving a high-paying job).*
- **B – Beliefs**: Notice what belief followed *(e.g., "I'm no longer valuable").*
- **C – Consequences**: Reflect on the emotional and behavioural outcome *(e.g., guilt, withdrawal).*
- **D – Disputation**: Challenge the belief—*Is it true? Is there evidence against it?*
- **E – Energize/Effect**: Adopt a more empowering belief *(e.g., "I'm building something more purposeful with my experience").*

This model converts limiting narratives into empowering perspectives by applying logic and reflection.

---

[18] The "ABCDE Model" is explained in greater depth in *Limitless Possibilities ~ YK Png.*(Available now on Amazon.com).

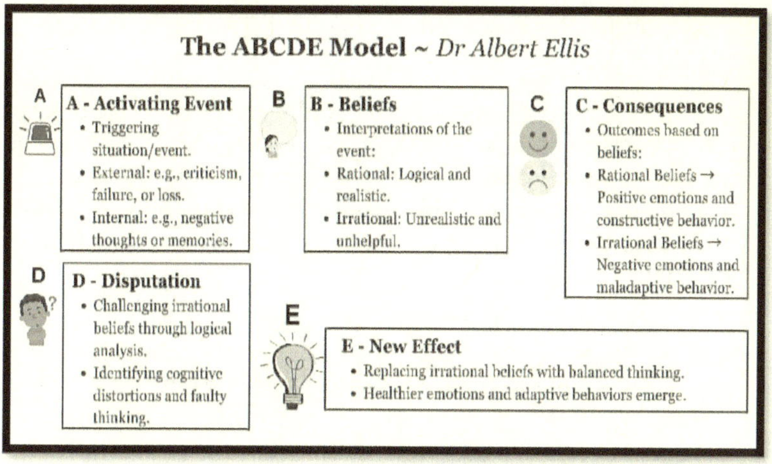

3. **Practice Mental Hygiene:** Mental well-being, like physical health, requires intentional care. Use daily habits like meditation, gratitude journaling, and positive affirmations to quiet the internal noise and strengthen emotional resilience.

Mini Reflection: *"If Not Now, When?"*

In moments of transition—whether you're contemplating a career pivot, starting a passion project, or redefining your life's pace—the greatest guide is not always a spreadsheet or a market forecast. It is often quiet introspection. This simple, profound question—*"If not now, when?"*—is the mirror reflecting where you are and where you long to be.

Many of us postpone meaningful change, telling ourselves we'll start "someday." But someday is not a day on the calendar. It's a delay tactic often rooted in fear, perfectionism, or external expectations. Asking *"If not now, when?"* invites you to interrupt that pattern. It challenges you to confront the true reasons behind your hesitation and to step into your potential before circumstances force you to.

- ***What beliefs or assumptions are holding me back?***

  In my own re-career journey, the resistance I faced was not loud fear—it was a quiet internal dialogue filled with questions: "Am I too late to start again?", "Am I wasting my time starting something I have never done before?", "Will my skills still be relevant in a different field?", "Can I create value outside the structures I had grown so comfortable in?"

  Upon deeper reflection, I realized these doubts were not grounded in reality but were inherited assumptions—echoes of societal norms about age, change, and success. When I voiced these internal questions to trusted mentors and friends, I found unexpected encouragement. They saw possibilities in me that I had momentarily overlooked. Their belief helped me see that the real obstacle was not external—it was the narrative I was telling myself.

Key Lessons from My Reflections:

- **Question Limiting Beliefs**: Many fears about re-careering stem from outdated assumptions, not reality.
- **Age and Background Are Not Barriers**: Reinvention is possible at any stage with the right mindset.
- **Your Skills Are Still Valuable**: Core competencies are often transferable across industries.

- **Seek Honest Support**: Mentors and peers can help you see possibilities you may overlook.
- **Redefine Success for Yourself**: True fulfilment comes from aligning work with personal purpose and values.

- ***How aligned is my current lifestyle with the future I envision?***

  This question requires brutal honesty. Are your daily routines moving you closer to the life you want—or anchoring you to a version of yourself you've outgrown? A common pitfall is staying in familiar discomfort simply because it's comfortable. But comfort zones, while safe, are often growth's greatest enemy.

  If you envision a more flexible, meaningful, or impactful life, it begins with alignment. Ask yourself: *Do my habits reflect my aspirations?* If your goal is freedom, but you're filling your calendar with obligations that drain you, it may be time to course correct.

- ***What small step can I take today to bring me closer to a life of meaning and freedom?***

  Big changes don't require dramatic leaps. Often, it's the micro-shifts that create momentum.

  In my journey, I made it a point to engage in at least one meaningful activity a day. These actions did not have to be major—they included catching up with friends or business networks over coffee, mentoring a junior, spending time with my wife at a museum or shopping mall, or enjoying a simple round of golf at the driving range.

  Between these moments, I dedicated time at home to work on building my business platform - coachtoring.com, posting consistently on LinkedIn and Facebook to brand myself and promote my services, and continuing my progress on writing my book.

  These small, consistent actions kept me connected to my larger purpose.

Practical Tool: A Simple Framework for Reflective Action

The ABCDE model helps reframe limiting beliefs, but awareness needs action. That's where the R.E.A.L. framework comes in.

R.E.A.L. supports ongoing reflection and momentum. If ABCDE clears the mental fog, R.E.A.L. provides the compass to navigate forward—one small, purposeful step at a time:

R – Recognize: Identify what you're feeling or experiencing right now. What emotions or thoughts are surfacing as you think about your transition?

Prompt: *What am I feeling about this phase of my journey?*

E – Examine: Explore the beliefs or assumptions behind those feelings. Are they grounded in facts, or are they inherited from societal norms or outdated narratives?

Prompt: *What belief is driving this feeling? Is it still serving me?*

A – Align: Reflect on how your current lifestyle, habits, and commitments align with your vision of the future.
Prompt: *What is one area of my life that feels misaligned with my goals?*

L – Leap: Identify one small, intentional action you can take today—however minor—to move toward alignment and purpose.

Prompt: *What's one step I can take in the next 24 hours to create momentum?*

This structured approach transforms insight into directed action. Reviewing entries over time reveals patterns and progress.

Summary

Chapter 11: Preparing for the Leap – Mental, Strategic, and Practical Readiness examines how successful re-careering or early retirement requires deliberate preparation across three critical dimensions: mindset, strategy, and practical execution. Making the leap is not just about financial calculations; it is a deeply personal process that touches identity, emotions, and self-belief.

This chapter guides readers through building the right foundations before transition. We explore how to de-risk the journey through financial planning, using strategies such as building buffers, securing insurance, and diversifying income streams. A Financial Readiness Checklist offers a clear, structured approach to assess your current standing.

Beyond financial preparation, we delve into emotional readiness—acknowledging identity shifts, social perceptions, and internal narratives that may arise. Readers learn techniques to engage their support networks, manage self-imposed stress, and reframe limiting beliefs through the ABCDE Model.

Through reflective practices like journaling or capturing digital notes, readers are encouraged to track emerging patterns and insights, strengthening clarity over time. Anchored by the reflection prompt "If not now, when?", the chapter emphasizes the importance of intentional action over endless preparation.

Key Takeaways:

- Preparation for major transitions must be **mental, strategic, and practical**—not purely financial.
- **Financial security** is foundational, but **emotional resilience** and identity work are equally crucial.
- Leveraging a **support system** and reframing internal narratives are powerful tools for navigating uncertainty.
- **Reflection practices** amplify clarity and surface deeper insights over time.

Practical Tips:

- Use the **Financial Readiness Checklist** to systematically evaluate your savings, expenses, risks, and opportunities.
- Apply the **ABCDE Model** to challenge self-limiting beliefs and cultivate empowering thought patterns.
- Engage a small circle of trusted allies to provide emotional and practical support during your transition.
- Integrate regular journaling or digital note-taking as a tool for ongoing reflection and clarity-building.
- When hesitation arises, ask yourself: *"If not now, when?"* to refocus on purposeful action.

In the next chapter, **Designing Your Unique Re-career Path**, we will shift from preparation to creation. You will explore how to craft a meaningful portfolio career, align your passions and skills with real-world needs, and learn from inspiring case studies of individuals who have successfully navigated their own re-career journeys.

Reflection Prompts & Mini Exercises

"Prepare internally and externally. Readiness is built before it is needed." ~ YK Png

---

1. Mental Readiness Check-In

Prompt:

- *What emotions arise when you think about leaving your current career or identity behind?*
- *How comfortable are you with uncertainty and temporary setbacks?*
- *What beliefs about success, failure, or security might be holding you back?*

Mini Exercise: Fear vs. Excitement List

- Draw two columns: "Fears" and "Excitements."
- List everything you fear and everything you look forward to in your next phase.
- Reflect: *How can you reframe at least one major fear into a challenge or opportunity?*

---

2. Financial Buffer Assessment

Prompt:

- *If your income stopped tomorrow, how many months could you comfortably sustain your lifestyle?*
- *Do you have enough insurance coverage to protect your family and assets during a transition?*
- *How diversified are your income sources beyond your primary career?*

Mini Exercise: Buffer and Risk Map

- Calculate your financial buffer in months (savings ÷ monthly expenses).
- List all active insurance policies and income sources.
- Identify one gap you can address within the next 30 days *(e.g., increase savings rate, review insurance coverage, create a side income stream)*.

---

3. **Identity and Emotional Anchoring**

Prompt:

- *How much of your self-worth is tied to your current job title, role, or professional identity?*
- *Without mentioning your job title, how would you introduce yourself to a new person?*
- *What personal qualities and passions define you beyond your work?*
- *Who are you becoming through this transition, not just what are you leaving behind?*

Mini Exercise: Identity Beyond Title Reflection

- Write 5 sentences starting with *"I am..."* focusing only on character strengths, passions, and values (not your job role).
- Reflect: *How can these qualities guide your re-career or new life design?*
- Choose one new role or community *(e.g., volunteer, advisor, hobbyist group)* where you can express these qualities.

---

4. **Support System Strengthening**

Prompt:

- *Who are your current "sounding boards" for major life decisions?*
- *Which mentors, coaches, or communities can stretch your thinking and belief in what's possible?*
- *How often do you seek advice, feedback, or encouragement—and are you open to receiving it?*
- *How can you become a support pillar for others during your own transition?*

Mini Exercise: Support Circle Audit

- Draw three circles: Inner Circle (closest, most trusted), Middle Circle (advisors, mentors), and Outer Circle (loose connections, acquaintances).
- Populate the circles with names.
- Identify one relationship to deepen intentionally over the next month through meaningful conversation or collaboration.

---

5. Action Readiness Self-Assessment

Prompt:

- *What is one action you've been delaying because you're "not ready enough"?*
- *What small, low-risk action could you take this month toward your re-career or next phase?*
- *What would you regret more in five years—trying and struggling, or never trying at all?*

Mini Exercise: "If Not Now, When?" Commitment Letter

- Write a short letter to your future self, explaining *"Why you chose to take action now?"*
- Outline one commitment you will make in the next 30 days *(e.g., submit an application, meet a mentor, test a new idea).*
- Sign and date it. Revisit the letter monthly for accountability.
- Celebrate completion, not outcome. Progress builds momentum.
- Journal how you feel after taking the step—you are now in motion.

Chapter 12: Designing Your Unique Re-career Path

"Your F.I.R(Re-career).E. journey is unique to you. Embrace it, navigate the challenges, and celebrate the joys along the way." ~ YK Png

---

Re-careering in today's world extends far beyond the notion of changing jobs. It represents a shift in mindset—from employment to intentional design. A modern re-career journey is about crafting a professional life that aligns with one's evolving identity, values, and lifestyle aspirations. It is an opportunity to shape a new chapter that is not dictated by circumstance or necessity, but by conscious choice and strategic planning.

This chapter explores the changing career landscape, practical portfolio career models, real-life examples across different life stages, and tools for designing a balanced, multi-dimensional professional life. The intent is not to offer a one-size-fits-all blueprint, but to present a flexible framework that supports personal reinvention on one's own terms.

The New Career Landscape: Navigating the Great Reconfiguration

The global workforce is undergoing a profound transformation. Traditional linear career paths are giving way to more **dynamic, adaptive models** of work. This shift—described by workforce strategists as the **"Great Reconfiguration"**—has been accelerated by technology, demographic changes, and evolving expectations around purpose.

This transformation is acutely felt in Singapore. While the CIMB Singapore Financial Independence Report 2025 notes that 63% of residents aim for financial independence between 40 and 60, many in this group also experience heightened financial anxiety. This gap—where desire for freedom outpaces confidence in traditional security—suggests conventional employment is often insufficient to support long-term goals. Portfolio careers, by diversifying income and leveraging expertise, offer a practical, empowering alternative.

Key advantages of a portfolio career approach include:

- **Risk Mitigation**: Multiple income sources provide a buffer against economic uncertainty. A slowdown in one stream does not derail overall financial stability.
- **Greater Fulfilment**: Individuals managing portfolio careers report significantly higher job satisfaction, driven by autonomy and alignment with personal interests *(McKinsey Report, 2022)*.
- **Lifestyle Integration**: A well-designed portfolio career can be shaped around preferred rhythms—allowing intensive consulting to be followed by quieter intervals for learning or family engagements.
- **Reinforcing Financial Confidence**: Rooted in proactive design and adaptability, a portfolio career helps professionals regain confidence and take strategic control of their income and future security.

My F.I.R(Re-career).E Journey: Designing a Purposeful Portfolio

The transition from a structured corporate role to a dynamic, multi-faceted portfolio was a deliberate process—rooted in strategic planning, continuous learning, and a desire to create meaningful, flexible work.

Today, this portfolio includes coaching, training, regulatory consulting, authorship, and mentorship. Each stream reflects a conscious alignment with personal strengths, interests, and impact areas:

- ***Professional Coaching - Empowering Transformation:*** *As a certified business and leadership coach, I support founders, SME leaders, and corporate professionals in unlocking their leadership potential. My coaching integrates proven models such as GROW and ICF Core Competencies to help clients gain clarity, embrace change, and lead with purpose.*

- ***Corporate Training and Course Development - Building Capability for the Future:*** *As an ACLP-certified trainer and courseware developer, I design and deliver learning solutions tailored to industry needs.*

Focus areas include:

- *Leadership development and high-performance cultures.*
- *Business acumen and financial literacy.*
- *Operational excellence and SOP development.*
- *Digital transformation and innovation.*
- *Sales, marketing, and brand storytelling.*
- *Organizational culture and values through my proprietary MPH Framework[19] (Mindset, Passion & Purpose, Habits).*

These programs blend best practices, real-world case studies, and adult learning principles to deliver sustainable capability development.

- ***Regulatory Consulting - Applying Niche Expertise:*** *With over 30 years in the pharmaceutical sector, I maintain industry relevance through regulatory consulting. I advise on product registration, compliance, and market strategy, providing the autonomy to balance consulting with other portfolio streams.*

- ***Authorship and Thought Leadership - Amplifying Impact:*** *Writing has become a powerful platform to scale impact. It enables the sharing of hard-earned lessons, practical insights, and inspiration with a broader audience.*
  Books authored include:
  - ***Limitless Possibilities*** *– a guide to unlocking personal and professional potential by cultivating mindset, passion, purpose, and habits. It distils three decades of corporate leadership and re-career lessons into a practical compass for leaders, professionals, and educators.*
  - ***F.I.R(Re-career).E: Work Less, Live More:*** *This very book, offering actionable frameworks for building a financially sustainable and values-aligned career. It is informed by lived experience, coaching engagements, and case studies from others who have redefined success on their terms.*

---

[19] The MPH Framework is explored in greater depth in *Limitless Possibilities ~ YK Png* (Available on Amazon.com)

- ***The BRIDGE Career Handbook:*** *Targeted mainly for graduates and young professionals, this book provides a core framework for career readiness and self-leadership.*
- ***The BRIDGE to Career Mastery: From Self-Leadership to Lasting Impact:*** *An expanded version of the Career Handbook, featuring more examples and a broader target audience, including founders and startups.*

  Through writing, I aim to empower professionals to challenge outdated paradigms, embrace possibility, and design a meaningful second career. Authorship has also positioned me for speaking engagements, partnerships, and further learning contributions.

- ***Strategic Projects and Mentorship - Investing in Future Innovators:*** *One of the most fulfilling aspects of this portfolio has been mentoring aspiring entrepreneurs, such as the NUS Graduate Research Innovation Programme (GRIP). By guiding early-stage innovators on business strategy, investor readiness, and strategic storytelling, I help shape the next generation of changemakers.*

This portfolio career was not built overnight. It was crafted through intentional steps over time. Key enablers include:

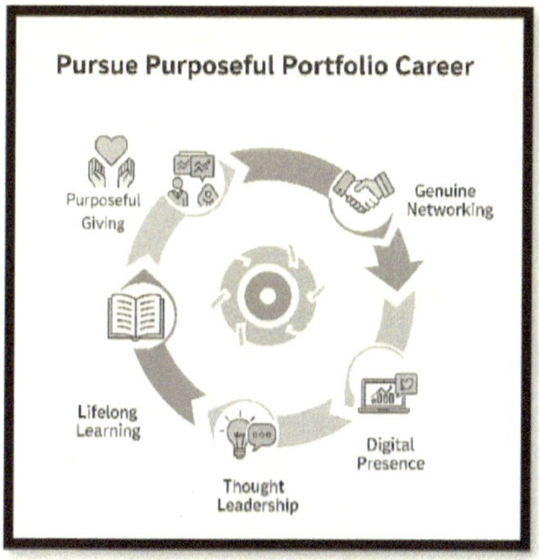

- ***Lifelong Learning:*** *Certifications in adult education (ACLP), professional coaching (PCTC, ICF ACC), digital marketing (NTU), and logistics and supply chain management expanded capabilities and kept skillsets relevant.*
- ***Purposeful Giving:*** *Pro bono coaching, mentoring, and participation in knowledge-sharing forums anchored this journey in contribution, not just commerce—adding depth and purpose to each role.*
- ***Genuine Networking:*** *Authentic relationships opened doors to training, consulting, and coaching collaborations.*

These connections created a virtuous cycle of referrals and co-creation.

- ***Digital Presence:** Platforms such as CoachToring.com, PharmacistCoaches.com, and active engagement on social media such as LinkedIn, Facebook, and Instagram helped build credibility and attract aligned clients.*
- ***Thought Leadership and Writing:** Publishing Limitless Possibilities and contributing to conversations on leadership, re-careering, and personal growth elevated visibility and reinforced professional identity.*

Key Lessons from My Re-career Journey:

- A portfolio career provides the flexibility to **align professional pursuits with personal passions** and lifestyle goals.
- **Lifelong learning, strategic positioning**, and a clear online presence are vital in building credibility and opportunities.
- **Giving back**—through mentoring, writing, and community engagement—adds a layer of meaning and fulfilment to the re-career journey.

Aligning Your Re-career with Your True Self

Designing a meaningful re-career path demands curiosity, courage, and clarity of intent—not someone else's formula. Some will pivot industries, others will launch entrepreneurial ventures, while some may transition gradually—balancing passion projects with personal commitments.

There is no universal path—only one that aligns with values, aspirations, and lifestyle priorities.

1. **Keep Learning - Stay Adaptable and Relevant:** In today's rapidly evolving world, what worked yesterday may not work tomorrow. The most successful professionals and entrepreneurs are those who embrace lifelong learning and adaptability.
    - **Invest in upskilling**. Stay ahead by continuously learning new skills, whether in technology, leadership, or industry-specific knowledge.

- **Embrace change**. The ability to adapt and evolve is what separates thriving professionals from those left behind.
- **Seek feedback**. Learning isn't just about formal education—it's also about gaining insights from experiences, mentors, and even failures.

2. **Build Meaningful Relationships - Grow Through Connection:** Success in a re-career journey is often tied to the strength of a professional network. Genuine relationships can lead to collaborations, mentorship, and new opportunities.
   - **Cultivate genuine relationships:** Networking isn't just about exchanging business cards—it's about building trust and adding value to others.
   - **Engage in communities:** Join professional groups, industry forums, and masterminds where one can learn from peers and contribute insights.
   - **Give before you ask:** Help others without expecting immediate returns—this generosity often leads to long-term, mutually beneficial connections.

3. **Leverage Strengths - Align Work With What Energizes You:** Strengths are superpowers. By focusing on what one excels at and enjoys, a career can be created that is both fulfilling and impactful.
   - **Identify unique skills:** *What do you naturally excel at? What activities put you in a state of flow?*
   - **Align work with passion:** When work excites, persistence and resilience come naturally.
   - **Delegate weaknesses:** Instead of struggling with areas that drain, collaborate with those whose strengths complement one's own.

4. **Create Impact - Let Purpose Guide Your Work:** True success is measured not just by personal gains but by the positive impact on others. Whether it's mentoring someone, creating solutions that improve lives, or giving back to the community, contributions shape a legacy.
   - **Share knowledge:** Whether through mentorship, training, or writing, help others grow.
   - **Focus on long-term impact:** Think beyond personal success—*how can your work leave a lasting mark on your industry or community?*

- **Lead with purpose:** Businesses and careers built on impact-driven goals tend to create more meaningful and sustainable success.

Embrace lifelong learning, cultivate strong relationships, leverage strengths, and make a positive impact to create a successful and fulfilling career. Keep pushing boundaries, stay curious, and strive to leave the world better than you found it.

The F.I.R(Re-career).E. journey is unique—shaped by aspirations, choices, and vision for the future. Embrace it with confidence, navigate the challenges with resilience, and celebrate every milestone along the way.

Tools to Define Your Portfolio Career

Once the foundation of your F.I.R(Re-career).E. journey is clear—that your path is uniquely yours to define, the next step is equipping yourself with practical tools to design it intentionally. Think of these frameworks as your compass and map—helping you chart a path that is both fulfilling and financially sustainable.

1. **Ikigai Framework - Finding Your "Sweet Spot":** The Japanese concept of Ikigai, or "reason for being," offers a meaningful starting point. It helps you identify where four key areas converge:
   - *What you love?*
   - *What you are good at?*
   - *What the world needs?*
   - *What you can be paid for?*

   This intersection often reveals the most sustainable and fulfilling career direction.

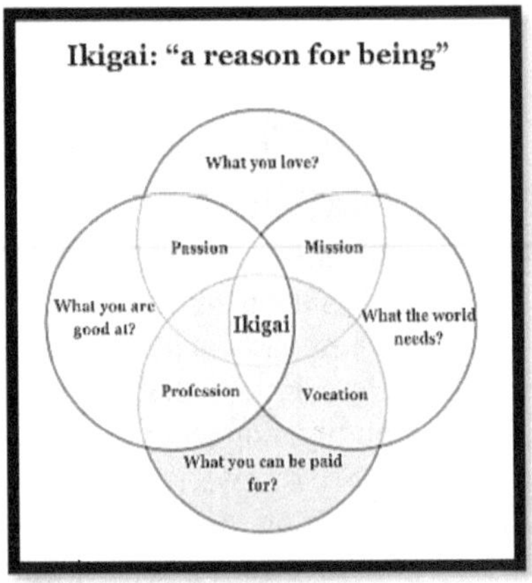

By reflecting on where your passion, profession, mission, and vocation intersect, you can discover deeply meaningful career directions.

Reflection questions to guide you:

- *What activities make me feel energized and inspired?*
- *What are the problems I am passionate about solving?*
- *What would people willingly pay me for?*
- *Where do my talents meet the world's needs?*

2. **Skills Matrix - Turning Strengths Into Opportunities:** Your skills are the raw materials of your re-career journey, but real leverage comes from knowing how to translate them into opportunities.

   How to build your Skills Matrix:

   - List down your technical skills, soft skills, certifications, and significant experiences.
   - For each skill, identify one or more ways it could be monetized—through freelancing, consulting, training, or creative work.

Example:

Skill	Opportunity
Public Speaking	Corporate Training, Emceeing
Financial Planning	Freelance Financial Advisory, Webinars
Writing	Content Creation, Copywriting
Project Management	Consulting for Startups or SMEs
Coaching and Mentoring	Executive or Career Coaching

3. **Market Demand Fit Analysis - Where Passion Meets Reality:** While passion drives, market demand transforms passion into a viable career. A fulfilling re-career sits at the intersection of what energizes you and what others will pay for. Understanding market trends ensures your skills align with real opportunities.

   How to Assess a Market Demand Fit:

   - **Browse Freelance and Project Marketplaces:** Explore platforms such as Upwork, Fiverr, LinkedIn, or Freelancer to identify high-demand skills and recurring service categories. Pay attention to the types of projects clients are posting and the rates being offered.

- **Research Industry Trends:** Study how your industry is evolving, what roles are being outsourced, which skills are becoming obsolete, and what new needs are emerging. Sector-specific reports, job boards, and trade publications can provide valuable signals.
- **Conduct Informational Interviews:** Speak with individuals *(e.g. mentors and certified coaches)* who have already transitioned into portfolio careers. Their first-hand experience can uncover hidden niches, pricing strategies, client expectations, and common mistakes to avoid.

Guiding Question:

- *Where does what I offer meet an existing or emerging need in the market?*
- *Are there underserved niches or untapped customer segments I can focus on?*

How to Start Small: Testing the Waters Before Full Exit

For many professionals considering a re-career, the idea of leaving a stable job can feel overwhelming.

Transitioning into a portfolio career does not always have to be a risky, all-or-nothing leap. In fact, many successful portfolio careers are built by starting small—testing ideas, gaining traction, and building confidence before making a full transition.

My Approach: *In my case, however, the path was different. My decision to leave the corporate world was not made hastily. It was a conscious and deliberate choice, rooted in a deep misalignment between my personal values and the company's evolving culture. Having achieved financial independence, I recognized that staying any longer would only prolong my sense of frustration and disengagement.*

Instead of "testing the waters" first, I made a decisive move—confronting the situation head-on and designing my exit strategy with clarity and conviction.

Key Takeaway from My Journey: My approach is not the conventional route, but it underlines three important truths:

- **Financial readiness gives you options:** When your basic financial needs are secured, you are no longer trapped by toxic environments or misaligned roles.
- **Values become non-negotiable:** You can prioritize purpose, impact, and well-being over survival.
- **You can transition with confidence, not desperation:** Re-careering becomes an empowering choice, not a forced reaction to circumstances.

That said, for many aspiring re-career professionals who are still building their financial runway or exploring new directions, starting small can be a highly effective strategy to de-risk the journey.

Here are low-risk ways to validate your re-career direction:

- **Offer Freelance Services Part-Time:** Start by taking on a few small freelance projects on weekends or evenings. This allows you to build real-world experience and client references while still maintaining financial stability.
- **Launch a Small Side Project:** Experiment with a manageable project, such as writing a blog, hosting a webinar, or offering a mini workshop. Watch how the market responds—are people engaging, signing up, paying?
- **Join Professional Networks and Communities:** Immerse yourself in the industry you want to move into. Attend meetups, join LinkedIn groups, or enrol in professional associations to build credibility and connections.
- **Volunteer or Intern in Related Roles:** If you are exploring a brand-new domain, volunteering can give you insider experience and help you assess whether you truly enjoy the work—without immediate pressure.
- **Pilot a Low-Risk Paid Product:** Instead of quitting to start a full-fledged business, offer a small paid service or product (e.g., an e-book, an introductory coaching package, a mini-course). Early sales and feedback will tell you if you're onto something viable.

Why Testing Matters:

- It validates your ideas with real-world feedback—not just assumptions.
- It helps you build momentum, testimonials, and credibility in your new domain.
- It minimizes financial and emotional risk, ensuring a smoother and more sustainable transition.

Whether you "start small" or "leap with intention," the principle remains: Your re-career is not a rigid path, but a dynamic canvas for purposeful reinvention.

Every step you take—big or small—is a brushstroke toward the future you are creating with purpose, passion, and courage.

Managing Multiple Roles and Income Streams

Building a portfolio career means embracing multiple roles and income streams. This dynamic model offers freedom and resilience, but demands intentional management of your time, energy, and brand. Success isn't about doing more; it's about doing the right things well and sustaining your energy.

Best Practices for Managing Multiple Roles

1. **Time Blocking - Protecting Focus and Energy:** When you are managing multiple professional identities, time blocking becomes your best ally.

   Dedicate specific days or hours to each role or project. Treat these blocks as non-negotiable appointments with yourself. This creates mental boundaries that enhance focus, reduce overwhelm, and help you fully show up for each endeavor.

   Example: *When I started managing business coaching engagements, regulatory service projects, and content creation, I allocated specific weekdays to each major focus area.*

   This discipline helped me stay present, productive, and energized—without feeling constantly pulled in different directions.

2. **Income Diversification - Building Stability and Growth: A** sustainable portfolio career balances predictable income streams with growth opportunities.

   In my case, having achieved financial independence before my corporate exit, I didn't need to rely on my portfolio career for stable income..

   My passive income—from carefully built investments and rental properties—formed the financial foundation that supported my F.I.R(Re-career).E. journey.

   This gave me the freedom to pursue multiple role-business coaching projects, corporate training, regulatory partnerships, courseware development, and authoring books—not out of financial pressure, but out of passion and purpose.

   However, if you have yet achieved financial independence, it is crucial to approach a portfolio career strategically. You need to balance:

   - **Base Income Activities**: such as long-term consulting retainers, stable freelance projects, or part-time contracts to ensure predictable cash flow.
   - **Growth Activities**: such as developing a new product, launching an online course, or building a personal brand, which may take longer to yield returns but have the potential for scalable growth.

3. **Clear Branding: Unifying Your Professional Identity:** One key challenge of a portfolio career is that you may wear many hats. Without a cohesive narrative, it can become confusing—to yourself and to your audience.

   The solution lies in clear personal branding. Develop a strong, unified "why" that connects all your activities, even if your "what" (the specific roles) varies.

   In my case, whether I am coaching entrepreneurs, delivering leadership training, providing regulatory services, or writing books, the unifying theme is clear: empowering individuals and organizations to unlock their full potential with purpose, passion, and peak performance.

You don't have to build your entire portfolio at once. Strategic integration—adding one role, one project, or one income stream at a time—leads to a more sustainable, enjoyable, and fulfilling re-career.

The beauty of designing your portfolio career lies in freedom and intentionality. You have the power to architect a life where multiple passions coexist, where work aligns with meaning, and where financial security and personal growth reinforce each other.

Overcoming Common Hurdles in the Early Re-career Phase

The journey of transitioning into a re-career can be fulfilling, exciting, and deeply meaningful. However, it is not without its share of challenges, especially the early phases, that are often accompanied by psychological, financial, and practical hurdles that require thoughtful navigation. Being prepared for these hurdles—and knowing how to navigate them—can make all the difference between a stressful experience and a rewarding one.

My Personal Journey: *Despite achieving financial independence before this shift, I experienced unexpected mental and emotional hurdles—adjusting to a new identity, building fresh routines, and facing the unfamiliarity of entrepreneurship.*

The F.I.R(Re-career).E. principles provided a framework to move forward with clarity, resilience, and renewed purpose.

Lessons from My Journey:

- True freedom is not just about having enough money — it is about mastering the emotional shifts that come with change.
- Letting go of ego, embracing simplicity, and finding joy in the small things can turn initial discomfort into newfound strength.
- Financial independence is the foundation; mental resilience builds the true re-career life.

The following are some common hurdles in the early re-career phase—along with suggested practical steps to ease the journey.

1. **Navigating Uncertainty and Financial Stability:** Without a stable paycheck, income volatility can cause stress—especially for those working toward financial independence.

   What You Can Do:

   - **Build a strong financial foundation**: Start with 6–12 months of emergency savings. This buffer gives peace of mind during slow months.
   - **Diversify your income**: Develop multiple income streams such as consulting, freelance projects, developing and selling online courses, or exploring passive income opportunities. Diversification reduces reliance on any single source and mitigates risk.
   - **Adjust your financial rhythm**: Embrace conscious spending and cultivate a mindful approach to your finances. This doesn't necessitate deprivation but rather an intentional simplification of your lifestyle, ensuring that your spending aligns with your values without sacrificing your quality of life.
   - **Detach identity from status**: Consciously release the ego's attachment to traditional career status or income. Embracing simplicity unlocks profound clarity and allow you to define success on your own terms, independent of external validation.

Mindset Shift: *Financial independence is the base, but mental resilience sustains the re-career path.*

---

2. **Developing Adaptability and Resilience:** New tools, shifting client needs, and evolving platforms demand a flexible, learning-oriented mindset.

   What You Can Do:

   - **Stay current and Continuously Upskill**: Make a commitment to regularly upgrade your skills, with a particular focus on digital engagement, new technologies, and innovative service delivery models. Lifelong learning is no longer optional but a strategic imperative.
   - **Experiment Boldly and Iterate**: Be willing to reimagine your services or offerings, perhaps in hybrid formats (e.g.,

online and in-person) or by targeting different audience segments. Test what resonates, gather feedback, and be prepared to pivot based on real-world results.
- **Lean into Discomfort**: Recognize that true growth often begins where your comfort zone ends. Embrace discomfort as a natural and necessary component of both personal and professional evolution. It signals that you are stretching beyond your current capabilities.

Mindset Shift: *Adaptability isn't optional; it's your new competitive edge.*

---

3. **Building Strong Networks and Continuous Improvement:** You are now your own brand. Your visibility, the quality of your professional relationships, and your willingness to contribute value to others directly drive new opportunities and sustained growth.

   What You Can Do:
   - **Network Intentionally:** Seek out and actively engage with events, masterminds, professional associations, or online communities that directly align with your re-career goals and values. Focus on quality connections over sheer quantity.
   - **Give Before You Ask:** Adopt a philosophy of generosity. Proactively share valuable insights, make thoughtful introductions between contacts, and genuinely support the growth and success of others in your network. Reciprocity often follows.
   - **Build Visibility Consistently:** Understand that building your personal brand is a cumulative process. Focus on consistent, small actions: one meaningful conversation, one insightful article published, or one collaborative project at a time.

Mindset Shift: *Authentic relationships are nurtured through genuine connection and generosity. Play the long game, focusing on building trust and mutual value.*

---

4. **Addressing Mental Health Challenges:** The newfound freedom of a re-career, particularly in solo pursuits, can paradoxically lead to issues such as isolation, heightened anxiety, or decision fatigue. The absence of traditional corporate structure requires intentional self-management.

   What You Can Do:
   - **Design Daily Structure:** Create purposeful routines that anchor your day. Integrate non-negotiable activities like physical movement, periods of quiet reflection, and dedicated learning time. Structure provides a sense of control and reduces overwhelm.
   - **Invest in Emotional Fitness:** Actively engage in practices that cultivate mental and emotional well-being. This could include mindfulness meditation, consistent journaling, or prioritizing social connections to counteract isolation.
   - **Seek External Support:** Do not hesitate to seek professional guidance. A coach can provide strategic direction, a therapist can help navigate emotional complexities, and a trusted peer group offers invaluable perspective and grounding.

Mindset Shift: *Your holistic well-being is not a luxury; it is your most critical asset. Guard it fiercely and invest in it proactively.*

---

5. **Managing Unexpected Expenses and Financial Resilience:** Unlike traditional employment where many benefits are covered, a re-career means you are responsible for all your overhead. Healthcare, software subscriptions, professional tools, and ongoing learning now come directly out of your own pocket.

   What You Can Do:
   - **Budget for Both Business and Life:** Establish separate financial accounts and distinct budgets for your personal living expenses and your re-career business operations. This clarity helps track spending, manage cash flow, and ensures financial control.
   - **Plan for the Unseen and Unanticipated:** Beyond obvious costs, factor in less apparent expenses such as specialized software, professional liability insurance, ongoing training

programs, and a contingency fund for unexpected challenges or opportunities.

- **Reinvest Wisely:** View investments in professional tools, continuing education, and efficient systems not as mere costs, but as strategic growth enablers. Prioritize investments that genuinely enhance your productivity, reach, or skill set.

Mindset Shift: *Robust financial discipline is not restrictive; it is the foundation that grants you the freedom to grow your re-career with confidence and stability.*

---

6. **Client Acquisition and Retention - A New Skillset:** In a re-career, clients do not simply materialize. Building and sustaining a consistent client base is a deliberate, ongoing process that requires proactive engagement, strategic positioning, and consistent value delivery.

   What You Can Do:

   - **Clarify Your Value Proposition:** Articulate with precision the specific problems you solve, the unique benefits you offer, and your ideal client profile. Clarity attracts the right opportunities and allows you to communicate your worth effectively.
   - **Build Credibility and Authority:** Consistently share your expertise and insights through various channels. This could include writing insightful blog posts, engaging on relevant social media platforms, delivering talks, or hosting informative webinars.
   - **Focus on Service, Not Selling:** Prioritize delivering exceptional value and cultivating strong client relationships. When you consistently provide outstanding service and genuinely help your clients succeed, authentic referrals and repeat business naturally follow.

Mindset Shift: *Visibility combined with consistent value delivery cultivates trust, and it is trust that serves as the most powerful magnet for attracting and retaining business.*

---

7. **Overcoming Self-Doubt and Imposter Syndrome:** Venturing onto new professional paths inevitably brings new insecurities. Even highly seasoned professionals can find themselves grappling with self-doubt or the pervasive feeling of imposter syndrome when starting fresh in a re-career.

   What You Can Do:

   - **Track Progress and Acknowledge Wins:** Maintain a dedicated journal or log of your accomplishments, positive feedback received, and lessons learned. Regularly reviewing these entries provides tangible evidence of your capabilities and progress.
   - **Surround Yourself with Encouragers:** Actively seek out mentors, peers, and communities who not only challenge you to grow but also provide genuine encouragement and upliftment. Their belief in your potential can be a powerful antidote to self-doubt.
   - **Reframe Fear as a Growth Signal:** Understand that feelings of fear or uncertainty often indicate that you are stepping outside your comfort zone and engaging in meaningful growth. View these emotions as natural companions on the path to expansion, not as signs to retreat.

Mindset Shift: *You are not starting from zero; you are building upon a rich foundation of accumulated experience, wisdom, and transferable skills.*

---

8. **Handling Inconsistent Workflows and Preventing Burnout:** The irregular demand often characteristic of re-careers can lead to cycles of overwork during busy periods and feelings of underwhelm during slower times. Both extremes can be emotionally and physically draining, potentially leading to burnout.

   What You Can Do:

   - **Adopt "Wave Planning":** Structure your time by scheduling distinct periods for focused work, dedicated learning and skill development, essential rest and rejuvenation, and proactive innovation or strategic planning. This approach balances effort and recovery.

- **Set Weekly, Achievable Goals:** Break down larger objectives into small, consistent weekly goals. Achieving these smaller wins builds momentum, reinforces a sense of accomplishment, and provides a clear direction during periods of fluctuating demand.
- **Prioritize Strategic Recovery:** Recognize that rest is not a reward for hard work but a fundamental component of sustainable high performance. Intentional periods of recovery fuel long-term creativity, enhance clarity, and prevent exhaustion.

Mindset Shift: *Pacing yourself strategically is not a sign of slacking; it is the cornerstone of sustainable high performance and long-term well-being in your re-career.*

---

9. **Handling Setbacks - Debriefing and Course-Correction:** Not every plan will unfold perfectly. Clients may disengage, projects might stall, or market conditions could shift unexpectedly. The re-career journey requires the capacity to navigate these setbacks without losing momentum or purpose.

   What You Can Do:

   - **Debrief Regularly and Course-Correct:** Establish a habit of reflecting on both successes and setbacks. Analyze what worked, what didn't, and what could be improved. Use these insights to intentionally adjust your strategies and actions moving forward.
   - **Cultivate Grit and Perseverance:** Develop a resilient mindset that views obstacles not as insurmountable dead ends, but as temporary detours. Embrace the belief that challenges are opportunities for learning and refinement.
   - **Stay Anchored in Your "Why":** Regularly reconnect with the core purpose and values that motivated your re-career transition. This deeply held *"why"* serves as a powerful fuel for perseverance through difficult times.

Mindset Shift: *Those who cultivate flexibility and embrace change are the ones who will ultimately go further. Resilience is your ultimate re-career superpower.*

---

10. **Leveraging Technology for Efficiency and Growth:** The sheer volume of available technology can feel overwhelming. However, when harnessed strategically, digital tools can unlock significant scale, enhance efficiency, and create new avenues for growth in your re-career.

    What You Can Do:

    - **Utilize Time-Saving Tools:** Explore and integrate technologies that automate repetitive tasks or streamline workflows. This could include AI-powered writing assistants, user-friendly design platforms, or various automation tools that free up your valuable time.
    - **Manage Your Business Digitally:** Adopt digital solutions for core business functions. Client Relationship Management (CRM) systems, online scheduling applications, and project management boards can centralize information and improve organization.
    - **Maintain Digital Curiosity:** Cultivate a continuous learning approach to technology. Experiment with new platforms, commit to regularly upgrading your digital literacy, and stay informed about innovations that could benefit your re-career.

Mindset Shift: *Technology is not a replacement for your unique skills and human connection; rather, it is a powerful multiplier that amplifies your capabilities and reach.*

F.I. First, Then R.E.: A Foundation for Freedom

As you reflect on the strategies, tools, and stories shared in this chapter, one message stands out with lasting clarity: the most empowered re-career journeys begin from a place of financial independence.

Financial Independence (F.I.) isn't just about having enough money to stop working—it's about gaining the freedom to start living and working on your own terms. It removes the fear of failure, reduces the urgency to monetize every venture, and allows you to re-career early (R.E.) with clarity, creativity, and confidence.

When you are no longer driven by survival, you gain the freedom to:

- **Say "No" with Conviction, On Your Terms:** Confidently decline roles, projects, or commitments that do not align with your core values or long-term vision. This ability to set boundaries protects your energy for purposeful engagement.
- **Say "Yes" to Passion-Driven Work, On Your Terms:** Embrace opportunities that ignite your curiosity and passion, even if their financial path is initially uncertain. F.I. provides the essential runway and psychological space to explore and build meaningful endeavors.
- **Build a Life and Career of Authentic Reflection, On Your Terms:** Construct a professional and personal life that is a true mirror of who you are and the unique impact you wish to make. This means designing your days around your deepest desires, driven by choice, not external expectation.

For a growing number of individuals, this expansive freedom is the ultimate aspiration—not a passive retirement from work, but an active and intentional reinvention of how work integrates into a life of purpose and fulfilment. It's about shifting from a life dictated by obligation to one driven by choice.

If you are just beginning your journey, dedicate your primary efforts to achieving financial independence as early and efficiently as possible. This involves a disciplined approach: save intentionally, invest wisely in diversified assets, and consciously reduce unnecessary commitments that drain your energy or financial resources. Laying this groundwork is the single most impactful step you can take.

Because when your financial foundation is strong and secure, your re-career choices are no longer dictated by the limitations of fear or the urgency of necessity. Instead, they are expanded by the possibilities of purpose, passion, and personal alignment.

Let your re-career be not merely a change in profession, but a profound life transformation—one that is bold in its vision, authentic in its expression, and truly limitless in its potential.

Summary

Chapter 12: Designing Your Unique Re-career Path focuses on how to intentionally design a life and career that aligns with your evolving values, purpose, and financial foundation. Re-careering is not a detour—it's a strategic and creative evolution of who you are and what you wish to contribute to your next chapter.

This chapter shifts the spotlight from the author's story to practical models, reflective tools, and real-world journeys that empower readers to take ownership of their own path. From exploring portfolio career options—like entrepreneurship, consultancy, creative work, and passion projects—to learning how to start small and manage multiple income streams, readers are equipped with strategies to move forward with clarity and confidence.

We emphasize that your journey is yours to shape, and no two re-career paths are the same. Tools for visioning, practical planning, and managing common hurdles such as time constraints, self-doubt, or financial uncertainty are shared to help readers take their first or next step.

The chapter concludes with a powerful principle: "F.I. First, Then R.E." By achieving financial independence first, you remove the pressure of survival and gain the freedom to re-career with purpose, creativity, and authenticity.

Key Takeaways:

- Re-careering is a deeply personal journey shaped by your passions, strengths, and values—not predefined roles or age norms.
- Portfolio careers offer flexibility and meaning; they can be designed around income diversification, freedom, and contribution.
- Financial independence provides the stability to take bold, values-aligned risks in your next chapter.
- Designing your path requires clarity, small experiments, and resilience—not perfection.
- Tools like vision boards, career maps, and personal mission statements can provide direction and inspiration.

Practical Tips:

- Use the **Re-career Visioning Canvas** to map your ideal lifestyle, values, skills, and opportunities.
- Begin with **low-risk, high-learning pilot projects** before fully transitioning.
- Identify and track **multiple income streams** aligned with your strengths and availability.
- Build your **support system**—mentors, peers, or coaches—to navigate early uncertainty.
- Revisit the mantra: **"F.I. First, Then R.E."** as a guidepost for sustainable and fulfilling decisions.

In the final chapter, **Living a Life of Purpose, Growth, and Fulfilment** delves into how engaging in meaningful activities, giving back to the community, and maintaining well-being contribute to a fulfilling re-career life.

Reflection Prompts & Mini Exercises

"Design begins with clarity, and clarity begins with reflection." ~ YK Png

---

1. **Re-career Vision Clarity**

Prompt:

- *What does your ideal day look like if career and income were not constraints?*
- *What types of work energize you, and which drain you?*
- *What problems in the world or your community do you feel compelled to solve?*
- *What kind of legacy do you want your next chapter to build?*

Mini Exercise: Ideal Week Visualization

- Block out a blank weekly calendar.
- Fill in your ideal work, learning, contribution, and leisure time—be honest and aspirational.
- Highlight themes and patterns (e.g., autonomy, creativity, impact).
- Use this as a guidepost for designing your re-career strategy.

---

2. **Portfolio Career Mapping**

Prompt:

- *What are 3 different roles or activities you'd like to explore or combine in a portfolio career?*
- *What skills or resources do you already have for each?*
- *Which income streams could be sustainable, and which would be passion-driven?*

Mini Exercise: Ikigai Alignment Map

- Draw four overlapping circles labelled:
    - *"What I Love"*
    - *"What I'm Good At"*
    - *"What the World Needs"*
    - *"What I Can Be Paid For"*

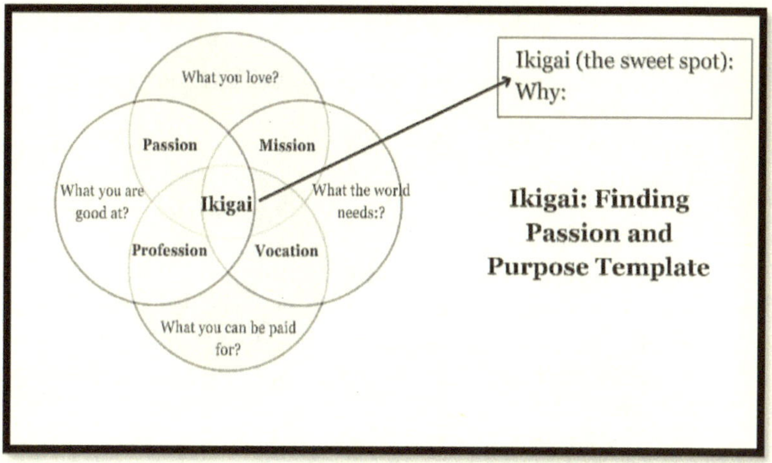

- Populate each circle with 3–5 responses using these prompts:
    - What You Love – *What energizes or excites you? (e.g., teaching, mentoring, creating)*
    - What You're Good At – *What are your natural strengths or learned skills? (e.g., communication, problem-solving)*
    - What the World Needs – *What challenges or causes resonate with you? (e.g., mental well-being, sustainability)*
    - What You Can Be Paid For – *What skills, services, or knowledge do others value? (e.g., coaching, consulting, digital content)*
- Explore the intersections:
    - Passion = *What You Love + What You're Good At*
    - Mission = *What You Love + What the World Needs*
    - Vocation = *What the World Needs + What You Can Be Paid For*
    - Profession = *What You're Good At + What You Can Be Paid For*
- Identify your Ikigai — the canter where all four areas intersect.
- Shortlist 1–2 ideas that reflect your Ikigai and can be tested or piloted in real-world settings.
- Optional next step:
    - Validate market demand with small experiments *(e.g., a freelance project, a workshop, or content series).*
    - Reflect monthly on alignment: *Is this work meaningful, sustainable, and aligned with your evolving values?*

3. Start Small, Start Smart

Prompt:

- *What's one idea you've been waiting to explore until "everything is perfect"?*
- *What's the smallest version of this idea you could try in the next 30 days?*
- *What's one fear or barrier stopping you—and what truth challenges it?*

Mini Exercise: Micro-Pilot Plan

- Choose one re-career idea *(e.g., side project, service)*.
- Define a version you can test in 2–4 hours a week.
- Set a clear goal: *"In 30 days, I will test [idea] by doing [specific action]."*
- Track learnings, not just outcomes.

---

4. Define Your 'F.I. First, Then R.E.' Strategy

Prompt:

- *Have you reached Financial Independence—or what's your target number?*
- *What trade-offs are you willing to make now to build that foundation faster?*
- *How would your re-career choices shift if money was no longer a constraint?*

Mini Exercise: Freedom Readiness Self-Check

- Review your current savings, passive income, and expense needs.
- Define your Freedom Number (monthly income needed to sustain your lifestyle).
- Write one sentence: *"I will accelerate my path to F.I. by [specific action]."*
- Reflect: *What would your Re-career look like if you were already F.I.?*

Chapter 13: Living a Life of Purpose, Growth and Fulfilment

"I am on a journey to live a life of purpose, growth, and Fulfilment." ~ YK Png

---

Attaining financial independence and entering the re-career phase represents a major life transition. Yet, beyond the milestone of financial security lies a deeper and more enduring aspiration: the pursuit of a meaningful and fulfilling life. True fulfilment is not measured solely by metrics such as net worth, career milestones, or material accomplishments. It is reflected in the intentional choices that shape each day—choices that align with deeply held values, purpose, and a sense of contribution.

The F.I.R.(Re-career).E journey is not simply about exiting the workforce or redesigning one's career; it is about redefining success and creating a life of purpose-driven action. It involves conscious decisions about how time is spent, how talents are used, and how personal growth continues across all domains—professional, emotional, intellectual, and relational.

Personal Reflections from My Re-career Path

Stepping away from a well-compensated corporate role to pursue a re-career aligned with personal values marked the beginning of profound personal transformation. While the initial transition brought uncertainty, it also opened the door to renewed energy, deeper satisfaction, and a stronger sense of purpose. Over time, it became clear that true success is not defined by the size of a paycheck or the prestige of a title—but by the quality of everyday experiences, the authenticity of contributions, and the capacity to live in alignment with what matters most.

Through business coaching, writing, and serving others in both professional and voluntary capacities, purpose became not just a guiding principle but a lived reality. Each initiative—from mentoring pharmacists and students, to consulting in companies and regulatory services—has reinforced a belief that significance is created not through intensity, but through intention.

This chapter outlines how financial independence can become the foundation for a more meaningful life—one shaped by purpose, sustained by personal growth, and enriched through contribution. It explores the mindset shifts, daily practices, and values-driven decisions that transform the re-career journey into a fulfilling and impactful life chapter.

Redefining Success in the FIR(Re-career)E Context

In conventional career paths, success is often framed through external validation—prestigious titles, escalating salaries, and societal recognition. These markers, while rewarding on the surface, may not always reflect inner fulfilment. It is not uncommon for high-achieving professionals to reach these benchmarks and still encounter a sense of disconnection or discontent.

The FIR(Re-career)E journey invites a conscious shift from externally defined success to an internally aligned version. It offers the opportunity to pause and reconsider the questions that drive professional and personal direction: *"What does success truly mean—beyond what society prescribes?"*

In the absence of traditional structures such as promotions or performance appraisals, individuals on a re-career path are responsible for defining their own benchmarks. Research by Deci and Ryan (2000) highlights three psychological drivers of enduring well-being: autonomy, competence, and relatedness. These elements—having agency, feeling capable, and being meaningfully connected—form the foundation of sustainable fulfilment.

This shift reframes the conversation from *"What do you do?"* to a deeper reflection: *"How does one live, contribute, and evolve?"*

The Three New Pillars of Success

As traditional definitions of success become less relevant in the context of re-careering, three essential dimensions emerge as a more authentic framework:

1. **Autonomy:** The freedom to shape time, environment, and professional pursuits in alignment with personal values. Success increasingly includes the ability to say "yes" to meaningful commitments—and "no" to obligations that no longer serve one's purpose.
2. **Contribution:** Engaging in work that generates impact beyond the self—whether through mentoring, volunteering, thought leadership, or community building. When individual strengths align with causes or communities that matter, the resulting fulfilment is both energising and enduring.
3. **Growth:** Lifelong learning, creative exploration, and personal development—not out of necessity, but out of intrinsic motivation. Success is reflected in the continuous process of becoming a fuller, wiser version of oneself.

Studies highlighted by the Harvard Business Review show that professionals who define success based on internal drivers such as purpose, contribution, and alignment report significantly higher life satisfaction than those focused purely on career status or income. This underscores a critical truth: success, when redefined through autonomy, contribution, and growth, becomes a way of being rather than a destination.

Reframing the Definition of Success

It can be helpful to reflect consciously on the meaning of success in one's own context:

- *Is the current definition inherited or intentionally crafted?*
- *Does it energise or constrain?*

A simple reflective exercise can anchor this shift.

> **Exercise**: Complete this sentence —
> *"To me, success means not my job title, but ______ [how I want to feel and contribute]."*
> Write your sentence down. Revisit it regularly.

This one small act of self-awareness can guide your decisions, priorities, and sense of fulfilment as you re-design your life.

Below are examples shared by others on the FIR(Re-career)E path:

- *"To me, success means not being a senior manager but waking up each day excited to teach and mentor young minds."*
- *"To me, success means not having a big title but having the freedom to spend my mornings with family and my afternoons building something meaningful."*
- *"To me, success means not managing large teams but helping others find clarity and direction through my coaching work."*

Such definitions reflect a deeper, more authentic version of success—rooted in intention, not convention.

Cultivating Passion, Purpose, and Well-Being in Daily Life

Living a meaningful life is not reserved for the few who make radical changes or chase extraordinary achievements. It is crafted moment by moment—in how one wakes up, what one chooses to focus on, how one practices self-care, and to whom one gives attention. Passion and purpose are not distant destinations—they reside in the present, in the deliberate, everyday choices made.

Upon reaching financial independence or starting a re-career, the urgency of survival gives way to a new challenge: *How can each day be made to matter?* The answer lies in intentional living, where time, energy, and attention are spent in ways that reflect what truly matters.

From Busy to Meaningful

In an always-on, hyper-connected world, it is easy to equate busyness with productivity, and productivity with purpose. However, these are not the same. Activity does not always equal alignment. When actions are driven by external demands rather than internal values, there is a risk of slipping into cycles of burnout, disillusionment, and emotional fatigue.

True fulfilment does not come from simply filling calendars. It comes from engaging in activities that not only utilize time but also uplift the spirit, restore energy, and reinforce a sense of meaning. Living intentionally means making conscious choices that reflect values, align with passions, and support emotional and physical well-being.

My Journey from Busy to Meaningful

For much of my corporate career in the pharmaceutical industry, I was immersed in driving outcomes—long hours, high demands, and constant pressure. While rewarding, it eventually became clear that success without alignment leads to burnout. My transition was a deliberate move to exchange intensity for impact.

Today, I guide organizations through business transformation and coach leaders to lead with clarity. I also find immense joy in offering pro bono coaching and mentoring—especially for students, fellow pharmacists, and colleagues—walking alongside them as they navigate career crossroads, seek direction, or embark on their own F.I.R.(Re-career).E journeys. My continued service to bodies like the Pharmaceutical Society of Singapore (PSS) and my work in regulatory consulting are deeply fulfilling because they are grounded in value, not just task completion.

These efforts—coaching, consulting, mentoring, writing—are all guided by the same principle: doing what matters most, rather than doing more.

My body of work—including Limitless Possibilities, The BRIDGE Career Handbook, The BRIDGE to Career Mastery, and now F.I.R.(Re-career).E—is the core of this commitment. This collection of books provides a progressive framework for designing a life of significance:

- ***Mindset & Performance:*** *Limitless Possibilities inspires transformation by aligning mindset, passion, and habits for peak performance.*
- ***Strategy & Mastery:*** *The BRIDGE Career Handbook and The BRIDGE to Career Mastery provide the robust strategic frameworks and practical toolkits necessary for career navigation and growth.*
- ***Freedom & Significance:*** *F.I.R.(Re-career).E culminates this journey, offering the definitive roadmap for individuals ready to move from financial security to life sovereignty.*

Together, these four books reflect my mission to help others design lives not just of conventional success, but of enduring significance.

Key Takeaways:

- **Purposeful living begins with self-alignment:** True fulfillment comes from aligning work and life with what truly matters, not constant activity.
- **Meaningful progress over busyness:** Shift from a task-driven mindset to a value-driven one to restore clarity, energy, and reduce burnout.
- **Passion is nurtured through contribution:** Creating impact in others' lives—whether through paid coaching or pro bono mentoring—cultivates personal meaning and motivation.

- **Significance comes from impact, not intensity:** Transformation is a shared journey where doing what matters most, rather than doing more, is the goal.

The commitment to well-being is non-negotiable for long-term fulfilment. The National Institutes of Health defines emotional wellness as "the ability to successfully handle life's stresses, adapt to change, and cope with adversity." This is not something stumbled upon by accident—it is built through consistent micro-practices that restore balance and foster resilience.

Micro-Practices That Build Macro Fulfilment

One does not need to overhaul their life to experience more purpose and well-being. The most sustainable changes often begin with small, intentional actions—done consistently. These micro-practices can be easily integrated into existing routines, without adding pressure or time drain.

Inspired by models like BJ Fogg's *Tiny Habits* and principles of consistent progress, these micro-habits help you shift from *"busy"* to *"intentional,"* one moment at a time:

- **Morning Anchoring (2–5 minutes)**: While brushing teeth, commuting, or waiting for morning coffee, mentally ask: *"What do I want to bring into today—calm, focus, empathy, clarity?"* A brief intention can shift one's mindset and set the tone for more meaningful engagement.
- **Purposeful Pauses (1–3 minutes)**: In between meetings, or high-focus tasks, take three deep breaths, step outside for a short walk, or simply stand and stretch. These small resets help reduce mental fatigue and keep individuals grounded under pressure.
- **Micro-Joys in Motion**: Infuse small moments of joy during the day. Listen to uplifting music while driving, savour a good coffee mindfully, or read a short article that sparks curiosity. These are not distractions—they are fuel for energy and emotional renewal.
- **Digital Edges (start small)**: A full digital detox is not necessary. Try no screens during lunch or wind down with five minutes of tech-free time before bed. These boundaries help create pockets of clarity in a noisy, always-on world.

- **One-Question Evening Check-In**: When preparing to sleep, ask: *"What moment today felt most meaningful or aligned with my values?"* No journaling is required—just a brief reflection to close the day with intention and self-awareness.

Research shows that professionals who incorporate such restorative practices experience reduced emotional exhaustion, greater mental clarity, and increased life satisfaction. Ultimately, it is not about doing more. It is about doing what matters—intentionally, meaningfully, and sustainably.

.Aligning Daily Choices with Passion and Purpose

Passion and purpose are not rare, life-altering discoveries. In reality, they often reside in the ordinary—embedded in the tasks, conversations, and quiet moments that energize and inspire you. Think of this as the practical application of finding your Ikigai (reason for being) on a daily basis

- **Passion** is what lights one up.
- **Purpose** is what grounds one in contribution.

Together, they fuel a rhythm of meaning and motivation in everyday life. If clarity is still sought, start by paying attention to these signals:

- *What activities make time fly?*
- *What topics are naturally gravitated toward in conversation or reading?*
- *When do you feel most alive, useful, or in flow?*

Now ask: *How can I intentionally create more space for these moments in my daily life?* Even 10–15 minutes a day devoted to something aligned with your passion or purpose can recalibrate your energy and, over time, reshape your life.

Reflection: A Daily Alignment Scan
To stay attuned to what matters, try this simple daily scan. Ask:

- *Did I do something today that energized me?*
- *Did I contribute to something larger than myself?*
- *Did I protect time for my well-being—emotionally, physically, spiritually?*

When these three questions are consistently answered *"yes,"* one is living in alignment—not just achieving goals but experiencing fulfilment.

Cultivating passion, purpose, and well-being is not about perfection. It is about presence. It is not about waiting for the ideal time. It is about choosing, today, to take small steps that align with what and who you care about most. When everyday choices reflect your inner compass, life becomes more than a checklist—it becomes a meaningful journey, lived one intentional day at a time.

Building a Sustainable and Fulfilling Lifestyle

As individuals journey beyond financial independence and re-career into a more intentional life, a deeper question arises—not just how one lives meaningfully, but also how lifestyle impacts others and the world. True fulfilment is not confined to personal growth; it also encompasses being a responsible steward of time, energy, and environment.

A sustainable and intentional lifestyle integrates not only passions and values but also the broader impact of choices—on one's health, communities, and the planet. It involves aligning how one lives with what one believes, while leaving a legacy of care and responsibility. Unlike the high-speed chase for success that often obscures environmental footprint or societal contributions, this lifestyle invites a slowing down and acting deliberately—for oneself and for the greater good.

Let's unpack what this truly means and how a life that is not just fulfilling, but also sustainable, can be built.

Understanding Sustainable Living

Sustainable living involves making conscious choices that reduce harm to the environment and contribute to long-term well-being—for both people and the planet. According to the United Nations Environment Programme (UNEP), sustainable lifestyles are about minimizing environmental degradation while promoting equity and quality of life for all (UNEP, 2022).

At first glance, sustainability may appear to be a global concern beyond the reach of an individual. Yet, it begins with the decisions made every day: what is consumed, how one travels, how resources are managed, and how one engages with communities.

Some of the most tangible benefits of sustainable living include:

- **Environmental Impact:** Small actions—such as reducing plastic use, consuming less energy, or choosing sustainable transport—collectively reduce one's carbon footprint and help preserve natural resources.
- **Health Benefits:** Sustainable lifestyles often involve eating whole, minimally processed foods, using non-toxic products, and spending time in nature—all of which contribute to better physical and mental health.
- **Financial Savings:** Energy-efficient appliances, conscious consumption, and mindful spending not only assist the planet but also reduce long-term costs.

When I made the shift to a more intentional life post-corporate, one of the most liberating changes was simplifying my material needs. I no longer needed to buy to impress or accumulate to validate success. I chose quality over quantity, and what started as an eco-conscious decision evolved into a mindset of contentment and clarity.

Embracing Intentional Living

If sustainability is about *"how"* one live, then intentionality is about *"why."*

Intentional living means making conscious choices that reflect one's deepest values and long-term goals. Instead of being swept up in autopilot routines or societal definitions of success, individuals live deliberately.

According to research from Weber State University (2021), individuals who live with intention report higher levels of clarity, well-being, and satisfaction. This is because their daily choices are aligned with a deeper sense of purpose.

Here's what that looks like in real life:

- **Enhanced Well-being**: When daily activities reflect who one is and what one believes in, stress is reduced, and inner conflict is avoided.
  For me, it meant transitioning from a high-pressure corporate environment to a portfolio career that includes coaching, training, and writing—activities that resonate deeply with my purpose.
- **Improved Relationships**: By living intentionally, one becomes more present with loved ones. Distractions are learned to be declined to prioritize meaningful connections.
- **Continuous Growth**: Intentional living naturally encourages personal development. Every choice becomes an opportunity to grow into a more authentic version of ourselves.

In my own journey, the transition to intentionality wasn't overnight. I had to unlearn habits shaped by decades in a performance-driven environment. For example, I began scheduling "non-productive" hours in my day—time to reflect, connect with nature, or simply be with family. These pauses, far from being wasted time, became my most nourishing moments.

Integrating Sustainability and Intentionality

The synergy of sustainable and intentional living is profound, as they complement and reinforce each other. When one is mindful of how they live, choices are naturally made that support long-term health—of oneself, one's communities, and the planet.

Here are some practical steps to integrate both into daily life:

- **Mindful Consumption:** Before acquiring anything, one can ask: *"Is this truly needed? Does it align with my values? What is its environmental or social cost?"*
- **Simplify Life:** Decluttering one's space, calendar, and even digital life reduces noise and enhances focus. Fewer possessions often lead to greater clarity, providing space to focus on what truly matters: relationships, health, and meaningful work.
- **Set Purposeful Goals:** Goals should not be chased merely because they appear impressive. Instead, one should ask: *"Does this goal align with the life I aspire to live?"* Goals should be revisited and refined regularly.

- **Engage in Community:** Whether joining a community garden, supporting local businesses, or volunteering for a cause, intentional living becomes richer when shared. During my re-career journey, collaborating with like-minded peers has added immense personal and professional value.
- **Create Rhythms, Not Rigid Routines:** Rather than building inflexible structures, one can create flexible rhythms—such as *"slow mornings"* on weekends, *"no-tech evenings,"* or family meals free from distractions. These rhythms build a life that feels both structured and spacious.

My Reflection: From Corporate Chase to Conscious Choices

In my earlier years climbing the corporate ladder in the pharmaceutical industry, I equated long hours with dedication and external achievement with self-worth. But no matter how much I achieved, something felt off. The stress, the busyness, the constant chase—it began to erode my sense of joy and clarity.

When I finally paused to reflect, I asked myself some difficult but essential questions: "What is the purpose of all this effort? Who am I becoming in the process?"

That moment of honest reckoning led me down a new path. Today, I live a portfolio life—coaching clients, facilitating workshops, writing books, and speaking on topics I care deeply about. My lifestyle may appear less "busy," but it is far more meaningful and aligned.

Key Takeaways:

- **Busyness Isn't the Same as Fulfilment:** Constant activity can create the illusion of success, but without alignment to values, it often leads to burnout and dissatisfaction.
- **Reflection is the gateway to intentional change:** Taking time to pause and ask meaningful questions can uncover what truly matters and inspire a shift toward purposeful living.
- **Fulfilment comes from alignment, not accumulation:** A meaningful life is built by aligning daily choices with personal values, rather than chasing external rewards. It's no longer about doing more but doing what matters.

- **Intentional Living Creates Sustainability:** Conscious decisions that support well-being, purpose, and balance lead to a lifestyle that is both impactful and enduring.

Building a sustainable, intentional lifestyle isn't about perfection; it's about progress with purpose. The F.I.R.E. journey is dynamic, evolving through awareness and guided by values. The small choices made each day—what we consume, how we live, how we connect—shape our legacy. When financial independence is paired with conscious living, we don't just escape the rat race; we build a life that reflects our deepest truths and supports the world we want to live in.

Living Fully: Balancing Purpose, Passion, and Well-Being

Living fully involves more than the pursuit of professional achievement or financial security. It reflects a deeper integration—of passion, contribution, and personal well-being—within the rhythms of daily life. Especially in the re-career phase, where work is often interwoven with identity and meaning, the ability to cultivate intentional balance becomes essential.

This stage is not about stepping away from ambition but about advancing with clarity and alignment. When daily choices reflect core values and authentic priorities, life transforms from a series of obligations into a coherent, fulfilling experience.

My Journey to Fulfilment—An Example, Not a Blueprint

As someone who transitioned from a structured corporate path to a re-career anchored in coaching, mentoring, and learning, I've come to appreciate that fulfilment goes far beyond titles or timelines. I chose to realign my life around purpose, not just productivity.

Along the way, I discovered that fulfilment emerged not from any one area, but from how they all came together:

- ***Lifelong Learning**: I discover new hobbies like pen-ink drawing, videography, and explored new competencies in* *digital marketing, logistics, and entrepreneurship—keeping my mind fresh and my skills relevant.*

- ***Travel**: From hiking in Tasmania to witnessing the Northern Lights, travel provided moments to reflect, connect deeply with loved ones, and reset. These experiences, often planned with my wife, became anchors in our shared journey.*
- ***Health**: Staying active—through golf, circuit training, or even National Day runs—helped me maintain the physical vitality and mental clarity needed for leadership and service.*
- ***Giving Back**: I found profound meaning in mentoring NUS students, coaching fellow pharmacists, and serving on boards. These aren't just activities—they are expressions of my purpose.*

This is my path to fulfilment—not a prescription.

Your FIR(*Re-career*)E journey will and should look different. The key is to identify your own sources of joy, meaning, and energy, and design your lifestyle around them.

Actionable Reflections for Your Own Journey

There is no one-size-fits-all approach to living fully. Each person's path toward fulfilment will look different, shaped by personal values, life stages, and circumstances. What energizes or grounds one individual may not speak to another. The reflections below are not a checklist to complete but prompts to help you explore what matters most to *you.*

Take what resonates, adapt what inspires, and leave what doesn't serve your journey.

- **Define Fulfilment**:
  - *What does a meaningful life look like beyond career success?*
  - *What are the values and experiences that truly matter?*
- **Stay Curious**: Consider experimenting with small, time-bound challenges—such as a 30-day exploration of a dormant interest or hobby. These micro-initiatives often uncover new sources of joy and potential.
- **Prioritize Well-Being**: Build consistent, sustainable habits that support rest, movement, and mindfulness. Protecting energy is a prerequisite for sustaining purpose.

- **Travel with Purpose** *(if it aligns with your lifestyle)*: Use travel not as an escape, but as an opportunity to reflect, bond with loved ones, or gain new perspectives—whether a weekend outing or a journey abroad.
- **Give Back Meaningfully** *(if this resonates with you)*: Consider mentoring, volunteering, or contributing in ways that align with experience and values. Service, when authentic, can be a powerful source of fulfilment.

Living fully is not about constant balance, but regular realignment. It is about designing a life where energy, time, and focus are directed toward what truly matters.

The Balancing Act of Fulfilment

Modern life often encourages compartmentalization, allocating work, health, relationships, and personal pursuits into separate silos. The FIR(Re-career)E mindset invites a shift from fragmentation toward integration. The essential question evolves: from *What am I achieving?* to *What am I nurturing?*

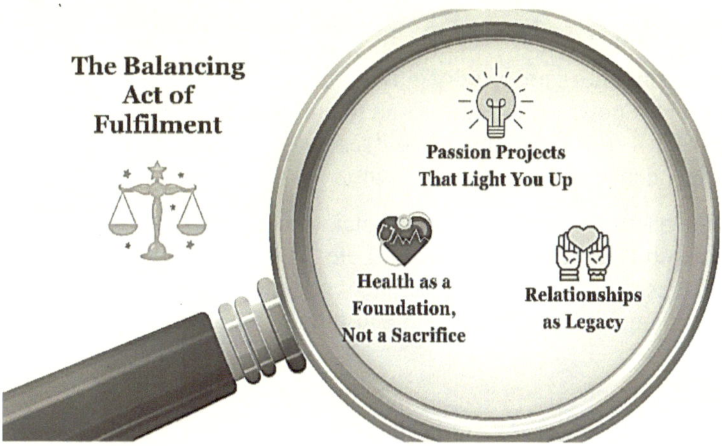

When individuals move from pursuing "more" to choosing what matters more, fulfilment is no longer about juggling—it becomes about aligning.

- **Passion Projects as Purposeful Expression:** Creative pursuits, volunteer efforts, or entrepreneurial initiatives that spark excitement are not indulgences—they are vital expressions of purpose. Such projects channel creativity, curiosity, and intrinsic motivation, often enhancing focus and fulfilment across other life areas.

- **Health as Foundation, Not a Sacrifice:** Health is not a cost of ambition, but its enabler. Physical and mental well-being provide the energy, clarity, and resilience necessary for pursuing long-term goals. Especially during the re-career phase, health supports continuity in purposeful work and meaningful living.
- **Relationships as a Living Legacy:** At life's end, individuals are seldom remembered for achievements alone. It is the presence, care, and connection they brought into relationships that endure. Deepening bonds with family, friends, and mentees forms a legacy far more powerful than accolades or status.

  The Harvard Study of Adult Development, one of the longest longitudinal studies ever conducted, underscores this truth: strong relationships are the most consistent predictor of long-term health and happiness.

Integration Over Perfection

Living fully does not require perfect balance every day. Rather, it involves regular recalibration—an intentional return to what matters most. This form of alignment bridges the gap between financial independence and meaningful living.

When passion energises, health sustains, and relationships enrich, the result is a lifestyle that feels whole. This is the deeper promise of FIR(Re-career)E—not merely to work less or retire early, but to live intentionally, purposefully, and fully.

The 3 Pillars of Fulfilment: Purpose, Balance, and Happiness

Financial independence unlocks more than the option to step away from traditional work—it creates space to design a life aligned with values, energy, and meaning. In this next phase, fulfilment is no longer defined by productivity or prestige. Instead, it is shaped by how intentionally one chooses to live each day.

The framework of Purpose, Balance, and Happiness offers a practical guide for navigating the post-F.I.R(Re-career)E landscape. It supports a shift from achievement-driven metrics to a more integrated, sustainable experience of life:

- **Purpose** provides a sense of direction and meaning, serving as an anchor for identity and contribution. A 2019 study published in *JAMA Network Open* found that individuals with a strong sense of life purpose experienced significantly lower mortality rates and greater psychological resilience—regardless of income, education, or overall health. In the context of re-careering, redefining one's purpose can enhance vitality, clarity, and long-term fulfilment.
- **Balance** encourages thoughtful allocation of time, energy, and attention across the domains of health, relationships, and growth. The *Harvard Study of Adult Development*, one of the longest-running studies on human well-being, consistently shows that individuals who maintain a balanced life—with emotional regulation and strong interpersonal connections—are more likely to experience sustained health and happiness over their lifespan.
- **Happiness** reinforces emotional well-being and connection to joy, beyond momentary pleasure. Martin Seligman's *PERMA model* from Positive Psychology highlights that true well-being is cultivated through Positive Emotions, Engagement, Relationships, Meaning, and Accomplishment. These elements become particularly salient in the post-career phase, as individuals seek deeper satisfaction and alignment with their values.

These three pillars are not abstract ideals—they are practical, evidence-based foundations for a life of purpose, vitality, and fulfilment after financial independence. When integrated with intention, they support not only sustained well-being but a redefined sense of success in the years ahead.

This framework encourages individuals to move beyond the question of *What am I retiring from?* and instead ask, *What am I now living for?*

- **Pillar 1: Purpose – The Anchor of Meaning:** Purpose is more than direction—it is a grounding force that transforms activity into contribution and achievement into legacy. Studies have consistently shown that individuals with a clear sense of purpose tend to enjoy better health, higher resilience, and longer lives.
  In the re-career phase, purpose is often redefined. Freed from formal job titles or corporate KPIs, individuals have the opportunity to revisit their "*why*." For some, this might involve mentorship or community service. For others, it could mean launching a cause-driven initiative, embracing artistic expression, or contributing through thought leadership.
  Personal Insight: *For me, coaching, writing, and mentoring aren't just roles—they are expressions of purpose.*
  They represent how I serve and grow at the same time. They bring me joy, challenge me to evolve, and allow me to pass on wisdom in a way that hopefully multiplies impact.

> **Reflection Prompt:** *"What would I still want to do—even if no one paid me for it?"*

- **Pillar 2: Balance – The Art of Harmonising Life Domains:** True balance is not about symmetry; it is about intentional alignment. It involves continually asking: *Do my daily choices reflect what matters most today?* Balance is the practice of allocating attention and energy in ways that sustain physical vitality, emotional resilience, and spiritual connection.
  The Self-Determination Theory by Deci and Ryan (2000) identifies three basic psychological needs that underpin fulfilment:
  - **Autonomy** – the freedom to make meaningful choices.
  - **Competence** – the opportunity to grow and master new challenges.
  - **Relatedness** – a sense of belonging and connection to others.

  When balance is lacking, one or more of these needs often goes unmet. In contrast, when life is structured to meet them consistently, individuals experience greater satisfaction and wholeness.
  Personal Insight: *After transitioning from corporate life, I learned that balance didn't mean doing less—it meant doing more of what mattered, with intention. That's why I began integrating exercise, morning reflection, catching up with friends, writing, and even unstructured time into my routine. These became anchors, not distractions.*
- **Pillar 3: Happiness – The Pursuit of True Happiness (*Eudaimonia*), Not Just Pleasure:** Happiness is often misunderstood as fleeting pleasure tied to external success. Yet, in the post-career phase, true happiness—what the ancient Greeks referred to as *eudaimonia*—is rooted in meaning, contribution, and personal growth.
  In *The Book of Joy*, Dalai Lama and Desmond Tutu introduce the Eight Pillars of Joy, which provide a framework for deep and enduring happiness:
  - **Perspective** – Shifting our viewpoint can change how we experience challenges.
  - **Humility** – Recognizing that we are part of something bigger than ourselves.
  - **Humour** – Finding joy in everyday moments, even in adversity.
  - **Acceptance** – Letting go of resistance to reality and embracing the present.

- **Forgiveness** – Releasing resentment to achieve inner peace.
- **Gratitude** – Focusing on what we have rather than what we lack.
- **Compassion** – Connecting with others through kindness and empathy.
- **Generosity** – Sharing our resources, time, and wisdom to create a more meaningful life.

Further, psychologist Martin Seligman's PERMA model provides a comprehensive framework for building lasting fulfilment:

- **P - Positive Emotions:** Cultivating joy, appreciation, and contentment in everyday life.
- **E - Engagement:** Immersing in activities that foster "flow" and personal mastery.
- **R - Relationships**: Deepening bonds that provide emotional support and connection.
- **M - Meaning**: Contributing to causes or communities greater than oneself.
- **A - Accomplishment**: Pursuing and celebrating progress toward meaningful goals.

These five elements help us move beyond *"feeling good"* to *"living well."*. They serve as guiding principles in defining and designing a fulfilling life. By integrating these aspects into our daily experiences, we can create a life rich with purpose, joy, and long-term satisfaction—one that extends beyond professional achievements and enriches every dimension of our journey.

Personal Insight: *In my FIR(Re-career)E journey, happiness has emerged not merely from freedom, but from the ability to live with intentionality. Whether hiking in nature, facilitating leadership workshops, or contributing to advisory boards, I often find myself in a "flow state"—a sign that the activity is both fulfilling and energizing.*

Reflection Prompt: *"What makes me feel deeply alive and connected to something larger than myself?"*
Your answer might uncover a current need.

Why These 3 Pillars Matter—Especially After F.I.R(Re-career)E?

The loss of structure, status, or routine following a career transition can be disorienting. Many individuals find themselves adrift, lacking the clarity once provided by a traditional professional role. The Purpose–Balance–Happiness framework does not seek to recreate old structures, but to replace them with intentional foundations for a new phase of life.

- **Purpose** offers direction and meaning in the absence of external validation.
- **Balance** supports sustainability and avoids burnout in this next chapter.
- **Happiness** ensures that fulfilment is not deferred but experienced in the present.

These pillars are interdependent. When one weakens, the others often feel the strain. A lack of purpose may manifest as restlessness; the absence of balance may lead to exhaustion; pursuit of happiness without meaning may result in emptiness.

Fulfilment is not static. It evolves. The key is to remain aware of these shifts and recalibrate accordingly. This is not a singular milestone to be reached, but an ongoing practice of realignment.

Guiding Question: *"Am I living in a way that reflects what matters most to me—right now?"*
If the answer is yes, continue on the path. If the answer is no, pause and reflect. Rebuild from these three pillars. In doing so, life becomes not just something to be managed, but something to be deeply lived.

Designing a Personal Fulfilment Plan

Reaching financial independence and transitioning into the F.I.R(Re-career)E phase often brings a shift in focus—from achievement to fulfilment. With time, autonomy, and experience now in greater supply, the key question becomes: *How can life be designed not just around freedom, but around meaning?*

Building on the Three Pillars—Purpose, Balance, and Happiness—a complementary framework grounded in positive psychology offers a clear path for translating reflection into intentional action. Centred on Pleasure, Engagement, and Meaning, these three elements form the foundation for designing a fulfilling life that extends beyond career success.

A Framework for Fulfilment: Pleasure, Engagement, and Meaning

Across cultures and life stages, researchers and practitioners have consistently identified three key elements at the heart of deep and sustainable fulfilment:

1. **Pleasure – Creating Space for Joy:** Pleasure encompasses experiences that bring genuine joy and emotional renewal. These are not fleeting indulgences, but regular, life-enhancing activities that uplift mood and replenish energy—whether through travel, nature, creativity, or quality time with loved ones.

> **Application**: Identify three activities that reliably bring you joy. Integrate them into your calendar regularly. Fulfilment is a result of what you prioritize, not what you hope will happen.

2. **Engagement – Cultivating Flow and Growth:** Engagement refers to the state of deep immersion in meaningful challenges—commonly known as *flow*. This occurs

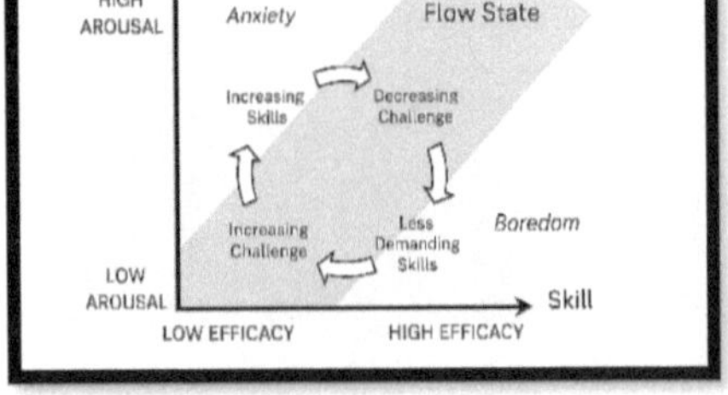

when skills are matched with purpose, and time seems to dissolve. Flow typically arises in activities that are both stimulating and aligned with intrinsic interests.

> **Application**: Identify an area where you can develop mastery—something that excites and challenges you. Make time for deep learning or creative pursuits that bring out your best.

3. **Meaning – Connecting to a Cause Beyond Self:** Meaning involves contribution to something larger than oneself—be it people, causes, or communities. It is the deepest layer of fulfilment, providing a sense that one's efforts matter and are part of a larger whole. This could take the form of mentorship, philanthropy, social impact, or knowledge-sharing.

> **Application**: Ask yourself, *"What impact do I want to leave on my family, my community, or my industry?"* Design your activities around that intention.

Personalized Paths to Fulfilment

One of the most liberating lessons in the F.I.R(Re-career)E. journey is this: there is *no one right way* to live a meaningful life after achieving financial independence. Fulfilment is not a one-size-fits-all formula. It is deeply personal, shaped by individual values, lived experiences, and evolving priorities.

Each individual's version of fulfilment won't—and shouldn't—look like anyone else's

My Journey to Fulfilment: *After more than three decades in the pharmaceutical industry—moving from frontline roles in hospital and community pharmacy to leadership positions in corporate—I had reached a point where I could have chosen a traditional retirement. But instead of stepping back, I chose to re-career.*

I founded CoachToring.com and PharmacistCoaches.com, merging my experience in healthcare and leadership with a passion for coaching, mentoring, and adult education. I wrote books to share insights and frameworks that had impacted my life, and I now spend my time empowering others to navigate transitions, unlock their potential, and live with clarity and intention.

The rewards—meaningful work, greater autonomy, and deep personal fulfilment. My journey is proof that it's never too late to redefine what matters, and that true purpose often emerges after the corporate title fades.

Fulfilment begins when we stop chasing someone else's definition of success and start building a life that truly energizes and sustains us.

Reflective Questions to Guide Fulfilment Design

To develop a personal plan for fulfilment, thoughtful reflection is essential. The following questions may serve as useful prompts:

- *If money was no longer a concern, how would I spend my time?*
- *What activities make me feel most alive and engaged?*
- *What do I want my legacy to be?*
- *Who are the people or causes I want to impact?*
- *When was the last time I felt deeply joyful, engaged, and purposeful?*

There is no need to have all the answers right away. Clarity often emerges from committing to honest self-inquiry and taking purposeful action.

A simple one-page fulfilment plan can provide both structure and flexibility. Below is a suggested format:

Area	Action Step	Frequency	Why it Matters
Joy (Pleasure)	*E.g., Attend monthly art class*	Monthly	Fuels creativity & connection
Growth (Engagement)	Learn to play the guitar	Weekly practice	Builds confidence & fun
Contribution (Meaning)	Mentor junior colleagues	Monthly session	Leaves a ripple impact

Fulfilment is not a final destination—it is a dynamic, lifelong practice. A personal plan that incorporates joy, engagement, and meaning provides clarity, but the real transformation lies in its consistent application. Financial freedom provides the time; a fulfilment plan provides the intention. When both align, life moves from being merely well-managed to being deeply lived.

Personal Fulfilment Plan Worksheet

Instructions: Take time to reflect on each section. There are no right answers—only *your* answers.

Step 1 - Define Your Vision of Fulfilment

- *If money were no longer a concern, how would I spend my time?*

☐ ______________________________

- *What does a truly fulfilling day or week look like to me?*

☐ ______________________________

Step 2 - Identify Your Joy Triggers: List three activities that consistently bring you joy and energy:

1. ______________________________
2. ______________________________
3. ______________________________

How often am I engaging in them?

☐ Daily ☐ Weekly ☐ Occasionally ☐ Rarely

Schedule these activities into your calendar for the next 30 days.

Step 3 - Engage in Deep Growth

- *What am I currently learning or mastering?*

☐ ______________________________

- *What new area would I love to grow in or explore?*

☐ ______________________________

Commit to one deep learning goal for the next 90 days:

☐ ______________________________

Step 4: Define Your Legacy

- *What do I want to be remembered for?*

☐ ______________________________

- *Who or what causes do I want to positively impact?*

☐ ______________________________

One way I will contribute this month:

☐ ______________________________

Final Reflection - Complete the sentence:

"A fulfilling life for me means..."

☐ ______________________________

☐ ______________________________

Next Review Date: ____________________

Keep the worksheet somewhere visible. Revisit it regularly *e.g. every 6 monthly)* as life evolves.

Integrating Fulfilment into the F.I.R(Re-career).E. Journey

Financial independence is often perceived as the ultimate milestone—a gateway to freedom from the constraints of the 9-to-5 routine. Yet in reality, it is not an endpoint. Rather, it marks the beginning of a new chapter—one rich with potential for deeper meaning, contribution, and growth.

The post-career phase is not about disengaging from life but fully engaging with it—living more intentionally, aligning actions with values, and designing days around what truly matters. While financial independence provides the freedom of time, fulfilment adds direction, depth, and emotional richness.

For many who reach this stage, the absence of structure and externally defined goals can lead to a sense of drift. Without a renewed sense of purpose, freedom can become a void. That is why fulfilment must be viewed not as a luxury but as a vital extension of financial independence—a dynamic process built on intentional living, self-awareness, and impact.

The Fulfilment Loop: Purpose → Action → Reflection → Growth

Fulfilment is not a static achievement; it is an ongoing cycle. This loop enables individuals to sustain vitality and alignment in the F.I.R(Re-career)E phase:

- **Purpose** provides direction, guiding decisions through clarity on values and desired identity: *"What matters to you most?"*, *"What kind of person do you want to become?"*
- **Action** transforms purpose into lived experience, reinforcing what matters through daily choices: *"What are you doing today that reflects that purpose?"*
- **Reflection** fosters alignment, encouraging evaluation of what energizes, depletes, or feels disconnected: *"Are you living in alignment?"*, *"What feels off?"*, *"What energizes you?"*
- **Growth** renews the journey, offering opportunities to stretch into new roles, skills, and contributions: *"What new habits, challenges, or contributions will stretch you next?"*

This cyclical process nurtures progressive fulfilment—not because circumstances are ideal, but because one remains engaged in a life of personal relevance and impact.

The key is not to "arrive," but to keep evolving.

> **Reflection Prompt:** Think of the last time you felt deeply engaged—time flew by, and you felt alive.
> What were you doing? Who were you with? What values were you expressing?

Live Intentionally, Not Passively

One of the most powerful outcomes of achieving financial independence is the ability to reclaim time. Without the demands of traditional work structures, individuals have the freedom to design each day with purpose. Yet this same freedom can lead to fragmentation or distraction in the absence of intentionality.

Practical strategies to support intentional living include:

- **Design days around energy, not just tasks:** Prioritizing activities that replenish vitality: *"What gives me energy?"*
- **Aligning commitments with values:** Accepting opportunities only when they reflect what is truly important. Say "*yes*" only when it aligns with personal values: Every *"yes"* is a *"no"* to something else. Be deliberate.
- **Keep a "Fulfilment Journal":** Regularly reflecting on what brought joy, usefulness, or dissonance during the week. Over time, these patterns inform a more aligned life rhythm.:
    - *What moments gave me joy?*
    - *When did I feel most useful?*
    - *What drained me or felt out of sync?*

Research shows that contribution to a cause beyond the self enhances long-term well-being and resilience. Impact does not need to be large-scale to be meaningful. Whether through mentorship, community involvement, or teaching, fulfilment is deepened when personal strengths are applied in the service of others.

Principles for the Fulfilment Mindset

Living with fulfilment after F.I.R(Re-career)E involves moving from obligation to intention. It is a shift toward designing a life that energises and sustains, rather than simply fills time. Key principles include:

- **Choose Contribution Over Comparison:** Value is not defined by external metrics but by where one's strengths and experience can make the most meaningful difference. Ask: *"Where can I add the most value with the freedom I've earned?"*
- **Design Around Energy, Not Just Time:** Aligning daily schedules with energising pursuits—such as mentoring, creating, or time in nature—nurtures long-term engagement.
- **Commit to Lifelong Learning and Curiosity:** As demonstrated by Carol Dweck's research on growth mindset, those who believe in continuous development tend to live with greater resilience and fulfilment.
- **Create Impact Beyond Self:** Fulfilment deepens when purpose is expressed through service—whether in professional mentorship, volunteerism, or personal acts of generosity.

My Journey: Living the Fulfilment Mindset

As someone who walked the path from corporate leadership to entrepreneurship, and now to coaching and authorship, I've learned that fulfilment doesn't come from any one role or title. It comes from doing work that aligns with who you are becoming—not who you used to be.

Every transition—pharmacist to regional director, trainer to coach, and author—challenged me to redefine success, reconnect with purpose, and recreate impact. And this reinvention never stops.

Fulfilment Is a Journey—Not a Checklist

Fulfilment is not a fixed destination. It is a lifelong process of recalibration, reflection, and renewed commitment to what matters most. The F.I.R(Re-career)E journey opens the door—but it is through intentional living that one walks through it with purpose and vitality.

- Fulfilment begins not with escape, but with engagement.
- It is not about doing more but doing more of what matters.

- It does not require dramatic change—only consistent, authentic steps.

> **Practical Next Step:** Revisit the **Personal Fulfilment Plan Worksheet**. Identify one meaningful action to take in the coming weeks - something that brings clarity, energy, or contribution. Over time, these small steps shape a life that is not only financially free but deeply fulfilling.

A Meaningful Chapter Awaits

The tools are in place. The foundation is set. The next chapter is not only possible—it is ready to be written. And the story, now, is one of growth, joy, and impact.

The author of that story is no longer bound by roles of the past—but free to design a life aligned with who they are becoming.

The author of that chapter is you.

Voices Across Life Stages: Purpose and Fulfilment at Every Phase

Fulfilment is not reserved for those at the end of a career journey. It is accessible—and essential—at every stage of life. Whether just starting out or stepping into a new chapter, individuals across generations face unique questions and opportunities for intentional living. These perspectives reflect how the pursuit of purpose and fulfilment can evolve with experience, awareness, and changing priorities.

- **Undergraduates – *"I'm still figuring things out."*:** This phase is defined by exploration, curiosity, and foundational choices. Asking meaningful questions early—about values, interests, and aspirations—lays the groundwork for a purposeful life. Small yet intentional actions such as engaging in volunteer work, pursuing passion projects, or maintaining a reflective journal can help translate personal ideals into lived experience. Fulfilment begins not with certainty, but with curiosity and alignment.

- **Young Professionals – *"I want more than just a paycheck."*:** In the early stages of a career, the pressure to succeed and establish stability can be intense. Yet this is also the time when habits, mindset, and the internal narrative of purpose begin to take root. Building a life where income and impact coexist—where momentum does not crowd out meaning—requires conscious choices. Fulfilment at this stage comes from balancing ambition with authenticity and aligning career direction with personal values.
- **Mid-Career Professionals – *"Is this really it?"*:** Many mid-career individuals find themselves questioning the trajectory they've built—prompted by burnout, stagnation, or a sense of disconnect. This inflection point is not a crisis, but an invitation to re-anchor in core values and reassess long-term direction. Fulfilment here may not require a dramatic exit, but rather a reframing of priorities, a renewed sense of contribution, or the pursuit of parallel paths that add depth and meaning to professional life.
- **Aspiring Retirees – *"I'm ready for a different kind of contribution."*:** Retirement is often viewed as a winding down. In reality, it can be a time of reinvention. With experience, wisdom, and increased autonomy, this phase offers the freedom to explore contribution in new forms—mentorship, volunteering, teaching, or community building. Fulfilment here often comes from legacy: not only what is left behind, but what continues to grow through the lives influenced and the values carried forward.

Across all stages, the search for fulfilment is a common thread. The expressions may differ—through learning, leading, mentoring, or serving—but the desire to live with intention remains constant. Financial independence is a powerful enabler, but fulfilment is what gives it direction.

Summary

Chapter 13: Living a Life of Purpose, Growth, and Fulfilment explores how fulfilment becomes the ultimate reward—and responsibility—after achieving financial independence and transitioning into a re-career. The chapter reframes financial independence not as an endpoint, but as the foundation upon which a more intentional, meaningful, and joyful life is built.

Drawing from reflective prompts, evidence-based practices, and personal insights, the chapter introduces the Fulfilment Loop—Purpose → Action → Reflection → Growth—as a dynamic framework for living with clarity and intention. It emphasizes that true fulfilment arises not from passive freedom but from engaged, values-aligned living.

Key themes include reclaiming your calendar with purpose, deepening personal growth through meaningful contribution, and recognising fulfilment as a continual evolution rather than a final destination. Real-life examples, including the author's own post-corporate journey, demonstrate how values, energy, and impact can guide a reimagined life of service and authenticity.

The chapter encourages readers to stay curious, courageous, and committed to evolving—even after achieving financial independence. Ultimately, it affirms that the next chapter of life is not written by default, but by conscious design.

Key Takeaways:

- **Fulfilment begins where financial independence leaves off**—it's built through purpose, growth, and contribution.
- The ***Fulfilment Loop***—Purpose, Action, Reflection, Growth—is a sustainable model for lifelong engagement.
- **Living intentionally** means designing days around energy and values, not just tasks or obligations.
- **Contribution** reinforces purpose and relevance, especially through mentorship, community involvement, or sharing one's knowledge.
- **Fulfilment is not a one-time achievement** but a journey of alignment and renewal.

Practical Tips:

- **Keep a weekly Fulfilment Journal** to track moments of joy, usefulness, and alignment.
- **Revisit your Fulfilment Plan Worksheet** and commit to one small, meaningful action each week.
- **Design your time around high-energy activities** that reflect your values.
- **Use reflective prompts** to stay aligned with your evolving sense of purpose and direction.
- **Embrace contribution** as a daily practice—impact doesn't need to be large to be meaningful.

This chapter concludes the book by returning the pen to the reader—reminding them that their next chapter is theirs to author. The journey toward financial independence and re-careering leads to the ultimate privilege: the opportunity to live with purpose, grow intentionally, and make a meaningful difference on one's own terms.

Reflection Prompts & Mini Exercises

"Fulfilment is not found—it is built through daily choices that reflect what matters most." ~ YK Png

---

1. Redefining Fulfilment for This Chapter of Life

Prompt:

- *What does fulfilment mean to you today, and how is it different from a decade ago?*
- *In which areas of your life do you feel most aligned? Where do you feel disconnected?*
- *What activities make you feel alive, purposeful, or deeply satisfied?*

Mini Exercise: Fulfilment Alignment Wheel

- Draw a circle and divide it into 6 segments: Health, Relationships, Contribution, Learning, Purpose, and Play.
- Score each area from 1 (low fulfilment) to 10 (high fulfilment).
- Choose one low-scoring area and write 2 small actions to raise your score over the next month.

---

2. Designing a Meaningful Contribution Plan

Prompt:

- *How do you want to make a difference in the lives of others in this next chapter?*
- *What skills, stories, or lessons could you share that might benefit others?*
- *What causes or communities do you feel drawn to support?*

Mini Exercise: Contribution Canvas

- List 3 ways you could give back—through mentoring, volunteering, teaching, or supporting a cause.
- Choose one and commit to a 30-day experiment *(e.g., weekly volunteer hours or mentoring a younger professional).*
- Reflect on how it makes you feel and what you're learning through the act of giving.

---

3. Energy and Purpose Calibration

Prompt:

- *Are you filling your calendar with tasks or with meaning?*
- *Which parts of your current routine bring joy or drain energy?*
- *If you had complete freedom, how would you redesign your ideal day or week?*

Mini Exercise: Purposeful Day Design

- Sketch out your *"ideal weekday"* from morning to night. Include activities that align with your values and energy rhythms.
- Compare it to your current schedule. What one adjustment can you make this week to bring your current day closer to your ideal?

---

4. **Reflecting Through the Fulfilment Loop**

Prompt:

- *What meaningful actions have you taken in the past month?*
- *What did those actions teach you about yourself or others?*
- *How are you growing from these reflections?*

Mini Exercise: Fulfilment Loop Journal

- Create a journal entry with these four headings: *Purpose – Action – Reflection – Growth.*
- Use this once a week to document a small moment where you felt aligned or inspired.
- Over time, look for patterns in what consistently leads to fulfilment.

---

5. **Living Forward with Legacy in Mind**

Prompt:

- *What do you want to be remembered for—not just professionally, but personally?*
- *If today were your last active day of contribution, what message or gift would you want to leave behind?*
- *Are you living your values out loud or keeping them hidden?*

Mini Exercise: Legacy Letter

- Write a short letter to your future self or loved ones summarizing what you hope your life stood for.
- Identify one small way to embody that message or legacy in how you show up this week.

Epilogue: A New Chapter, A Life Reimagined

Financial independence and re-careering are not destinations—they are catalysts for transformation. They offer the freedom to question convention, challenge limiting beliefs, and design a life that reflects one's deepest values and aspirations.

The journey through F.I.R(Re-career)E has been about more than mastering financial strategies or navigating career pivots. At its core, it is a redefinition of success—moving from accumulation to alignment, from obligation to intention, from burnout to fulfilment. It is about reclaiming the most valuable resource of all: time.

Each chapter of this book was crafted to equip individuals with practical tips, frameworks, and reflective prompts to guide decisions across life stages. But the true power lies not in the pages, but in how one applies the insights with clarity and courage. Whether the path ahead involves launching a portfolio career, simplifying life, giving back to society, or simply enjoying greater freedom with loved ones—F.I.R(Re-career)E is a reminder that purposeful living begins not at the end of a career, but with each intentional choice made today.

This is not an ending, but a new beginning.

My Journey

Looking back, pursuing financial independence and re-careering early was never about escaping work—it was about finding meaning. It was about aligning what I did with who I was becoming. The journey wasn't always clear or linear, but each step brought me closer to a life of purpose, freedom, and fulfilment. Writing this book is part of that evolving journey. I hope it inspires others to take their first step—intentionally and confidently—wherever they are.

A Final Word: Your Turn to Begin

"Don't just make a living—design a life."

The tools are in your hands. The decision is yours. Work less. Live more. On your terms.

Further Reading from the Author

Limitless Possibilities: Unlock Your Potential Today!

Limitless Possibilities is YK Png's first book—an empowering guide for those seeking deeper meaning and direction in life and career. It introduces two practical frameworks developed by the author:

- The **MPH Framework** (Mindset, Passion and Purpose, Habits) helps individuals build strong personal values and intentional habits that support growth and fulfilment.
- The **BRIDGE Elements** (Brand Yourself, Right Attitude, Interpersonal Skills, Development, Gain Influence, EQ) offers tools for navigating career progression and leadership development.

Together, these frameworks provide clarity and confidence for personal transformation and professional success.

Limitless Possibilities is available on **Amazon** in both **English and Chinese** editions. It complements *F.I.R(E). – Financial Independence Re-career Early* by focusing on the inner mindset and values needed to pursue a life of purpose, contribution, and growth.

The BRIDGE Career Handbook
Practical Strategies to Build Your Brand, Network, Influence & EQ for Career Success

The ***BRIDGE Career Handbook*** is a tactical field guide specifically for new graduates and early-to-mid-career professionals. It provides a step-by-step approach to applying the six BRIDGE elements (Branding, Right Attitude, Interpersonal Skills, Development, Gaining Influence, and Emotional Intelligence). This handbook is a practical resource filled with actionable tools, templates, and exercises designed to help readers build confidence and navigate common workplace challenges. It focuses on bridging the gap between academic achievement and career success.

The BRIDGE to Career Mastery
From Self-Leadership to Lasting Impact

The BRIDGE to Career Mastery is an expanded playbook designed for a wider audience, including experienced professionals, entrepreneurs, and founders. While it builds upon the core BRIDGE framework, this book goes beyond foundational skills to focus on long-term career mastery and creating lasting impact. It includes new chapters on financial literacy, work-life balance, and, most notably, a new pillar on "Coaching & Mentoring", positioning it as a guide for those who seek not only to advance their own careers but also to elevate and guide others. This book is a complete guide to intentional growth and sustained success.

Bibliography

Books

- Becker, G. S. (1964). *Human capital: A theoretical and empirical analysis, with special reference to education*. University of Chicago Press.
- Bridges, W. (1991). *Managing transitions: Making the most of change*. Da Capo Lifelong Books.
- Burchard, B. (2017). *High performance habits: How extraordinary people become that way*. Hay House.
- Covey, S. R. (1989). *The 7 habits of highly effective people: Powerful lessons in personal change*. Free Press.
- Csikszentmihalyi, M. (1990). *Flow: The psychology of optimal experience*. Harper & Row.
- Dalai Lama, & Tutu, D. (2016). *The book of joy: Lasting happiness in a changing world*. Avery.
- Dweck, C. (2006). *Mindset: The new psychology of success*. Ballantine Books.
- Ferrazzi, K. (2005). *Never eat alone: And other secrets to success, one relationship at a time*. Currency.
- Fisher, K. (2019). *Paths to wealth through common stocks*. Harper Business.
- Fogg, B. J. (2019). *Tiny Habits: The small changes that change everything*. Houghton Mifflin Harcourt.
- Garcia, H., & Miralles, F. (2016). *Ikigai: The Japanese secret to a long and happy life*. Penguin Books.
- Gardner, C. (2006). *The pursuit of happyness*. Amistad.
- Goleman, D. (1995). *Emotional intelligence: Why it can matter more than IQ*. Bantam.
- Goleman, D. (2006). *Social intelligence: The new science of human relationships*. Bantam Books.
- Grant, A. (2013). *Give and take: A revolutionary approach to success*. Viking.
- Grant, A. (2013). *Give and take: Why helping others drives our success*. Penguin Books.
- Grant, A. (2021). *Think again: The power of knowing what you don't know*. Viking.
- Housel, M. (2020). *The psychology of money: Timeless lessons on wealth, greed, and happiness*. Harriman House.
- Ibarra, H. (2003). *Working identity: Unconventional strategies for reinventing your career*. Harvard Business Review Press.
- Kabat-Zinn, J. (1990). *Full catastrophe living: Using the wisdom of your body and mind to face stress, pain, and illness*. Delta.
- Kahneman, D. (2011). *Thinking, fast and slow*. Farrar, Straus and Giroux.
- Kiyosaki, R. T. (1997). *Rich dad poor dad: What the rich teach their kids about money that the poor and middle class do not!*. Warner Books.

- Knowles, M. S. (1980). *The modern practice of adult education: From pedagogy to andragogy*. Cambridge Books.
- Kolb, D. A. (1984). *Experiential learning: Experience as the source of learning and development*. Prentice Hall.
- Locke, E. A., & Latham, G. P. (1990). *A theory of goal setting & task performance*. Prentice Hall.
- Pink, D. H. (2009). *Drive: The surprising truth about what motivates us*. Riverhead Books.
- Ramsey, D. (2013). *The total money makeover: A proven plan for financial fitness*. Thomas Nelson.
- Robin, V., & Dominguez, J. (1992). *Your money or your life: 9 steps to transforming your relationship with money and achieving financial independence*. Penguin Books.
- Seligman, M. E. P. (2002). *Authentic happiness: Using the new positive psychology to realize your potential for lasting fulfilment*. Free Press.
- Seligman, M. E. P. (2011). *Flourish: A visionary new understanding of happiness and well-being*. Free Press.
- Siegel, J. (2022). *Stocks for the long run*. McGraw Hill.
- Stanley, T. J., & Danko, W. D. (1996). *The millionaire next door: The surprising secrets of America's wealthy*. Longstreet Press.
- Vaillant, G. E. (2012). *Triumphs of experience: The men of the Harvard Grant Study*. Harvard University Press.
- Walker, M. (2017). *Why we sleep: The new science of sleep and dreams*. Scribner.
- Waldinger, R., & Schulz, M. S. (2023). *The Good Life: Lessons from the World's Longest Scientific Study of Happiness*. Simon & Schuster.
- Warren, E., & Tyagi, A. W. (2005). *All your worth: The ultimate lifetime money plan*. Simon & Schuster.

Journal Articles

- Aditya Birla Capital. (n.d.). *Term Deposit vs Fixed Deposit: Key differences*. Retrieved June 17, 2025, from https://www.adityabirlacapital.com/abc-of-money/term-deposit-vs-fixed-deposit
- Alimujiang, A., Wiensch, A., Boss, J., Fleischer, N. L., Mondul, A. M., McLean, K., ... & Pearce, C. L. (2019). Association between life purpose and mortality among US adults older than 50 years. *JAMA Network Open*, *2*(5), e194270. https://doi.org/10.1001/jamanetworkopen.2019.4270
- CIMB Singapore. (2025, April 16). *2 out of 3 Singapore residents aspire to achieve financial independence between 40 to 60* [Press release]. The Straits Times. https://www.straitstimes.com
- Deci, E. L., & Ryan, R. M. (2000). The "what" and "why" of goal pursuits: Human needs and the self-determination of behaviour. *Psychological Inquiry*, *11*(4), 227–268. https://doi.org/10.1207/S15327965PLI1104_01

- Doran, G. T. (1981). There's a S.M.A.R.T. Way to Write Management's Goals and Objectives. *Management Review*, *70*(11), 35–36.
- Duffy, R. D., Douglass, R. P., & Autin, K. L. (2016). Career adaptability and academic satisfaction: Examining work volition and self-efficacy as mediators. *Journal of Vocational Behaviour*, *94*, 102-111.
- George, L. S., & Park, C. L. (2016). Meaning in life as a predictor of mortality across adulthood. *Journal of Positive Psychology*, *11*(6), 613–621. https://doi.org/10.1080/17439760.2016.1157061
- Hill, P. L., & Turiano, N. A. (2014). Purpose in life as a predictor of mortality across adulthood. *Psychological Science*, *25*(7), 1482–1486. https://doi.org/10.1177/0956797614531799
- Kahneman, D., & Deaton, A. (2010). High income improves evaluation of life but not emotional well-being. *Proceedings of the National Academy of Sciences*.
- Pennebaker, J. W. (1997). Writing about emotional experiences as a therapeutic process. *Psychological Science*.
- Ryan, R. M., & Deci, E. L. (2000). Self-determination theory and the facilitation of intrinsic motivation, social development, and well-being. *American Psychologist*, *55*(1), 68–78.
- Steger, M. F. (2012). Making meaning in life. *Psychological Inquiry*, *23*(4), 381–385.

Websites and Reports

- American Institute for Economic Research. (2019). *Older workers on the move: Re-careering in later life*.
- American Psychological Association. (2020). *The role of social support in stress management*.
- Buffett, W. (n.d.). *Various speeches and writings on financial discipline and investing principles*.
- Case studies from *The Pursuit of Happyness* (Chris Gardner) and *The Huffington Post* (Arianna Huffington).
- Central Provident Fund Board (CPF). (2023). *Integrated Shield Plans and ElderShield/CareShield Life*. https://www.cpf.gov.sg
- Central Provident Fund Board (CPF). (2023). *Retirement planning guide*. Singapore Government. www.cpf.gov.sg
- Central Provident Fund Board Singapore. (2024). *Understanding CPF LIFE and retirement planning*. www.cpf.gov.sg
- CFA Institute. (2020). *Essentials of Investment Management*. https://www.cfainstitute.org
- Consumer Financial Protection Bureau. (n.d.). *An essential guide to building an emergency fund*. https://www.consumerfinance.gov/an-essential-guide-to-building-an-emergency-fund/
- DBS Bank Investor Relations. https://www.dbs.com/investor
- DBS Bank Ltd. (n.d.). *Maximise interest with DBS Multiplier Account*. Retrieved June 17, 2025, from https://www.dbs.com.sg/personal/deposits/bank-accounts/multiplier

- Elim Chew interview: CNA Luxury. *Why 77th Street's founder left retail to fund startups and social causes*. https://cnaluxury.channelnewsasia.com
- Fidelity Investments. (2022). *The power of compounding interest.*
- Fiig Securities. (2016, November 23). *Capital Structure – A detailed assessment*. Retrieved June 17, 2025, from https://www.fiig.com.au/research-and-education/fiig-research-news-item/2016/11/23/capital-structure---a-detailed-assessment
- Gallup. (2021). *The impact of coaching on employee engagement.*
- Gates Foundation. (2023). *Melinda Gates: Creating impact through philanthropy*. https://www.gatesfoundation.org.
- Glaeser, E. L., & Gyourko, J. (2018). The Economic Implications of Housing Supply. *Journal of Economic Perspectives*, *32*(1), 3-30.
- Global Property Guide. https://www.globalpropertyguide.com
- GROW Model. (n.d.). *A simple framework for coaching and mentoring*. https://www.mindtools.com.
- Harvard Business Review. (2019). *The case for lifelong learning*. https://hbr.org.
- Harvard Business Review. (2020). *Lifelong learning and the future of work*. https://hbr.org.
- Harvard Business Review. (2020). *The role of career coaching in job search success*. https://hbr.org.
- Harvard Business Review. (2021). *Reinventing your career at any age*. https://hbr.org
- Harvard Business Review. (2023). *Why redefining success leads to more fulfilment*. https://hbr.org/2023/05/redefining-success-life-satisfaction
- HM Revenue & Customs (UK). gov.uk
- Inland Revenue Authority of Singapore (IRAS). iras.gov.sg
- Institute for Financial Literacy Singapore (IFL). *Understanding Investment Risks*. https://www.moneysense.gov.sg
- Institute of Mental Health (IMH) & Duke-NUS Medical School. (2021). *The Impact of Purpose and Social Connection on Wellbeing Among Older Adults in Singapore*. https://www.duke-nus.edu.sg/care/publications/reports
- Interventional News. (2020). *Micro-practices for burnout prevention and emotional wellness*. https://www.interventionalnews.com/micro-practices-emotional-wellness
- Interventional News. (2020). *Micro-practices for burnout prevention and emotional wellness*. https://www.interventionalnews.com/micro-practices-burnout-prevention
- Invesco ETFs. https://www.invesco.com
- Investopedia. (n.d.). *Exchange-Traded Fund (ETF): What It Is and How It Works*. Retrieved June 17, 2025, from https://www.investopedia.com/terms/e/etf.asp
- Investopedia. (n.d.). *Real Estate Investment Strategies*. https://www.investopedia.com

- Investopedia. (n.d.). *The Most Affordable Way to Buy Gold: Physical Gold or ETFs?*. Retrieved June 17, 2025, from https://www.investopedia.com/articles/investing/031913/most-affordable-way-buy-gold-physical-gold-or-etfs.asp
- iShares by BlackRock. https://www.ishares.com
- Life Insurance Association Singapore (LIA). (2023). *Insurance coverage gap studies and consumer guides*. https://www.lia.org.sg
- LinkedIn Talent Solutions. (2022). *Job Seekers Trends in Singapore*. https://business.linkedin.com
- Microsoft. (2020). *Satya Nadella's vision for a learn-it-all culture*. https://www.microsoft.com.
- Ministry of Finance Singapore. mof.gov.sg
- Ministry of Health Singapore. (2023). *CareShield life overview*. https://www.moh.gov.sg
- Ministry of Health Singapore. (2023). *Healthcare financing and MediShield Life*. https://www.moh.gov.sg
- Ministry of Health Singapore. (2023). *Integrated shield plans and medisave usage*. https://www.moh.gov.sg
- Ministry of Health Singapore. *MediShield Life Overview*. https://www.moh.gov.sg
- Monetary Authority of Singapore (MAS). (2021, October 4). *Guidelines on Licensing, Registration and Conduct of Business for Fund Management Companies [SFA 04-G05]*. https://www.mas.gov.sg/regulation/guidelines/sfa04-g05
- Monetary Authority of Singapore (MAS). (2022). *Consumer guide to life insurance*. https://www.mas.gov.sg
- Monetary Authority of Singapore (MAS). (2022). *Residential Property Loan Guidelines: MSR and TDSR Framework*. https://www.mas.gov.sg/
- Monetary Authority of Singapore (MAS). (2022). *Your guide to life insurance*. https://www.mas.gov.sg
- Monetary Authority of Singapore (MAS). *Guidelines on Licensing and Conduct of Business for Fund Management Companies (SFA 04-G05)*. https://www.mas.gov.sg/regulation/guidelines/guidelines-on-licensing-and-conduct-of-business-for-fund-management-companies
- Monetary Authority of Singapore (MAS). *Guidelines on Standards of Conduct for Marketing and Distribution Activities by Financial Institutions (FSG-G02)*. https://www.mas.gov.sg/regulation/guidelines/guidelines-on-standards-of-conduct-for-marketing-and-distribution-activities
- MoneySense Singapore. *Income Protection Insurance*. https://www.moneysense.gov.sg
- National Endowment for Financial Education (NEFE). (2016). *Debt Reduction Strategies Study*. www.nefe.org

- National Institutes of Health. (2016). *Emotional wellness toolkit.* NIH. https://www.nih.gov/news-events/news-releases/emotional-wellness-toolkit.
- National Institutes of Health. (2016). *Emotional wellness toolkit.* U.S. Department of Health and Human Services. https://www.nih.gov/health-information/emotional-wellness-toolkit
- National University of Singapore Centre for Ageing Research and Education. (2019). *Productive ageing and well-being.* https://medicine.nus.edu.sg/ageing/research/research-centre-care/
- Nikko Asset Management. https://www.nikkoam.com.sg
- OECD. (2017). *Health at a Glance 2017: OECD Indicators.* https://www.oecd.org/health/health-at-a-glance-19991312.htm
- OECD. (2021). *Insurance resilience in the face of disasters.* https://www.oecd.org
- Oliver Wendell Holmes Jr., *Speeches 72* (1913) (address delivered at the Justice Oliver Wendell Holmes Dedication Day, Washington, D.C., Mar. 8, 1913).
- PMC. (2024). *Relationship between Family Variables and Career Adaptability.* https://pmc.ncbi.nlm.nih.gov/articles/PMC11428647/
- Positively Productive. (2023). *How productivity is impacted by seasonal energy.* https://positivelyproductive.com/seasonal-energy-productivity
- Psych Central. (n.d.). *Intentional living: Why and how to start acting with purpose.* https://psychcentral.com/health/intentional-living
- Reclaim.ai. (2025). *Time blocking: The complete productivity guide.* https://reclaim.ai/blog/time-blocking-guide
- Sangare, D. (2025). *Redefining success: Beyond paychecks and job titles.* LinkedIn. https://www.linkedin.com/pulse/redefining-success-beyond-paychecks-job-titles-d-sangare
- Singapore Exchange (SGX). https://www.sgx.com
- SingSaver. *Best ETFs to Invest in Singapore.* https://www.singsaver.com.sg
- SPDR ETFs. https://www.ssga.com/sg
- Starbucks. (2017). *Howard Schultz: The vision behind Starbucks.* https://www.starbucks.com.
- Sustain Your Style. (2023, July 27). *6 life-changing benefits of leading a sustainable lifestyle.* https://www.sustainyourstyle.org/en/blog/2023/7/27/6-life-changing-benefits-of-leading-a-sustainable-lifestyle
- The Association for Financial Counselling & Planning Education (AFCPE). (2020). *The Importance of Insurance in Financial Planning.*
- U.S. Internal Revenue Service (IRS). irs.gov
- United Nations Environment Programme (UNEP). (n.d.). *Sustainable lifestyles.* https://www.unep.org/explore-topics/resource-efficiency/what-we-do/sustainable-lifestyles

- Urban Redevelopment Authority (URA). (2023). *Private Residential Property Price Index*. https://www.ura.gov.sg/
- Vanguard. (n.d.). *Prepare for the emotional side of retirement*. https://ownyourfuture.vanguard.com/content/en/learn/living-in-retirement/be-prepared-for-the-emotional-side-of-retirement.html
- Weber State University. (n.d.). *How being intentional can help you on your road to success*. https://www.weber.edu/academicpeercoaching/blog/being-intentional.html
- World Bank. *Housing and Mortgage Market Reports*. https://www.worldbank.org
- World Economic Forum. (2023). *The future of jobs report 2023*.
- World Health Organization. (2022). *Workplace mental health and well-being*. https://www.who.int
- Yung Pueblo. (2025). *The 3 pillars of happiness*. Substack. https://yungpueblo.substack.com/p/the-three-pillars-of-happiness

Acknowledgments

This book is the product of not just personal experience, but the collective wisdom, support, and encouragement of many individuals who have shaped my journey and inspired this work.

First, I would like to thank my family—for their unwavering support, understanding, and belief in this vision. Your patience and encouragement gave me the space to reflect, create, and pursue this purpose-driven path.

To the subject matter contributors—**Martin Toh**, **CW Tan**, and **Anna Png**—thank you for sharing your expertise, insights, and time. Your contributions added depth and practical value to this book, and your work continues to make a meaningful impact in the lives of many.

My inspiration in writing this book comes from many individuals that I have coached and mentored. Many have asked how I managed to achieve financial independence and re-career before reaching the conventional retirement age. Their questions and words of admiration prompted me to document my journey and insights—so that others who aspire to achieve F.I.R(Re-career).E may benefit as well.

A special thanks to ChatGPT, Gemini by Google, and DeepSeek for helping to refine my writing and clarify my ideas. Their assistance significantly improved the quality, coherence, and structure of the content, and supported the development of some of the key images and visual aids in the book.

To every reader embarking on the F.I.R(Re-career).E journey—thank you. This book is written for you. May it serve as a guide, a mirror, and a catalyst as you design a life aligned with your values, passions, and purpose.

Finally, to the younger version of myself who once questioned the status quo and dared to believe there was a better way—this book is your answer.

~ YK Png

About the Author and Contributors

YK Png (FPSS. ACC. PCTC. ACLP.)
Author | Certified Coach | Educator | Pharmacist | Founder, CoachToring.Com

YK Png is a multiple award-winning pharmacist turned coach, adult educator, course developer, author, and the founder of Coachtoring.com (formerly PharmacistCoaches.com). With over two decades of experience spanning pharmacy practice, regulatory affairs, senior corporate leadership, entrepreneurship, and talent development, he brings a multidisciplinary and pragmatic lens to personal growth, career transitions, and purposeful living.

Having successfully re-careered from a senior corporate executive into a portfolio career as a coach, trainer, regulatory pharmacist and author, YK now shares his journey and insights in *Financial Independence, Re-career Early: Work Less, Live More*. This book, along with his earlier title *Limitless Possibilities*, reflects his mission to empower individuals to pursue clarity, autonomy, and fulfilment—aligning their careers with purpose and their lives with what truly matters.

Martin Toh (CFP. ChFC. ESP.)
Financial Services Director, AIA Singapore | CEO, RTP Organization

Martin Toh is Financial Services Director (High Net Worth District) at AIA Singapore and CEO of RTP Organization. Since 1998, he has built a strong reputation in high-net-worth planning, estate and succession advisory, and agency leadership.

He holds CFP®, ChFC®, and Estate Planning certifications, and is also a certified Enneagram Coach—bringing psychological insight into strategic financial planning. Martin is the creator of the PASS framework and has received numerous accolades including MDRT membership, Pinnacle District award, and induction into the AIA Hall of Fame.

In this book, Martin shares his frameworks and field-tested strategies to help readers navigate critical life and financial transitions with clarity and confidence.

CW Tan (ACCA)
Financial Planner

CW Tan is a financial planner specializing in comprehensive financial planning services for individuals and families in Singapore. Her passion lies in promoting financial literacy and long-term investing through clear, evidence-based education.

As the subject matter expert on investment strategies in this book, CW contributed insights on building diversified portfolios, understanding risk-return trade-offs, and making informed decisions across market cycles. Her work is grounded in the belief that sound investing should be accessible, practical, and purposeful.

Anna Png
Certified Real Estate Consultant | Property Wealth Strategist | Founder, Churros Factory

Anna Png is a licensed real estate consultant known for her dedication to helping clients make informed property decisions. She is passionate about guiding individuals and families in building long-term value through property ownership.

She is also the founder of *Churros Factory*, a homegrown brand launched in 2014 that has gained a loyal following for its handcrafted churros. Her entrepreneurial journey reflects a blend of creativity, resilience, and customer-focused excellence.

In this book, Anna contributes her expertise to the property chapter, offering practical frameworks and real-life considerations for using property as a strategic asset in financial independence and retirement planning. She believes that property decisions should be both data-informed and life-aligned.

www.ingramcontent.com/pod-product-compliance
Lightning Source LLC
LaVergne TN
LVHW100249210926
848480LV00003B/872

9789819436859